Goodness beyond Virtue

Jacobins during the French Revolution

Patrice Higonnet

Harvard University Press
Cambridge, Massachusetts
London, England
1998

About the cover: Jean-Baptiste Regnault's *Liberty or Death* was painted during the Terror of 1793–1794 and was presented in the 1795 salon. The Genius of France, borne aloft by faintly tricolor wings, hovers in allegorically universal space far above the terrestrial globe. Opposite a blackened Death sits the serene, white-robed Jacobin Republic with bundled Roman fasces at her feet. In one hand, she holds the sans-culottes' favored cap, the phrygian bonnet of liberty, worn in ancient times by emancipated slaves. With the other, she lifts a masonic triangle, a symbol of equality. She rests on steps that lead perhaps to a celestial tribune the likes of which was used by orators in clubs and Convention alike. Innocent and Christlike, the naked Genius smilingly urges the virtuous but hesitant citizen-spectator to choose between Jacobin liberty and death, between good and evil.

Copyright © 1998 by the President and Fellows of Harvard College
All rights reserved
Printed in the United States of America

Library of Congress Cataloging-in-Publication Data
Higonnet, Patrice L. R.
Goodness beyond virtue : Jacobins during the French Revolution /
Patrice Higonnet.
p.   cm.
Includes bibliographical references and index.
ISBN 0-674-47061-3 (cloth : alk. paper).
ISBN 0-674-47062-1 (pbk. : alk. paper)
1. Jacobins—France.
2. France—History—Revolution, 1789–1799— Societies, etc.
I. Title.
DC178.H54   1998
944.04—dc21
98-10187

To the memory of Clarence Crane Brinton, my predecessor
in the teaching of the French Revolution at Harvard University

Crane Brinton was born in Winsted, Connecticut, in 1898, the son of Eva Josephine Crane and Clarence Hawthorne Brinton. Educated in public primary and secondary schools, he entered Harvard College in 1915 and graduated summa cum laude in 1919. He received his doctorate at Oxford in 1926. His book *The Jacobins: A Study in the New History,* a work of enduring value that is often cited in these pages, was published in 1930.

A Wilsonian democrat, Brinton had an abiding detestation of the use of force in domestic and international affairs. Throughout his life, he remained loyal, in his own words, to "the basic belief of my youth in the rightness . . . of human reason." During the Second World War, Crane Brinton served in the Office of Strategic Services.

A wise and learned man, invariably polite and kind, Crane Brinton died, bravely, after a long illness in 1968.

Acknowledgments

My thanks go to current and former students who were kind enough to read this book in manuscript: David Bell, Erika Dreifus, Christina Jurgens, Jeremy Kleiner, Gerard Livesey, Edouard Metrailler, Jeremy Popkin, Michael Puri, Joel Rainey, Ron Schechter, and Celia Whitaker.

I am grateful also to those colleagues and friends who took time to read all or some of these pages: Keith Baker, Seyla Benhabib, Arthur Goldhammer, Anne Higonnet, Edward Keenan, Joan Landes, Richard Pipes, and Paolo Viola.

I am especially grateful to Steven Kaplan for a detailed and informed reading.

I owe a great deal—more than I should!—to Elizabeth Hurwit's patient and invariably insightful editorial comments.

Margaret Higonnet will find in the more thoughtful pages of this book the echoes of her own voice.

Contents

History is the "Place La Morgue" where everyone seeks
the dead kinsmen of his heart.

Jean-Paul Richter

Introduction

> What a terrible illusion it is to have to recognize and sanction in the rights of man, modern bourgeois society, the society of industry, of universal competition, of private interest freely pursuing its aims of anarchy, of self-estranged natural and spiritual individuality, and at the same time to want to annul the manifestations of the life of this society in particular individuals and simultaneously to want to model the political head of that society in the manner of antiquity.
>
> Karl Marx and Friedrich Engels, *The Holy Family*

*J*acobinism's doubled message was of individual becoming and altruistic involvement. Its core belief was that mankind could best realize its true self in the politicized context of a universalist republic. Only in that ideal setting could men and women, as individuals in their own right, fully become what nature and reason wished for them to be, namely, the free and active citizens of a harmonious state. Jacobins praised heroes who had found themselves in universalist sacrifice on behalf of a nation, humanity, or some imagined and enlightened community, for some truth larger than themselves. Jacobins easily experienced that spontaneous empathy which Rousseau described as the surest foundation of virtuous sensibility.

Of course, this book treats Jacobinism's decay into terrorism. But it rejects the idea that the essence of Jacobin politics culminated in the immoral and useless Terror of 1793–94. It holds that Jacobinism can still be a model for modern democrats.

It grants that the Jacobins' terroristic choices were not fortuitous. Jacobins not only invented positive verbal and iconographic vocabularies of freedom and conciliation, they also concocted negative themes of persecution that any fool might easily understand. All Jacobin *patriotes* some of the time (and some, no doubt, all of the time) were more intent on hounding counterrevolutionary, and often mythical, *aristocrates* than on asserting enlightened principles of civility.

Nonetheless, this book downplays the causal relevance of terroristic mythologizing to Jacobin thought and action. The Jacobins' drift to terror had less to do with either the excluding words of Rousseau or the need to find practical solutions to immediate problems (such as war, civil war, and inflation) than with unthinking and intolerant instincts whose roots were buried in the depths of their unconscious selves.

Jacobins were enlightened libertarians who to their own uncomprehending dismay found themselves reenacting a past of persecution that they desperately wanted to deny. They experienced as a living nightmare what the great counterrevolutionaries of their times, Burke and de Maistre, fantasized as a beloved dream: that the memory of age-old values would prove stronger than the appeal of universalizing reason.

In the beginning, then, the Jacobins manifested a doubled and reconcilable but also unstable inspiration, at once individualistic and communitarian. It is important to keep this division—and instability—in mind because it sets up the framework of the two basic dimensions of Jacobinism's history.

First, as a divided ideology Jacobinism was inherently conditioned to secrete rhetorics of reconciliation and compensatory enmities. Precisely because their worldview was dualistic Jacobins instinctively developed images of togetherness, as well as unalloyed (and unifying) detestations of those who refused their proffered friendship. Second, Jacobins automatically assumed that Jacobinism could not stand still. Because its fragile and demanding nature did not allow for negotiation, because all problems as they arose were to be resolved ideologically and not pragmatically, Jacobinism—thought the Jacobins—would either fall back or move forward. It required commitment. It could not pause. Time and time again, Jacobin politics excluded those revolutionaries (Monarchiens in 1789, Feuillants in 1791, Girondins in 1793, Indulgents in 1794) who feared to go further.

Depending on the moment, the arguments that were used to exclude did of course vary in their focus (the monarchy in 1791, the war in 1792, the price of bread in 1793, the Terror in 1794). However, we should not place too much importance on any particular reason. Factionalization arose not from its varied rationalizations but from a more simple issue: immobilization or dynamism. Would the Feuillants carry the Revolution with or without the king? Would the Gironde agree to deal with the populist sans-culottes or not? What really mattered was that those Jacobins who reluctantly concluded that the Revolution should stop ceased to be Jacobins; they were instantaneously rejected by their former friends, however politically correct their committed past or their socially minded arguments might be.

Alas, the cure was worse than the disease. Jacobinism, or so true Jacobins intuited, had to move forward. But when it did so, this ecumenical worldview foundered on the issue of class and class formation. From its essence, Jacobinism necessarily denied the existence of class divisions. When these hurdles proved insuperable (as in Lyons in 1793 and in Paris in early 1794), Jacobinism faltered.

And when it did so, the punitive instinct of the Jacobins, derived from long habits of absolutist politics and intolerant religion, was to resort to terror. This trend bred even more enemies and served, in the long run, to make Jacobinism's failure more certain.

A red thread runs from Jacobinism's dual structure, to the perpetual motion of revolutionary politics, to the emergence of class consciousness, and finally to the Terror.

It is often (if somewhat exaggeratedly) said that historians, like cuckoos as it were, instinctively place their work in frames devised by more noble thinkers for some literary purpose, like epic, romance, comedy, or farce. Taken in that light, the story of the Jacobins is like a tragedy, its mainspring an instinctive and self-destructive desire of the noble-minded to resolve by force the consequences of contradictory desire and flawed ambition.

Ideally, Jacobinism's four trajectories (ideological, chronological, social, and atavistic) should be addressed on a single front. But we dissect to understand, and we murder to dissect. To grasp the wholeness of Jacobin thought, politics, failures, and solutions, I have disaggregated what a Michelet or a Macaulay would, no doubt, have effortlessly presented as an organic whole.

The book therefore begins with an account of events that tries to trace the Jacobins' relentless, driving, and excluding pursuit of their twinned and, at times, contradictory concerns: private rights and public good. But Chapter 1 has other incidental assignments as well. It sets signposts for the general reader. It serves as an introduction for the subsequent presentation of Jacobinism's divided ideals. And it also works backward to highlight the hidden agendas of the Jacobins, which (in my view) a narrative of events does not reveal directly but nonetheless relentlessly implies, namely, the lurking presence in Jacobin thinking of both quasi-monarchic authoritarianism and quasi-religious, moralizing, and judgmental suspicions of dissent.

In the next four chapters, the text goes on to describe the place of individualism and universalism in the Jacobins' unformed sensibility before 1790–91 and in their consciously articulated ideology after that. At stake (as argued in Chapter 2) were the rights and social space of *private* persons, male or female, rich or poor, white or black. Jacobins abolished slavery on February 4, 1794. They also assumed the equal right of women to inherit, rights that were complemented (as discussed in Chapter 3) with the rights and autonomy of civil society vis-à-vis the state. "Civil society" is a useful but vexingly fluid and originally Hegelian term. Here, it means those aspects of social and public life—such as property rights and professional loyalties—that lay between the realm of the purely private (the family, essentially) and the explicitly political (public institutions of representation or administration).

Chapters 4 and 5 describe the other and *universalist* half of the Jacobins' worldview, which centered on their driving concern for the nation and the public good. Overall, then, the point of Chapters 2 through 5 is that Jacobins—though ensconced in a world of "bourgeois" values—were also able to soar above them, from time to time in any case. Jacobins often were at once utopian dreamers of a kind and, in their day-to-day politics, practical, hard-hearted, or even cruel men of affairs who ruled with a rod of iron. (Why and how that doubled human condition could have come so sharply into being is left to the penultimate pages of the book.)

Chapters 6 through 9 describe the various contradictions and solutions that flowed from the Jacobins' divided way of looking at the world, simultaneously privatist and universalist, involved in the world and indifferent to its calls. At stake here was the Jacobins' paradoxical situation as the free-minded servants of a tyrannical, terrorizing state, as universalists who had become terrorists (see Chapter 6). After Jacobinism's theory, at once individualist and universalist, comes its increasingly schizophrenic and illiberal practice.

At stake also were the many solutions the Jacobins instinctively developed to cope with a view of life that was at odds with itself. A number of these palliatives were inclusive in their purpose, such as their belief in familial unity and in the natural unity of creation (described in Chapter 7) or their rhetorics of reconciliation and harmony (described in Chapter 8). Other stratagems, however, were darkly threatening. Jacobins loved their fellow men; but (as shown in Chapter 9) they also loved to hate the chosen "enemies of the people."

In the last chapters of the book the argument circles back on itself. These pages provide a reflection on the distant causes and effects of Jacobinism's contradictions and decay.

In Chapter 10 the book locates a first cause for the breakdown of Jacobinism's fundamentally humane purpose in the differing shapes of social life that prevailed in the different parts of France. It moves from place to place but finds a common intersection in the varied interplay of class formation and Jacobin ideology. For Jacobin thoughts and words were more or less the same everywhere, though with different effects. The text concludes (audaciously, perhaps) that in 1793–94 Jacobin ideology, regardless of its stated words, worked well in those parts of France where incipient class lines were muted, and foundered most completely where nascent lines of class were amplified by revolutionary struggle. There, in Lyons, in Paris, Jacobinism became fierce and terroristic as ancient instincts provided horrendous solutions to unforeseen contention.

The penultimate chapter of the book takes this insight on the social ecology of Jacobinism's failures and successes as the start of a retrospective speculation on Jacobinism's close and distant origins in prerevolutionary French ways of thinking about the relationship of the self to public authority. It argues that Jacobinism was born at a unique sociological moment in the social history of the Western world, a moment set in France (and elsewhere) between two points: one marked by the decay of an older—traditional and hierarchic—society of interlocking social orders and estates where the identities of the king's subjects were defined by the privileges of the groups to which they belonged from birth or chance; and the other, organized around the modern—and warring—principles of individual rights, divisive class consciousness, and democratic rule.

Students of other national histories will readily recognize this accessible—and even classic—sociological reasoning, since most societies (except for America, perhaps) are said to have moved or be now moving, each in its own way, through those selfsame stages, from organicist to mechanistic themes, from *Gemeinschaft* to *Gesellschaft*, from group allegiance to more individuated forms. (Blessed by the gods, nearly from the start Americans have lived in and conceived of their society as one without a feudal past.)

Chapter 11 also incorporates a line of reasoning less sociological than political and cultural. Briefly stated, it argues that when absolutism sagged, gradually at first, after 1750, and then quite suddenly, in 1787–1789, French citizens showed themselves prone to thinking about public life in a unique and moralizing manner. Revolutionary Jacobinism, it asserts (and on faith, to be sure), emerged from this doubled and prerevolutionary context of classless, sociological transition and "post-absolutist" definitions of the private and the public. Regardless of their wealth and rank, regardless of circumstance also, Jacobins were moralizing and highly critical citizens who wanted blameless public and private lives to overlap equally and completely without reference to caste or class.

In many ways, this book follows the recent and brilliant revisionist argument of François Furet, who saw revolutionary Jacobinism as a self-referential ideology that moved with little regard to ambient social life. But it tries to extend and modulates that view in two ways.

First, it argues that the relevant frame of Jacobin politics goes beyond a free-floating ideology to involve the wider context of lived and experienced Jacobin culture as well. In other words, Jacobins' thinking, as regards both their private and public lives, encompassed not just the realm of high ideas but also the broadest range of human feelings, with all the passions that ordinary men and women ceaselessly churn over: hope, love, friendship, desire, the joy of achievement, the fears of failure, disappointment, solitude, and death.

Of course, Jacobinism can be approached (somewhat naively) as the ideology of a particular class at a particular moment in time or, more daringly and with extreme literary and theoretical sophistication, as a high, discursive statement that moved from one symbolic trope to the next. But in the end, what historians have to say about the Jacobin project will have more force, I feel, if their description also brings into play the many yearnings and emotions—spoken and unspoken—that structure our banal, experiential present and our more noble goals as well.

To describe that worldview, I have throughout relied on Jacobins' own words as often as seemed feasible. About two hundred clubs are mentioned here. Much emphasis is placed in these pages not just on the self-conscious feats and speeches of the Jacobin "stars" in Paris, but on the accounts—occasionally unpublished—of provincial Jacobins, that is to say on words and facts that are quite mundane but have a ring of authenticity. In that same frame of mind, I have often juxtaposed statements of great and obscure Jacobins in small towns and in the capital. Though Jacobinism was hardly of a piece, its various insights—and banalities—were, or so it seems to me, different sides of a single truth.

Second, this book departs from revisionist thought by emphasizing the idea that Jacobinism's decline into terrorism derived neither from its undeniable self-referentiality nor from the obvious contradictions of Jacobin culture, but from an unconsciously internalized legacy of intolerance. The Jacobins were voluntary activists, to be sure, but they were also prisoners of a checkered and rejected past.

Many historians will flatly deny this positive view of Jacobinism's twinned essence and of its revolutionary representativity.

Looking forward, some modern revisionist historians will suggest that Jacobinism was far more lopsided than I have argued here. They will surmise that its individualist component was inconsequential, and that the Jacobins' decline into terror did not have that much to do with a clerico-monarchic past. They will say instead that the Jacobins' monistic and Rousseauean interpretation of popular sovereignty fated them to destruction.

Looking backward, other historians (less numerous, I believe) will argue that the Revolution was well under way before Jacobinism ever emerged. They will query my view on the overlap of Jacobinism and *L'Esprit de la Révolution* (as ran the title of a small book written by Saint-Just in 1791). The term "Jacobin," after all, derives from the nickname that stuck to the Paris club after it leased its headquarters from some Jacobin monks, and this the *clubbistes* did not do until October 27, 1789. (A more serious point might be that there could not really be any Jacobins until the club network had acquired nationwide relevance, which only happened a year after the fall of the Bastille, if then.)

And in a different but equally disbelieving register, many historians who are primarily interested in visible social forms will in one way or another insist on the fundamental idea of Marxian eschatology, namely, that every successive "class" which (supposedly) came to power between 1789 and 1793 (liberal nobles in 1789, upper middle class in 1791, middle and lower middle class in 1792–93, and so on) brought forward its own discontinuous brand of Jacobin ideas, each one strikingly different from the last.

In sum, for some historians, we have Jacobinism distinct from the Revolution; for the revisionists, we have Jacobinism as ongoing continuity toward terror; and for the Marxists, we have any number of Jacobinisms, each different from the others.

By strong contrast, the basic assumption of this book is that Jacobinism was the quintessence of a single (if always changing), complex, divided, but ultimately liberal sensibility—or *esprit révolutionnaire*—that was superimposed on threatening, inherited, and unspoken apprehensions which perniciously denied consciously held principles, and eventually overwhelmed them.

This book also holds that the roots of Jacobin ideology existed latently as a sensibility before the Revolution, long before Jacobinism found physical embodiment in the clubs: Jacques-Louis David's *Oath of the Horatii* of 1785 prefigures 1789, just as his portrayal of Brutus of early 1789 is itself a stepping stone toward the High Jacobin painting in late 1793 of David's murdered hero, Marat.

John Adams wrote that the American Revolution was first made in the hearts and minds of the people; that is my view of Jacobinism as well. Events may well have brought Jacobin sensibility to self-conscious, ideological crystallization, but they hardly created it.

The overall narrative strategy of this book, then, is to use an introductory and sequential account of revolutionary politics to highlight the doubled, individuated, and communitarian goals of Jacobin sensibility. A concern for the social and cultural ecology of Jacobin ideas—both before and after 1789—will show how these happy tensions became irreconcilable contradiction that brought Jacobinism to catastrophe.

More than half a century ago the intellectual historian Daniel Mornet wrote that the origin of the Revolution is one story and the history of the Revolution is another. That is *not* the view I take. An insistence on the dynamic movement of revolutionary politics, a focus on Jacobinism's divided goals, a concern for nascent class lines, and a larger need to ruminate on hidden and ancient causes are the sequential frames of this book.

Finally, the last chapter denies the supposed connection of 1789, a glorious revolution, to the dismal Russian Revolution of October 1917. By understanding the differences between these two revolutionary situations we can grasp better why 1789, unlike 1917, was a great and inspiring moment of world history, a moment we should ponder and put to good use in the management of our own affairs.

In sum, we need to separate the nobility of the Jacobins' message from the flaws, errors, and liabilities of the Jacobins. Their bungled inception of parliamentary democracy—interesting in itself as a cautionary tale that all democrats should heed—is one thing. But Jacobinism's complementary and democratic definition of self and universalist community is something else indeed.

If the French Revolution were over, as is often said today, then how dim would become Western culture's expectation that willed and collective action can meaningfully inflect the vast and grinding "impersonal forces" which invariably bear down on our isolated private lives.

The prospects of such a failure are so discouraging that they cannot be true. Despite their gruesome failure, we are still today the heirs of the Jacobins' hopes and disappointments, even as we see that their fall was fated.

In the optic of this book, to paraphrase Baudelaire, the Jacobins, for better and for worse, are our models and our companions, the heralds of our future, "nos semblables et nos frères."

A Narrative of the French Revolution from a Jacobin Perspective

The Revolution! An unutterable word. Who can claim to understand clearly and precisely that set of events, alternatively glorious and deplorable, some of them the fruit of genius and daring, or again, of the most respectable integrity, and others born of the most perverse iniquity.

Jeanbon Saint-André (a member of the Committee of Public Safety)

How can one conceive of an event like the French Revolution?

François Furet, *Penser la Révolution française*

A narrative of Jacobinism's revolutionary trajectory has two assignments. It exists in its own right. It aims to give a generally accessible account of political unfolding. It emphasizes implicit causes (like cultural instincts or the Jacobins' sense of the revolutionary dynamic). It does not depend on an explicit but illusorily precise, quasi-theatrical presentation of events. It remembers that most contemporaries lived the Revolution as an incomprehensible experience, as a volcanic eruption or as a torrent, to use an expression favored at the time by the Swiss writer Benjamin Constant and by many others. With hindsight, that is to say, with a knowledge of the Revolution's origins and conclusion, we can today present its history in an orderly way; but we must remain cautious and modest in our hopes of recapturing the past "as it really was."

Another more critical assignment—and one that hardly overlaps with the first—is to introduce a thematic understanding of Jacobinism's central problems: What was Jacobinism about? Who was a Jacobin? Why did it decline into terrorism? Was terror inherent in Jacobinism's goals? Was the *dérapage*—or "sliding out" of the Revolution—implicit in its ideological structure? Could a great man—Mirabeau, for example, had he not died in early 1791—have arrested the drift of the Revolution in the years 1792–1794 toward universalism run wild? Or was terror the result of unspoken but painful cultural legacies (as I argue in this book)? In other words, does a clear and logically compelling line run directly from some flaw in the libertarian Declaration of the Rights of Man in August 1789 to Robespierre's authoritarian rule of virtuous terror in 1794?

Here the first problem, of course, is that even the plainest narrative of the Revolution presupposes antecedent choices. Historians with a basically *institutional* and political agenda will distinguish three phases of revolutionary history:

1. The breakdown in June and July 1789 of the old, simultaneously traditionalist and absolutist monarchy;
2. A constitutional phase in two parts: constitutional monarchism from June 20, 1789, to August 10, 1792, when the monarchy was overthrown; and constitutional republicanism from August 1792 to June 2, 1793;
3. A democratic authoritarian republic that begins with the exclusion (on June 2, 1793), travels through the arrest and execution of the legally elected Girondin deputies, and ends with the fall of Robespierre on July 27, 1794 (9 Thermidor, Year II).

Historians with a rigorous *social* agenda have a different scenario. Because they consider institutions superstructures that both express and conceal deeper social layering, Marxist accounts of revolutionary politics ordinarily identify four phases:

1. The collapse of a traditional, hierarchic, rural, and organicist society of estates in the summer of 1789 with the fall of the Bastille on July 14 and the abolition of feudal privileges on the night of August 4;
2. A fragile and unstable alliance during the years 1789–1792 of the entire propertied class dominated by liberal landed nobles and the

upper-middle-class commercial notables (the Monarchiens and the Feuillants), culminating in the Le Chapelier law of June 1791, which outlawed trade unions and in effect defined labor as a commodity to be bought and sold like any other;

3. An alliance after the February 1793 food riots in Paris of the urban poor on the one hand and, on the other, the middle- or lower-middle-class, propertied, bourgeois Jacobin democrats, momentarily indifferent to the class interests of the rich;

4. The gradual destruction of the increasingly dangerous, sans-culotte, "popular movement" by the middle-class Jacobin democrats; November 1793 marks the beginning of the process with the faltering of the dechristianization campaign sponsored by the populist Hébertists; other phases include the execution of these sans-culotte leaders in March 1794 and the militarized destruction of politicized populism in the spring of 1795.

By contrast, for the "moderate left," nationalist historians of the late nineteenth century who wanted to disengage the French Revolution—which they saw as the inspiration of the liberal-minded Third Republic—from worldwide revolutionary violence and terrorism, the most significant events of the decade were the declaration of war on April 20, 1792, and its convoluting effects. Their sequential analysis also outlined four phases:

1. Initial French defeats at Longwy and Verdun, which led to the fall of the monarchy on August 10, 1792, and to the September massacres from the second to the sixth;

2. Victory in late 1792, starting with the battle of Valmy on September 20 and the consolidation of the parliamentary republic;

3. Renewed defeat in the spring and summer of 1793 and the ensuing rise of terror with the creation of the Revolutionary Tribunal as a consequence of events like the counterrevolutionary insurrection in the Vendée on March 13, 1793, and the betrayal of General Charles Dumouriez in the first week of April;

4. Renewed military success with the victory at Fleurus on June 26, 1794, and the end of the Terror in July.

In this "Third Republican" view, the Terror had little to do with either the cultural shape of French society at the time of the Revolution or the principles of 1789. These nationalist historians blamed the Terror on France's sempiternal, malevolent, and reactionary enemies. Hide one of two warring duelists from view, said the Protestant and Republican historian Charles Seignobos, and the learned feints of the one visible combatant look like the incoherent gyrations of a madman.

The history of Jacobinism presented in these pages by no means denies the relevance of institutional, social, or military events to Jacobinism's unfolding. It matters, for example, that the harvest of 1790, the quietest year of the Revolution, was excellent. Conversely, the fear of imminent defeat and terrible retribution that filled all hearts in August and September 1792 is also significant.

Nonetheless, this narrative focuses much less on the "material" or military history of the Revolution than on the ideologized development of the Jacobins' spoken and unspoken ways of thinking. Revolutionary politics were politics of passion and, as such, more cultural than social or economic in their origins and unfolding, even if social and economic forms were both critical cause and effect of cultural belief.[1]

This account describes Jacobinism's starting point as a prerevolutionary *sensibility,* an unshaped but libertarian and modernizing aspiration reflected in the endlessly varied ways that human beings express the different sides of their being (in their views, for example, of familial life, professional roles, property, sexual morality, and the like).

But it also holds that after 1789, Jacobinism grew more coherent and more politicized, gradually until 1791, and rapidly so in 1793–94 when set at fever pitch in Paris. At that point heretofore shapeless yearnings became the articulated parts of a coherent, systemic, and dictatorial *ideology.*

In the nation's capital, during the so-called Year II (from September 1793 to September 1794), Jacobinism had a base (the clubs), a votive figure (Rousseau), recognized martyrs (Marat among them), and, of course, an overwhelming weapon: the militarized and terroristic—if chaotic—state machine that ruled over what was then in many ways the world's most powerful and technologically advanced society.

It was also then and there (in Paris, in 1793–94) that triumphant Jacobinism began to self-destruct. The Jacobins created the Terror; but they despised it also, and with it, we can conjecture, themselves.

But who were the Jacobins who carried this doctrine forward? By 1788 tens of thousands of French men and women shared an unformed sensibility and unbeknownst to themselves were Jacobins-to-be. In the summer of

1789, when political events first crystallized this enlightened and liberalizing mood, hostile to privilege and "despotism," as *esprit révolutionnaire,* and when royal officials vanished as if into thin air, hundreds of thousands supported the aims of the dedicated "patriots," many of whom would soon become hard-core Jacobins.

At the Festival of the Federation, on July 14, 1790, when the Revolution's universalist goals seemed self-evidently practical and true, millions appeared to be Jacobinically inclined. The largely bloodless Revolution of 1789–90 gave Jacobinism an almost universal audience. But in 1792–93, as Jacobins grew more strident and militarized Jacobins were known as such—and feared—its appeal declined. Paradoxically, Jacobinism's support shrank as its power expanded and its principles sharpened. And in the summer of 1794, when Jacobinism had become a highly self-conscious and tyrannous ideology, adamant Jacobins were fewer still. What the Revolution had granted, it also took away. Finally, by late 1799, when Jacobinism had become an elaborate rhetoric of deception and self-deception, almost no one still admitted to being a Jacobin.

We cannot easily assign numbers to these estimates. At one time or another, about six thousand Jacobin or popular societies came into being. Crane Brinton calculated that about one million people joined one of these clubs, about half of them in 1793–94. He also believed that perhaps as many as one half of the *clubbistes* remained so for a long period from the time of their signing on.[2] (Louis Sébastien Mercier, a Conventionnel who lived through it all, was quite wrong to argue later that the Jacobins of 1794 were as different from those of 1791 as the Spartans were from the Frenchmen of his own times.)[3] Brinton suggested that self-identified Jacobins (Jacobin sympathizers who at some point joined a club) may have numbered about 2 percent to 4 percent of the French population taken as a whole. (Other estimates are only half as great.)[4] At Marseilles Jacobins counted for 4.4 percent of the population, and around Rouen, 5 percent.

Precise numbers are not to be had. Sources are incomplete or biased. Many membership roles were destroyed. A more evocative statistic is that as many perhaps as one adult French male in six or seven was at some moment committed to Jacobinism, an extraordinary figure for the times, and one that prefigures the mass political commitments of our own day.

How did Jacobinism develop? In the initial days of the Revolution, which culminated in the Festival of the Federation, ecumenical and reformist thought miraculously swept the field. Old institutions either vanished or blended harmoniously into the new, as happened with the coming together of the ancient monarchy and the new Constituent Assembly.

Then came two years or so of anguished and rising contradiction beginning in the summer of 1791 (with such awesome and earlier premonitions during the summer of 1790 as the divisive promulgation of the Civil Constitution of the Clergy on July 12, 1790). In this intermediate and still more or less constitutional phase, which ended in the late summer of 1793, Jacobin sensibility developed ideologically. On the left, a countervailing popular consciousness also coalesced. The term "sans-culotte" came into general use. And on the right, disenchanted Catholics broke with the Revolution altogether. Within the Jacobin camp, anxieties likewise arose in some quarters as the Revolution continued. A key event in this drift from harmony to disharmony and from sensibility to ideology was the king's flight to Varennes in late June 1791. An open schism developed between progressive Jacobins and the more cautious Feuillant Jacobins.

In late 1791 the Revolution moved steadily to the left, toward greater universalism in both fact and symbol. Orthodox Jacobins were convinced that unless the Revolution moved forward, it would collapse, and with it their dream of regenerated man. At the behest of the Girondist Jacobins, in April 1792, war was declared against the reactionary Austrian and Prussian monarchies.

In the early summer of 1792 unexpected military failure precipitated ongoing ideological transformation. The Jacobins drifted to universalizing republicanism. The monarchy's fall on August 10, 1792, accelerated the repression of the religious and political right. A special tribunal was created on August 17, 1792, which decreed the first condemnations to the guillotine. Then came the September massacres, which the Montagnard Jacobins condoned. Another schism followed during the winter of 1792–93, this time between the Girondin Jacobins, who wished to stop the Revolution—just as the Feuillants had tried to do a year before—and the Montagnard Jacobins, who remained eager to work toward ideologically determined goals and who were ready to forge a political alliance with the Paris poor regardless of the social cost.

In the last moments of this intervening period—that is to say, during the thirty months that stand between the harmony of 1789–90 and the terror of 1793–94—Jacobinism in early 1793 evolved steadily toward ever more ideologized and illiberal goals. These goals may have been embedded in it from the first, but at this point they began to take on dominant and horrendous relevance.

In Jacobinism as it had evolved by late 1793 authoritarian universalism crowded out the liberal-minded individualism that at first, in 1789, Jacobinism had intended to enhance. Nationalism prevailed over internationalism; terrorist intolerance over political liberty; and the use of the French language over dialects. The women's movement was broken.

A third and frenetic phase of revolutionary politics runs from the late fall of 1793 to July 1794. High Jacobinism, now a full-blown ideology best expressed by the intolerant orthodoxy of its "great high priest," Robespierre, eliminated all of its rivals, left and right (terms that, incidentally, were invented in Paris at this time). As it did so, Jacobinism also emptied from within, torn apart by its own contradictions and by its terrorist pursuit of abstract and communitarian values, which appeared increasingly meaningless or positively dangerous to most French men and women. Here was universalism inverted and run wild.

In May and June 1794 the rule of law was suspended with the "laws of Prairial," a denial of humane legal principles that made it possible for the Jacobins to condemn their enemies at will, oftentimes by declaring them to be Girondins, a category damned not just in their fratricidal eyes but in the eyes of the "law."

Robespierre's friend Georges Couthon explained it all in early June 1794, a few weeks before his own death. These new (and in fact outrageous) laws were, he said, perfectly fair and just. Under the Old Regime, arcane judicial procedures had served some purpose. At that time, he added, "moral proofs had counted for nothing." But now, Jacobins were easily able to know in their conscience which of their enemies were truly guilty of counterrevolutionary offense.

A final period in the explanation presented here runs from Robespierre's fall in July 1794 to Bonaparte's rise to power on 18 Brumaire, Year VII (November 9, 1799). It centers on the alternatively pathetic and irritating efforts of the chastened ex-Jacobins around Sieyès to muddle through by simultaneously affirming and denying their Jacobinical, Roman-Republican principles. Behind this communitarian screen, however, the late neo-Jacobin regime asserted unchecked individualism, in economic life especially. Communitarian universalism survived largely in increasingly mendacious symbols and in ever emptier and official forms.

Jacobinism begins as divine comedy (1789–1791), becomes tragedy (1793), and ends as intermittently bloody farce (1795–1799).

French Politics on the Eve of the Revolution

That the Old Regime collapsed is in retrospect unsurprising. Nevertheless, its demise came as a shock to many contemporary pundits who remembered that for over a century the Old Regime had lurched bumblingly but successfully enough from one financial crisis to the next. Arthur Young, a failed English agronomist and self-styled oracle, predicted that the French aristocracy would emerge strengthened from this test.

A fortiori, the dramatic rise of Jacobin republicanism was most definitely not in anyone's mind at the time. Some events (like the revolutions of 1848 or the coming of the two world wars) confirm widespread expectations. But many others, like the fall of communism in our own time or the rise of Jacobinism in the period 1789–1794, come as complete surprises.

The pattern of day-to-day politics during the two decades of the Old Regime contributed to contemporaries' lack of foresight. In 1789 the forces of immobilism seemed strong, although they were, in fact, quite weak. During the 1770s and 1780s the deeper but still invisible effect of the monarchy's intermittent cardiac arrests had been to widen the scope of pre-Jacobin sensibilities. Their immediate effect, however, had been to strengthen the hand of the absolutist monarchy's most important (and, at that time, only organized) enemies. In the 1780s the nation's highest and aristocratized law courts, the Parlements, were ideally situated to complain. The noble Parlementaires had selfish goals, but a genuine hostility to absolutist "despotism" motivated them. For some years the Parlementaires remained quite popular because their enemy—namely, royal absolutism—was also the enemy of enlightened public opinion. The enemy of my enemy is my friend.

Incoherently managed, unable to pay its way, unable and unwilling to coerce, the monarchy in the summer and fall of 1788 had no choice but to turn to the nation and convoke the neomedieval Estates General, which had last been convened in 1614. Though brought together at Versailles on May 5, 1789, as delegates of the traditionally sanctioned three estates (the church was the first; the nobles, second; with everyone else—rich or poor—third), the members of the Third Estate, after weeks of hesitations, proclaimed themselves on June 17, 1789, a sovereign National Assembly, whose members were beyond the king's writ. But that proclamation was not fated to have occurred. Had the king's first minister, Jacques Necker, been a wiser man and not allowed events to drift, who today would know the name of Robespierre?

In any instance, having crossed their Rubicon, and although elected as the mandated representatives of traditionally defined corporate groups (provinces, baillages, estates, towns, guilds, and so on), the newly elected deputies easily fitted themselves into their new and more elevated role as national representatives. A few did suggest on July 7, 1789, that they should go back to their electorate to secure new instructions; but they were overruled. Henceforth, deputies were to vote not collectively as before, by order or estate, but one by one, as members of a single, and in this instance, self-appointed National Assembly (also called the Constituent Assembly since it was drafting a constitution).

The deputies' assumption that the whole of popular sovereignty rested on the nation's representatives (that is, themselves) ultimately became a cardinal principle of Jacobin constitutional thinking, and one that, by way of comparison, the American system explicitly denied. There, the thirteen constituent states of a federal republic continued to exercise some sovereignty. But the French instinctively reasoned quite differently.

After desultorily staging an aimless political and military coup (by forbidding the deputies to meet as a National Assembly and by bringing mercenary troops to Paris), the king called off his soldiers and yielded. The conservative majorities of the first two estates also gave in. When the poorly defended Bastille (with its seven political prisoners) fell to a crowd of Parisians and disaffected soldiers on July 14, 1789, the king did nothing about that either, rather to the surprise of the deputies, who were at first distressed by the news of this overt and popular attack on the monarch's fortress and prerogatives. They feared militarized retribution, but it did not come.

In the following days the multisecular royal bureaucracy vanished. On July 23, 1789, two related royal officials, Louis Jean Bertier de Sauvigny and Joseph François Foulon, who had been peripherally involved with the Paris food supply and were suspected of peculation, were murdered by a Parisian mob, just as the captured governor of the Bastille and others had been lynched a week before. Future leaders of Jacobinism, Barnave especially, exonerated the murderers, an ominous first step to the general suspension of the rule of law in 1794. Were not the people sovereign? asked Barnave in 1789. Were not these two officials somehow immoral? "Was not their blood impure?" (Looking forward, it is appropriate to note that Barnave was executed in November 1793, by which time he too had become an "enemy of the people.")

Then, in late July 1789, the Great Fear (Grande Peur, a rural panic) ran through the countryside. Though few were killed, many lordly castles were attacked and feudal parchments burned. French peasants did not want to pay feudal dues any longer. (In some regions, they were still quite burdensome.) Many nobles sought refuge in the cities where new revolutionary authorities more or less maintained law and order. Hysterical rumors of foreign invasion swept the nation.

Georges Lefebvre in the 1930s described with memorable skill the conjunction of revolutions (urban, rural, aristocratic, and middle-class reformist) that made it impossible for the monarchy to resist these coterminous waves of complaints.[5]

All over France, in the south, west, and northeast especially, new town administrations were created, as were municipal militias called National Guards. (In Paris these units took shape on July 13; in Angers, on the nineteenth.) Now the deputies and their friends had actual power as well as theoretical sovereignty.

In central Europe, after 1848, traditionalist monarchies could rely on both nobles and peasants to shore up their questioned cause. But in France during the early summer of 1789 political traditionalism, unmourned and without an audience, decomposed in a matter of days, not weeks, and across the board.

The abrupt end of the Old Regime in the summer of 1789 and the quasi-unanimous acceptance of a single and new national and popular sovereignty after that profoundly influenced the Jacobins' revolutionary ways of thinking. It mattered greatly to the Jacobins that the peasants had proved to be the allies of the Revolution. And it mattered also that they had actually seen universalist political wholeness in action. In the summer of 1789 the Old Regime had died as if by magic, and the news of its fall had rallied all hearts. The entire revolutionary career of the Jacobins can be seen as an elaboration on a remembrance of things just passed, as an effort to recreate the unanimity of 1789–90.

Once again, then, who could be called a Jacobin in this early summer of 1789? No one, of course, if we take the question in a strict sense. The word did not yet exist. It was only on September 21, 1792, that the *clubbistes* officially and defiantly took up as their own this insulting nickname, from the leased Jacobin convent where the Paris club settled in 1789. In the last days of 1789, after six months of Revolution, France still counted less than twenty societies or clubs that would later become part of the Jacobin network. And nearly one year later, in early September 1790, there were still no more than 140 towns with a club. (France in these same months was redistricted into 40,680 municipalities.)

Card-carrying Jacobins (later in Paris they actually did carry red cards) at first numbered few. Strictly speaking, at this early date the only certified Jacobins were those committed deputies in the National Assembly who met as a kind of club or lobby to coordinate parliamentary stratagems.

And yet, in a large and truer sense, in 1789 much of the French nation, and certainly many of the French citizens who called themselves *patriotes*, were "potential" Jacobins because Jacobinism was the essence of the wider *esprit révolutionnaire* they shared.

All patriots understood diffusely what Jacobins were beginning to understand more precisely, namely, that absolutism was really despotism, that privilege was unnatural, that sovereignty was sited in a united, fraternal, and newly moralized nation-state whose aim was to empower every individual citizen, and perhaps every citizeness as well.

1789–1791: Universalism and Individualism Reconciled

Immediately, in the summer of 1789, the National Assembly interpreted the events at hand (the fall of the Bastille, the Great Fear, the breakdown of the older law and order) as the self-evident justification for a restructuring of every French political institution without exception. That goal, of course, had certainly not been consciously formulated in the first weeks of the year when the quite moderate and pro-monarchy *cahiers de doléances*, or grievance books, had been drawn up all over France as a guide to what the conjoined estates should do. But it was in the nature of an ongoing Revolution—and of many-layered Jacobinism—that they should always deepen and reinvent themselves as they moved from one critical moment to the next. In any case, all of the great reforms of 1789–1791 reflected the synthesis of individualist and communitarian values soon to become explicitly central to the Jacobin ideal.

The universalist nation was made more real, at the level of symbol especially. Provincial borders were wiped out and departments created, each one of these administrative entities small enough for every citizen to walk to its capital or *chef lieu* and participate in local politics. France was given a national flag (the white of the monarchy flanked by the blue and red of Paris). The country also became a national customs union, as Britain had been for nearly a century and as the United States had just become. On September 13 the deputies decided that France, as one nation, could have but one representative assembly. A senate or a house of peers was ruled out. French law, though not yet codified (that would not happen until 1804), was at least standardized and nationalized, as were eventually weights and measures. Citizenship became a meaningful public concept.

Symbolically, on October 5, 1789, after women had marched to Versailles to secure bread (its cost in 1789 was nearly twice what it had been a year before), Louis, surrounded by sixty thousand people, was forcibly brought back from Versailles, the absolutist capital of the kingdom, to Paris, the *national* capital of France. (Orthodox Jacobins sometimes described Paris as the nation's *ville centrale,* central city, because the term *capitale,* in the words of the Girondin Jacobin Rabaut Saint-Étienne, "could not be accorded to the principles of equality.")

Popular sovereignty was broadly acknowledged. In December four and a half million adult males (out of France's approximately twenty-seven million people) were given the vote, making the franchise broader in revolutionary France than in many American states at the time. And in another universalistic move, on May 15, 1790, the deputies refused to back Bourbon Spain, whose king was Louis's cousin, in its quarrel with Britain over Vancouver Island. Instead, they declared peace, as it were, on the entire world: "The National Assembly declares that the French nation will refuse to undertake any war of conquest and will never employ its forces against the liberty of any people."[6]

The individuation of French civil life in these early months was even more exaggerated. Indeed, so strong was this unprecedented and ideologically motivated liberal drift that it stands as a first *dérapage* of revolutionary politics. Enthused, the deputies set upon the rules in many domains: social, political, economic, industrial, commercial, artistic, fiscal, judicial, familial, and matrimonial. The list of corporate or ancient institutions that were suppressed in the first twenty months or so of the Revolution included the law courts, guilds, estates, the privileged position of the church, hospitals, universities, and associations of all kinds. In every realm, the traditional hierarchies and corporate institutions that for centuries had enabled French men and women to define themselves were sacrificed in a bonfire of inherited tradition without precedent in European history: "War unto privileges and the privileged," the marquis de Mirabeau asserted on August 16. "Privileges are useful against kings, but they are hateful against nations, and ours will never have a public spirit until it has been delivered of them." Proudly, the Constitution of 1791 began not with a description of what it was, but with a long, presentist, and antitraditional list of over twenty institutions of the Old Regime that were gone forever, starting with nobility and peerage, and ending with irrevocable religious vows and any "unnatural commitment."

True enough, the day-to-day workings of ordinary life remained nearly unchanged. Landed property was not transferred from one social group to another. Rents were still due and bills had to be paid. Likewise, compensation was awarded to dispossessed owners of offices or privileges, to bishops whose bishoprics had shrunk or vanished, to judges whose judgeships were suppressed, and so on. Yet, the legal bases of nearly every existing social arrangement were thoroughly transformed.

The end of the feudal system was a particularly important landmark in this individualization of society. This close to a thousand years of history was implicit in the juridical annihilation of the three estates on June 17, 1789; but it was made wholly explicit in the assembly's decisions of the night of August 4, 1789 (whose unfolding, as will be seen, had been prepared in what became the first Jacobin club). In a partially orchestrated cascade of self-denial, one privileged deputy after another renounced the feudal and traditional advantages that had been cherished for centuries by the entire possessing elite, noble and non-noble, of the French nation.

Within hours, some other deputies tried, fitfully, to limit in practice the application of the drastically individuating principle they had just enacted. Distinctions were made between honorific feudal dues (which were once again declared abolished) and "real" feudal dues (which were converted into property rights), but to no avail. Successive Jacobin factions would abandon the defense of these feudal remnants one by one and, eventually, without compensation. On July 13, 1793, all feudal titles were ordered burned. On October 22, 1793, the Jacobin-dominated Convention also made it illegal to recycle feudal dues as part of a moneyed payment due by lessees to lessors.

These were important decisions. By dissolving feudalism on terms favorable to the peasantry and deleterious to the landlords, the Jacobins guaranteed the neutrality and perhaps the loyalty of most peasants to the cause of the Revolution, if not precisely to their own version of it. In 1793 and 1794 peasants hardly took up the cudgels for either Brissot or Robespierre (or for or against the Directory after them). But in the main, outside the Vendée, Britanny, and some small areas of southern France, neither did the peasantry choose to fight *against* the Jacobins.

This was a great achievement, especially when set in world perspective, as the Italian Marxist philosopher and politician Antonio Gramsci (1891–1937) wisely understood.[7] By winning over some peasants and neutralizing the rest (as nineteenth-century Italian liberals were not able to do) revolutionary Jacobinism laid the lasting foundations in France of a progressive alliance between the urban middle class and a landowning peasantry, a means of enlightened governance that came to fruition in the years 1871–1940, during the Third French Republic.

Another early landmark in the actuation of the revolutionary defense of individual rights was the Declaration of the Rights of Man, initially discussed on July 6, 1789 (that is, more than a week before the fall of the Bastille) and enacted on August 26, 1789. The inspiration for this document, which defined the rights of individual citizens, was mixed. Historians of ideas have learnedly traced the wording of the text to varied individualistic and libertarian sources: Locke, the Physiocrats, Cesare Beccaria, and Voltaire especially as regarded articles 7, 8, and 9 with their generous definition of civil rights in criminal cases. The text also paid silent tribute to American precedents, to Virginian legislation especially.

It differed, however, from the contemporaneous American Bill of Rights in one all-important way. In the American Constitution, the Bill of Rights was not free standing. It was instead conceived as a series of amendments added in 1790 to the Constitution of 1789. To justify their principles, American libertarians from that day to our own have had to be constitutionalists as well.

Significantly, the Monarchiens, joined by Mirabeau, also failed in their efforts to insert the French declaration within a larger—and limiting—constitutional document,[8] a failure that foretold the Jacobins' eventual rejection of constitutional procedure for the sake of some higher truth.

With the end of feudalism and the Declaration of the Rights of Man came yet another critical and individuating decision, in March and June 1791. At the behest of Isaac Le Chapelier—one of the first Jacobins in June 1789 and, as it happens, a victim of the Jacobin guillotine in late 1793— the National Assembly, mostly drawn from liberal and nonindustrial professions (the law, the church, and the army)[9] outlawed guilds, labor unions, and employers' associations.

The Le Chapelier law of June 14, 1791, which Karl Marx rightly described as the most important piece of social legislation of the entire French Revolution, made of labor a commodity bought and sold by workers and employers. Henceforth, in social and economic matters, the function of the "night-watchman" state would be to enforce rather than examine contracts, as had been true before 1789 for traditionalist reasons, and as would again be true in the middle decades of the twentieth century for Keynesian reasons.

Civil society was thus severed from both tradition and the state. In theory if not yet in fact, unbridled individualism had become the Jacobin law of the land.

A truism of current political theory holds that all "totalitarian" regimes (fascist or communist) detest intermediary bodies. (Pluralist democracies, by contrast, are of their nature based on the cohabitation of explicitly or implicitly distinct social, economic, or cultural groups.) In this context, Jacobins could indeed be seen as precursors of the gulag except that they did not intend the abolition of intermediary bodies—especially those of feudal origin—to give a free hand to a more interfering state. They sought, through antitraditionalism, to widen the scope of private consciousness within a free-standing civil society that by definition was protected from state action.

The Jacobins' decision to make of French public life a tabula rasa clearly brings grist to the mill of another recent trend, politico-philosophical interpretations of revolutionary politics. The indifference to the feudal past of the deputies of 1789 also relates to current views on the discursive nature of revolutionary French politics, to the "invention" of the French Revolution, and to the "self-referentiality" of Jacobin words.

For the historicizing appropriators of modern literary criticism, which often treats the words of texts in relation to each other rather than to some external referent, the Jacobins' apparent disregard for society as it was and had been serves to justify the notion of Jacobin politics as some kind of abstract and free-floating "discourse." Much is to be said for this point of view. Revisionist historians have a case that can be inflected and expanded, but which is difficult to confound.

From 1790–91 to the Summer of 1792: Mistakes and Contradictions

For more than a year, from the summer of 1789 to the summer of 1790, proto-Jacobin *patriotisme* rallied nearly unanimous support. It crested with the Festival of the Federation, on the anniversary of the fall of the Bastille, when National Guards and Jacobins from all over France converged to celebrate in the nation's capital. But in late 1790–91 this unity so dear to the Jacobins began to crumble.

Some of the assembly's legislation had a stabilizing effect: the abolition of feudalism, as has been said, delivered to the Jacobins a peasant audience. Likewise, the Declaration of the Rights of Man of August 1789 was broadly accepted. Even during the Revolution's darkest hour, its aura made it impossible to envisage a return to the unreconstructed ways of the traditionalist Old Regime, as royalists (vainly) advocated until 1814 when they finally dropped most of their obscurantist and anti-individualist pretensions.

But many other measures taken in these first months of the Revolution were profoundly destabilizing. Some of these upsetting reforms were unavoidable given the Jacobins' worldview as children of the Enlightenment. In May 1791, for example, civic rights were extended to people of color born of free parents; and in September 1792 divorce by mutual consent was also recognized in law. The assembly likewise decreed in favor of partible inheritance not just for males but for females also.

Many other decisions, however, were essentially provocations for those whose will and reason had accepted the Revolution but whose heart and imagination were still set in the ways of the Old Regime. The deputies gained little, for instance, by abolishing titles and honorific distinctions in June 1790 when it became illegal for Frenchmen to call themselves barons, counts, or dukes. (The same stipulation applied in the United States, but nobles were fewer even in Virginia than they were in the most modern parts of France.) Conservatives (like Necker, the de facto prime minister, preoccupied with material social distinctions) and radicals (like Marat, intent on structural political and economic change) were either hostile or indifferent to this symbolic gesture. But the pointless abolition of hallowed titles was much praised by key Jacobins like Brissot, who were more interested in symbolic fraternity than in the ongoing business of daily life.

The Civil Constitution of the Clergy, which the assembly ratified on July 12, 1790, was especially destructive, indeed, disastrous. It brought out the Jacobins' instinct of intolerance and saddled them with endless problems. This "constitution" brought together a series of measures passed in the preceding months to regulate the place of the Catholic Church in French life. It ended the church's privileged place in public life, a change nearly everyone understood to be inevitable. But it went far beyond that. Religious vows were declared no longer binding. Contemplative orders were dissolved. The new arrangement also provided for the reshaping of episcopal sees (some had been large and rich, others small and poor). Importantly, it also decreed the confiscation of church lands in exchange for state stipends, reinforcing a decision made in November 1789.

These formerly clerical lands, which in some departments accounted for as much as one quarter of arable land, came up for sale as *biens nationaux*. Receipts were to guarantee the value of the paper money, the *assignats,* which the *patriotes* had simultaneously decided to float. In some places many peasants, including poor ones, did manage to buy land. But city people, many of them Jacobins, got the lion's share of this booty. In western France especially, where church holdings were extensive, much bitterness surrounded these divisions.

The revolutionaries had mixed motives in enacting this counterproductive legislation. Generally, *patriotes* felt that the church could not be allowed to continue as a free-standing intermediary institution between state and citizen. Like every other body, the church would have to fit into the new cultural and political order of unmediated citizenship.

Many deputies also were freethinkers, who exaggerated the cultural and political weakness of the church. They had taken note of the brutal manipulation of the church elsewhere in Europe by Catholic and non-Catholic monarchs alike. Yet others were Gallican Catholics, religious nationalists of a kind, who resented the pope's influence on the French church. A few, finally, were doctrinally rebellious, neo-Calvinist Jansenists, among them Armand-Gaston Camus (a canonist), Henri-Baptiste Grégoire, and Jean-

Denis Lanjuinais, all of them important Jacobins. Proudly, Grégoire noted in his memoirs that in Naples citizens used the terms "Jansenist" and "Jacobin" interchangeably.[10] Needless to say, all of these statements gave Catholics pause, as did the creation in September 1790 of a Jacobin club in the papal enclave of Avignon.

The church might have accepted the loss of its privileges. On April 12, 1790, the deputies had already refused to declare Catholicism the national religion.[11] But devout Catholics could hardly live with a Civil Constitution that also provided for the election of Catholic priests and bishops by all French citizens, including, of necessity, Protestants, Jews, and avowed freethinkers.

On August 24, 1790, as a public but not as a private person, the French king ratified the Civil Constitution. That is, Louis XVI agreed as a public official to accept its legality; but as a devout believer, he refused to accept the clerical ministrations of priests who had agreed to it. (A nonjuring priest would accompany him to the scaffold in January 1793.)

At first, a fearful pope also remained publicly silent, although he had privately condemned the Declaration of the Rights of Man in a secret consistory on March 29, 1790, a decision of which the king had been privately apprised. But one year later, on April 13, 1791, the pope openly denounced the new arrangements. For good measure, the pontiff also denounced as "monstrous" the revolutionaries' defense of liberty of thought. En masse the Roman bishops rejected the reforms. When oaths were demanded of priests and officials, a growing number of intransigent priests and their peasant audience began to move against the Revolution.

A generation ago, Marxist historians saw these rural choices as a function of economic rather than religious options, but scholars today are less sure.

In some parts of western and eastern France, 85 percent of local priests refused to comply. Law and order broke down in many areas. In February 1791 thousands of hostile Catholic National Guards met at Jalès, an omen of future troubles. Matters worsened when the assembly (which in May 1791 had reasserted the right of adamantly Catholic, pro-papal, and nonjuring priests to say mass in private places) nonetheless and disquietingly ordered that lists of "nonjurors" be drawn up. Under pressure from the clubs and from the Paris *sections* (geographical divisions), the assembly also decided on November 27, 1790, to require all priests to take an oath of loyalty to the Revolution. In Nîmes intransigent Catholics were prosecuted for inciting civil unrest. In Paris nonjuring nuns were whipped by crowds. On July 11, 1791, Voltaire's remains were transferred to the Pantheon, which, until shortly before, had been the Church of Sainte Geneviève, dedicated to the capital's fifth-century patron saint.

Some Jacobin-dominated regional authorities were even more truculent in their anticlericalism than were the nation's highest officials. Everyone took sides. In the years to come more than 30,000 priests fled abroad. From 1793 onward about a thousand more were executed. On the other shore hundreds of enlightened or impoverished and patriotic parish vicars and curates[12] accepted the Civil Constitution regardless. Many of them joined the clubs. Moreover, behind these revolutionary priests, the entire Jacobin machine swung into perfervid action, in the south and southeast especially.

The Jacobins' enthusiastic endorsement of the abrogation of the church's right to manage its own affairs stands as the first, massive instance of their fatal desire despotically to overextend the limits of the public sphere. In 1790–91 the church was goaded into overt opposition to the Revolution, as was the king, whose role had shrunk drastically. If the National Assembly was everything, as it had declared in June and July 1789, what then was the king? The revolutionaries' first response was opaque, but many worried royalists, Louis XVI included, could read between the lines.

The bastard solution of Jean-Joseph Mousnier (1758–1806), a pro-monarchist patriot, was to say, nebulously, that the king was the "executive" branch of the state; but according to the new constitution, which made the ministers he appointed largely powerless, Louis XVI's only true prerogative (granted to him on September 15 by a vote of 673 to 352) was an unworkable right to veto legislation suspensively, a surefire recipe for devastating unpopularity. As Robespierre put it on May 18, 1790, the king was not the representative of the nation but the "commis et le délégué de la nation" (the clerk and delegate of the nation). In September 1790 Marat dared to attack the king openly.

When in early 1791 the monarch decided to exercise his veto powers, the Jacobin clubs became more radical. On January 24, 1791, the Paris Jacobins circularized their affiliates on the disturbing activities of a conservative association, the Friends of the Monarchic Constitution; and on March 28, 1791, they succeeded in getting the Paris municipality to shut down this rival group, establishing a pattern of silencing and censorship that political progressives accepted as wholly normative.

In response to these Jacobin moves, not just the monarch but many confirmed patriots also began to feel that the Revolution was going too far too fast. In the National Assembly Barnave (still a Jacobin but soon to be a former one) urged that the clubs be denied the right to file petitions. Then, on May 9, 1791, his friend and ally Le Chapelier (another soon-to-be former Jacobin) explained that the clubs, though wonderful instruments of public and political education, ought not to become self-regarding "corporations."[13] In retaliation, in late May 1791 in the Jacobin club, Robespierre tried to push Barnave's friends off the key Committee of Correspondence.

In short, by the summer of 1791, revolutionary left and Catholic right were far more aggressive than they had been a year before, and within the left, the Jacobin "party" had begun to break up.

To complicate matters, Louis began to demonstrate a newfound resolve. In December 1790 the king had sounded out foreign monarchs to see if he could count on their help. By February 1791 he was planning his escape. In April 1791 the crowds that kept him from leaving Paris for the neighboring Chateau of Saint-Cloud gave him further offense. Then, on June 5, the assembly deprived him of his right to pardon convicted felons.

On June 20, 1791, at midnight, the king fled from Paris, not to the northwest, toward Rouen, as Mirabeau had sensibly advised the year before, on the grounds that from this provincial place he might rally some heretofore silent and monarchic majority that would be prorevolutionary and antifeudal but socially conservative and loyal to the king. Louis's oversized carriage rolled instead (and very slowly) toward Austrian-controlled Belgium, then under the sway of France's national enemies. One day later he was ignominiously captured by locals in the town of Varennes and brought back to the capital under the silent and condemnatory stare of tens of thousands of Parisians. "As poor peasants," wrote Carlyle of Louis and his wife, "how happy, worthy had ye two been! But by evil destiny, ye were made a King and Queen . . . and so, both an astonishment and a byword to all times."[14]

Louis was formally exonerated one month later by Barnave and his disconcerted and waveringly Jacobin friends, who felt they had no choice but to use the monarch's vestigial claims to sovereignty to stop the radicalization of the Revolution. They suggested—absurdly—that Louis XVI had been kidnapped, although no one believed them. They also tried to emphasize the role of property. Only wealth, Barnave reasoned in an un-Jacobinical sort of way, could enable private persons to be impartial and civic-minded. (While awaiting execution in late 1793, Barnave was to write the first economistic explanation of the French Revolution.)

Most Jacobins, however, reasoned quite differently from their erstwhile hero. Their tentative confidence in the monarchy was irretrievably damaged. Where Barnave reacted to unexpected revolutionary dysfunction by reinforcing monarchism, his fellow Jacobins gravitated instead toward more universalism and popular sovereignty. Badly shaken, the Jacobin clubs convened special sessions. Some of them met all night long. Wild rumors swept their networks.

Earlier in the year, in March 1791, Louis had still been broadly popular. An illness of his had elicited a flurry of concerned messages from loyalist Jacobin clubs. Moulins had declared him to be "the best of kings." But by the summer the Jacobins' royalist devotion had evaporated. Many clubs (Montpellier and Perpignan especially) openly argued for the proclamation of a republic, as some of the Parisian popular societies had been suggesting for a few weeks already. Some provincial clubs wanted to proclaim the deposition of the king in favor of his son, who would be advised by a council, a solution other more cautious clubs noisily decried. Many Jacobins began to think of themselves as betrayed citizens who would have to punish an aberrant and devious father-king.

A thread runs to the execution of the king in January 1793 (and henceforth, no doubt, to the Terror) from the Jacobins' panicked reaction in 1791 to Louis's—for them—sudden decision to desert. For with the events of the summer of 1791, and their eventual antimonarchic sequels, revolutionary Jacobin politics came to its first major crisis.

True, already in the fall of 1789—that is, before the clubs had come into being nationwide—the patriotic Monarchiens had dropped out of the revolutionary movement. Likewise, in May 1790, Mirabeau and Lafayette had attempted to make of their Society of 1789 a counterweight to the club. (About 10 percent of the Parisian Jacobins had followed the two men into that disguised opposition.) But Mirabeau had been careful not to break openly with the mother society, to which he later ostentatiously returned when his divisive maneuver fizzled.

But on July 16, 1791, Barnave's followers, the Feuillants, irrevocably broke away. The next day a Republican crowd of five thousand (small by Parisian standards but large as revolutionary crowds went) gathered at the Champ de Mars where the Eiffel Tower stands today. In response, Barnave's two most important allies, Lafayette, the commander of the Paris

National Guard, and Jean-Sylvain Bailly, a famous astronomer who had become the mayor of Paris, ordered troops to fire on the people. Dozens of Parisians were killed in this Massacre of the Champ de Mars. Hundreds more were briefly arrested, and nearly all of them resurfaced in the next years as militant sans-culottes. Danton, the most prominent of the Parisian radicals, fled to Britain. Camille Desmoulins and Marat dropped out of sight.

On September 3, 1791, a revised Barnavian constitution was promulgated by a new Legislative Assembly (it had been elected on August 27, 1791, all previously elected deputies being ineligible for reelection, as Robespierre had proposed). Louis accepted it two weeks later.

Self-servingly, Jacques-Guillaume Thouret, a leading moderate and a famous jurist and publicist, explained that "the revision [of the Constitution] is complete. It may cause the privileged classes to complain because not a single abuse has been restored. But it will satisfy all the enlightened partisans of monarchic government." (Thouret too was executed in 1794.) Meanwhile a Feuillant newspaper in Lyons summed up Barnave's moderate and anti-Jacobin line: "The people are sovereign; but it would be injurious for it to exercise that sovereignty."[15] Thus the Jacobin network split apart.

At first, in July 1791, a mere fifteen clubs nationwide sided with the left Jacobins against Barnave's dissident Jacobins. Many Jacobins simply withdrew. Participation in national and local elections fell from one-half to one-fourth of the electorate.

By late September 1791, however, nearly all of the provincial societies had changed their minds and rallied behind Brissot, Jérôme Pétion de Villeneuve, and Robespierre, now working in close accord. Translated, this leftward shift of the clubs meant that after the king's flight in June 1791, most Jacobins at large had instinctively concluded that the solution to revolutionary dysfunction was not to stop the Revolution, and consolidate its individualistic achievements, but to move it forward, toward more universalistic goals. They did not believe Barnave when he warned that doing so would threaten property rights.

An untoward sign for the Feuillants came in November 1791 when Pétion (along with Robespierre considered the great heros of the Paris Jacobins) was elected mayor of Paris over the once immensely popular Lafayette. (Pétion, a future Girondin, was to commit suicide in June 1794.)

Constitutional monarchy rapidly lost its aura. The club at Limoux expressed most Jacobins' new point of view when it wrote to the Legislative

Assembly in Paris that it could recognize the king but could neither love nor respect him.[16] When Louis once again in November 1791 decided to use his veto power (as it happens, to protect the rights of individual émigrés to come and go as they pleased), the clubs sprang back to life.

Another galvanizing event was the assembly's decision to release the once mutinous "soldiers of Chateauvieux," who had been condemned to hard labor by their mercenary—and reactionary—Swiss commanders in 1790. Louis had been slow in acquiescing to their pardon. In late February 1792 at the seaport of Brest, where they were imprisoned, ten thousand people joined the local *clubbistes* in a celebratory march to their prison.

The popular sans-culotte movement, which was to the left of even the left Jacobins, strengthened day by day. After the Massacre of the Champ de Mars, far-left journalists like Marat had had to go underground. But in the early winter of 1791–92 Marat and Danton, who had returned from abroad, were once again deeply involved in Parisian politics.

True, when the new Legislative Assembly met in Paris in October 1791, 264 deputies joined the Feuillants and only 136, the Jacobin club.[17] More to the point, however, in the provincial clubs Barnave's Jacobin audience was consistently shrinking.

More able to influence opinion, the left-Jacobin Brissotins launched a press and propaganda campaign for an objective they thought would help them control the revolutionary state: war. Ostensibly they aimed to attack Austria and punish it for protecting counterrevolutionary noble émigrés, the bêtes noires of the *clubbistes*. (The club at Tain had urged the sequestration of their property in November 1790 already.)[18] In reality, however, the left Jacobins hoped to use war fever to unite the nation behind their universalizing program.

In and out of the Paris club, Brissot, Henri-Maximin Isnard, and Jean-Louis Carra (a wild journalist and convicted thief) pushed hard for warlike measures, a daring and desperately foolish policy that their fellow Jacobin Robespierre (a resolute antimilitarist) was unable to resist. Gradually nearly all the leading Jacobins of the day (Pierre Vergniaud, Armand Gensonné, Marguerite-Elie Guadet, Claude Fauchet, and Condorcet, a convinced pacifist!) fell in step behind Brissot. In early 1792 five clubs, including Dijon, Clermont, and Caen, circularized other societies for support.[19] Ninety percent of the clubs that are known to have expressed views on this issue were pro-war.[20]

The Civil Constitution of the Clergy was the *patriotes'* biggest mistake. Declaring war on April 20, 1792, was their second-worst move. The war went badly. Unexpected military defeats stoked radical feeling. Governmental receipts had been catching up with expenses but the war soon disrupted state finances hopelessly. Refractory, nonjuring priests were ordered deported. In May 1792 François de Neufchâteau, an ordinarily conservative man, urged the Paris club to demand that suspects be disarmed without due process. Robespierre denounced courtiers and noble-born army officers, who were—he said—conspiring against liberty.

Influence slipped away from the Legislative (still called National) Assembly, where the left Jacobins composed only a small minority of the *patriote* party and drifted instead toward the Paris Jacobin club, from which Barnave had long since been excluded and where, in the early summer of 1792, Robespierre was gradually displacing Brissot as the leading radical Jacobin.

Another phase of political change—or decomposition—opened in mid-June 1792, when Louis XVI, who in March 1792 had named a Girondin cabinet (known at the time as "the Jacobin ministry") in order to expose its incompetence, dismissed these Jacobin ministers. (An insolent letter sent by the minister Jean Marie Roland but drafted by his wife had triggered the monarch's indignation.) In defiant response to the king's show of independence, on June 20, 1792, a crowd, abetted by the Girondin Jacobin mayor of Paris, Pétion, forced its way into the royal palace and demanded that Louis put on a red Phrygian bonnet, of the kind worn in ancient times by freed slaves, now a symbol of patriotic zeal. Some clubs (Rouen and Le Havre) protested; but most of them defended the Parisians and the Girondins. The size of the Jacobin club network reached a new peak. Only in 1794, with state help, would it rise to that same level of intensity.

Appalled, Lafayette asked the assembly on June 28, 1792, to dissolve the Jacobin clubs, but to no avail. The assembly's Feuillant majority, hesitant, discredited, and powerless, neither blamed nor supported him. In the clubs provincial Jacobins, as might be expected, reviled their former hero. At Tulle a *clubbiste* declared Lafayette all at once Cromwell, Marius, and Sulla.[21]

By the summer of 1792, all patriots understood that the constitutional monarchy was in its death throes. So, for that matter, did the king and queen, but they persistently and foolishly believed that matters had to worsen before they could improve. Nearly fifty clubs called for the king to yield and bring back Roland and the Jacobin ministry. Then, on July 25, 1792, the poorly advised commander of the invading Prussian army, the duke of Brunswick, signed a manifesto (written by a French noble émigré) threatening to destroy Paris if the royal family were harmed in any way. Four days later, Robespierre, in the Paris club, asked for the removal of the king and the calling of a new constitutional convention. On August 3, 1792, forty-seven of the forty-eight Paris *sections* also demanded the removal of the king.

The role during the next two weeks of the Jacobins in the actual overthrow of the monarchy is not clear. They appear to have been guided by a *directoire secret* (secret directory committee). But some Jacobins at least were decidedly instrumental in this second revolution. Jacobins were especially active in winning over to insurrection the thousands of provincial volunteers who had headed for the capital in response to the dubiously legal call of many local clubs to march and "defend freedom." (The ones from Marseilles had set off on July 2, 1792, singing a hymn that has ever since borne their name.)

In the first week of August 1792 the *fédéré* militiamen, the Paris crowd, and the radicalized Jacobin clubs acted in harmony. On August 9 the already Revolutionized Paris Commune or municipality, which exercised authority over the capital's National Guard, was deposed and replaced by an even more radical Commune where sans-culottes played an important role. Together, *fédérés,* Jacobins, and the new Commune forced the hand of the disoriented, bewildered ex-Jacobin Feuillants in the National Assembly.

On August 10, 1792, the monarchy fell in a minibattle that ironically began more or less by accident, well after the king had yielded and been marched off to safety—and prison. Six hundred soldiers died—most of them Swiss guards murdered by the Parisian crowd after they had surrendered. Four hundred attackers also died, an unwanted and unforeseen human cost that made it impossible to let bygones be bygones. A less bloody battle might have made the mere deposal of the king feasible. But the ferocity of this urban conflict made revenge and, in its wake, the Terror far more likely.

It bears mentioning that of all the figures of the revolutionary decade who had military force at their disposal, Louis XVI alone consistently refused to use it. The Jacobins, who claimed to be the modern party of humanity, were in practice more than matched by Louis and his ancient Christian scruples.

At the front, a dismayed and disillusioned Lafayette went over to France's Austrian enemies, who ironically imprisoned him for five years as a dangerous revolutionary. (George Washington, president of the newly reconstituted American republic, vainly pleaded for the release of this honorary American citizen whose child was his godson.)

Jacobinism had turned another corner. Royalist newspapers were shut down. Jacobins decided that only Jacobins had the right to speak. As Saint-Just would later explain, henceforth, only the friends of liberty had the right to enjoy the fruits of liberty.

From August 1792 to June 1793: The Jacobins' Rise to Power

> To kill a king, and become the horror of respectable nations and persons? But then also, to save a king; to lose one's footing with the decided Patriot . . . The dilemma presses sore; and between the horns of it, you wiggle round and round. Decision is nowhere, save in the Mother Society and her Sons. These have decided, and go forward; the others wriggle round uneasily with their dilemma-horns, and make way no wither.
>
> Thomas Carlyle, *The French Revolution*

The Jacobins cheered the end of the monarchy. Two hundred and fifty societies sent messages to the newly elected Convention to hail the proclamation of the new republic on September 22, 1792.

Nonetheless, the politics of August–September 1792 occasioned the second great split in the Jacobin clubs. The Feuillants of course were long gone; but a new struggle pitted against each other the two wings of what had been in the fall of 1791 a unified Jacobin left. This second internal split of late 1792–93, between the Girondins and Montagnards, was felt more deeply by the provincial clubs than even the painful division of 1791 between the Feuillants and the Paris Jacobins.

Since the spring of 1792 the left-leaning Girondin Jacobins had either steered the revolutionary state or been close to doing so. The fall of the monarchy, although not their doing, did not displease them. The king after all had tried to force them out in June. Moreover, in September many Girondins were returned to power, among them Roland, who was once again made minister of the interior. Nor did the Girondin Jacobins mind the forced sale of émigré estates, the placing of their relatives under policy surveillance, the removal of the king's name from all documents, or the suppression of religious orders. The Girondins also supported the suspension on August 25, 1792, of the earlier laws that provided for the compensatory repayment of canceled feudal dues.

But the Girondin Jacobins, who had in the past steadily pushed for the radicalization of revolutionary politics, grew increasingly worried about the continued leftist drift of events. Ideological extremists were accumulating power, they thought, at the expense of the legal authorities (that is, themselves) and this trend they did not like, although they themselves had been ideological extremists when out of power only the year before.

Late in the summer of 1792 the Girondins were increasingly troubled by the scattered arrests of their former enemies, the Feuillants, whose unhappy fate suddenly seemed relevant to their own. Troubling also for the Girondins was the creation on August 17, 1792, at the prompting of the new sans-culotte–dominated Paris Commune, of a special tribunal to judge crimes supposedly committed by the (constitutionally sanctioned) royalists during the (illicit) overthrow of the monarchy. This first wave of terror was not extensive, but a number of prominent conservative figures and journalists were nonetheless executed.

These Parisian developments made the Girondins anxious, just as the first massacre of counterrevolutionaries in Avignon in October 1791 had. The threatened Girondins did not approve when Danton, the new minister of justice in Paris, who derived his true power from his links to the new self-appointed and populist Paris Communal government, granted amnesty to the man in charge of that initial slaughter, "Coupe-tête" (head-chopper) Jourdan. (Jourdan was so wild that he was ordered executed by his fellow Robespierrist administrators in May 1794.)

Nor did the Girondins like Danton's egalitarian rhetoric. They worried about a greater and destabilizing involvement of the poor in public affairs. The Girondins were dead set against the Paris Commune, or municipal government, which some weeks back had fallen into the hands of truculent sans-culottes. Rural unrest was also much more widespread in 1792 than it had been in 1790 or 1791.

Like the Feuillants in the late summer of 1791, the Girondins of late 1792 decided that the Revolution had gone too far. As a former mayor of Lyons wrote in November to Roland: "The scene has changed: laws which before the 10th of August were favorable only to our enemies are now the [last] safeguard of liberty."[22]

The September massacres in Paris (and by imitation in many other cities like Versailles and Reims) were the very heavy straw that broke the Girondins' eroded patience. About thirteen hundred prisoners, many of them apolitical common criminals and prostitutes, were hacked to death. (Rates of execution from jail to jail varied between 1 percent and 97 percent.) It is difficult to ascertain the deeper causes of this horrible bloodshed, which was unimaginable before it occurred. One possibility is to see it as a populist throwback to ancient destructive habits: under the pressure of events, consciously phrased principle yielded to primitive blood lust, the likes of which had not been seen in France since the messianic wars of religion in the late sixteenth century.

If set in that context of inherited impulse, the September massacres of 1792 were for the sans-culottes what the Terror of 1794 was to be for the more educated and propertied Jacobins. In any instance, what mattered politically was that most left Jacobins reacted passively to these massacres. When urged to protect these victims, Danton is said to have responded, "Fuck the prisoners."[23]

One might add in passing that although often represented in literature and film—especially in their German variants (notably by the playwright Büchner in his *Death of Danton* of 1834)—as a fatalist and preromantic victim of Robespierrist tyranny, Danton was in fact a sensual, vulgar, theatrical, unprincipled, and venal man, an *a*typical Jacobin in most respects except for his nationalism and his cult of dynamism. His obvious energy and his genuine oratorical talents brought him to early prominence, but in an ideologically determined setting, the man was no match for Maximilian Robespierre, his doctrinal and triumphant nemesis.

The September massacres and the left Jacobins' tolerance of them mattered a great deal to the Girondins, not because such acts of popular violence particularly offended their quasi-populist principles but, more simply, because they had nearly been its victims. On September 2, 1792, Robespierre and Marat had tried to have Brissot and thirty of his friends arrested. Without Danton's grudging interference, the Girondins would have been in jail during the massacre, and they would surely have been killed as well.

To make matters worse, after the fact, the left Montagnard Jacobins did not condemn the massacres at all. Far from it, as shall be seen below, Robespierre explained that these murderous attacks had been the work of "un mouvement populaire et non une sédition partielle" (a popular movement and not a seditious riot as has been ridiculously supposed).[24] Even a moderate Jacobin like Grégoire shunted responsibility for these dreadful acts away from the actors and toward an exculpating cultural context inherited from the Old Regime. The massacres, he explained some months later, had been "the fruit of a government without morality, and the depravity of a court that had raised its scandalous triumphs on the debris of morality."[25]

For a few days after the slaughter the Girondins continued to hesitate. Should they break with the Jacobin movement altogether? At first, Carra and Antoine-Joseph Gorsas, their leading journalists, defended the massacres as a welcomed, necessary, and purging step. But gradually the Girondins, as the Feuillants had before them, turned to the right in order to stop the Revolution and to consolidate their hold over national politics. Their new immobilizing resolve was strengthened by echoes of yet more killings in the provinces, and by the victory of Valmy two weeks later on September 20, 1792, which stopped the allies' invasion of France and made further radicalization seem less necessary. Also relevant to the Girondins' newly found determination to halt the Revolution was the convening of the recently elected and more prestigious Convention on the next day.[26]

By late September 1792, then, the leading Girondins had made up their minds to speak out on behalf of law and order. Like those other ex-Jacobins, the Feuillants of September 1791, the Girondins had become in September 1792 defenders of the revolutionary status quo. On October 29, 1792, Jean-Baptiste Louvet assailed Robespierre as an "insolent demagogue."

As will be seen, the split between Girondin Jacobins and Montagnard Jacobins is a set piece of a Marxist revolutionary historiography that highlights economic interest and class analysis. Many historians have insisted that the two groups were different on other grounds as well (religion, for example). Nonetheless, a close reading of their fundamental opinions (rather than of their opportunistic statements) reveals that Girondins were no less Republican than Montagnards and no less anticlerical (indeed, with some exceptions, they were perhaps more hostile to the nonconstitutional, populist church than was the Montagne). Nor were Girondins more constitutional and legalistic. When out of power, they had passively allowed the crowds (then favorable to them) to invade the Tuileries Palace in April

1792 and the National Assembly in June 1792. Likewise, in April 1793, they would try to impeach Marat, who was at the time both the president of the Paris Jacobins and an authentically elected deputy as well. And years later, in September 1797, those of them who survived accepted the mildly leftist military coup d'état that led to the illegal purge of a representative assembly whose control they had lost to constitutional monarchists in the previous and fair elections. Indeed, many Girondins lived on to serve Bonaparte's autocratic militarism as well. Nor were the Girondins more rich, more bourgeois, more interested in industrial development, or, in a word, more capitalist than their rivals.

The essence of the problem was elsewhere. Specifically, in the fall of 1792 the Girondin Jacobins, who were linked to one another by ties of friendship and mutual interest, were then governing and instinctively assumed that the Revolution would have to be stabilized to be saved, whereas the Montagnard Jacobins (then in opposition) thought that salvation lay in a move toward intransigent universalism, with popular help if need be.

For the Feuillants, after the flight of the king to Varennes in June 1791, slowing down the Revolution suddenly seemed imperative. In the fall of 1792, after the September massacres, the Girondins made a similar decision. They had changed their mind. The best way to preserve Jacobin ideals, they now thought, was for the Revolution to stand still. Indeed, the Girondins' conservative turnabout of late 1792 not only echoed Barnave's reversal in 1791, it also heralded Robespierre's own future course, when in the winter of 1793–94 he too attempted to slow the dynamic of revolutionary change by disengaging Jacobinism from its sans-culotte allies.

By the fall of 1792 issues in the capital were clearly drawn, even more so than in 1791 because the Parisian popular movement had a tighter structure. Girondin insiders who still controlled the government after the election of the new Convention on September 21, 1792, decided to confront the Montagnards directly.

On October 8, 1792, the Girondins (backed by several provincial clubs) proposed both the creation of a departmental guard for the Convention and an official inquiry on the origins of the September massacres. They attacked Danton, whom they rightly suspected of having stolen public monies.

But the Montagnards were equally determined to impose their interpretation of the massacres. On October 8, 1792, the *Journal de la correspondance des Jacobins* claimed that the prisoners had been responsible for the

September massacres because they had intended to escape and kill the companions of absent volunteers: "you can understand that when the horrible plot was discovered the people wreaked a terrible vengeance."[27] On November 5, 1792, Robespierre asked rhetorically if the revolutionaries had wanted a "Revolution without revolution . . . Who can indicate with precision," he asked, "the point where the flood of popular insurrection must break? And if that is a price to be paid, what people could then ever shake the yoke of despotism?"[28]

On November 30, 1792, the Paris club decided that the September massacres had saved the Revolution. Jacobin orators defended the sans-culotte–dominated Paris Commune. They attacked the Girondins, once their fellow Jacobins. Jean-Marie Collot d'Herbois went one step further: without the massacres, he said, liberty would not exist.

In a famous debate with Louvet, on the Convention floor, Robespierre managed to convince the hesitant members of the Plaine—the silent and undecided majority that was afraid of popular violence but did not want the Revolution to falter—that on this issue the Gironde was wrong and the Montagne was right.

The deputies tabled the Girondins' proposed inquiry into the cause of the massacres; Robespierre made a triumphal entry into the Paris Jacobin club that same day. The Jacobins of Nîmes likewise resolved that an *Adresse à tous les Républicains de France* of Brissot, who had recently been excluded from the Paris club, was motivated by a "secret intrigue."[29]

Then in late 1792 came the trial of the king. Pierre Louis Bentabole, a deranged Jacobin extremist, soon to become a violent terrorist, had already in October asked for the death penalty for Louis. On November 20 secret and incriminating documents were discovered in an iron safe that had been hidden by order of the monarch in a wall of the Tuileries Palace the year before. On December 2, 1792, the popular revolutionaries of the Paris *sections*—and many provincial clubs as well—urged the Convention to proceed with the trial, as did Robespierre on December 3.

The Girondins did not want to bring the king to trial. To do so would only radicalize the Revolution, which was what they wished to avoid above all else. But they had no choice. Opinion went against them. On December 11, 1792, the inexorable procedure was set into motion.

The Girondins hedged their arguments. They agreed the king was guilty. Should he be executed? No, they argued. But if he were condemned to die, should the execution be ratified by a plebiscite that the partisans of the death penalty might lose? Yes, they responded.

By implication, the desperate Girondins found themselves denying the Convention's right to rule as a wholly sovereign body. For Pierre Vergniaud, the Gironde's greatest orator and a former president of the Paris Jacobin club, the deputies as representatives of the sovereign people had many prerogatives, but those did not include the power to try the king. Brissot described the Montagnards, who rejected the idea of a plebiscite, as "ambitious imbeciles" bent on violating the sovereignty of the people. Gensonné attacked the Jacobins as a "faction" that encouraged sectional insurrection against the sovereign nation. But Vergniaud, like many Girondins, went on to vote for the death penalty. The uncommitted deputies of the Plaine took note of the Girondins' inability to act forcefully and in concert.

Wordsworth, who was in Paris at the time, later wrote eloquently of Brissot's friends in his *Prelude,* "That Heaven's best aid is wasted upon men who to themselves are false."

Given the Jacobins' confused interpretations of popular sovereignty, the Montagne's retort to the Girondins' call for a popular vote was predictable. If the Convention had had the right to proclaim a republic on September 22, 1792, why did it not have the right to condemn the king in January 1793? The Montagnards loftily refuted the Gironde's evocation of popular sovereignty and its call for a referendum, a stance they surely understood completely since it had been their own in the recent past: Danton and Robespierre, for example, had both argued for that selfsame democratic and consultative solution in the summer of 1791 after the king's flight to Varennes, when they hoped to mobilize the electorate against the National Parliament so as to dethrone the king.

By January 1793, however, times had apparently changed. A popular vote, they explained, was at that moment practically undesirable because the provincial electoral assemblies were already in disarray. If Louis's fate were referred to these local assemblies, they concluded, more confusion would ensue. Proposing a plebiscite was a counterrevolutionary measure. Needless to say, the Montagnards also concluded that the Girondins had themselves become factional *aristocrates.*

Clearly, the different words spoken by these two warring groups of Jacobins must hold our close attention. But Jacobins, especially in Paris, in both club and Convention, were highly educated men who could with ease rattle off this Voltairean idea of toleration or that idea of Rousseauean general will. To justify what really mattered to them—first, the advancement or the retrogression of the Revolution at any given moment; and second, the suppression or encouragement of popular revolutionaries—both progressive and regressive Jacobins knew precisely which kind of argument they should use.

During the trial of the king, some "pre-Freudian" Jacobins might choose to say that the king was a mythic figure whose body had to die if the nation were to live. But other Jacobins could conclude instead that rationally appraised, his death would cause more problems than it would resolve.

On January 20, 1793, Louis XVI, "the last king of France" as Jacobins liked to say, was condemned to death. He was executed the next day. Two days later, a noble-born Jacobin, Louis Michel Le Peletier, who had voted for his execution, was in turn assassinated by a suicidal royalist.

The first months of 1793 were a period of intense psychological radicalization and institutional disorganization. Financial credit dried up. The distribution and transportation of food to Paris (never well organized) was made more difficult by the cavalry's requisition of draft animals. Domestic and international problems piled up as well. On February 1, 1793, France declared war on England and, for good measure, on the Netherlands and Spain, too. (Russia, Naples, and Turkey would also join the anti-French coalition.) Inside France, in the west, the peasants of the Vendée rose up in revolt on March 11, 1793. Many local patriots were brutally murdered by the rebels. In the first week of April 1793, General Dumouriez, the commanding, pro-Girondin general on the Belgian front, went over to the enemy. He was, after Lafayette in August 1792, the second commander-in-chief to defect in less than a year.

At this juncture, the Montagnards' instinctive response—namely, to speak in more universalist and audacious terms—seemed to make increasing sense to desperately anxious pro-revolutionaries and, in the Convention, to the hesitant, fearful deputies of the Plaine.

Montagnard Jacobins everywhere vociferously advocated arresting more people. They also wished to give more leeway to the crowd. In ordinary times law and order and the free exchange of goods and money would have been their strong preference. But now an ancient instinctive thought took hold, namely, that military repression was the best way to deal with what they considered an anomalous penury of supply. It increasingly seemed to the propertied, ordinarily enlightened Montagnards that the un-committed rich were being selfish. They were not virtuous. As Saint-Just said of those Conventionnels who did not want to kill the king, "they lacked energy." They deserved punishment.

Inside the Convention the uncommitted deputies of the Plaine inclined to that same view. They too were hostile to direct popular involvement in pol-itics, but they also thought that the Girondins were pusillanimous and du-plicitous men who had changed their mind too often, on the rights of crowds, the sanctity of the law, virtue, energy, and the proper embodiment of sovereignty.

On October 11, 1792, the Girondins had still managed to secure nearly every place on the prestigious Constitutional Committee. But after the death of the king on January 21, 1793, the moderate allies of the Giron-dins increasingly gave them up for lost. It seemed more than ever unthink-able to the Plaine that the Revolution could be saved if it did not go for-ward, as the Montagnards had been arguing all along (and as the Girondins, of course, had also argued from late 1791 into early 1792).

Paradoxically, then, in the spring and summer of 1793, many moderate revolutionaries of the Plaine concluded that they had no choice but to accept temporary measures of extralegal coercion in order to uphold the parliamen-tarian and individualist values they had earnestly proclaimed in 1789.

On February 22, 1793, the Marseilles club circularized the network and asked for the recall of the Girondin Conventionnels. The Limoges society, which had sided with the Gironde on January 28, 1793, moved back to-ward the Montagne on February 25.[30]

Of course, it was difficult at first for left Montagnard Jacobins and right Girondin Jacobins to see one another as mortal enemies. They had been like brothers only a few months before. On March 17, 1793, four days after the creation of an extraordinary Revolutionary Tribunal, which the Girondins had fully supported, François Buzot and Robespierre met once again. For a brief time, it seemed as if the rift between the two camps had been bridged, fraternally. But accord among these varying left and right Ja-cobins was impossible. The Revolution could not simultaneously go for-ward and stop.

To mark their new stance of conservative resistance, in April 1793 the Girondins tried (and failed) to convict Marat, who had been elected to the

Convention by the city of Paris. A point of no return now ensued. On May 31, and once again on June 2, the Parisian crowds and militia (eighty thousand men in all) organized by the sans-culotte–dominated Paris Commune and abetted by the Jacobins, surrounded the Convention hall.

A few weeks before, on March 8, the authorities had easily dissolved a similar sans-culotte move against that same assembly, which the Jacobins had *not* encouraged. In June, however, the unchecked sans-culottes successfully demanded the expulsion and arrest of the legally elected Girondin deputies. After some hesitation, the centrist deputies of the Plaine gave in. Key Girondins were expelled. Some escaped. Others were placed under house arrest. Most were executed five months later.

Attendance in the clubs, which had slackened a bit, picked up once again as the tempo of radicalized politics quickened also. Jacobinism had reached another important turning point. In August 1792 Jacobins had decided that only they could speak, and so it was that on December 4, 1792, the Girondins had made it a crime for newspapers to advocate a return to the monarchy. But now, in June 1793, the victorious left Jacobins decided that only some of the *clubbistes* could speak. After July 23, 1793, it became an offense to obstruct their meetings.

The ancient and illiberal side of the Jacobin sensibility was given free rein.

From July 1793 to July 1794: Jacobin Politics in a Social Void

> Thus, in Milton, did the monsters of the deep devour with rabid greed the breast of the very being that had given them life.
>
> José Marchena, a Spanish liberal imprisoned in France as a friend of the Girondins, speaking of the rivalry between the Girondins and the Montagnards

In the summer of 1793 many provincial Jacobins whose lives were still unperturbed found it hard to grasp the various issues and events in Paris. "How will you establish laws on foundations that are constantly thrown up by the volcano of anarchy?" asked the *Vedette de Besançon*. "[How can you place laws] on the uncertain bases of a public opinion that is excited or corrupted at will by the party that masters it?"[31] Provincial Jacobins believed the republicanized Revolution should go forward legally. They asked two related questions: Was it legal to exclude legally elected deputies? The answer was clearly "no." And were the Montagnards a faction, or were they the voice of Jacobin opinion? Here answers were more varied.

In many parts of France, in western France and Normandy especially, local clubs, nearly without exception, sided with the legally elected Girondins. Likewise, in the southwest, where the local clubs sided with the Montagnards in Paris, many disgruntled Girondin Jacobins (as at Marseilles) managed to ensconce themselves in the *sections*. In central and eastern France, by contrast, where Girondin opposition was unstructured, most of the *clubbistes* responded quite quickly to the Montagnards' call for a deepening of revolutionary ideology.

Local conflicts and proximity to the power of the capital were keenly relevant to these divergent provincial options, which were also affected by antecedent cultural and social provincial contexts. In southeastern France, for example, where sociability was intense and densely organized, and where the Civil Constitution of the Clergy had been overwhelmingly accepted by the local clergy, entire communities went over to the side of the more progressive, activist Montagnards. There, civil war divided not leftist Montagnards and rightist Girondins, but mainstream local Jacobins and the populist far left that was allied to the Paris Jacobins for tactical reasons.

Likewise, in modernizing cities and protoindustrial centers where social differences of class were consciously apprehended and institutionally embodied in rival clubs that had different social profiles (as in Bordeaux, Arles, Aix, and Nîmes) the Montagnards' decision to go forward and realize their ideological worldview, in momentary tandem with the sansculottes, struck a leftist chord with some people at least.

On balance, however, provincial middle-of-the-road Jacobin clubs were, at first, indignant; and ensuing divisions deepened when anti-Parisian Jacobin revolutionaries were joined in opposition to the Montagne by all those—royalists or Republicans—who, since the summer of 1789, had been nursing a silent grievance of some kind against all Jacobins of the right or of the left.

It was as if a dam had broken. The intra-Jacobin, Parisian quarrel of Girondins and Montagnards over making a deal with or against the Paris crowd left in its wake a slew of mini–civil wars whose social and cultural origins were very broad.

In March 1793 Vendéen peasants had been the first to organize a serious rebellion. Then, on July 13, 1793, Charlotte Corday murdered Marat. Robespierre had despised the utterly unrespectable Marat, who was less convinced about the merits of individualism than were most Jacobins. But his death muted this discordant past and made of Marat the premier martyr of the Jacobin Revolution.

After this came the news that at Lyons the momentarily victorious anti-Jacobins had executed Joseph Chalier, the Montagnard mayor of the city, whose image now joined that of Marat and Le Peletier in the Jacobins' imaginary pantheon. On July 23 the city of Mayence, on the Rhine, which the French had occupied and garrisoned in October 1792, surrendered. Finally, on August 27, 1793, the naval base and fleet at Toulon went over to the invading English.

Different places produced different kinds of anti-Montagnard coalitions (as will be seen in Chapter 10). In the west peasant rebels had since March 1793 co-opted reluctant nobles, and had in turn been co-opted ideologically by glib royalists and nonjuring clergymen. In Lyons the anti-Jacobin enemies of the Montagne, though confirmed Republicans for the most part, remained well to the right of mainstream Jacobins. In Marseilles, by contrast, the local foes of the lower-middle-class Montagnard Jacobins in the club were the genuine (if middle-class) Jacobins in the *sections* who were real revolutionaries in most respects but were nonetheless determined to resist Parisian interference in their local affairs.

And yet, in the space of weeks, the indomitable Paris-directed Jacobin Montagnards pushed back all of their enemies. Thinking in absolute terms gives one a transcendental indifference to the odds of failure. The Jacobins had become the architects of a "mythic present."[32] Henceforth, explained one of their numbers at Bourg-sur-Rhône, "we will not have to grub through the history of Greece and Rome to find legislators and heroes."[33]

On the one hand, Jacobin leaders really did struggle heroically. Universal military conscription (the *levée en masse*) was decreed on August 23, 1793. Lyons was recaptured. The English were beaten in the north; the Spaniards, in the south. Thanks to a young Corsican artillery officer with a funny name, Napoleone de Buonaparte, Toulon was besieged and retaken on December 19. On December 23, 1793, the Vendéen army in the west was broken up.

On the other hand, with resistance came terror. In the summer of 1793 the ingredients of rampant state-decreed terrorism began to coalesce. Its ostensible cause was the sense that "these were the times that tried men's souls." War and civil war made the Jacobins' collective dictatorship seem more acceptable, to them in any case. Its precedent was the execution of the king in January. Its means were the gradual suspension of law. Its driving motive was the hatred of faction. Its mainspring was the moralization of politics and the demonization of Jacobinism's enemies, critical themes to which I will often return. Its words came from the hegemonic assemblage of formulaic recipes that were taking on a demonic life of their own.

And once state-sponsored terror began in earnest, in October of 1793, nothing could arrest it. Desmoulins wept at the trial of the Girondins, but in vain. Terror now fed on its own self. As Paul Barras (a noble-born Jacobin terrorist) pithily explained, "Il faut terroriser ou s'attendre à l'être" (Your choice is to be terrorized or to become a terrorist).

Cowed, galvanized, silenced, or enthused, millions decided to follow the lead of the militant Jacobins, who at this point composed surely no more than a small minority of the urban possessing class. On August 23, 1793, the Jacobins decreed that the resources of the entire country would be mobilized behind the faltering war effort, whose organization was directed by Carnot, a Jacobin of sorts. International trade, mining, and metallurgy all came under state control. Symbolically, the single state manufacture of rifles in Paris in 1794 produced more than five hundred weapons daily, a huge number by the standards of the day. By September 1794 the armies of the republic numbered over a million men.

The Jacobin majority of the Convention also reorganized the revolutionary government once again, but in a manner far removed from what had just been voted on August 10, 1793, with the enactment of a new constitution.

In theory, the new Jacobin charter was latitudinarian: it had an unusual libertarian clause that allowed rebellion in the name of violated freedom (the "law must protect public and private liberties against oppression by those who govern"). But more to the point was the Jacobins' decision not to apply this constitution until the war had stopped. In the summer and fall of 1793, constitutional procedure was not the Jacobins' first concern.

Some of these changes had already begun in the spring of 1793. On April 5 the Revolutionary Tribunal, established in March, had seen its powers extended to enable it to prosecute more or less at will. Likewise, on April 6 the Convention, Girondins included, decreed the creation of an omnipotent Committee of Public Safety (CPS), backed by a Committee of General Security (CGS).[34] That delegation of powers to the CPS and the

CGS was of course required by the Jacobins' belief that the single and elected assembly held all sovereignty and that executive power could be exercised only dependently by a committee which—in theory—remained a mere branch of the unicameral legislature.

Then, in midsummer 1793, the left Jacobins turned the screws tighter yet. They managed to pack all of the Convention's key committees. On July 27, 1793, Robespierre joined the CPS, which he never (despite appearances) tyrannized but whose spokesman he nonetheless became. The Robespierrist and neoclassical painter David was the most famous member of the neighboring CGS. To make sure that the writ of the Jacobins in Paris would not be ignored, eighty-two Conventionnels *en mission*—most of them Montagnards—were delegated as pro-consuls in the provinces. Provisioning Paris was handed over to a Subsistence Commission with power to purchase grain abroad and to requisition it at home. Ironically, this modernizing step elaborated ancient monarchic and patriarchal practices rather than reversing what had existed before 1789. (Tocqueville in the 1850s would take historical note of such continuities.)

In the provinces the administrative business of government was in theory still entrusted to local and elected representatives; but revolutionary business (suspects, the controlled economy, requisitions of goods and services, provisioning the army) was increasingly placed in the hands of appointed officials who ordinarily worked with the clubs. These in turn became cogs in the Parisian Jacobins' new system of government, which had been officially decreed on July 25, 1793. Together with the Committees of Surveillance, created in March of 1793 (whose membership often overlapped with that of the clubs), the Jacobin societies became the provincial mainstay of the national state-machine, a complete turnabout from what had been their self-defined role of 1789–90, when the clubs had presented themselves as removed and impartial critics, as friendly, nonparticipating observers.

In brief, France in late 1793 approximated a single-party state, with the Jacobin clubs as its fundamental cells. The arithmetic of club foundations is eloquent on this score. They were few at first in 1790. Many more came into being around the time of the king's flight to Varennes. And in the spring of 1794 they reached their high-water mark.

January 1790:	less than 50
August 1790:	90–150
November 1790:	200

December 1790:   300
March 1791:   543
May 1791:   745
July 1791:   833
September 1791:   1,000
December 1791:   1,250
December 1792:   1,500
December 1793:   2,000
Spring of 1794:   6,000

These clubs, though all known in 1794 as "popular societies" or *sociétés populaires,* were not all of the same ilk. Quite varied in membership and motivation, they reflected the instability of Jacobin ideological intensity and membership.

Some of the popular societies of 1794 really were clubs, the linear descendants of the private societies of 1789. In the countryside, however, many were no more than ephemeral village assemblies that met only a few times, probably at the behest of visiting administrators. At Melun an official remarked in late 1794 that "the larger part of the societies that were set up in rural communes were only there in name."[35] More important, in the larger cities (like Marseilles, Lyons, and Lille) many of the new clubs were not clubs at all; they began as popular assemblies whose aim, ironically, was, if not to struggle against the more bourgeois Jacobin clubs, at least to make known their own distinct and non-Jacobin voice.

Overall, then, three different types of associations were originally at stake: (1) the Jacobin clubs proper, where Jacobin ideology was gradually articulated and applied; (2) the original *sociétés populaires,* which at first were also voluntary but had a different social base and whose definition would change completely in the spring of 1794; and (3) the official *assemblées sectionnaires* (or *sections,* for short), which also had a popular audience—at first—but which were legally empowered associations.

Thus, in essence the clubs, societies, and *sections* were initially quite distinct entities. The Jacobin clubs and the original *sociétés populaires,* which more or less opposed them, were private associations. They might claim to represent the nation as a whole, but that claim was derided by anti-Jacobins.

By contrast, the *assemblées sectionnaires,* which corresponded to the officially created geographical *sections,* were legally constituted, representative assemblies. They were town meetings of a kind where any citizen had the legal right to speak. Indeed, in September 1793, when the Jacobins were eager to slow down popular participation in Parisian politics, attendance at such meetings was paradoxically subsidized by the state in a kind of collective and compensatory bribe to the militant sans-culottes, whose political autonomy was in fact being reduced, appearances notwithstanding.

But the identification of these various associations, which is important to a clear narration of events, is often baffling because the two principles at hand—namely, political choice and relationship to public authority—did not necessarily overlap. "Private" clubs might be to the right or the left of the "public" *sections.* Lineups varied from place to place. In Paris the *assemblées sectionnaires* were to the left of the Jacobins; but that was not the case in many other parts of France. In Lyons, for example, anti-Jacobin socially conservative Republicans took over the *sections.*

And Marseilles was even more complex. The Parisian Jacobins, had they focused on finding similarly minded class allies in that city, should have sided against the local club, which had fallen into the hands of local Hébertists of a kind, and with the Marseillais *sections,* whose members were socially more like themselves. But (as will be seen in Chapter 10) because the petit bourgeois Marseillais Hébertists were highly efficacious, and because the bourgeois Jacobins of the Marseillais *sections* had foolishly sided with the Girondins in Paris, the bourgeois Parisian Jacobins who were sent to Marseilles decided to side with their "class enemy" for the sake of tactical success, a fact which reminds us that the cooperation of the (bourgeois) Jacobin *clubbistes* in Paris with the (lower-middle-class populist) *clubbistes* in Marseilles (which at first glance seems straightforward institutionally) represented a complex arrangement. Indeed, a seemingly commonsensical statement (that the Parisian *clubbistes* "naturally" supported their peers in Marseilles) necessarily conceals a basic aspect of Jacobin politics, namely, that to maintain the dynamic of Revolution mattered more to the Parisian Jacobins than did the establishment of class-based alliances.

Overall, then, an involved situation existed until early 1794, when it was drastically simplified: first, because in the late summer and early fall of 1793 the Jacobins militarily repressed the bourgeois-dominated *sections* of the southern cities; and, second, because in the winter of 1793–94 the

Parisian Jacobins all but destroyed the leftist sans-culottes and Hébertist-dominated popular societies and *sections* of the capital.

At this point, the differences among clubs, *sections,* and popular societies—which because of their different social audiences had been so important a few months before—lost their relevance.

In Paris, some voluntary popular associations had already fused of their own accord with the domesticated and paid *assemblées sectionnaires.* (A few of them, even before the king's flight to Varennes in 1791, had voluntarily affiliated themselves to the club.) In 1793–94 others were forced to do so. In other northern cities like Reims and Rouen, popular associations were likewise absorbed into Jacobin-controlled bodies or shut down.

Expressive of their new subservience, all subsisting entities—whether Jacobin clubs, popular associations, or urban *sections*—were without exception given a similar regulated status and ordered to take on the name *sociétés populaires.*

In sum, the term *sociétés populaires,* which was commonly used to describe the clubs in the spring of 1794, had meant something quite different a few months before, and hence the oft-cited statistic of "six thousand societies" is much less clear than one might think.[36]

From late 1793 to July 1794 terror increasingly became the Jacobins' chief means of government. It was on September 5, 1793, that the Convention—ostensibly to placate the sans-culottes—decided that "Terror was the order of the day."

The power of the Revolutionary Tribunal dramatically expanded on September 17, when the Convention approved a "law of suspects" so vaguely defined that it might apply to anyone. Eventually, as many, perhaps, as 800,000 people were so designated. Without a *certificat de civisme,* which Committees of Surveillance and Jacobin clubs could withhold at will, ordinary people became defenseless.

Further landmarks came with the execution of the former queen, Marie Antoinette, on October 16, 1793, despite the absence of proof against her. Jacobins thrilled to the news of the death of the "Austrian Messalina," as at Angoulême, on the following Sunday:

[T]o the cries of "Long Live the Republic, Long Live the Mountain," the popular society and the people who are constantly in attendance at its meetings went to the foot of the Tree of Liberty to give thanks to the divinity that has rid France of this fury. A choir sang the sacred hymn ["La Marseillaise"] and citizens whose hearts were still oppressed by the weight of the existence of this monster withdrew, singing cries of joy whose same refrain always was "Long Live the Republic! Long Live the Mountain!"[37]

The Girondins who had been under mere house arrest since June were also executed in late October 1793.

After that, Jacobin terror swelled unchecked, and on June 10, 1794 (22 Prairial, Year II)—at the united prompting of Robespierre, Couthon, and Barère—the Convention in essence suspended the rule of law everywhere. Trials became a cruel travesty. On May 10, 1794, the king's sister, a wholly insignificant person, was executed for no reason whatsoever. One or two clubs asked for the execution of the king's ten-year-old son! In the summer of 1793 eleven people had been put to death monthly. That figure rose to 134 in early 1794 and 800 in May, June, and July 1794. In Paris 1,251 men and women were condemned to death between March 1793 and June 1974, and 1,376 more between June 10 and July 27, 1794. Small and insignificant numbers by the standards of our own times, but an extraordinary and, of course, ominous departure from previous norms. All in all, about 20,000 people were guillotined or shot "legally." Half a million more were arrested at one point or another.

More people yet died in the course of military repression, more than 250,000 in the Vendée alone,[38] many of them in ways so horrible as to conjure for us the death camps and massacres of modern times. On December 10, 1793, for example, Carrier in a report to the Convention wrote that "58 individuals, designated by the name of refractory priests, arrived at Nantes from Angers; they were immediately imprisoned on a boat on the Loire; and last night, were swallowed up by that river. What a Revolutionary torrent the Loire is!"[39] After January 1794 sadistically punitive Republican expeditions, many of them headed by generals close to the Parisian sans-culottes, ravaged this hapless area, ostensibly to make sure that it would not rise again. Republican soldiers made collars with the ears of their victims. Children were bayonetted to death. Vendéens were called a *race de brigands*. In some places the size of population fell by nearly one half. Even the countryside of the Vendée was demonized. Though flat in actual fact, Barère portrayed this landscape as mountainous and threatening, deserving somehow of punishment. In their punitive zeal, the Republican troops destroyed even some pro-Republican villages.

The Jacobins also used terror retroactively, as it were, to punish the notorious enemies of the people, a vast category that ranged from the very rich and much despised tax farmers, who had collected the indirect taxes of the Old Regime, to the friends of yesterday, like the Feuillants or the Girondins. And in a drastic reversal of the pattern of Jacobin–sans-culotte cooperation that had prevailed from April to September 1793, the Terror also claimed victims among the leaders of the popular movement.

Relations between the Jacobins and the Parisian sans-culottes, always complicated, had improved by April of 1793 with an alliance over food policy. When in December 1792 the Conventionnels decided that inflation was the root cause of the nation's economic woes, they engaged in price setting, but only as a temporary measure. Isolated Conventionnels *en mission,* like Nicolas Maure, a Montagnard Jacobin, had likewise sporadically "taxed" food, but only to maintain local law and order. The Jacobins' basic preference for laissez-faire was quite plain, and on June 3, 1792, they symbolically and collectively participated in a *fête* honoring Jacques Simoneau, the mayor of a market town close to Paris who had been murdered by a price-fixing mob. It was therefore unsurprising that in February 1793 the Jacobins, including even Marat, once again criticized sans-culotte involvement in the food riots of the day. Robespierre declared such mundane concerns to be "unworthy" of a Republican people.

On May 4, 1793, however, at the height of the Montagnards' struggle against the Gironde and a time of bread shortages and sharply rising prices, the Paris club reversed itself and began to actively support the enactment of price controls for food. At stake, no doubt, was Robespierre's genuine (if calculating) sympathy for all those who (like himself) had once been poor, humiliated, or scorned. But more present in his thinking and in that of his fellow Montagnard Jacobins was the realization that the defense of the free trade of grain had become politically and socially destructive. Jacobins who refused to accept this shift were pushed aside. Striking a bargain with the Parisian crowd became *the* point of reference for the orthodox Jacobins. *Hic Rhodus, hic salta!*

Other decisions followed from that new and fundamental choice. Public welfare was secularized, and on March 19, 1793, the Convention decreed the creation of a *caisse nationale de prévoyance,* the first—if shadowy—

scheme for a modern guaranteed minimum wage. On April 11, 1793, the forced circulation of paper money was decreed. On May 4, when the Girondins had not yet been excluded, the Convention, after another popular demonstration, decided to control the price of wheat and flour. Traders were required by law to register their stocks. On July 26 the death penalty for hoarders was instituted. On September 5 crowds invaded the Convention to demand yet more. On September 11 and 29, that chamber passed a general maximum price (the *maximum*) for every commodity. Few of these rules were ever enforced, but prices were set at 33 percent above those of 1790 and wages at 50 percent above the 1790 level. On February 24, 1794, a national schedule of prices was created, a set of laws that were in the main to be repealed half a year or so after the fall of Robespierre in December 1794. Bread was rationed. Jacobins and sans-culottes alike kept a close watch on bakeries.

In these same weeks (on June 14, 1793, specifically) the Convention also recognized every citizen's right to instruction and to material help in cases of extreme need. Jacobins likewise agreed to a forced loan on the rich and to the creation of the sans-culotte militias, the fifty-odd *armées révolutionnaires*. Staffed by militants and city thugs, a number of them from the fringes of the middle classes, these armed units, which numbered forty thousand, prowled through the countryside, pressuring the peasants for food. They often worked in close collaboration with local sans-culottes and were particularly active "dechristianizers" in the fall of 1793.

And yet, though they thought they had no choice but to work with the sans-culottes, the Jacobins were nonetheless quite determined *not* to share power with these people. Jacques Billaud-Varennes, though close to the sans-culottes, warned, "it is in the Convention that national drives must begin." "The sword of Damocles," he reminded one and all, "must henceforth hover over the entire surface of the nation."[40] The Jacobins' urge to domination did not wane. They and only they, in the Convention and in the clubs, were entitled to act as the repositories of the people's will. The Jacobins' desire to reassert their authority grew in direct response to the rising voices of the sans-culottes.

Old Regime administrators had considered the plebs a hungry beast. It might be cajoled but it was always dangerous. The Jacobins' instinct was to favor the crowd instead. But like their monarchic predecessors, they had no intention of ever losing control of the social and political machine.

On 14 Frimaire (December 4, 1793) the Jacobinized Convention decided to appoint national agents to enforce the Convention's will in the provinces. The number of officials employed in the central ministries—about four thousand—was by now eight times what it had been in 1789. The Jacobin clubs were also brought under closer Parisian control. "The popular societies must be the arsenals of public opinion," explained the Committee of Public Safety, "but it is up to the Convention and it alone to set the goal where opinion strikes."[41]

The sans-culottes, for the first of two times, misjudged their situation. They became more rather than less truculent, and with predictable results.

The first spokesmen of the popular movement to feel the wrath of the Jacobins were the *enragés*, the most authentic leaders of the Parisian poor, who denounced daily the misdeeds of the *aristocratie bourgeoisie*, the new aristocracy of wealth, which they thought the Jacobins should punish more severely.

Earlier in 1793 the *enragé* leader Jacques Roux had justified the food riots, which Robespierre had then decried. As spring turned to summer, Roux's speeches became more insistent, more inclined to divide the world into poor and rich (some of whom were Jacobins) than to see it as a battleground between moral and immoral men as the Jacobins still did: "Liberty is a hollow sham," he wrote, "if one class can deprive another of food with impunity. Liberty is meaningless where the rich may exercise the power of life and death over their fellow men with impunity."[42] Roux demanded that the death penalty be decreed against usurers and stock-jobbers.

On June 30, 1793, twelve prominent Jacobins went to the Cordelier club and bullied its members into expelling Roux and his ally Jean Théophile Leclerc. Hébert and Marat joined in. Roux, said the Friend of the People, was "un homme très dangereux," and his fellow *enragé* Jean Varlet was an "intrigant cupide." Then, in the fall of 1793, Roux was arrested, released, and rearrested. He committed suicide in jail on February 10, 1794, after embracing the public prosecutor: the man after all was only doing his Republican duty.

In a parallel move, in late October 1793, the Parisian women's clubs in Paris, which had close links to the sans-culottes (especially the Society of Revolutionary Citizenesses, which had worked with the *enragés*), were also shut down. Though straightforward political strategy was probably uppermost in their minds, the Jacobins also decided that the involvement of women in politics ran against nature's dictates. Anatomy was political destiny. "Each of the two sexes," explained the Montagnard Jacobin Jean-Pierre Amar (who had recently fathered an illegitimate child), "is called to a particular type of occupation . . . Its sphere of action is circumscribed within that circle which it cannot cross, because nature, which has set these limits to man, imperiously demands it."[43]

The struggle over dechristianization in November and December 1793 was yet another step in the Jacobins' reassertion of their right to rule over their sans-culotte allies. Anti-Catholic dechristianization had many roots, from a generalized anti-clericalism to local and specific hatreds of the church, as in the Nièvre, in north-central France, for example.[44] Its effects were widespread. In Paris the sans-culotte–dominated and dechristianizing Commune ordered the capital's churches to be closed. The constitutional bishop of Paris publicly renounced his priesthood. All over France, priests were humiliated, ridiculed, beaten, or imprisoned. Twenty thousand of them abjured, of whom six thousand chose to marry.

To many Jacobins, this anticlerical and roughly institutionalized popular violence, though more or less tolerable doctrinally, seemed politically threatening. On this matter Danton and Robespierre for once were of one mind.

Robespierre attacked Hébert directly on this issue on November 9, 1793, on the floor of the Paris club. Eight days later he underscored the diplomatic problems that dechristianization was creating for the Revolution. On November 21, he attacked atheism, and on December 8, 1793, the Convention reminded the nation that freedom of religion was recognized by law. Henceforth, in principle at least, forced dechristianization gradually lapsed. (In the anticlerical south it went on and peaked in the early spring of 1794.)

The CPS and the clubs sought to subdue rather than destroy the sans-culottes. Once victorious, the Jacobins were eager to forgive their populist rivals. But the handwriting was on the wall.

For the second time the leaders of the Parisian sans-culotterie misread their cues. On March 4, 1794, the Cordelier club proclaimed the need for yet another insurrection. At first, the Jacobins responded generously. They visited their rivals to arrange a reconciliation. But when the Cordeliers decided to continue their insurrectionary propaganda, the Jacobin CPS struck back and easily won the day. The Hébertists had limited appeal, whereas that of the Convention, which stood for the nation's will, was great.[45]

On March 24, 1794, Hébert was executed. On March 27, Barère, on be-half of the CPS, asked for the dissolution of the *armées révolutionnaires*. The export of many commodities was once again allowed. The govern-ment's right to control wages was reasserted, and in state-owned works pay packets were actually lowered. The value of paper money, which had risen in late 1793, now declined again. Thirty-nine Parisian popular soci-eties were shut down. Those that remained often became cautious, espe-cially as the more conservative Parisians, sensing the way the wind was blowing, began to return to the *section* meetings they had feared to attend.[46] Sans-culottes were purged from state institutions, particularly the ministry of war, where many of them had found employment in 1793. Ja-cobin Conventionnels *en mission* openly criticized the effect of the *maxi-mum*. Price controls, they argued, disrupted the workings of supply and demand, and providing for the militarized nation's needs was a priority that mattered more than wages.

In early May the Paris Commune was packed with friends of Robes-pierre. In mid-July the Incorruptible One also denounced a series of ban-quets the sans-culottes had organized. At the Jacobin club Couthon dared to say of the forty-eight populist and Parisian *assemblées sectionnaires* that they were like the "spectacle hideux du fédéralisme." When Robespierre's moment of need rolled around in Thermidor (July 1794), the popular movement's will to struggle had for many weeks been broken, as he then found out to his great dismay.

The sans-culottes were bewildered by the Jacobins' about-face. At first, they complained vociferously, unable to understand why their familiar words could no longer convince. Then, discouraged, they fell mute, espe-cially as they were worn down by months and years of cold and hunger. They felt they had been betrayed.

In these dark moments, it is true, the Jacobins were still able to act in hu-mane and constructive ways. On December 19, 1793, the Convention voted to create free, public, and subsidized primary education, France being the first modern nation to do so. More grandly yet, on February 4, 1794, France abolished slavery; again, it was the first modern nation to do so, and at a time when the enslavement of blacks was a recognized part of American constitutional arrangements. Indeed, the liberalism and human-ity of the Jacobinism on this issue is particularly eloquent since many of the most radical philosophes had been strangely ambiguous or silent on the abomination of black slavery. (All of them condemned, by contrast, the enslavement of whites by whites.) It was also in these early days of 1794 that the festivals of the republic reached their apogee.

But terrorism was a cancer that wasted all of Jacobinism's achievements.

As one way out of the dilemma they faced, the Jacobins could have stopped the Terror. Many of them contemplated such a course. From February 1794 to the end of their rule in late July 1794, Robespierre and his closest friends often spoke of the need to stabilize the Revolution. Many people expected Robespierre to take this initiative, especially at the time of the Festival of the Supreme Being in May 1794.

Indeed, some Jacobins around Danton and Desmoulins, the so-called Indulgents, openly proclaimed their opposition to an ongoing terror whose first steps they had praised. Their aim, from early December 1793 onward, was to silence the populist extremists and to return to legal normalcy, with freedom of the press especially. For many weeks, in the winter of 1793–94, during the struggle with the popular left especially, Robespierre and his closest orthodox Jacobin associates hesitated about this growing force of moderate opposition. Should they destroy it or accept its message? But if the Terror stopped, what would follow? They too might be swept aside. Besides, many were suspicious of Danton's dishonest demagogy and of Desmoulins's superficiality.

In the spring of 1794 the hard-core Jacobins Robespierre spoke for finally decided to treat the Indulgents not as ideological allies (which they were, basically) but as members of yet another faction unconcerned about the public good even when they seemed to be working for it. If the Dantonists had ever been right, the Robespierrists concluded, it was for the wrong reasons.

On January 10, 1794, Desmoulins had almost been excluded from the Jacobin club. Robespierre rescued him on that day of troubles: they had known each other for years and were both graduates of the lycée Louis-le-Grand in Paris. But afterward the Indulgents lost ground steadily. One of their chief allies, Philippe Fabre d'Eglantine, was arrested on a justified charge of corruption, and some weeks later the hard-core Jacobins in the CPS finally decided that Danton's and Desmoulins's (and Fabre's) executions could no longer be avoided. It took place on April 5, 1794.

Jacobinism, though seemingly more efficient, was grinding to a spiritual halt. Frenetic persecution everywhere engendered leaden and factitious orthodoxy. In the eloquent words of Saint-Just, the Revolution was "frozen." Within the provincial clubs, no one dared openly to oppose the theatrical posturing of the Robespierrists. By the thousands, however, rank-and-file Jacobins voted silently, with their feet. Attendance in the clubs fell off sharply.[47] The "nondeeds" of ordinary provincial Jacobins became a silent language more eloquent than the highly articulate but formulaic speeches of High Jacobins in Paris.

Robespierre himself was unable to decide. For many weeks in June and July 1794 he stopped attending the meetings of the CPS, as if unwilling to go either forward to more Terror or backward to the rule of law. Many Jacobins, we can wager, felt these same doubts.

Everyone feared for his life and safety, and property owners feared for their possessions as well. Even confirmed Jacobins thought they might at any moment become suspects. Everyone was disgusted by the bloodshed of terrorist repression, which repentant Jacobins at Tulle later (in the Year III) described, no doubt sincerely, as "un système anti-social et anti-humain."[48]

Military events, which had been an ostensible justification of the Terror's inception in the summer of 1793, also began to work in reversed gear when, on June 26, 1794, a French army won a decisive victory over the Austrians at Fleurus in Belgium.

For years the Jacobins had detested factions and lived in fear of dire conspiracy. Ironically, they were about to be proved right but, as it happens, by their own covert ministrations, because the Revolution's only consequential conspiracy was the one that was staged against Robespierre by his fellow Jacobins in the fourth week of July 1794.

The plot to overthrow Robespierre brought together four groups: (1) left Jacobins like Collot d'Herbois, a failed playwright who had been close to the executed Hébertists and to the popular revolutionaries; (2) terrorist Jacobins notorious for their brutality and cruelty like Joseph Fouché, Barras, Carrier, and Jean Tallien, who had been excluded from the Paris club on June 14, a sure sign of impending doom; (3) neo-Jacobin technocrats like Lazare Carnot and Jean-Baptiste Lindet, who had accepted Jacobinism less for the power of its ideology than for its organizational energy; and (4) Barère, "the Anacreon of the Revolution," a former Feuillant and a former Girondin, who had made his mark as the all-purpose impresario of Jacobin unity.[49]

On 8 Thermidor (July 26, 1794) the plotters, acting in concert, attacked Robespierre verbally on the Convention floor. That night, he defended himself one last time—and quite successfully so—in the Paris Jacobin club; but given the bureaucratized nature of the club's membership, that success no longer meant very much.

The next day the conspirators set on Robespierre once more on the Convention floor. Disoriented and confused, he voluntarily abandoned the podium. The Convention then ordered him arrested. Later that night he was released by order of the Paris Commune, which had been purged earlier in the year of militant sans-culottes and was staffed by Robespierre's supporters, as was the Paris club. By leaving jail, Robespierre made of himself an outlaw who had defied the Convention. If captured, he would no longer have to be tried.

But even at this juncture, rebellion was clearly hard for him. Jacobins, after all, were men of order. While signing an insurrectionary manifesto, Robespierre, ever dutiful, paused, and turned to ask: "but in whose name?" Couthon, his friend, then sighed: "Nous n'avons plus qu'à mourir" (All that is left for us to do is die).

When the Convention's troops burst into the Paris City Hall at two in the morning of 10 Thermidor, a number of Jacobins (including, it was said, Robespierre) killed themselves or tried to do so. More impassively, on his way to execution later that day, Saint-Just turned toward a poster of the 1793 Constitution and said, "Yes, but I am the one who made that."

The defeated leaders of Jacobin orthodoxy were mocked by the crowd as their tumbril worked its way to the Place de la Révolution.

From 1789 onward, the Revolution had been lived day by day as an incoherent succession of unforeseeable events—often as a melodrama and at times as a buffoonery. Now, suddenly, with the death of Robespierre-the-tyrant, in an unexpected moment of Aristotelian anagnorisis, of epiphany, the events of the Revolution became all at once and retroactively a linear and plotted tragedy that had come to an inescapable turning point. Thermidor, thought the remaining Jacobins, would enable them to find their way at last; but of course it signaled their imminent fall instead.

From Thermidor, Year II (July 1794) to 1799: The Irresistible Rise of Napoleon Bonaparte

The Paris club that had supported Robespierre on 8 Thermidor endured several days of disarray after his sudden overthrow and demise.

But in the provinces, without exception and often enthusiastically, local Jacobins welcomed the fall of the hated "tyrant." In hundreds of clubs Robespierre was denounced in late July and early August 1794 as the hypocritical, feline, bloodthirsty incarnation of every evil, as a modern Satan.

It was Jacobins who had raised Robespierre and his friends to power and it was Jacobins also who unseated him. Robespierrist terrorism was overthrown not by an anti-Jacobin ground swell of opinion but by the men and women who had once been convinced of its necessity.

In the summer of 1794 the more honest and successful anti-Robespierrist conspirators thus aimed to reverse the sinister application of Jacobin principles but not to abandon the principles themselves. The individualism of private life harnessed to the universalism of public life remained their cherished goal. At Millau the *clubbistes* decided quite logically that since they too had been oppressed by Robespierrist tyranny, they should use his fall as an opportunity "to become more energetic and to come out of that . . . paralysis and compression in which popular societies had been placed by the system of terror and despotism of the faction that has just failed."[50]

And yet, of course, 9 Thermidor marked the beginning of the end for Jacobinism. Its death throes would haltingly structure the anticlimactic politics of the late 1790s, through the last year of the Convention, which broke up in the fall of 1795, and through the Directory, which subsisted until Bonaparte's military coup of 18 Brumaire (November 9, 1799).

During these four years, Jacobins and former Jacobins fell into three groups. The most important is identified with the name of Sieyès, although the author of *What Is the Third Estate?* became a ruling director only in the so-called Second Directory of 1797–1799.

Ideologically, Sieyès helped develop and articulate Jacobin doctrine. (He had initially been a fairly active member of Bonneville's Cercle Social.)[51] But the practical working out after 1789 of the principles he had voiced earlier caused him growing anguish.

Institutionally, Sieyès had refused to take sides when the Feuillants split from the Paris club in 1791. This was an offense that was hard to forgive in 1793–94, and the man probably owed his life to the vote he had cast in favor of the execution of Louis XVI in January 1793.

Sieyès and his friends hoped to steer a middle course between the other two groups, the resurgent royalist right and the ultrademocratic, explicitly communistic left. "Pour éviter carybde, ne tombons pas dans scylla."[52] In addition to irreconcilable royalists, to the right of Sieyès's neo-Jacobins stood the *réacteurs* or Thermidorian opportunists, former Jacobins (indeed, some of them former and brutal terrorists like Tallien) who were ready to do just about anything (including making a deal with the royalists) to remain in power, keep their money, and save their skins. Many of these sinister ex-Jacobins hit upon the happy idea of distinguishing themselves from the Robespierrists by focusing on the issue of vandalism. Robespierre clearly had been one, they said (this was not true); and just as clearly, they added, they had never agreed to the desecration of France's past (which was true only in the sense that they had never been consulted about this issue). Citing their noninvolvement in vandalism, the *réacteurs* attempted to make others believe that they had really been anti-Robespierrists all along.

To the left of Sieyès remained hard-core Jacobins, still completely taken with the universalist and ideological message of 1793–94, a message that, idealistically, they intended to carry out in a nonterrorist parliamentary way. Many provincial clubs followed that militant lead. "What!" wrote members of the club of Bédarieux to the National Convention on 24 Fructidor, "Citizen Representatives: will you allow a government to be attacked just because a scoundrel abused that same type of government to oppress patriots? Will you give as much weight to liberty and to vile intriguers?"[53] Similarly, the Jacobins of Saint-Étienne urged that "death strike pitilessly all enemies of the people and liberty."[54]

In the late summer of 1794 this last provincial and dedicated Jacobin phalanx, ensconced in the clubs of Chambéry, Dijon, Macon, and Marseilles, advocated continuing the war against selfish *aristocratie*. Encouraged by this provincial response, relayed by the Jacobin press, Collot d'Herbois, in Paris in the fall of 1794, made a famous speech on the Convention floor to urge the remaining Jacobins to vigilance and energy. Many of these small-town Jacobins reasserted their claim to represent popular sovereignty, an argument endorsed by some subsisting Parisian popular societies.

Inexorably, however, left Jacobinism was rejected by both the popular movement and the possessing elite. It lost one political battle after another. Prominent radicals were shunted aside. Many Jacobins of 1794 were deported. In Paris the Convention and the courts unanimously condemned Carrier, the most notorious Jacobin Cordelier terrorist of all. In the provinces, where the police was indifferent to their fate, many former Jacobins were murdered by the friends and relations of their executed enemies, as happened openly in the streets of Lyons from mid-February 1795 onward. A list of Lyonese Jacobins together with their addresses was published in Switzerland to make sure that no one would be overlooked. A few days after these outrages, the unscrupulous Thermidorian Joseph Rovère, a former Jacobin and a genuine scoundrel, dared to justify the lynchings of his erstwhile friends: "If you yourself do not punish these men, then every Frenchman will have the right to do so."[55]

A turning point was reached in April and May 1795 when a handful of Jacobin Conventionnels responded sympathetically to the last and failed sans-culotte insurrections in Paris. After a show of military force, the popular revolutionaries surrendered and the few Jacobins who had supported them were arrested. Tried and condemned some months later, these Plutarchians—Gilbert Romme, Pierre Soubrany (a marquess), and Jean Goujon, often known as the Prairial martyrs—stabbed themselves in the dock hoping to make of their suicidal death an example for a wayward nation.

Squeezed between the far right and the far left, the Jacobin clubs went into eclipse. At first, Sieyès's mainstream Thermidorians, still unsure of themselves, allowed the clubs to subsist. If Sieyès worried that the clubs might again become a fulcrum for left opponents of the regime, he also feared the royalist right. He knew how useful the clubs had been as a means of government in 1793–94.

On balance, however, the governmental, middle-of-the-road neo-Jacobins soon deemed it wiser to shut the clubs down. On 22 Brumaire, Year III (November 12, 1794) the Convention ordered the Paris club dissolved, on the grounds, not altogether unfair, that it was not truly a "popular" society. On October 16, 1794, clubs were ordered to submit their membership lists. They were forbidden to affiliate or correspond with one another. Many clubs dropped out of sight altogether. Within the clubs, attendance plummeted yet further. Club committees ceased to meet, except for special commissions designed to hound former terrorists. Many club archives suddenly vanished. In many places the *clubbistes* took care to burn them. In late August 1795, on 6 Fructidor, Year III, the remaining extant provincial societies were shut down—some of them on charges of continuing terrorism, and others because they were said to be royalist.

The theoretical, politico-sociological argument most commonly used to justify these closures was hardly new. It had been bruited in 1791. The clubs were decried as particularist institutions, as corporations that had no place in the Republican system, where no institution could interpose itself between the citizen and the state. Within a month of Robespierre's fall, Jean-Jacques Cambacérès, who would become second consul after the coup of 18 Brumaire, which made Bonaparte first consul, had made clear the need for an unmediated, unfettered, and centralized government: no particular authority, no assembly outside the state could claim to represent the nation. The National Convention, he went on, "alone deserved the confidence of the people." To gain the people's trust, it would have to "push aside everything which weakens its authority, and reduce as much as can be done the intermediaries which might find themselves between it and the people."[56]

But even after the suppression of the clubs and the death of the Prairial martyrs, Jacobinism did not vanish all at once. Every tolerated resurgence of the left, which the Directory allowed whenever it worried about rightist insurrections, led to renewed and intense networking on the lines of what had existed before 1794. In 1798 at least three hundred Constitutional Circles and three hundred other political societies came once more to life. (Some think that the true figure is four times as large.) These groups actively propagandized. They relied heavily on the press, attacked royalists, managed elections, and tried to act in concert.

The most famous of them was the Parisian Manège, which met in the former royal palace of the Tuileries as had the Jacobin-dominated Convention of 1793–94. The club enjoyed brief success. It soon counted three thousand members, two hundred and fifty of them deputies and many of them former prominent Montagnards of 1793–94.

But it did not last long. Sieyès, who for a while had thought of encouraging these neo-Jacobins, soon changed his mind. On 26 Thermidor, Year VII, Fouché, now minister of police, ordered the Manège closed. The club had lasted a mere thirty-eight days.

A map of Jacobin clubs under the Directory recalls the spontaneous establishment of clubs in 1791 rather than the state-imposed pattern of 1793–94. It also foreshadows the sites of late-nineteenth-century French Republican liberalism, a geographical continuity that links revolutionary Jacobinism to the liberal principles of the Third Republic.

Unencumbered by left and right (or so they wished themselves to be) the mainstream Jacobins around Sieyès developed their modest program. Their first task was political: never again would the threat of terror be used against them. They were not adverse to using force against their enemies, especially against the church. But they were extremely legalistic and bureaucratically inclined in their dealings with one another. Individual rights would not ordinarily be waved. The laws of 22 Prairial (June 10, 1794), which had legalized the Great Terror of June and July 1794, were immediately repealed, as was the law of suspects a few months later. Eventually, surviving Girondins were readmitted to the Convention. The state was at once shrunk and protected from political infection from below: the election of bureaucrats that had been decreed in 1789 was suspended, as was the election of officers in the army that had been common in 1793.

The second goal of Sieyès and his group was to reduce the state's control of the economy. Production in state-owned arsenals dropped off rapidly. Coal mines that had been nationalized because their owners had collaborated with the Austrians were reprivatized. The dream of compulsory and free primary education was abandoned, as was the practice of price supports. On December 24, 1794, the Convention abolished the *maximum*. Paper money became nearly worthless. The *assignats*—which urban artisans ordinarily received as payment—had remained more or less at par for about a year; but in 1792 their worth fell abruptly. By January 1793 they fetched only one-half of their face value; and in May 1795, no more than 8 percent of par. The condition of the poor deteriorated correspondingly. In 1795–96 Paris counted ten thousand more deaths than births. Many people froze or starved to death. Suicide rates went up.

In tandem with this disengagement of the state from the economy came the further circumscription of the sans-culottes. On August 14, 1794, Jacobin deputies voted to end the compensatory fee that had been paid to the poor for attending the (infrequent) meetings of the *sections*. In Germinal and Prairial (April 1795), as has been said, the army suppressed the last and fitful sans-culotte insurrections, which, as would become common in nineteenth-century Parisian revolutions, opposed a quite clearly bourgeois and conservative west Paris to a popular and insurrectionary east Paris. In these same months the neo-Jacobin regime likewise turned against the more extreme Babouvists, the group named after Gracchus Babeuf (1760–1797), whose communist conspiracy of 1796 was also a striking premonition of nineteenth-century European politics.

The sans-culottes had wanted bread. Babeuf went much further. He abandoned their dream of state-controlled bread prices and argued instead for the wholesale abolition of private property. His coup had some military support, but it was easily suppressed, if only because the third-ranking Babouvist leader was a police spy.

All of this is not to say that the Directorial neo-Jacobins around Sieyès suddenly and massively turned their back on either the Revolution or the Enlightenment. On the contrary, many French institutions of higher learning—a number of them extant today—were created at this time. The neo-Enlightenment Ideologues who argued for the relevance of Enlightenment universalism were held in high esteem by the regime.[57] Many of them held prominent offices.

Indeed, the Directorials consolidated many of the Revolution's most durable achievements. Administration was improved. The judicial system and the jury system acquired greater consistency.[58] Paper money, wholly worthless by this point, was finally given up. France gradually returned to the gold standard, as contemporaries wanted and expected. The nation's debt was consolidated and its yearly deficit curtailed. Taxation was made more methodical and military conscription codified. The regime also encouraged the standardization of weights and measures, the use of which, explained the minister in charge, would further the development of "public reason."

Much was to be said for this watered-down but more efficient program. It was less civically oriented to be sure: unlike the suspended Constitution of 1793, the Constitution of 1795 made no mention of a right to insurrection; and unlike the Constitution of 1789–1791, it included a declaration of duties and responsibilities as well as of human rights. It was also more commercially minded. Still, its tone was recognizably Jacobin.[59] In fact, Sieyès's actions can be read as a last-ditch effort to preserve as much of Jacobinism's principles and achievements as the French nation could accept after having suffered from the Jacobins' terrorist excesses. And there is no doubt that his compromising stance was much preferable to what would soon prevail from 1799 to 1814–15, with Bonaparte's endless warmongering, dictatorship, and pointless and reactionary policies. (In 1802 the first consul, uncoerced, restored slavery in the French colonies and, at home, once again recognized the privileged position of papalist Catholicism.)

But in order to secure his more or less enlightened and Jacobin program, Sieyès and his friends would have had to make of Jacobinism a modern and parliamentary party. They would have had to step back from Jacobinism's moralizing judgments and its fears of conspiracy. They would have had to accept the idea that other political families had a right to exist and to rule. More practically, the Jacobins would have had to accept the verdict of the polls and decide conclusively that popular sovereignty was incarnate in the results of free elections. In the late 1790s, however, the fearful ex-Jacobins—though resolutely antiterrorist—could not bring themselves to accept that consensual vision.

Unable to take that extra step, unwilling and afraid to give up power, Sieyès and his former Jacobins chose instead to steer a middle course between parliamentary rule and the darker sides of Jacobin principle. Anticlericalism rose to fever pitch. More priests were deported in 1798 than in any other year of the Revolution. In late 1797 Sieyès also arranged to pass a law depriving all the noble-born of French citizenship, regardless of their opinions, a tangentially racist statement with unpleasant connotations. The use of the revolutionary calendar was made compulsory, as was addressing strangers in official correspondence with the pronoun *tu*. Deputies and judges were dressed up in ridiculous pseudo-Roman, Republican costume, designed as it happens by the painter David. The regime also encouraged the quasi-religious civic cult of the Theophilanthropists. (A former Girondin Jacobin, Louis-Marie La Revellière-Lépeaux, played a particularly important role in this cult.) Some, like Germaine de Staël, even toyed with the idea of staging a conversion of the French to Protestantism, more than two centuries after the death of Calvin!

All of this activity enabled Sieyès's system to stumble forward for some months and years. In western France and Paris émigrés and royalists were successfully repressed, as the Parisian sans-culottes and Babouvists had been in 1795–96.

But nothing could make up for the political sterility of the regime, not even the ever more complicated constitutional provisions Sieyès brought forward from time to time. (In 1795, the Conventionnels had already passed a law—instantly and universally decried—which required that two-thirds of the deputies returned to the new assembly be drawn from the discredited Convention.)

Inevitably, from year to year, the prospects of the Directory worsened steadily. Wars of aggression—consciously provoked after 1796 especially—were, when lost, destabilizing. So were victories, which lessened political tensions but made repression of the right and the left harder to justify. The peace of Campo-Formio between France and Austria, which Bonaparte negotiated in October 1797 after a string of stunning victories in the spring, allowed domestic quarrels to revive and increased the prestige of the generals at the expense of the regime.

A first step to political self-destruction came when the Directorials concluded that they had no choice but to stage a coup against their legally elected opponents. In September 1797 Catholic or socially conservative Republicans like Carnot were purged, arrested, or deported to Guyana, where many died a tropical, slow death known as the "dry guillotine." Then, in May 1798, Sieyès's allies forced out the legally elected parliamentary left consisting of about one hundred and twenty neo-Jacobin deputies.

By 1799 the situation of the regime was rather like that of Robespierre in early July 1794, with few allies on either left or right and not that many followers in the center either, the difference being that Robespierre had decided to carry through to the end and died for his beliefs, whereas Sieyès was far more cautious. (Robespierre once described him as the mole of the Revolution.)

On 18 Brumaire (November 9, 1799), after some initial shufflings, the Directory was easily toppled in a bloodless military coup orchestrated by Lucien Bonaparte (once a Jacobin and soon to be a prince); by Sieyès (once a Jacobin more or less and soon to be a count and very rich); and by General "Buonaparte" (who had been imprisoned in August 1794 as a Robespierrist Jacobin and who would soon crown himself emperor of the French).

As the Corsican pithily explained in his first proclamation as first consul, "the Revolution was over."

The Politics of Covert Sensibility: An Individualist and Universalist *Dérapage*

> For I have learned
> To look on nature, not as in the hour
> Of thoughtless youth; but hearing sometimes
> The still, sad music of humanity,
> Not harsh nor grating, though of ample power
> To chasten and subdue.
>
> William Wordsworth, "Lines Composed a
> Few Miles above Tintern Abbey"

Conceptually, the *histoire événementielle* of the Revolution is initially disconcerting. For many puzzled readers, the first ostensible message of a narrative account of revolutionary politics is that a confusing number of factors contributed to Jacobinism's unraveling catastrophe. Contingency, war, the economy, bad luck, bad judgment, incoherent private purpose: all of these do loom large.

It is striking also that a chronological account of politics does not even tell us when the Terror actually began. Was it when Barnave excused the murder of Foulon and Bertier on July 23, 1789? when Lafayette ordered his soldiers to fire on peaceful Republicans in July 1791? after the fall of the Tuileries Palace in August 1792, when the Parisian crowds murdered hundreds of defenseless Swiss guards? Or did it begin with the kangaroo courts of the September massacres one month later? Was the death of the king in January 1793 the point of no return? Or did that come with the execution of the Girondins in October 1793?

Henry Ford's unfriendly verdict on the merits of Clio's craft readily comes to mind. Upon reflection, however, there is much to be learned from a narrative of Revolutionary politics. For one thing, it highlights the contradictory nature of Jacobin goals. In the name of universalistic values (citizenship, the nation) the Jacobins drifted to brutal excess in 1793–94. (This is the collectivist and celebrated *dérapage* of the Revolution.) But their individuating zeal in 1789–1791 was as wild as their universalist tyranny was to be in 1794. (At stake here are the skewed Declaration of the Rights of Man of 1789 unaccompanied by a declaration of responsibilities; and the Le Chapelier law of 1791.)

Jacobin terrorism of the Year II was without historical precedent. Yet, no society before or since was ever so radical in asserting the unalloyed rights of *individuals* as the Jacobin-dominated, Barnavian France of 1789–1791. As for the later years of Jacobin domination, namely 1793 and 1794, though other bourgeois owners of property in other climes and times have also straightforwardly defended their material rights, no other national Parliament has ever decreed the death penalty for the mere discussion of agrarian communism, as did the Convention of 1793, dominated by High Jacobins like Robespierre, Couthon, Saint-Just, and Danton.

In short, a narrative of events reminds us there was not one *dérapage* of the Revolution but two, individualist and communitarian, a telling duality at the heart of Jacobin principle.

Another and equally important lesson embedded in the narrative is that the Jacobins were nearly always under terrific pressure. In the thirty-odd weeks that ran from March to October 1793, when the Terror came fully into its own, they faced problems that must have seemed insuperable. They endured no less than four civil wars (in the west against royalist, Vendéen peasants; against assorted Republicans at Lyons; against the Girondins in Normandy; and against fellow Jacobins in Marseilles). In addition, they experienced uncontrolled inflation; a dislocated economy; a losing war against nearly all of Europe; the defection of the French commander in chief, Dumouriez; and the murder of Marat, their most notorious leader. As Robespierre put it in February 1794: "we have to admit that we were more guided by the love of the public good [*l'amour du bien*] and by our feeling for the needs of the Fatherland [*les besoins de la Patrie*], than by an exact theory or by precise rules of conduct, which we did not have the time even to envisage."[60]

This cascade of catastrophes tells us that, of necessity, Jacobins had to deal with unforeseen situations from instinct. They did not have time to debate and experiment. And their instincts (carried forward from prerevolutionary times) were deeply illiberal, as a narrative clearly shows time and time again.

In principle, Jacobins tolerated dissent, but only in the sense that they were willing to wait a short while for it to abate. They could not see that honest men of good faith might consider a political problem in different ways. They were suspicious of their own best and former friends and assumed every enemy was an *aristocrate,* an immoral conspirator who should not be just overcome but punished.

Generally, conservative historians—including Tocqueville among them—have (wrongly) tried to connect Jacobin intolerance to prerevolutionary inexperience or incompetence. Jacobins, in this view, drifted to authoritarianism because their private backgrounds were inadequate. But this is much too personal a view. The link of past to present was strong, but it worked on a different, deeper plane.

In the 1780s, because of their libertarian and religious past, revolutionary Americans managed to elaborate a social and political system that durably blended the private and the public, and reconciled (however lamely) individuated capitalism with a Republican, universalist sense of commonly held responsibility.

In the 1790s, by contrast, the French—prisoners of a thousand years of monarchic and religious habits—failed in that same quest. Behind the Jacobins' willfulness stand both a regal sense of the public sphere and a regal disdain for the rights of those who might be in the way.

In 1789 it certainly seemed that the idea of absolutist monarchy had died in all hearts. But the quasi-mystic loyalty that the French had once felt for their father-king had merely transmogrified into a new, quasi-mystical entity, the People. It is revealing that so many of the symbols the Jacobins used to represent and explain their cause and principles were familiar royal images, like the monarchic Hercules and the ludovician sun.

The mechanics of Saint-Just's politics, for example, have clear links to the hallowed principles of absolutist monarchy. In the older monarchic perspective, every subject had a perfect right to communicate vertically and frankly with the sun king at Versailles, whose decisions regulated the entire state machine. But no subject could communicate horizontally with any other subject. For the Robespierrist Jacobins of 1794, in much the same way, every club had the obligation to communicate with Paris, but citizens had no right to come together outside the clubs to form distinct centers of opinion. For the Jacobins, in the end, the nation could speak but with a single voice, their own.

On January 21, 1793, when they chose to execute Louis XVI on the Place de la Révolution—heretofore the Place Louis XV and known today as the Place de la Concorde—in front of the statue of Liberty that had replaced the equestrian statue of Louis's grandfather, the Jacobins attempted to underscore the destruction of the old monarchy by the new republic. But what we also see in this ritual murder on one of the great royal squares is a continuity of majestic public purpose that links the Jacobins of 1793 to an ancient political system they genuinely detested.

Clerical legacies, both good and bad, were also relevant. Perspicaciously, Baudot, a friend of Danton, once remarked that Jacobins "wanted to apply to politics that same equality which the Gospels grant to all Christians, but this does not mean that we also wanted to share property or land, because nowhere does the Gospel say that you must share your goods with your neighbors, though it does everywhere say that you must help him in his need."[61]

How appropriate and symbolic the remark of some civic-minded (and coached?) seven-year-olds, in the Beauce, near Paris, who having received their first communion proclaimed in 1790 that they had just become "members of the august body of Christian citizens."[62]

Paul's epistle to the Galatians likewise has "unearthbound" words that could easily be amended to express the Jacobins' collective sense of their ostensibly earth-bound and areligious mission:

> [B]efore faith came, we were kept under the law, shut up unto the faith which afterwards should be revealed . . . But after that faith is come, we are no longer under a schoolmaster . . . There is neither Jew nor Greek, there is neither bond nor free, there is neither male nor female; for ye are one in Christ Jesus.

Substituting "Nation" and "Revolution" for "Christ" underscores the similarity of the Jacobins' universalist message to the religious message it sought first to supplant and later to destroy.[63]

All historians of Jacobinism have speculated—as they should—on the extent of the Jacobins' knowledge of Rousseau. But when it comes to gauging the roots of Jacobin sensibility for both good and evil, it is useful to re-member that many more of them had read the Gospels than the *Social Contract*. Jacques Brival, a Jacobin Conventionnel at Tulle, reminded his audience that Rousseau had been the first writer to use the word "sublime" to describe the Scriptures.[64]

Augustin Cochin (who wrote before the First World War and propheti-cally criticized modern totalitarianism even before it existed) linked the Terror not to religion at all but to antireligious fervor, that is, to the En-lightenment. Jacobinism, he argued, was about Voltaire and Rousseau; and the politically excluding method of the Jacobins after 1789 related socio-logically to the literally intolerant tactic of the prerevolutionary phi-losophes. The revolutionary guillotine, he suggested, excluded radically, and so had the prerevolutionary philosophes done their best to crowd out and exclude their intellectual opponents. "Before the bloody Terror of 1793, there was in the Republic of Letters a dry terror, with the Encyclope-dia project as the Committee of Public Safety, and d'Alembert as Robes-pierre."[65]

But Cochin's argument becomes more interesting if pushed further back in time. For the prerevolutionary intolerance of the philosophes was itself a copy of earlier modes of thought.

Consciously, the philosophes and the Jacobins abominated intolerant re-ligiosity. "The religious spirit," wrote Holbach, "was and always will be incompatible with moderation, sweetness and humanity. Thus religious morality can never serve to render mortals more sociable."[66] Regardless of such disclaimers, we can nonetheless see that both groups argued with a suspiciously religious fervor. In its uncompromising intransigence, Robes-pierre's anticlerical Jacobinism bears a disturbing likeness to the High Catholic and absolutist intolerance of Bishop Bossuet in the reign of the sun king.[67]

In the past the church had been sacred. Only it had a right to public exis-tence. The church did not claim the right to force the conscience of individ-uals, but other forms of public worship were anathema. For the Jacobins as well, intolerance in the name of truth was no sin. The Convention was the Jacobins' holy temple. The nation's salvation was their alpha and omega.

"May the people rise up!" wrote Camille Desmoulins derisively in his libertarian attack against Robespierre's defense of terror in March 1794, "when the Dominicans in Spain burn some unfortunate heretic, they never fail to sing 'Excurgat Deus, may God the Father rise up.'"[68] The joke of a former priest who had become a Jacobin and who proposed at Poitiers to light an "auto-da-fé" of all theological books on the "altar of Philosophy" was likewise less funny than he thought.[69]

Inherited ways of church and state marked the Jacobins' way of thinking, as did more broadly diffused, socially dominant assumptions. Even Jacobin individualism was not just militarized but aristocratically self-assertive. How curious that at Lille a heroic soldier should have received from the club a sword suitably inscribed with Bayard's famous sixteenth-century knightly motto: "without fear and without reproach."[70]

In their conscious theorizing, for example, Jacobins accepted fully the Enlightenment idea that crime and punishment were individuated problems. They too believed, in the celebrated words of Jeremy Bentham, that the punishment should be made to fit the crime. Victims of revolutionary "justice" were tried and sent to the guillotine one by one. We should also note that the Jacobins did not ordinarily stoop to torture or desecrate their victims' bodies.[71]

And yet, the blind practice of Jacobin purges shows us that liberal thought ultimately mattered less to the Jacobins than age-old punitive intent. Their true purpose, as that of premodern justice—we cannot forbear from thinking—was not to apportion individuated blame but to punish by example. The public execution of the Old Regime had been "a ceremonial by which a momentarily injured sovereign (was) reconstituted,"[72] and much the same can be said of the ritual of the supposedly more modern Jacobins.

The Jacobins could not, of course, explicitly approve of the revolutionary crowd's brutality during the September massacres of 1792. But neither could they condemn this spontaneous upsurge of popular indignation, which aimed to restore the wholeness of a revolutionary people through blood sacrifice. Jacobins were much less free of their private and public pasts than they thought. Benjamin Constant (1767–1830) put his finger on this theme in 1815. The revolutionaries of 1789, he wrote, "saw in the history [of the Old Regime] a small number of people, or a single person, endowed with great power, who caused great harm; but their anger was directed against the wielders of that power rather than against their power as such. They were more interested in displacing than in destroying it."[73] Habits of democratic tolerance do not come naturally or quickly.

Indeed, this view of deep, dark cultural and social continuities pertains to many levels, from high monarchic and clerical principles to specific aspects of daily life. Far fewer Jacobins than is often supposed were embittered men for whom the universalism of the Revolution was no more than a pretext to settle old scores. But nationwide, personal animosities did saturate the daily life of subjects under the Old Regime, who lived on top of one another figuratively and literally, in crowded cities, in compacted villages, and in closed guilds where one person's advancement often came at the expense of another's.

The Old Regime was an unusually litigious society, an especially anxiety-provoking situation since laws were extremely complicated and the limits of jurisdictions unclear and conflicting. The course of any lawsuit was unpredictable and potentially disastrous. Denunciations of neighbors or rivals to the authorities were quite commonplace.[74]

In 1789 many old scores—both private and semipublic—were waiting to be settled. In the Ariège, for example, at Pamiers, the Conventionnel Marc Vadier managed to have his old enemy Darmaing, who had become a judge, arrested and executed, only to be pursued after the fall of Robespierre by Darmaing's son.[75] In revolutionary Geneva, which closely followed French politics and was annexed by the French in 1798, nearly all of the four hundred people convicted by its Revolutionary Tribunal in July and August 1794 (thirty-seven of whom were sentenced to death) had been prominent in repressing a patriotic insurrection of 1782.

Thus local ties bound universalist-minded Jacobins not just to civil society but to uncivil hatreds. Many a purge or denunciation was little more than an opportunity for getting even. In premodern Paris, before the invention of the elevator, rich and poor lived side by side or, more precisely, floor by floor, with indigents on the less accessible higher levels; and many a politicized accusation in 1793 had less to do with the events of the day than with the poor's embittered memory of ostentatious and prerevolutionary display by their richer neighbors.[76] At Lagny one *clubbiste* sensibly complained, "most of the time, we deal with personal problems, which wastes precious time."[77] Two Conventionnels *en mission*, Claude Laurent and Florent-Guiot, concurred: "Generally speaking, the system of denunciation is too established in the [clubs], which busy themselves exclusively with recriminations that mask personal hatreds."[78]

Jacobin terrorism was not of a piece. Without its ideological justifications, without guidance from Paris, local terror could never have arisen. And yet, the background of many a punitive local act was strikingly banal and nonideological. Even visiting Conventionnels like Claude Javogues[79] might use their newly found, Jacobin-inspired power to come home and work out their own private sadistic impulses, especially since these were sanctioned in many minds by the age-old instinct of exemplary and redemptive punishment.

Alain Corbin has portrayed 1792 as a "watershed year," which marked the point when an ancient "sacrificial system" began to break down, at least for those who had been touched by the Enlightenment.[80] This judgment no doubt holds true for most Jacobins most of the time; but many of them, obviously, did not understand, or in any instance accept, the idea that ideological rivalries might be sublimated rather than summarily and brutally resolved.

What weighty problems! A narrative of events cannot do justice to all of Jacobinism's cultural and ideological complexities. But it does outline the contours of its contradictory components. And it helps us to gauge the weight of a rejected past in its descent toward terrorist abuse.

The Limitless Claims of Individual Liberty

Daylight is not more pure than the depths of my heart.

Racine, *Phèdre*

"*A*nd so began the most noble Revolution that has ever honored humanity," wrote Robespierre after the fall of the monarchy in August 1792. "Or better yet," he went on, "the only Revolution whose purpose is worthy of man himself, because it finally rests political societies on the immortal principles of equality, justice, and reason."[1]

To create a free society that was also rational, just, and fraternal was the Jacobins' great desire. In the world as it might become, all things great and small would remind man of his free, harmonious, integrated, and independent self. All of life should and—they earnestly thought—would eventually revolve around the rights of free individuals, whether economic or matrimonial, legal or educational, religious or secular. Every human being—regardless of age, class, race, or gender—would realize his or her innermost being: "man everywhere has the same rights; these rights are the legitimate exercise of his faculties."[2] In his message to the club at Poitiers, to which he had offered his manuals of civility, Pierre Lavrault reminded the *clubbistes* that "we must teach men to love and respect one another because it is by respecting others that you get others to respect you."[3] For the Jacobins of 1789–90, who would soon become the unwitting architects of blind terror, a moralized polity—a republic, in a word—could not exist if a single innocent citizen were unjustly punished or oppressed. "The arrest and punishment of an innocent person," explained the Jacobin Conventionnel Brival to fellow Jacobins from the neighboring city of Tulle, "is a calamity which can only increase the enemies of the Revolution."[4]

"Happiness is a new idea in Europe," said the arch-Jacobin Saint-Just, who could easily have added that in the Jacobin scheme of things, individual well-being, self-respect, and freedom were coterminous. In that view the defense of the public good made for both "common happiness in general and for the happiness of every private person."[5] Jacobins thrilled at stories that described the sudden ecstasy of men and women liberated from mind-forged or earth-bound manacles, like the freed prisoners of the Bastille or the Swiss soldiers of Chateauvieux condemned to hard labor and later released. They found particular satisfaction in hearing of priests and nuns who had liberated themselves from inhuman vows and were now able to find marital bliss in each other's freely chosen company.

Although nation building and the assertion of class as a social category were perhaps the indirect and postrevolutionary consequence of Jacobinism's rise and fall, the Jacobins' conscious desires were elsewhere. Freedom and the well-being of mankind were their first goals. Even in the difficult days of 1793 and 1794, the Jacobins remained convinced that individuals had rights because nature, reason, and God had meant for men and women to be free agents, or subjects and not objects. In a common trope of revolutionary parlance, the Revolution had not just created but had also returned to regenerated citizens the eternal rights that despotism had unjustly suppressed.

Since the Jacobins considered self-expression a basic, natural human right, they were united in wishing to guarantee the right to free speech. Well into the Revolution, after the death of the king and on the eve of ensuing terror (on March 3, 1793), a Jacobin club that was struggling to make sense of its situation might still remind the public that the "goal of all patriotic societies has been to gather, develop, communicate, and spread all possible Enlightenment, all knowledge, ever further; to form a public spirit, to fortify it . . . to instruct the people of its rights, to teach it to respect its duties, to inspire it with a love of the fatherland, to persuade it to submit to and obey the law."[6] Robespierre put it pithily in May 1791: to speak and to communicate one's opinions is a natural right and "a need of the soul."[7]

Thus the rules of many clubs were designed to make it possible for every member to have his say. At Moret, not far from Paris, the club set up a special committee at whose meetings members who feared to address a larger group might find the courage to speak up: "the only purpose of this committee . . . is to enable citizens to make those statements which they might otherwise not make because of their timidity or their inability to speak to a large audience."[8] No one could speak a second time until all those who had something to say had spoken. Not allowed to interrupt, members were enjoined to listen to all speakers, who were under an obligation to speak politely, to the point, and not too often. At Ozoir-la-Ferrière the *clubbistes* adopted a procedure guaranteeing access to the podium because "it is evident that without this rule, it would not be possible for us to understand one another and for our society to reach the goal it has set for itself."[9] To ensure fluidity and free access to the podium, presidents of clubs held office for one month only and, as a rule, were not eligible for immediate reelection. The Jacobins' increasingly intolerant stand after August 1792 was a definite break with their attitude in the first and more generous days of the Revolution. In May 1791, when the National Assembly sought to limit the clubs' right to correspond with one another, Robespierre was asked to draw up an address on freedom of the press.

The Jacobins hailed individual becoming in all of its many forms. Individualistic meritocracy and worldly success were proof for them of talent and of moral worth rather than of self-seeking greed. Though of different minds about the value of experience, education, and native ability, all Jacobins believed that every man—and perhaps every woman—had the right to compete fairly to secure the knowledge, property, and influence he deserved, provided of course that private achievements had been made compatible with the public good. All for one and one for all. Jacobins loved to recount the feats of champions, of humble men who had striven and deservedly succeeded. They wanted to sing the praises of such people loud and often.

Jacobins carried over this principle of beneficent individuation into many domains. As children of the Enlightenment, they stridently opposed the idea that men were born with unequal rights. They despised distinctions and social ranking based on race or birth, inherited nobility being only the most obvious of these nefarious barriers. Racial or at least genetic justifications of exclusion—against the noble-born, as it happens—were eventually invoked by the Jacobins but not until much later, in the fall of 1797, when

Jacobinism was close to breaking down completely. In August 1794, by contrast, on the Convention floor, Tallien, a former Jacobin terrorist, asked rhetorically: "What does it matter to me that a man be born a noble if his behavior is good? What does it matter to me that a man be born a plebeian if he is a scoundrel?"[10]

The issue of individual rights was well defined by Sieyès in his famous pamphlet, *What Is the Third Estate?* "The final cause of all the social world," he wrote, "should be individual liberty." Doubtlessly, Sieyès's text was also—among many other things—an unconscious prefiguration of revolutionary dictatorship because it postulated both the indivisible oneness of the sovereign nation and the exclusion of political dissidents. But his conscious and primary purpose, like that of most true Jacobins, was to wage an anti-absolutist defense of private rights.

As lovers of threatened freedom and of a fragile human race, Jacobins were also keen students of human nature. Individuals were ordinarily created good, they knew, but in France as it then existed many individuals had become quite bad. Some of their contemporaries—transformed by the Revolution—might become angelic: Marat, for example, was for those who loved him a saintly figure. David's celebrated portrait of the *Ami du peuple*[11] presents him as a sacrificial, quasi-religious, feminized, Christ-like victim: "Marat died for you."

But men were complicated creatures whose individuality could easily become tyrannical. "The best of princes is nothing more than a crowned bandit . . . We must never lose sight of this verity, which rests on both experience and [our understanding of] human nature."[12] "Les passions," explained Robespierre in a debate on shortages and on the need to control food prices, "déclarent la guerre à l'humanité souffrante" (Passions declare war against suffering humanity).[13] Around every corner lurked the threat of corruption, and Jacobins often expressed shock when some former political ally suddenly became *corrompu.*

It mattered politically therefore that every Jacobin be trained to read the actions, the motives, and the faces of every individual friend and foe, and of themselves as well. In the middle decades of the nineteenth century, Turgenev wrote that the heart of the person closest to us is like a dark forest; today, as heirs of modernism's queries, we are more despondent yet. Man, for us, cannot read the wishes even of his own heart. Jacobins thought the reverse. For those who had political discernment, the human condition— and the human face—were open books that any sincere person might learn to read: "Just by looking at him," said a Paris Jacobin of a man he had just denounced, "I would pronounce him guilty."[14]

Jacobins were confirmed individualists who reasoned from intimate conviction. Like Rousseau, they assumed that one's heart and conscience—that is, the core of one's self—might remain pure though one's actions might seem blamable to the ill-intentioned. (Rousseau, an intransigent moralist, wrote of his older, beloved, self-indulgent, and faintly promiscuous companion, Mme. de Warens, a one-time police spy, that she had made mistakes but that her heart was pure.) Jacobins deftly distinguished action from intent, an echo also, perhaps, of both Christian belief and Old Regime jurisprudence. For the judges of ancient French common law, intent (the *question intentionnelle*) had often mattered as much as the actuality of criminal action. Had the accused *willfully* wronged another? That had been a favored issue of criminal legislation before 1789, and the Jacobins carried this way of thinking (as they did much of the traditionalist sensibility) into their modern life. Indeed, after Robespierre's fall in July 1794, the chastened and newly anti-terrorist Thermidorian Jacobins seized on the issue of confused intentionality (as opposed to willful involvement in terrorist excess) to explain why they had heretofore gone along with the Terror in the first place. Terror, explained the anti-Robespierrists at Tulle, had obviously been the conspiratorial achievement of wicked men with hidden motives. Fortunately, provincial Jacobins like themselves could learn from their mistakes. Now, to despise terrorist hypocrisy, it sufficed "to deepen our understanding of both the conduct and the character of those who still defend it."[15] The Terror of 1794, thought the Jacobins of 1795, had not been a fated or structured event of which they had been the unwitting architects. It had been instead the work of malevolent deceivers and hypocrites like Robespierre (who had been punished) and of his deceived followers (for whom bygones should be bygones.) They asked, not "Did you commit such and such an act (in 1794)?" but rather, "in committing this barbarous act, were you acting from public necessity or private cruelty . . . Were you an accomplice or a passive victim of Robespierrist tyranny?"[16] This approach, though opportunistic, also spoke to their way of thinking about human nature. Jacobins studied their own actions closely, and as a rule these seemed to them to have been morally laudable: "I shall open my mind to you," said Saint-Just during the trial of the king.[17]

Jacobins much preferred sincerity to grace: "La politesse," remarked a Jacobin Conventionnel, "n'est pas une vertu républicaine" (Politeness is not a Republican virtue).[18] Jacobins, in their own opinion at least, were open, passionate, modest, and above all truthful. In their questionnaires and public confessions, Jacobins emphasized not just externally visible acts but inner emotion and character. They did not ask, "What did you do when you heard of the death of the king?" They wondered instead, "How did you feel when you heard this news?" and "Were you pleased to see that the nation had been restored to its rights when the goods of the clergy had been confiscated?"[19]

In large part because they valued individual intent so highly, these pacifistic and bourgeois engineers of the heart hesitated for many months, in 1792–93, to condemn the repulsive violence that had become second nature to some in the Parisian crowd. Most Jacobins found it hard to complain on this score because they "knew" that the prorevolutionary sansculottes were childlike innocents. Popular actions might seem bad, but the poor (like themselves) were uncorrupted individuals who could not really err. In late September 1792 Danton, who had just allowed the murder of hundreds of prisoners, said of the Parisian crowd, "le peuple . . . en masse est toujours juste" (The people as a whole is always just).[20]

Nevertheless some of the Jacobins' enemies were obviously bad. Émigrés and royalists were visibly selfish, proud, and truly nasty *(méchants)*. But other, more devious individuals had motives that were harder to unmask. Especially trying were two-faced men *(hommes doubles)*. As dedicated connoisseurs of dissimulation, Jacobins constantly ripped apart the "veils of duplicity."[21] They carefully distinguished between left-wing *hypocrites du patriotisme* (the supposedly egalitarian leaders of the sans-culotte movement who claimed to be more revolutionary than even the Jacobins) and right-wing hypocrites (the supposedly Christian but in reality, sanguinary, nonjuring Catholic clergy. Also to be despised were "arch-hypocrites," former Jacobins who had gone over to the side of immobilism. These included the pro-monarchy Feuillants of 1791, who claimed to be revolutionaries but had now changed their views about the king; and the Girondins of 1793, who claimed to be revolutionaries still but had become hostile to the Parisian sans-culottes and wanted to stop the Revolution. These were the mendacious *tartuffes de la Révolution*.

In consequence, Jacobins made the baring of the heart in publicly staged introspection an important aspect of revolutionary ritual. In both the National Assemblies and the clubs, the Jacobins were addicted to self-criticism, and from time to time patriots were expected to provide long autobiographies to prove that their conduct had been blameless from the start.

Jacobins cherished these moments of moral self-exposure reminiscent of prerevolutionary Catholic confessions. They often availed themselves of such occasions to recount their entire personal history, including that of their prerevolutionary life, which became in these personalized narratives, the long prologue to the intense, third, and triumphal act of revolutionary drama.

Jacobins keenly scrutinized their friends, their enemies, and themselves. Conscience was for them, as it was for Rousseau, truth's chosen censor. Its strong voice, they thought, vitiated the need for an intermediary priestly caste of learned men. The Rémois Jacobins, for example, found choosing deputies simple. They voted for those who could neither listen to "private solicitations" nor "lie to their conscience."[22] For these neo-Protestants of a kind, conscience—not priest or church or club—mediated between man and God and nature. Jacobins yearned to make the mechanics of social life obvious and ubiquitously transparent. Man, they posited, could become a better citizen by becoming the attentive listener to his own inner voice.

Those who had been misled and repented deserved some forgiveness. Nevertheless, no one committed crimes inadvertently, including those who had sinned from weakness. Those men who really wished to hear their conscience could always do so. Jacobins believed in moralized, individual self-assertion. They instinctively rejected negotiated consensus.

*A*s unabashed admirers of the self, Jacobins also defended economic and professional individualism. They believed in the overall social usefulness of entrepreneurialism. Jacobins generally disliked the constraining network of guilds that had regulated wages and conditions of work before 1789, often (though the Jacobins usually chose not to notice this) to the satisfaction of working artisans.

As individualists, Jacobins were adamant partisans of private property, which they imagined to be a guarantee of liberty. They detested the very idea of agrarian communism. Here and there, after 1792 especially, the populist proponents of "an agrarian law," modeled on that of ancient Rome, argued—or were said by the Jacobins to argue—for a massive distribution of wealth. But overwhelmingly, Jacobins were hostile to this communistic vision. For them, in Danton's words, moral equality was a necessity, but material equality was an obvious impossibility. Jacques Monbrion (a left Jacobin in the radical city of Marseilles) urged all revolutionaries to be on their toes: "Every time that someone says 'you should have half the property of your neighbor'; shun that man! He is a veritable enemy of the Constitution; he wants you to misinterpret equality so that he can slander the Declaration of the Rights of Man."[23]

Although only one Frenchman sold wheat for every three who purchased it, Jacobins were convinced that the internal free trade of grain was in the general interest. Eventually, under the pressure of politics and circumstance, Jacobins did support price controls; but that was certainly not part of their original plan.

Because such privatist endorsements are at the heart of modern capitalism, it is not inaccurate in some simple and *prima facie* sense to describe Jacobins as (confused) "precapitalist" actors. Many historians have indeed focused their entire interpretation of Jacobinism on just that point. However, it is important to remember that for the Jacobins, economic issues were less an end in themselves than the extension of other principles—freedom especially. Jacobins interpreted what would seem to us to be economic measures of exclusion through the screen of their moralized and individuated sensibility. For example, they momentarily accepted the exclusion of impoverished domestics from the franchise (and at times excluded them from their own clubs). Such a step strikes us necessarily as being intensely sectarian. But many Jacobins tentatively reasoned in this matter that they were excluding domestics for their own good, in part at least, because the very poor were easily coercible and were not capable of being citizens.

Likewise, the Jacobins' exclusion of bankrupts from club membership, as proposed by the club at Bayonne,[24] had less to do with a desire to protect property than with their value judgment of such people as individually irresponsible. In the same way, when he spoke up in the Paris club *against* this provincial measure, which had also figured in the Constitution of 1789–1791, Robespierre referred not to money but to moral worth. Bankrupts, he reasoned, were usually innocent individuals who had fallen prey to moneyed interests. They were hapless people (perhaps like his absent and delinquent father) who had not been rich enough to pay their debts during troubled, revolutionary times and deserved a second chance.[25]

Tellingly, the Jacobins, though partisans of economic individualism, had a moralized, precapitalist, and Jeffersonian detestation of credit, debt, hoarding, stockjobbing, banks, and speculation, which they saw as so many forms of antisocial and antinational betrayal. In their view, these sophisticated instruments of moneyed gain diminished human freedom.

Indeed, Jacobins rejected these capitalist tools for the same reason that they accepted private property. Banks and usurers were in practice the small holder's most confirmed enemy, just as small holdings were for them—as for the radical Whigs of England and America—a guarantee of freedom. Ends mattered to them more than means: at Pau, the Jacobins were pleased when someone offered to make cheap shoes for the army, but they paused when other shoemakers and tanners complained about unfair competition.[26] Jacobins understood that they should not consider the price of the soldiers' shoes only. They also had to give thought to the livelihood of struggling cobblers. The dictates of intersecting supply and demand might be good but they might also be quite bad.

The Jacobins' suspicion of capitalism taken as an end in its own right does not, however, mean that the Jacobins were economic primitives who did not grasp the concept of capitalism. "Do you want to keep peasants from feeding grain to their pigs?" asked an experienced *clubbiste,* "then reduce the price of pork and lard."[27] Girondins during the winter of 1792–93 liked to point out that subsidizing state-run bakeries would make bread scarcer because it would drive other bakers out of business. Saint-Just, one of the loftiest and most radical of all Jacobins, similarly warned in November 1792 that the shortages inflation would necessarily engender might incite peasants to withhold their grain from the market. In his response to a defense of life insurance couched in strict economic terms by Étienne Clavière (a Geneva-born Girondin Jacobin who in 1787 founded the first French life insurance company before the Revolution),[28] Robespierre did not point-blank deny the value of insurance or of the notion that money could be made that way. He merely expressed a preference for mutual assistance as a more apt manifestation of the "general sensibility that is one of the bases of humanitarian service."[29]

Jacobins realized full well the complex and technical effects of capitalism and private property. But they were determined to find their place between the rejected extremes of collectively held property and private greed. They understood that buying and selling could aggravate or generate social inequalities. But they also wanted to believe that some of the mechanisms of individualistic capitalism might be accommodated to civic republicanism. Joint stock companies, for example, did not have to be instruments of selfish profit. At Châtelleraut the Jacobin club considered floating shares to create a company that would make sabers, with the profits going to the poor, so that no shareholders could derive any personal gain.[30] Capitalism and capitalistic tools were acceptable to the Jacobins when proved compatible with the moral health of Self and Nation.

Although some Jacobins like Fouché (a former priest and later under Napoleon duke of Otranto) railed in 1793–94 against the *riches égoïstes,* most Jacobins accepted economic inequality because they—like Aristotle—reasoned that a man might be more generous if he were rich than if he were poor. In fact, a newly enriched man would be made more generous from remembering his earlier misfortune.

The Jacobins' endorsement of private property also depended on their sense that individuated economic forms were far better than what had been before. Jacobins defined economic individualism (capitalism) as a new alternative to antique feudal, statist, and nonmonetary relations of power, rather than as an alternative to some future collectivization of economic life (though they did gradually do that as well, after 1794 especially).

They perceived a social choice between new, unfettered, and liberating monetized exchange on the one hand and, on the other, politicized (feudal or absolutist) state-directed relations, many examples of which existed already in an age of enlightened despotism. Which was the freer, they wondered, the worker who sold his labor to the highest bidder, or the tenant forced by his "patriarchal" seigneur to use a banal oven to bake his daily bread? As Jean-Pierre Gross explains in his insightful *Fair Shares for All: Jacobin Egalitarianism in Practice,* like Voltaire, the Jacobins considered independence more important than equality.[31]

Jacobins despised not just traditional economic corporatism (in theory especially) but cartels and economic associations, which in their eyes defended selfish and vested interests instead of protecting the poor. At Dijon, in 1795, the *clubbistes* denounced "an infamous coalition of tanners and of the richest cobblers."[32]

In this same register, Jacobins disliked primogeniture because it made some rich and others poor while crippling the rights of many individuals. This custom—which had been the prerevolutionary rule in many provinces of southern France especially—vitiated the right not just of younger sons but of women also, a category that, as Mme. Roland pointed out, might ironically include the suddenly dispossessed mother of an ungrateful eldest son and heir.

In October 1793 the Jacobin-dominated Convention likewise opened the law courts to all citizens. *Avocats* and *procureurs* (of whom they had been suspicious since 1790, when the order of barristers had been dissolved and lawyers forbidden to wear a distinctive costume) would no longer have a monopoly on pleading before the courts. Ordinary people would have their say as well. For the Jacobins, to paraphrase the words of C. L. R. James, "every [talented] cook could govern."[33]

In sum, then, as far as they could see, modern, small, and private property was basically a good thing. Jacobins, although eager to please deserving artisans or peasants, were nonetheless fierce and self-assured when faced with opposition to the idea of private property, either from the communistically minded on the left or from the traditionalists on the right.

Jacobins could easily turn a deaf ear to social complaints when they felt that their—and society's—basic interests were at stake. Aggressive or surly workers who came to the clubs to complain about their employers were often rebuffed. After the enactment of price and wage controls, *clubbistes* were quick to remind workers that it might be illegal for them to demand higher wages. They severely reprimanded workers who refused to work long hours or who did not show up for work, especially if their labors were connected to the war economy (and in 1793–94, even the harvest was considered war-related work). With the advent of a new calendar and ten-day week in the fall of 1793, idling on Sundays became one more counterrevolutionary offense. Slackness in the state-run armaments industry—known for its harsh conditions and rife with complaints—was particularly censured. In the spring of 1794 the Committee of Public Safety, keener on productivity than on the workers' welfare, reconsidered pay scales in these establishments and switched from paying workers by the day to paying them for piecework.[34] Though key workers might be exempt from the draft, they were subject to heavy fines and arrest for misconduct on the shop floor. Alcohol was not allowed in these factories. Workers who dared to complain were told that they had no cause to do so because their representatives (the political leaders of the sans-culotte movement) had acquiesced to the new wage scales.

The Jacobins' assumptions on the supposed overlap of the national good and the private gain of the propertied (themselves) extended quite far: the *Chronique du mois,* a representative Girondin journal, suggested that its essays would surely be "useful to bankers, financiers, and merchants who must know our internal and external state in order to establish in their transactions commercial relations that assure our national fortune as they augment their own wealth."[35]

In brief, then, Jacobins certainly believed in private property; but economic individualism was not predominant in the Jacobin frame of mind. If Jacobinism transformed tradition to make the world safer for capitalism's unfolding, that was definitely not the conscious goal of the *clubbistes*. It makes more sense to remember instead that their attitude related to a long-held and characteristic French interest in private motivation, which reached back to La Rochefoucauld in the seventeenth century and, in times closer to their own, to writers like Vauvenargues and Chamfort (who was, as it happens, driven by the Jacobins to suicide in 1794).

The Jacobins despised self-assertive insolence, arrogance, pride, and the display of wealth or knowledge by the learned and the rich. They knew that wealth had a social cost. Poverty for them gave a presumption of goodness; as riches did of vice. Jacobins were not much attracted to the Physiocrats' belief that greater profit regardless of social cost was good because it led to more investment and more growth.

*B*ut why did only *some* hearts incline to goodness? In the Jacobins' eyes, no one was born bad. Even nobles, even those who had been brought up to be vain and selfish, might become good Republicans. Moral regeneration through accession to virtuous citizenship was one of their most cherished themes. Jacobins believed (at times) that even their worst enemies were morally vulnerable: "the traitors who threatened to cut the throats of their fellow citizens are torn by burning remorse and are burdened by the shame of appearing horrible in the eyes of humanity."[36]

To understand why it was that some men became *patriotes* while others inclined instead to manifestly immoral *aristocratie,* Jacobins often stressed the effect of context. A negative environment, they knew, dulled the voice of conscience. As they reflected on April 9, 1792, on the actions of their enemies, the Jacobins of Tulle understood that they should not hate the deceived rank and file of *aristocratie:* they had been carried away "by the rage that is a natural response to the crimes of the factious . . . The blame for them lies squarely in the circumstances in which we were through no fault of our own."[37] The boundary between the private and the public was often porous, and Jacobins assumed as matter of course that public corruption could spill over into the souls of the private persons who were exposed to it, or vice versa. In a corrupted royal court or palace, for example, no courtier could hope to remain pure. Monarchy spoiled everything it touched.

But because men had free will—even at Versailles—Jacobins ultimately insisted on assigning guilt and responsibility precisely and individually. In their view, although a wicked family ambiance might well lead to crime, individuals could rise above their familial circumstances as they could rise above any handicap. When quondam friends attempted to embarrass the Montagnards by mocking them for including in their ranks a close relative of the king, Philippe Égalité, duc d'Orléans, who in his role as a Conventionnel had voted for the death of his royal cousin, the Montagnard Jacobins responded that being born into a family of tyrants had nothing to do with the case. Jacobins rejected the Old Regime idea of collective familial responsibility, which held that any personally innocent person might have to share the guilt and punishment of others to whom he was somehow connected. (Robespierre's first publication as a young man had been an impassioned statement against the Old Regime principle of collective familial guilt.) After 1792 writing to relatives who had emigrated was punishable by death but having such relatives was not per se a legal offense, and the Jacobins who urged the imprisonment of the émigrés' relatives often claimed to be doing so for the prisoners' own good, as a protective measure.

Only in extreme cases and under great pressure did Jacobins agree to deprive their victims of all legal rights irrespective of individual circumstance. British and Hanoverian soldiers were indeed ordered shot upon capture. Relatives of émigrés and royalist counterrevolutionaries were eventually detained as hostages. In early 1794 all nobles, regardless of their politics, were likewise deemed militarily dangerous and banned as a group from the capital and some maritime cities.

But such collective interdicts were justified pragmatically and without reference to principle. Jacobins understood such steps to be temporary and exceptional. Although the Jacobins did legislate the confiscation of a dead victim's property and recriminalize suicide (by arranging for the de facto punishment of a victim's survivors), these penalties were intended to deter future criminals rather than prove guilt by association.

Like the Old Regime, and unlike recent totalitarian governments that hid their death camps and gulags from open view, the Jacobins also believed in public executions. But their theory of public punishment, on the face of it at least, differed from that of the Old Regime in one essential respect. The purpose of prerevolutionary punishment had been to restore community norms irrespective of individuated concerns. The more brutal the punishment (like breaking on the wheel), the better. By contrast, the rationale of Jacobin punishment was (ostensibly) to appease public opinion by carefully selecting culprits who had already been proven guilty in a court of law. It was essential for the Jacobins that criminals first be judged one by one—even if they were also made to stand side by side in *fournées* (or batches)—and then, if convicted, be executed one by one. Just as Jacobins who joined a club took their oath of loyalty separately, so were culprits executed singly. Plans for multiple guillotines were never implemented, though they were known to be technically feasible. Abroad, in Germany for example, French guillotines were often represented as complex machines with rotating razors that might decapitate hordes of innocent victims indiscriminately and collectively, but such machines were never built.

Jacobins had great faith in man's ability to choose to be a law-abiding citizen, and they also set great store by man's virile will, that is, by every individual male's ability to weigh his motives and act upon the world. "We are arbiters of our destiny," explained Robespierre after Louis's flight to Varennes. How else could kings be overthrown?[38] Jacobins commonly assumed their enemies to be weak, indecisive, and feminine. "Soft" and "pleasurable" were not for them commendatory terms. In their speech, Jacobins often coupled "fanatical and timorous." They spoke the "langage mâle de la vertu." They believed in a self that was at once passionate and controlled. "L'Empire," wrote Saint-Just sententiously, "est aux phlegmatiques" (dominance comes from self-control), which was not to be confused with passivity. "Le calme," he also wrote, "est l'âme de la tyrannie, la passion est l'âme de la liberté" (Calmness is the soul of tyranny, and passion the soul of liberty). A true patriot, he thought, brought together "la froideur de l'esprit, le feu d'un coeur ardent et pur" (a cool spirit and the fire of a pure and ardent heart).[39]

Will and its companion, passion, were the perfect inversions of moderation and hypocrisy, traits the Jacobins methodically attributed to their enemies. A petition of Jacobin artists made this point nicely. "Hypocritical priests used to say: know how to defeat your passions—and they called that morality. The active and warm-blooded Republican must say: leave man his passions, but know how to direct them. Passions give men energy. A man without passion is a federalist and a moderate, or a hypocritical Feuillant, incapable of great things."[40] The Jacobins saw Hercules as the proper symbol of revolutionary might. Both male and female symbols of revolutionary principle and power were interchangeably monumental.

For those regenerated men who did control their revolutionary selves, no mission could ever be impossible. Jacobins felt that the fate of the world was in their hands. They did not know the meaning of boredom. They lived intensely. They knew they could reshape history. They felt pity mitigated by contempt for foreign patriots who had failed to defend their own liberty. On October 23, 1792, the Jacobins of Toulon ordered the Polish flag, which had adorned their hall, removed: the Poles had not fought to the death. They had yielded and agreed to live under "l'esclavage des tyrans" (the slavery of tyrants).[41]

Some historians have inferred that the Enlightenment's redefinition of gender roles (men are public and heroic; women, private and chaste) engendered widespread anxieties of self-definition during the Revolution. This argument has considerable merit if set in a larger social context; but for their part the Jacobins were resolute political actors.

They inclined to categorical and trenchant judgment. They had no trouble distinguishing the healthy from the pathological, patriots from aristocrats, the masculine from the feminine, the heroic from the pusillanimous, the general from the particular. Those that were not with them were against them. "All the monuments of history testify," the abbé Grégoire explained during the king's trial, "that royalty and liberty are like the principles of the Manichaeans, in eternal battle."[42] The stock Jacobin portrait—as David's of Marat—sets clearly delineated features against a stark, contrasting, monochrome background. Jacobins were not interested in nuance. They emphasized man's power over nature, as well as his autonomy and ability to forge his own destiny. The Jacobins were persistently perplexed by the presence of the poor, the destitute, and the sick.

They were even tempted to think that the desire to exercise one's will also separated the helplessly mad from the sane and the vigorous. It was hard for Jacobins to accept the idea that any human being might not want to become the able-bodied, happy, healthy, and alert citizen of a regenerated republic. "If we are agreed that no portion of humanity should suffer . . . let us put inscriptions above the gates of our asylums which declare that they will soon disappear. For if, when the Revolution has ended, we still have some unfortunates among us, our revolutionary labors will have been in vain."[43]

In the eyes of the Jacobins, kindness and charity were civic obligations. Misfortune and accidents were part of life. Moreover, the Jacobins did not expect the destitute to be humble or deferential to their betters as in the mythology of the Old Regime. Nonetheless, in the Jacobins' perspective, not all the poor deserved their help. A strong will distinguished the deserving worker from those who had to beg and plead. Many Jacobins decried *l'aristocratie de la pauvreté,* poor people who did not try to improve their condition and who abusively claimed a (selfish) right to live at the expense of hard-working citizens.

In (universalist) theory, Jacobins were sympathetic to the urban poor. In (propertied) practice, they did not like to have their hand forced. They had a sharp eye for the "audacious importunity [of] clever and hypocritical beggars."[44] They were keener than the monarchy had been to remove beggars from the streets. The Convention did not abolish the older *dépôts de mendicité,* now called *maisons de répression,* and this new nomenclature made Jacobin sense: in a republic, the presence of able-bodied beggars was an insult to hard-working, law-abiding citizens. In Jacobin legislation, indigents were required to return to their home municipalities, as the English poor laws of the time also decreed.

*W*omen and their relationship to both men and nation likewise occupied the Jacobins. In Mme. de Staël's novel *Delphine,* written in 1802 but set in Paris in 1790–1792, Léonce, the unreformed reactionary hero explains to Delphine, a quasi-Protestant modernizer, that "une femme ne sauroit avoir trop d'aristocratie" (a woman cannot be too haughty or aloof.)[45] Jacobins thought the reverse. To be sure, many other matters (the safety of the nation, conspiracies against liberty, the gap between poverty and wealth) mattered more to them than the question of women's social role. Men's clubs outnumbered women's clubs by about one hundred to one. Nonetheless, women's issues were quite crucial. No major Jacobin figure remained silent on the woman question, which every Jacobin club had to resolve for itself.

In many ways, the Jacobins revealed themselves to be less than progressive on women's issues. On October 30, 1793, for instance, the Jacobin-dominated government and courts ordered women's clubs shut down, just as they decreed the execution of the queen on October 16; of Olympe de Gouges (a feminist publicist who had published a Declaration of the Rights of Women in September 1791) on November 4; and of Mme. Roland on November 8. It is also true that Robespierre railed against women for suggesting that only *aristocrates* believed in the sexual specificity of talent and occupation. When women were invited to participate in Jacobin *fêtes* or celebrations, it was usually to serve the food or clean up. In December 1793 at Chateauroux, the *clubbistes* endorsed the suggestion that "the *citoyennes*, our sisters, members of this society should sweep the hall every five days [that is, twice in every *decade*] and that men not be charged with this task; the citizen-president of the club consulted our sisters to find out if they were amenable to this proposition, which they unanimously adopted."[46]

A number of Jacobins made extreme antifeminist statements. At Toul the Jacobins resolved that women who had entered the benches reserved for men should be arrested.[47] Jacobins berated women for being untrustworthy or lukewarm in their commitment to the Revolution. They accused women of spreading defeatist rumors and giving aid and comfort to their émigré relatives abroad and to the nonjuring, antirevolutionary Catholic clergy at home. At Arles the club insisted that hesitant wives commit themselves to revolutionary principle by spitting on consecrated hosts.[48] At Mouzeuil a local Jacobin reported with glee that his fellow revolutionaries had staged, in his own words, an unusual auto-da-fé with ecclesiastical ornaments that were set on fire on the body of a female counterrevolutionary who had just been shot: "what caused us the greatest pleasure," he added, "was that all the women came to warm themselves by this fire whilst having a patriotic nip."[49]

Many clubs discussed the need to compel young women and widows to marry veterans, or recognized sans-culottes, or men less rich than themselves. Jacobins were perhaps too (condescendingly) ready to warm to the theme of Republican motherhood, which relegated women to private life, albeit on new grounds. "Enter within," exclaimed the Jacobins of Grenade, a small town near Toulouse, "among your brothers, fathers, and spouses to find the principles whose first duty it will be to teach to your children."[50]

Moreover, in the Jacobin scheme of things, women clearly belonged to a second sex whose first duty was chastity. They were intent on preserving the sexual innocence of young women especially. In Republican allegorical painting, women—when not fully clothed—bared shapes and breasts that were more nurturing and maternal than seductive and erotic. The unmarried, virginal, and Republican Charlotte Corday, who had internalized this ethic, bristled when her judges implied that she had taken lovers and had had children by them. A favored technique of revolutionary prosecutors was to portray anti-Republican women—the queen especially—as promiscuous, unnatural Messalinas or, worse yet, as lesbians. (Accusations of masculine homosexuality were never used to justify punishment, not even by implication.) At the same time, many Jacobins like Fabre d'Eglantine (who invented the name of the months on the revolutionary calendar) or Amar (who presented to the Convention the case for shutting down the women's clubs) had sordid and exploitative sexual pasts.

Overall, then, Jacobins perceived Republican femininity as conciliatory rather than participatory. They took it for granted that male and female gender roles, though complementary in both politics and nature, were of necessity quite distinct. In a discussion of adoption one aristocratic Jacobin who believed that children spontaneously imitated the parent of their own sex, urged that widows and widowers be allowed to adopt children of their own gender only. Regardless of its effects,[51] the motivation of revolutionary legislation allowing divorce probably had less to do with the Jacobins' concern for women than with their interest in the abstract principle of natural rights taken without regard to gender.[52]

And so it was that in this domain Jacobins often took back with one hand what they had given with the other. They both applauded women who cross-dressed as soldiers and congratulated them on returning to civilian life when their identity had been revealed, like the *citoyenne* Brunel of Nay, who had fought at the front on the *avants-postes* but had come home "by the delicacy that was inspired by her modesty."[53]

True, Jacobin women could become more assertive: when a Jacobin orator at Vire suggested that rich women be made to pay the wages of National Guardsmen, a female spectator immediately responded that women would be quite glad to mount guard themselves once they had been admitted to membership in the clubs. Similarly, at Eguilles, in the more radical Var, the Marseillais Jacobin Monbrion organized an armed company of women in the local National Guard. About one hundred women are thought to have joined the army under false identities. Collot d'Herbois, a radical and populist Jacobin, hailed one of them as a hero—an intrepid warrior—who though female by sex was male by spirit.[54] It was suggested here and there that women form entire battalions in the National Guard.[55]

Ordinarily, however, Jacobin women were Jacobins first and women second. Even the most militant Parisian women tailored their radical requests to sexual roles acceptable to men. The members of the radical female club, the Citoyennes Républicaines Révolutionnaires, believed, for example, that women should hunt down traitors at home while men fought with the army at the front. By and large, Jacobin women accepted—no doubt with reluctance in many cases—the Jacobins' Rousseauean naturalizing distinction between public man and private woman, a great handicap, obviously, in the formulation and assertion of their claims.

As a consequence, the Jacobin woman tended to do her work outside the clubs. Women often aimed to raise the awareness of other women by participating in parades or, more prosaically, by presenting their own quotidian and Republican example. At Reims, for instance, the women members asked a visiting Conventionnel if he had brought his wife along, as they wished to present her with a tricolor belt.[56] Many Jacobin women saw the Revolution as an opportunity to widen the moral scope of their domestic tasks, and some Jacobin men encouraged them to do this: "Sisters and friends," explained a Jacobin at Ruffec, "you form opinion . . . It is before your tribunal that politics must submit its operations and the warrior triumphs."[57]

Overall, however, in historical perspective, the uncertainty of the Jacobins' commitment to the promotion of woman as citizen is far less surprising than the very fact of their interest in the question. The most thoughtful Jacobins—especially when arguing from rationality rather than natural law—understood that equality of the sexes followed from the logic of their ideals. In July 1790 Condorcet, the most lucid of the Jacobin feminists, wrote that the distinctive characteristic of humans was that these "feeling creatures" were able to reason about their moral rights, and that "women who have these same qualities, must necessarily have equal rights. Either no individual of the human race has true rights, or all have them equally; and to vote against the rights of others, on grounds of religion, race, or sex, is to abjure one's own rights."[58] More mutedly, Sieyès likewise abstractly understood that a universalist definition of citizenship implied that women would eventually become full-fledged members of the political community. Jacobins were, in any case, already prepared to grant many social rights to women, as witnessed, for example, by a law of June 10, 1793, which gave women and men equal rights—and an equal say—in the distribution of common lands.[59] It is of critical importance that Jacobins laid the groundwork for women's right to inherit property equally, surely their most important durable gain during the entire Revolution.

Jacobins had some practical sense of the difficult situation women faced in civil life. They were moved by the plight of women who had fallen on hard times. Whether married or unmarried, the companion of a fallen soldier was in their view entitled not just to sympathy but to material help. Although the police of Old Regime Paris had routinely ignored such cases, Jacobins disliked instances of domestic violence. At Callas, in the Var, the *clubbistes* urged the local authorities to prosecute a man who was a notorious wife beater.[60] Many Jacobins understood the Revolution to have been made in no small part by and for women.

The presence of women as spectators in the clubs challenged many (and for all we know, most) Jacobin societies. In the spring of 1792 many women began to attend the meetings ostentatiously, bringing with them knitting for soldiers at the front and bandages to be made for the wounded, thereby serving the republic twice, by their work and by their presence at a revolutionary gathering. At Reims on January 1, 1792, the *clubbistes* voted to admit women, with men sitting on one side of the hall and women on the other. In February 1792 the Paris Jacobins (whose locale was also used by the Fraternal Society of One and the Other Sex) also discussed the idea of letting women deliberate on the floor of the club as members of visiting delegations.[61]

The presence of women soon led to other proposals: that they be admitted as members plain and simple and, later, that they be involved in the governance of the clubs. After the fall of the radical Hébert in March 1794, when female *clubbistes* at Reims decided to boycott the society because of disparaging remarks by some members about citizenesses, the secretary of the society noted that "every member has sharply felt this absolute isolation of a sex that is dear to all Jacobins."[62]

Women also figured prominently in the *fêtes* organized by both Jacobin clubs and Jacobin-dominated municipal and other governmental bodies. Because these celebrations attempted to represent the entire nation and the whole of humanity to itself, no parade could be staged without the participation of both sexes in roughly equal roles.

At times, as at Castres, women refused to form clubs of their own, preferring to belong to societies where membership was open to citizens and citizenesses alike. In the end, however, about fifty Jacobin women's clubs were created, many of them in southwestern France (as at Alais, where the women's club was the first to be denounced by the conservative press, Bordeaux, and Montpellier). The most famous were in Dijon (with four hundred members) and in the populous city of Lyons, where women from thirty-one different popular societies, with broad social origins,[63] met periodically in 1791 and 1792 to coordinate their efforts.[64] Women also played an important political role in the club at Marseilles. Many French women were drawn to Jacobinism, as were many foreign women, among them Mary Wollstonecraft and Helen Mariah Williams, both close to the Girondin Jacobins and, it might be added, resolutely hostile to the Terror.

To be sure, Jacobinism's response to the women's issue was regionally as well as ideologically conditioned. Conspicuously, women's clubs were unknown in rural, Mediterranean, and patriarchal Provence, where, by contrast, the network of men's clubs was the densest in the whole of France. Nonetheless, overall, Jacobin women's clubs were highly visible, and women worked hard—with only moderate success, it must be said—to establish national networks. In Paris a Dutch woman, Etta Palm d'Aelders, hoped to create a women's club in every one of Paris's forty-eight *sections,* all of them connected to one another and to provincial counterparts.[65] And in September 1792, female *clubbistes* from Dijon and Cusset met to consider the possibility of setting up a National Confederation of Patriotic French Women.

*T*he individuality of children and young people was yet another Jacobin concern. They deemed the reshaping of young minds a priority, but they also believed that the creation of a universal system of primary education could unite the Revolution's universal and individualist aspirations. If no "true talent was lost or neglected," if every individual's right to be himself or herself was fostered in state-run schools, who could then object to the hierarchic differentiation of reward and social function that prevailed in society at large? Clubs were eager to attract the young, and the society of Magnac, in the Haute Vienne, took pride in its membership of "étudiants et . . . patriotes de la ville."[66] In Normandy, at Saint-Gilles-de-la-Neuville, the members of the local club (the Popular Society of Perfect Unity) serially invited all of the commune's children in groups of four to attend its meetings.[67] About fifty Jacobin youth clubs came into being, the most active of them in Toulouse, often under the aegis of Jacobin-minded priests who had accepted the Civil Constitution of the Clergy. The purpose of these youth clubs was not to amuse but to educate and to shape character; at Vitry-le-François children "too young to benefit from its instruction" were excluded from membership.[68] Similarly, at Tonneins the *clubbistes* agreed to allow youths at the meetings but only after they had learned the Declaration of the Rights of Man by heart. By 1793–94 military training had also become a focus of youth club life.

Youth, education, and politics also came together in the revolutionary catechisms taught by government order in the schools, works that focused on the heroic actions of soldiers, especially the adolescents François Bara and Joseph Agricol Viala, who had died more or less voluntarily on behalf of the republic. Their example was widely celebrated. A *fête* in their honor was scheduled for 10 Thermidor (but was abruptly canceled).

The Jacobins' concern about youth and education was neither opportunistic nor calculating. It instead fit with their larger interest in the self-development of all citizens. It was hardly fortuitous that Grenoble, for example, which had one of the liveliest women's clubs, should have had a youth club also. Joseph Chalier, an admittedly eccentric Jacobin, argued that France did not need an army because it was itself an army of twenty-five million citizens. Women and children, he explained, also have a patriotic heart. Laclos, a conservative Jacobin, on the occasion of the king's flight in June 1791 urged that the king's fate be the object of thousands of petitions which might be signed by both active and passive citizens, women, and children, albeit on three different registers.[69]

In the Jacobins' renewed universe, men could rise above themselves, and children like Bara and Viala could become immortal. As Robespierre boasted, France alone had thirteen-year-old heroes. To Bara's mother, a guest of the Convention, a Jacobin explained that she had lost nothing: "your son is not dead; he has received a new existence; he is born to immortality."[70]

Indeed, a paradoxical sign of the sincerity of the Jacobins' interest in youth was the gradual disappearance of the youth clubs as they generally merged with the clubs for adults, sometimes on order of the authorities. Because the Jacobins believed that young people could achieve great things in a regenerated republic, the age limit for joining a club was gradually lowered from twenty-one to eighteen and, in some places, sixteen. (Young people also came to the clubs with their parents. At Rabastens the club ruled that no one under the age of twelve could attend.[71] The romantic writer Charles Nodier remembered having spoken to the Besançon club when he was only eleven.)

*T*he concepts of individualism and the natural right of man to freedom also supported the Jacobins' noblest decision, the abolition of slavery on February 4, 1794.[72] As in the case for women, the record of French Jacobins on this issue was inconsistent, as was the line followed by Jacobins residing in France's distant colonies. Until 1791, not a single French club, for example, took the trouble to correspond with the French abolitionist society, the Society of the Friends of Blacks, which modeled itself on the London Committee for the Abolition of the Slave Trade. In the club at Nantes, a trading seaport, the left Jacobin Fouché was obliged in March 1791 to disavow a public letter sympathetic to blacks that he had written to Brissot.

The first cause of the Jacobins' hesitation was obvious. Jacobins were men of property who knew that French manufacturing, to some extent, and French commerce, especially, depended on profits made from slavery, whether directly through the slave trade or indirectly through commerce with the sugar islands. Theoretically minded Jacobins also pointed out that the juxtaposition of freedom for some and slavery for others (however puzzling it might seem at first glance) was not unknown. Had that not been true in ancient Athens, and was that still not true in the newly founded United States?[73] Moreover, with blacks in France numbering fewer than five thousand in 1789, their presence at home was not of concern.

After 1792 another reason for the Montagnard Jacobins' reluctance to become involved with the question of slavery developed: the Girondin Jacobins had been close to abolitionist circles in 1789–1792. Indeed, under the pseudonym of Monsieur Schwartz (the German word for "black") the more or less Girondin Condorcet had denounced not just the slave trade but slavery itself as an unnatural crime. Tactically, therefore, to abolish slavery was to say, for the Montagnards, that the Girondins had been right about something after all.[74]

Nonetheless, some Jacobins were from the first concerned with slavery. In 1788 Brissot—who became in early 1792 the most prominent radical Jacobin of the day—had been a founding member of the Society of the

Friends of Blacks. In February 1790 he attacked the "commercial spirit" that made of slavery an exception to French liberty: "Liberty for us, chains for others. And these people claim they are the friends of Liberty!"[75] Many Jacobins realized from the first days of the Revolution that slavery and the Declaration of the Rights of Man were utterly incompatible.[76] In May 1791, after Robespierre had been elected president of the Paris society, much was made of the simultaneous exclusion of a slave owner and admission of a "mulatto." In December 1791 it was precisely on the issue of slavery that Brissot focused a victorious struggle inside the National Assembly against the more cautious Feuillant Jacobins who had lost control of the clubs earlier that fall.

Many revolutionary women who wished to inflect the Rights of Man as the Rights of Man and Woman naturally understood how Jacobin principle placed women, blacks, and Jews on the same footing. So did—in reverse—the more conservative *clubbistes:* an anti-Semitic Jacobin at Strasbourg openly linked his hostility toward Jews to his sympathy for the threatened prosperity of slave traders.[77]

However, just as Jacobins eventually understood that it was intellectually absurd to emancipate some Jews and not others, so did they eventually grasp the connection between freedom at home and freedom in the colonies. The survival of slavery, they knew, vitiated their claim to represent universalist humanity. Peicam de Bressoles in his *Fête Américaine,* presented at the Opéra Comique in August 1794, included in his wide panoply of symbols a black man; a white man; a black baby; a white baby; busts of Marat, Le Peletier, Bara, and Viala; and a Tree of Liberty, all of them cherished symbols of Jacobin politics.

Gradually, momentum for the emancipation of slaves grew in both the Jacobin clubs and the press. The noble-born Jacobin La Rochefoucauld first proposed it on the night of August 4, 1789. By 1791 many Jacobins wished to grant civic rights to free blacks and to "mulattos" of mixed African and European origins, many of whom were free already. Then, in March 1792, the issue of the rights of black slaves also came to the fore. Progress was slow, but many clubs praised the assembly for whatever faltering steps it might be taking in that direction. In the spring of 1794 nearly three hundred Jacobin clubs congratulated the Convention on its abolition of slavery.

In short, the end of slavery, like the defense of individual rights in general, was an integral part of Jacobins' ideology, even if, as often happened, the full implications of their libertarian thinking developed only gradually. Ensconced as they were in France's villages, towns, and cities, it was hard for the Jacobins to see the logic of their point of view. But in the end, they did see it.

We often think of Jacobins as resolute collectivists, as terrorists who were willing to pay any price to save their Revolution. But one must remember also that the Jacobins were first and foremost confirmed apologists of individualistic values.

3

The Indisputable Claims
of Civil Society

There is a natural, essential, and general order that encompasses the
constituent and fundamental laws of all societies, an order from which
societies cannot depart without ceasing to be fully social.

Pierre Iréné Dupont (de Nemours), *De l'Origine*
et du progrès d'une science nouvelle

*R*ights, but no rights: during the Great Terror of 1794, Jacobinism
foundered on this unresolvable aporia. Events challenged the assertion the
Jacobins had begun with, namely, that every person had a right to be himself, whether noble-born or not, white or black, male or female, rich or
poor, young or old.

Their view of civil society also changed over time. In the beginning, they
wished to leave it largely as it was because they thought that society would
bloom harmoniously and of its own accord if the institutions of public life
were made more rational and natural.

This modest stance sharply distinguishes the Jacobins from modern totalitarians (National Socialist, fascist, and communist), whose leaders invariably assumed that brutal and constraining social principles were essential to their future prospects, however mild their actual beginnings may
have been. In these modern and oppressive settings, the rights of groups
took precedence over the rights of individuals from the first. Long before
they seized power, Hitler, Lenin, and Mussolini all assumed that man and
society would have to be reshaped drastically, probably through terror.

But Jacobinism hardly did so. For these modern-minded secularists, civil society and the family as well existed in their own right. They were not the adjunct of Christian metaphysics or fortuitous politics.[1] Moreover, the Jacobins' eventual drift away from their initial tolerant perspective was never made theoretically complete—far from it! At Thonon the *clubbistes* urged that overeager patriots remember the "true sentiments of the Republican who must both respect properties and scrupulously enforce the law that protects them."[2] At Ars-en-Ré the local Jacobins decided in October 1793 to burn some feudal documents but also took care to preserve those "which justify real property."[3] In Paris Robespierre once reminded the Conventionnels that the first objective of the Revolution was no more than "the peaceful enjoyment of liberty and equality . . . We do not intend to cast the Republic in a Spartan mold."[4] Saint-Just, a perfect symbol of Jacobin intransigence, made the same point more poetically on March 12, 1794. In the ancient republics of Sparta and Athens, he explained, "happiness in its finest day [was] . . . a plough, a field, a cottage protected from the state's exchequer, and a family protected from the lust of brigands . . . The people's liberty," he went on, "is in its private life. Do not disturb it. The force of the government . . . should aim to protect that simple state against force itself."[5]

The Jacobins' cautious endorsement of limited change was clearly stated and, it may be added, quite typical of their age. In the north-Atlantic world of the late eighteenth century, it was commonly assumed that the individuation of social forms required some—but not much—supplemental economic engineering. Adam Ferguson and other members of the Scottish school, though eager to assert the autonomy of civil society and to describe its history,[6] believed that economics and politics could not be wholly torn asunder.

What was to be made of individuals who had no property at all? Were they really free? How could the nonpropertied be guaranteed access to property? And how could one answer these questions without throwing society into chaos? The Jacobins cautiously understood such hopes and doubts—though few of them had heard of Ferguson—because all of them, we can wager, had heard of Rousseau. In his view socially disabled private persons who did not participate in collective political life were not really free. Even the rich who lived in a monarchy were spiritually chained and fettered. Like Rousseau, the Jacobins wondered how a society might be reformed for the sake of all without brutalizing the few. They knew, as did their master, that the legislative role of any state, however democratic, ought always to be constrained.

Our own place in world history enables us immediately to grasp that the civic equality of varyingly advantaged individuals is hardly to be achieved irrespective of material reality. It was the Jacobins' historical (mis)fortune to live at a time when that message had not yet been driven home by the long and painful sequence of events that has shaped our own industrial and postindustrial understanding of modern history's weighty messages.

*T*he Jacobins' prudent endorsement of civil society presents a telling clue to another important theme in their history, namely, their place in French social hierarchies. In no small part, the Jacobins accepted society as they knew it because they were comfortably ensconced within its folds.

In the nineteenth century conservative historians believed the reverse to be true. Hyppolite Taine (1828–1893) for example, who combined in his writings the social and racial prejudices of the northern French bourgeois toward southern plebeians, mocked the Jacobin club in the Mediterranean seaport of Marseilles as

> a rendez-vous for nomadic interlopers, vagabonds, persons without fixed callings, the lawless bullies, and blackguards, who, like uprooted, decaying seaweed, drift from coast to coast, from the entire circle of the Mediterranean Sea; a veritable sink filled with the dregs of twenty corrupt and semi-barbarous civilizations. Marseilles belongs to the low class, 40,000 needy adventurers of which the Club is the leader.[7]

This biased—one is tempted to say, foolish—judgment reflected the adversarial social and political climate of the day. Taine despised Jacobinism, which he took to be the root cause of the insurrectionary Paris Commune of 1871, and whose violent denunciation of bourgeois life he found appalling. Taine then telescoped 1793 and 1871, in order to conclude all too hastily that the revolutionaries of 1789 could not have been ordinary members of the middle classes because the middle-class people of his day (he thought) were fated by History to be the victims of terrorism rather than the terrorists themselves.[8]

Crane Brinton, sixty years ago, and Michael Kennedy, more recently, have studied the social antecedents of the Jacobin *clubbistes* in great detail. Their work enables us to correct Taine's prejudiced misjudgment, even if their findings are—of necessity—based in large part on police listings that were drawn up *after* the fall of Robespierre, when many Jacobins were covering their revolutionary tracks or dropping out of sight completely.

Jacobins were largely of a middling, decent sort. Musing back on his younger days, Napoleon himself owned to having been a Jacobin, at Valence, in the Rhône valley. "There were some good Jacobins," explained the emperor. "It was a time when any faintly noble soul had to be a Jacobin. I myself was one, like yourself, and like thousands of other well-meaning people."[9] He did not add that he had been the club's librarian and secretary, and was urged to be its president.

Club profiles varied from region to region. The number of priests and nobles who joined varied greatly, as did over time the number of skilled artisans, from 26 percent to 32 percent, and peasants, from 8 percent to 11 percent. Exceptions did exist. At Tulle, an arms-manufacturing center in central France, the first artisan joined the club in November 1790. By 1791 41 percent of the members were manual workers; by 1794, 58 percent were. Likewise, in the north, near Rouen, and in southern France, in the Drôme and in Provence especially, Jacobinism had a large rural audience. In some rural, southeastern subdepartmental *cantons,* nearly every village had a club. Nationwide, however, and from first to last, including the terrorist days of 1794, Jacobinism was basically a blend of an urban middle-class or upper-class leadership with a middle- and lower-middle-class audience.

Most Jacobins were propertied, and some privileged, men of substance whose cultural instincts and ideology—or wishful thinking—far more than envy, greed, or personal circumstance drove them to extremes.

The average Jacobin was a reasonably prosperous town dweller. Every French city with more than 4,000 inhabitants had a club, as did 97 percent of those with over 3,000 and 87 percent with over 2,000, a statistic whose full meaning registers if we recall that only 14 percent of French municipal entities (most of them rural, of course) had a club at all. It is no coincidence that clubs were most common in eastern and southeastern France, where cities with a nucleated population of 2,000–5,000 were most common also.[10]

The Jacobins valued belonging to a community. They were emphatically not strangers to the towns whose clubs they joined. They were not marginal. In Toulon, for example, members of the local club's key committees were required to be over thirty, to be natives of the city, and to have lived there for four years, unless they displayed such obvious *civisme* as to make these norms irrelevant.[11] Conditions of morality were often imposed for membership and some clubs secretly investigated postulants.[12] At Le Havre, upon hearing that an "honorable citizen" had found himself unable to pay off a small debt, the *clubbistes* raised the money on his behalf to save him "from the shame and disgrace of defaulting on his payments."[13] They did so out of a desire to meet the norms of respectability as well as those of fraternal solidarity.

Even the most militant and abstract-minded Jacobins thought of themselves as representatives of their home communities, as defenders of a lived, extant, and acceptable social order. They believed in unanimity from below rather than in centralized government imposed from above. "Renounce the ancient mania of governments who wished to govern too much," Robespierre urged on May 10, 1793, "leave to the communes the right to regulate their own affairs in everything that does not essentially affect the general administration of the republic."[14]

Militant Jacobins existed not as single political actors but collectively, as members of local clubs. Moreover, their associations, though obviously affected by ongoing and changing political consciousness, had strong, prerevolutionary local roots. Militant Jacobinism evolved from established, prerevolutionary local sociability.

A few clubs (though many fewer than was once thought)[15] had their origin in the 1,800 Masonic lodges created in France since 1770. In 1789 the Grand Orient Masonic order alone had 635 affiliated lodges in 395 French cities. Prerevolutionary Masonic societies also informed Jacobinism as "laboratories where new values were produced."[16] The Masonic ideals of domestic virtue and philanthropy bore a strong resemblance to similarly enlightened Jacobin preferences.[17] (A fair number of Masons were Protestants like the Nîmois minister Jean-Paul Rabaut Saint-Étienne.)

Lodges provided continuities in procedure, sociability, and outlook. In theory if not in fact members of lodges before 1789 and of clubs after that related to one another democratically, as friends and colleagues, without reference to social rank. Prerevolutionary Masons, like the Jacobins of 1793–94, felt they had a mission. Masons and Jacobins alike assumed that a small and self-defined but representative minority (themselves) held the key to the well-being of the larger community. Georges Couthon, a feared member of the Committee of Public Safety, was the most prominent Jacobin to have been a Mason.[18] Camille Desmoulins struck a chord in 1790 when he used Masonry as a metaphor for the clubs. The Paris society, he wrote, was the Grand Orient of the Friends of the Constitution in all of the nation's eighty-three departments.[19]

Other established forms of local sociability were also relevant to the genesis of the clubs. At Bergerac forty-two of the fifty-eight members of the Société Mesmérienne joined to create a club in 1789. In Grenoble many early Jacobins were members of a philanthropic society that had been founded by municipal notables to raise money for local hospitals. Many former local *parlementaires* (that is, members of the office-holding, neo-aristocratic judiciary) had belonged to this club.[20] Antecedents also included musical societies and "museums," or private institutions of learning focused on advanced prerevolutionary ideas (in Bordeaux the *musée,* founded in 1782, had as its motto "liberty, equality," and as its emblem, an eagle breaking its chain). In Colmar a smoking club became a Jacobin society. At Castres a club grew out of a newspaper-reading society founded in 1782, which had then subscribed to the *Gazette de France,* the *Mercure historique,* the *Courier de l'Europe,* and the *Courier d'Avignon.*[21] At Dijon the women's Jacobin club developed in part to take over social tasks from excluded Catholic religious orders.[22]

In other instances, the new clubs brought together individuals who had heretofore been more or less formally in touch with one another about the arts or philosophy, as happened with the members of the prerevolutionary French Linnaean Society, which counted among its postrevolutionary "graduates" a number of prominent Jacobins and other political figures: Louis Bosc, Jacques Creuzé-Latouche, Henri Grégoire, Gilbert Romme, Antoine Fourcroy, and Jean Hassenfratz.[23] It has likewise been suggested that the Breton club at Versailles, which evolved in May 1789 into the Jacobin club of Paris, was itself a distant offshoot of the Patriotic Society of Breton at Rennes, the site of heated prerevolutionary electoral politics and patriotic opposition to the local nobility.[24] Some Jacobin clubs had also mutated from local assemblies of National Guardsmen. Ambulatory clubs without a fixed base did exist, in the Vendée, for example, where Jacobins were few. But such associations were quite rare.

Many *clubbistes* had known each other for years in varied capacities, especially in the smaller towns where a club might have no more than twenty or thirty members. At Marseilles many of the club's founders were old grads from the Collège de l'Oratoire.[25] Signatures of members on founding charters were often grouped by neighborhoods, another telltale sign.

Significantly, Jacobin *clubbistes* felt strongly that towns should have but a single club. Of course, that monistic goal could not be managed in large cities. Nantes, with 60,000 inhabitants, had three clubs. Bordeaux (the fourth-largest city in France, with about 110,000 inhabitants) had thirteen between July 1789 and June 1791 and five in 1791–92. Beaucaire, famous in medieval times and still a meaningful trading town, had six. In Paris, when the Jacobin clubs and the *assemblées sectionnaires* were relabeled *sociétés populaires* in 1793, the capital counted over twenty deliberating associations of one kind or another. From start in 1789 to finish in 1795, Paris spawned more than one hundred clubs and protoclubs within its city walls.

Still, in the whole of France, only about two hundred communes counted more than one club.[26] By more than ten to one, single-club towns outnumbered multiclub cities. Overall, Jacobins wanted to represent both a single ideological truth and the public opinion of an entire community. It made no more sense to them to have two clubs in one town than to have two National Assemblies in one country. At Reims members of one club were required to swear that "they would never leave this club in order to join another club in the same city."[27] At Toulon the members of an existing club asked the municipal government to forbid the creation of a second club. (Their motion failed, and six months later the rival *clubbistes* were involved in a fistfight.)[28] The Paris club reinforced this drive to singleness by refusing affiliation to more than one club per town.

The anomalous cohabitation of two or more clubs in a single city usually resulted from long-standing feuds. In small towns and villages tension might run high between Jacobins who were vintners and Jacobins who grew wheat. One of the two clubs created at Saverne, in Alsace, for example, had a distinctly more rural membership than the other. Such relatively innocuous distinctions often became lethal in 1793–94 when animosities were politicized and one group of local revolutionaries secured the ear of the centralized state representative in order to push aside or kill their age-old local rivals.

At Pertuis, a small city in the Vaucluse, a visiting Jacobin opined that the existence of two rival societies was due to "their private interests and inveterate hatreds, many of which went back more than twenty years. Their supposed zeal for liberty and the Constitution masks their mutual animosity . . . They called their personal enemies the enemies of the Revolution."[29]

By and large, however, a club represented an entire town, and club networks aimed to reflect regional sociability. From early 1790 onward, clubs in large cities "networked" (or, in the parlance of the time, "fraternized") with one another. They also spawned smaller clubs in neighboring towns and villages. It often happened that the clubs of neighboring villages related to each other only distantly through their vertical affiliation to some distant mother society. In the spring of 1790 the patriots of Strasbourg invited to their city the National Guardsmen from a large swathe of eastern France, an example copied all over France. In the Vaucluse and the Drôme, where clubs were particularly numerous, thirteen such regional congresses were held between February 1792 and June 1793.[30]

The lines that led from a parent club to its subsidiaries often followed established social ties. In their request for affiliation with the regional capital, Montpellier, the *clubbistes* of Agde explained that what drew them to the larger city was "the links that already bind us, those of the former and actual administration, the ties of commerce, and above all the esteem we have for your society, based on the reports of those of our compatriots who have visited you."[31] "The tree of liberty," wrote the Jacobins of Bourbourg of themselves, "is the social tree."[32]

These linked origins speak not just to the rooted nature of Jacobinism but also to the determination of individual Jacobins who used their older contacts to achieve their newly conceived political purpose. It is unreasonable to think of the Jacobins as a class-based party whose associative expressions emerged spontaneously from some determining, class-conscious, Paris-dominated, and Hegelian bedrock of "class-for-itself." Jacobins were willful and efficient organizers.

Dedicated to the well-being of their hometowns, the Jacobins labored to make sure that the new judicial and educational institutions just created by the revolutionary National Assembly would be located in their own towns, to the friendly detriment of their neighbors. Competition over this matter was often fierce. No stone or argument was left unturned; and in one mountainous region the citizens of a downhill town argued for their site's natural superiority over another town's location higher up by reasoning that in order to come to them, their neighbors could walk downhill, whereas they would be required to walk uphill to meet their rivals!

Clubs argued for special exemptions from all kinds of rules that might well apply to the larger nation but not to them. Strasbourg, for example, sought to be made a free port. At Bischwiller the Jacobins complained about a law forbidding the export of Alsatian hemp to the Frankfurt fairs.

This ruling seemed to them part of a "treasonable plan" to wean citizens from the Revolution.[33] Clubs lobbied for local industries. They defended the right of municipalities to search incoming and (especially) outgoing carts that might be removing food from their hometowns. The configuration of local passions might well determine local responses to some national trajectory.[34]

Jacobins often espoused ancient local grievances. At Saint-Servan, in Brittany, the Jacobins affiliated themselves with many clubs near and far, including the London Corresponding Society. But they studiously ignored the Jacobin club in the nearby rival seaport of Saint-Malo, just across the bay.

Jacobins boasted of the entrepreneurial zeal they extended on behalf of their communities. (The first title of the Riom society was the Society of the Friends of the Constitution and of Rural Economy.) The minutes of the clubs teem with schemes for local improvements of all kinds.

Economic growth was a common concern. In Bordeaux Jean-Baptiste Boyer-Fonfrède tried to enlist Jacobin support for the creation of an English-style textile factory. At Tulle soap was on the agenda. The Montpellier club considered the shipment of coal and the erection of new windmills to grind wheat.

Other clubs had more fanciful public goals, with plans for the construction of roads, road signs, harbors, and improbable canals from Poitiers and Niort to Châtellerault or from the Rance to the Villaine; for draining swamps or growing hemp for ship's riggings; for laying down pipes to supply water; for creating slaughter houses, street lighting, and mail service; or for a campaign to familiarize peasants with the potato.[35] No concern was too mundane for the Jacobins.

The improvement of public health preoccupied them. At Villecroze the *clubbistes* asked for the appointment of a "communal physician because by this means, indigents will have their maladies attended to as well as those who live in opulence."[36] Many clubs did their best to keep heretofore religiously run hospitals afloat. They discussed health insurance schemes and the distribution of free medicines. They proposed asylums for the mentally ill. At Cherbourg the local club demanded that employers compensate injured workers.

Finding food—always a source of concern, especially in revolutionary times—was particularly important to the Jacobins. From 1792 onward, grain was increasingly scarce. In 1793–94 peasants and bourgeois producers alike became reluctant to exchange a valuable commodity for increasingly valueless paper currency. With nearly one million men under arms in 1793, the government exacerbated food shortages by making feeding the soldiers the nation's first priority. Cities would somehow have to manage with whatever was left over. In the grain-exporting areas, clubs urged their fellow citizens to be generous. But elsewhere, *clubbistes* ranged far and wide either to find food for their hometowns or to convince national and departmental officials who controlled food reserves to release some locally rather than sending all to the front or to distant cities.

Even at the height of the Terror, clubs also went out of their way to protect their fellow townspeople. Local Jacobins could struggle mightily against their neighbors, win, and then forget to forward the case of their defeated opponents to the Revolutionary Tribunal in Paris.[37] At Lagny, not too far from the capital, when the baron de Marguerittes was arrested, the local society began by sending him a certificate of patriotism. When that did not prove to be enough, they sent a delegation to Paris to secure a (temporary) stay of execution.[38] Some clubs also complained about military exactions.

Clubs did sing the praises of national (and therefore distant) heroes like Marat and Le Peletier. But many clubs also had local votive figures of their own, regional martyrs, or for that matter purely local figures who had made good.

Jacobins, always forceful, in time grew relentlessly sectarian. But that change surprised even them. In their private lives they were often neighborly, cultivated, and polite persons. In his early days at Arras, Robespierre wrote neoclassical, mannerist love poetry of a most laudable and stilted kind. The *clubbistes* were respected, respectable people who were so involved in the life of their community that to be excluded from a club was not just politically dangerous but socially disgraceful as well. At Lagny the "committee for purges" charged the club's secretary to contact excluded members personally "so that they would not be exposed to receiving [news of] their exclusion publicly."[39] Many clubs (Paris and Dijon among them) had *défenseurs officieux* whose task it was to dispel the suspicions that weighed on every heart, of includers and excluders alike.

So strong was the localist impulse of the Jacobins' sensibility that it took them some time to understand the implications of their more sustained and ever more ideological worldview. Initially, in the period 1789–1791, the clubs acted as semisecret societies, often requiring from their members a promise of confidentiality regarding their proceedings. Members could invite only one friend at a time. Registers of visitors were closely kept. Important sessions were not open to nonmembers.

Only as the Revolution proceeded did clubs take on their role as agencies of public and politicized knowledge, not just for themselves but for the entire population of their towns and cities. Étienne Clavière, a leading Jacobin financier, suggested countering the insinuations of the émigrés by circulating a petition to the people proving the sincerity of the Jacobins' motives and by making the meetings of the clubs public. By late 1791 clubs eagerly welcomed visitors to their now public debates.[40] It mattered immensely "that all civic and Republican-minded men not be kept away from our society, regardless of what their circumstances were or might now be."[41] The Grenoblois Jacobins in April 1790 were the first to hold public assemblies. The Strasbourg club soon followed, and the Marseillais went one step further by making of their assembly hall "a gathering place and refreshment center."[42] Some clubs, as at Toulouse, slid into the public limelight gradually, by having two kinds of meetings, some open and some not, and then gradually dispensing with private sessions. The first public meeting of the Paris Jacobins took place in mid-October 1791, and thereafter open sessions became the norm throughout France. Spectators who had once been excluded were now actively recruited. At Libourne a gallery collapsed under their weight.[43]

Jacobin club members soon came to see themselves as participating in the same galvanizing relationship to their hometowns as the Convention did to the Grande Nation, and they underlined this shared local and national identity by adopting the Convention's rules of order as their own. But one type of concern did not exclude the other. At Courthézon, in the Vaucluse, in one afternoon the *clubbistes* decided in quite rapid succession to deal with the stray dogs that were damaging the local vineyards and to burn symbolically "the red flag of anarchy."[44] At Saint-Céré local Jacobins questioned, on lofty grounds indeed, the right of Rousset to carve out his garden from common lands: "private and particularist interests," they concluded, "must yield to the public good and no sacrifice is too costly when the happiness of the people is at stake."[45]

*J*acobins had a lively sense of social responsibility, and that apprehension spilled over into their handling of social relations generally. Whenever circumstances made it feasible, they perceived fellow urban workers as needy and deserving fellow citizens. At Vire some *clubbistes* thought workers should have the right to strike. But Jacobins strongly believed in hard and productive work as well.

Jacobins held that man—whether rich or poor—realized his potential through work effected in fruitful cooperation with others and with nature, an encompassing view that aggregated manual and mental work, artisanal and bourgeois status. The corporate structure of the Old Regime, they thought, vitiated honest effort. Before 1789 workers had often been shiftless. In the nation's central library, Roland explained, the idleness of indolent runners during monarchic times had been an insult to the "impatience of learned men and artists" eager to get their books.[46] In April 1793 Robespierre did explain that the poor had a right to work. But he also assumed that this right was an obligation. The Jacobins considered idleness a reprehensible trait shared by nobles and the feckless poor. Saint-Just and many others attributed the poor's lost desire to work to the moral climate set by the monarchy. "You must force people to do something, to have a profession . . . In our homeland, what are the rights of those who do nothing there?"[47]

Whereas buying and selling were socially unproductive, the productive, socially useful habit of work, manual work especially, was much to be admired. At Romans a manufacturer who had set up a factory to provide local employment because he believed in the *bien public* and not his *intérêt particulier* found a receptive audience when he explained to the club that the local youths had heretofore been culpably idle. Young people should be reminded that "only work will ready men for virtue, idleness being the mother of every vice."[48]

And thanks to the Revolution, they assumed, all citizens could now become truly useful. At Saint-Malo, when it was pointed out to some *citoyennes* who had offered to work benevolently for the families of departing soldiers that many poor women would like to do this but could not afford to do so, the club itself stepped into the breach and offered a subsidy to make such employment feasible.

Jacobins might be unsympathetic to morally degenerate beggars, but they were by contrast extremely sympathetic to the unemployed who sought work. "If there are no useful works to be commissioned," explained the Conventionnel Louis Guyton-Morveau to the Dijon *clubbistes*, "then we shall have to commandeer useless ones."[49] At Aix, in 1791, the club asked for the creation of a workhouse for the unemployed. At Tonneins, a member who urged the *clubbistes* to find work for former "manoeuvres de la manufacture de tabac" (workers at the tobacco manufactory) was warmly applauded for his "zèle charitable."[50] Jacobins expressed hostility to employers who dismissed workers they might not need but could afford to keep.

Needless to say, Jacobin attitudes to workers' complaints varied a good deal. One of the reasons the Jacobins endorsed paper money was that local workers received it for pay; but at Boulogne, when exasperated artisans finally refused to accept paper after all, the local Jacobins turned around and rescinded their support of this fiat currency. In that same spirit of social friendship many clubs went out of their way to lower or waive entrance fees, whose purpose was not to be a barrier but, more mundanely, to raise needed cash for mailing, heating, lighting, and printing costs.

Jacobins did their best to further the concerns of their local peasant neighbors, who were referred to in their "politically correct" verbiage as *cultivateurs* rather than *paysans*.[51] Jacobins, of course, strove to suppress feudal dues, and a few of them also favored the sale of confiscated émigré properties to peasants in small lots. They similarly urged the dismissal of ancient lawsuits relating to the peasantry.[52] They extolled patriotic peasants who had paid their taxes, sold their foodstuffs for paper money, and agreed to serve in the army. Jacobins gave peasants wise advice on choosing crops and using fallow lands.[53] They often defended traditional communal rights. They concurred at Aix when a *clubbiste* reminded his colleagues that a feudal custom attached to the sale of wine had been in the interest of the rural poor and should be retained "because the Nation has today taken the place of the [Cathedral] Chapter."[54] At Callas, in the Var, a region with strong individualistic traditions, Jacobins nonetheless defended the municipality's right to own common lands. They urged the city authorities to prosecute aggressive and selfish individuals who had appropriated and seeded tracts that were communally owned.[55]

The *clubbistes* worked hard to proselytize potential allies in the countryside, and with some success, particularly after 1791. At Marcillac, in the Aveyron, local vintners proudly informed the regional club in Rodez that the members of the Jacobin society they had formed were nearly all "cultivators." At Cugnauz, in the Haute Garonne, thirty-three of the forty-nine *sociétaires* were agriculturists. At Arpajon, in the Cantal, a predominantly peasant Jacobin society was used as a springboard by a local leftist, Jean-Baptist Milhaud, to capitalize on local rural radicalism.[56] By 1795 perhaps more than one Jacobin in ten was a peasant. Of course, Jacobins also expected peasants to toe the mark, pay taxes, serve in the army, speak French, and behave as citizens, all of which—to say the least—were not the goals peasants had in mind when they rose up in many parts of France in 1789. But even those demands were for the peasants' good, according to the Jacobins.

In both town and country, then, Jacobins espoused social life as they found it, and their aesthetics and intellectual principles placed them in the mainstream currents of French cultural life. In countless ways, the Jacobins—with some conspicuous exceptions of those hostile to higher learning—were the children of the rationalist Enlightenment. At Lagny the *sociétaires* went so far as to distinguish between destructive and "reasonable" animals.[57] They believed in individualism, government by discussion, statistics, meliorism, and science. They valued debates and the freedom to choose (as in elections) because these allowed the voice of reason to emerge.

Jacobins took pride in the Enlightenment's scientific achievements. They were interested in lighter-than-air balloons, and the French army of 1792 was, as it were, the first military in history to rely on its air arm.[58] Jacobins were also fascinated by the communicative possibilities of electricity. They subsidized a visual telegraph. After 1792 they relied on new, standardized ways of mass-producing weapons. Many Jacobins were intrigued by medicine and surgery. The extended use of the guillotine might be said to be a ghoulish by-product of that interest. They commonly referred to aristocratism as a gangrenous disease, and to their purges as scalpels.[59]

Scientific figures like Benjamin Franklin were Jacobin heroes. Tom Paine, whose name represented practical common sense, was made an honorary French citizen and invited to sit in the National Convention. (He narrowly escaped execution in 1794.) Jacobins did not believe in dreams, omens, and superstitions. To be told that they were unconsciously carrying forward in a secularized register many of religious and monarchic France's ancient instincts of intolerance would have distressed them greatly.

Jacobins were no less representative of their times in embracing the nonscientific, nonrational force of "nature," whose beneficent hand they saw at work in any number of domains. Jacobins were strongly pulled by natural law, natural religion, and the countryside. Although they often used scientific metaphors, they clearly preferred symbols drawn from nature, like sheaves of wheat, trees, and cornucopias. Ordinarily, their *fêtes* were staged outdoors in open rather than enclosed spaces. Indeed, the *clubbistes* sometimes met outdoors as well. At "Tonneins-la-Montagne" the ceiling of their meeting room was painted over to look like the sky: dark blue with stars.[60] Kant's aphorism on the starry heavens above and the moral law within readily comes to mind.

Unlike nineteenth-century bourgeois figures, Jacobins did not praise peasants as such or criticize urban workers as such. But they did prefer country to town. Lyons, wrote Mme. Roland, who was city-born and -bred, "is a cloaca that gathers unto itself the most disgusting refuse ever produced by the old regime."[61]

Jacobins had a strong prejudice for the beloved eighteenth-century fiction of the Republican yeoman farmer of Jeffersonian fame. Regardless of their private situation as urban dwellers, Jacobins saw the world through Rousseauean and ruralist lenses. Agriculture, wrote Saint-Just, was "the mother of [good] mores."[62]

At ease as they were with their world socially and intellectually, Jacobins—at first—had no trouble getting along with local officials, who, they assumed, were equally mindful of their neighbors' stated needs. Why else would they have been elected? Indeed, the Jacobins had organized themselves specifically for the purpose of explaining to the people the sensible decisions that had just been taken for them by the nation's newly chosen representatives. In the words of a conservative Thermidorian who chastised them at Auch in 1795 for having strayed from that purpose, their task was to be in "fraternal surveillance of the authorities."[63] In 1790 their most controversial demand was that public officials deliberate publicly so that their own task of friendly, constructive criticism might be made more efficacious. Had not Rousseau told the Poles that in a well-ordered republic, "every citizen shall at every instant feel himself in the public eye"?[64]

As the Revolution progressed, however, this era of good feelings soured. As early as mid-1790, in a decision eventually overruled by the National Assembly in Paris, the municipality of Dax ordered the local club shut down. After the king's flight to Varennes in June 1791, unpleasant instances of rivalry between club and elected officials became all too common, and relations between Jacobins and local officials did not improve until the triumph of the Montagnards in June 1793, at which point the *clubbistes* themselves became the nation's governing officials.

During those intervening months, from mid-1791 to mid-1793, the clubs (which now represented active minorities of unusually engaged patriots) increasingly bickered with the mainstream, middle-of-the-road municipalities, whose basic inspiration was perhaps not much different from their own but whose sense of urgency was more muted.

Even then, the stated Jacobin motive for attacking local officials was that they—the Jacobins—understood what was best not just for themselves but for the entire community, including, of course, its elected functionaries. Unlike the Bolsheviks, who always saw themselves as a class-based party fated to struggle violently against another previously dominant social class, the Jacobins liked to believe that community-wide harmony was imminent.

In any instance, after mid-1793, when the Jacobins managed to capture municipal offices nationwide, the question of Jacobin relations to local officials largely lapsed. At Bourbourg, in the words of Georges Lefebvre, the club treated the municipal officers as if they were "a subordinate body."[65] In Toulouse forty-two *clubbistes* held municipal office between 1789 and 1795; in Strasbourg, eighty-three did.[66] In January 1795 a Conventionnel on a visit to Tulle naively congratulated himself on the presence of all of the town's officials in the club that day. (For good measure he added that if he had been born at Tulle, he too would have become a *clubbiste*.)[67] In many towns the meetings of the clubs were timed *not* to coincide with municipal meetings so that the Jacobins could attend both venues. A similar mechanism enabled Robespierre and Danton to make nearly the same speech first in the Paris club and then on the Convention floor.

$\mathcal{M}$any social historians have worked hard to show that some Jacobins, specifically, the Girondins, were more prone to accept civil society as it then existed than were the Montagnards. This view broaches a fundamental problem of revolutionary politics. Can we say that by 1792 distinct social classes already existed and that conflicting versions of Jacobinism (Girondin or Montagnard) corresponded to these new social rankings?[68]

In 1793 the Girondins certainly *seemed* to be more accepting of civil society as it then functioned than did the Montagnards. Since the late summer and fall of 1792, the Girondins had become hostile to the Parisian sans-culottes, who wanted to push forward a revolution that they, the Girondins, wished to direct and stabilize.[69] And as the Girondists lost power in early 1793, they did indeed make many conservative statements on a wide range of subjects including economic life and free enterprise. But these appearances are deceiving. Their more conservative words in 1793 resulted from their realization, after many hesitations, that a new approach was required if they were to retain their influence and stop the Revolution with the help of new allies to the right.

In 1791–92, during an earlier incarnation and when out of power, these same Girondins had often argued the reverse of what they chose to say in 1793. The latter-day Brissot, for example, did indeed defend property, but in 1791, in his *première manière,* he spoke as a militant abolitionist and presented himself as a victim of planter capitalism. François Xavier Lanthenas, another prominent Girondin, had struck a similar leftist tone in November 1791, if in an altered register. "The bourgeois," he explained, "wants to put himself in the place of the noble, and not allow the artisan to take his. However, the artisan is the true defender, the sincere friend of the Revolution. He alone forms the National Guard . . . He alone frequents the electoral assemblies. Finally, he alone is worthy of liberty, because he alone has good morals."[70] But by 1793 Lanthenas had become one of Brissot's closest associates.

Such gyrations were not isolated cases. In their earlier guise as leaders of the leftist opposition, Girondins made hundreds of progressive statements, on any number of themes, all of which are at least as meaningful as the conservative statements they were to make in the spring of 1793 when struggling against the Montagne, now increasingly prone to communitarian statements that would please the Parisian crowd.

In September 1791 Brissot, then still a progressive *clubbiste,* denounced the attack of Le Chapelier (an ex-Jacobin) on club affiliation. But after the September massacres, in November 1792, when the Revolution—he thought—had become too threatening, Brissot executed a volte-face and attacked Jacobin affiliation with much the same words he had used against Le Chapelier the year before. The Paris club had become a kind of "Holy See." Affiliation, Brissot decided, was a non-Republican hierarchic humiliation of smaller club by larger club.

Instead of seeing the Montagnards as representing the middle class and the Girondins as the party of the *grande bourgeoisie,* we should note that *all* Jacobins, once in power, were suddenly able to see how politically dangerous it was to let the Revolution unfold toward an unfettered universalism.

A truly useful comparison of Girondin Jacobinism and Montagnard Jacobinism would juxtapose statements made by the groups at hand when in similar strategic and political situations. Not too much importance should be placed on the formal content of such and such statement for or against property, for or against slavery, for or against the rule of law, for or against concessions to the sans-culottes, or for or against the death of king.

Social origin was not, of course, wholly irrelevant to the debates between Girondins and Feuillants in 1791 or between Girondins and Montagnards in 1792–93. A Jacobin's attitude toward the Revolution's progress might depend on either his relationship to power (was he for personal reasons a client of those who ruled?) or his antecedent social rank and wealth (which often determined one's choice of friends). A Jacobin who changed his mind about the revolutionary movement and modulated his social *discours* accordingly might well give a thought to his personal wealth and status.

But the effects of material interest on the opinions of the warring Jacobins were weak and were mitigated by many other factors ranging from personal character,[71] to private situation or office, to a tendency to moralize one's own position and demonize one's enemies. And in any case, some Girondins remained relatively daring to the end; consider Rabaut, again, a partisan of civic *fêtes,* of nationalism as a modern substitute for religion, and of greater material equality. Since it is rare, he wrote on January 19, 1793, for the rich to give up their wealth, they must be compelled to do so, "by force or by law."[72] Moreover, the cross-class Jacobin ethos was so powerful that dropping out of Jacobinism usually meant falling into a politically and ideologically debilitating void. Ex-Jacobins did not become royalists or traditionalists. Instead, they often retreated from public life. The alternative to Jacobinism for ex-Jacobins was not reaction politics but political impotence.

The basic conservatism of all of the Jacobins' social thought generally did not escape contemporary observers. In the summer of 1793 the sans-culottes, the Parisian *enragés* especially, accused even the most radical Jacobins of being too tolerant of greed and insufficiently universalist. From this far-left point of view, all Jacobins were at fault because all of them tolerated existing civil life and social structures.

On the right, many property owners mocked the Jacobins for speaking universalist words while remaining quite bourgeois in their deeds. Conservative accusers focused on two points: that the Jacobins had purchased the *biens nationaux,* and that they used their privileged role in the new regime to avoid the draft.

The *biens nationaux* were in the main confiscated church property.[73] At times, Jacobins urged municipalities to buy these properties for the common good. At Castres, for example, they proposed that the city buy a wheat-grinding mill up for sale. Much more frequently, however, the Jacobins purchased these properties themselves, another sign incidentally of their wealth and status. At Aix the *clubbistes,* who counted for 3 percent of the population, bought 33 percent of the *biens nationaux.* This example could be multiplied a thousandfold. Many a nineteenth-century, Catholic, and bourgeois family fortune was founded on this financially sound but theologically uncertain and revolutionary base. Jacobins liked to think that they were working for the Revolution when they purchased these properties. Peasants should be grateful: weren't Jacobin purchases reducing the national debt? "This is a relief [for peasants] because it is the only way to amortize debts on which [they] have to pay hefty interest payments."[74]

Jacobins benefited in other material ways from the Revolution as well. At Toulon the Jacobins armed a ship for privateering with, as it happens, a Jacobin crew. Many clubs suggested that confiscated noble estates be redistributed, but only to patriots, that is, to themselves. At Artonne, a small country town in central France, the local club demanded that a tax be levied on the rich and then decided that "the members of this society will be exempt from the tax."[75] In the same vein, it may well be that many of the Catholic priests who opted in 1790 for Jacobinism and the Civil Constitution of the Clergy looked forward to the rapid acceleration of their clerical career. Nuns who had no institutional future in the new church were less prone than priests to Jacobinical conversion.

Many Jacobins also managed to circumvent military conscription, the most painful burden imposed by the Revolution; its enactment in March 1793 triggered open rebellion in the Vendée and sullenness in many other parts of France. The current form of "La Marseillaise" is in the declarative nominative ("let us march"), but the original text ran instead in a more imperative mode ("march!"): *marchez,* not the modern *marchons.*

Of course, many Jacobins were proud to serve. At Strasbourg and Bordeaux members who did not volunteer were required to explain why. In some places volunteering for the army was so widespread that it severely depleted the ranks of local Jacobins. But many others dodged conscription, either by joining the National Guard, which, though often "requisitioned," was ordinarily exempted from frontline service, or by hiring a replacement or working in an armaments factory. It has been suggested that the *clubbistes* who were most patriotic were often older men beyond the reach of the draft. Younger members were less fervent. In the club at Lons-le-Saulnier stony silence met a suggestion that all the youthful members of the society be asked to choose between expulsion from the club and joining the army.[76] At Bergerac a Jacobin asked his peers if it would be proper for him to hire a replacement. Although he was eager to join the army and leave, his wife was desolated by this prospect. In the end, the club decided that "he might be as useful to the public good at home as he would be on the nation's border."[77]

Many contemporaries naturally took such discrepancies as proof of the Jacobins' hypocrisy—a telling accusation because the Jacobins themselves were so quick to accuse their enemies of that same vice. But a more convincing explanation also comes to mind. Jacobins were sincerely dedicated to organizing all of society around the rights and needs of individuals like themselves, manly, young to middle-aged, propertied. It seemed self-evident to them that what was good for Jacobinism was necessarily good for the nation. When rural and especially urban discontent had made that view empirically untenable, Jacobin social conservatism and institutional self-enhancement began to resemble self-preservation. By 1794 the Jacobins' universalist words resonated as false and hollow, first to others, and then to themselves. But this transformation is not proof of some earlier dissimulation.

The Jacobins of 1789 did not—and could not understand—that the decline of traditional corporatist social forms would soon feed the creation of new and shattering relationships of class. When class-consciousness and the desire to protect property at all cost appeared, Jacobin universalism faltered. The interpretation of Jacobinism by the German philosopher Friedrich Hegel (1770–1831) centers on this issue.[78] In his view the Jacobins failed because they misread the reality of everyday life and insisted instead on the false transcendence of "absolute freedom," by which he meant a false and abstract conception of freedom that was defined without reference to the actual cultural needs and possibilities of civil society.

As a mundane example of Hegel's perspective, consider the revolutionaries' rational uniformization of weights and measures—from pounds and inches to kilograms and centimeters. It succeeded because it made sense culturally and economically, whereas their no less rational but overly abstract restructuring of time—dividing the day into twenty rather than twenty-four hours—failed because it was practically and culturally pointless. The same could be said of an unimplemented plan that aimed to divide France administratively into rational squares regardless of history or geography.

For Hegel, Jacobinism's central flaw was its inability to transform society so as to give meaning to its message of social unity. When the Jacobins of a small French town in southwestern France faced an anticlerical policy that few of their fellow townspeople wanted to secure, they explained that "having destroyed despotism, it was time for the people to rise to the level of the Revolution."[79] Hegel's point was that the Jacobins ought instead to have brought the Revolution to the level of the people. Rousseau, when he drew up constitutions for Corsica and Poland, remembered that societies are resistant to massive change.

Jacobins, unable or unwilling to transform civil society, Hegel went on to argue, inexorably drifted to terror, which was for them a kind of escapist fantasy.[80] (Furet likewise writes that on 9 Thermidor an "alienated" society was "restored to its former self.")[81] In the spring of 1794 Robespierre proposed that although terror without virtue would be tyranny, virtue without terror was weakness. But a Hegelian would suggest that their recourse to terror was instead proof of weakness.

Hegel's reasoning, doubtlessly suggestive, needs to be amended (drastically) in different ways. First, as a great philosopher but an uncritical historian, Hegel had no interest in the internal dynamic of a divided Jacobin ideology. He focused exclusively on Jacobinism as a whole, and on its relation to social configurations, which in his scheme were also uncritically defined. Second, Hegel precipitously assumed that the cultural and social rift could be resolved only by terrorism. But not all political groups resolve their ideological or political contradiction as brutally as happened in 1793–94. Finally, the relevant historical evidence clearly shows—in contradistinction to Hegel's argument—that some Jacobins did *try* at least to bring greater equality to civil society than any of them had thought feasible at first.

Although a wholesale social restructuring was the very thing they did *not* want, many Jacobins did want to do something. In March 1793 Danton insisted that citizens could expect only an equality of rights *(l'égalité des droits)* but in August of 1793, Félix Le Peletier spoke of the equality of enjoyment *(l'égalité des jouissances)*. From late 1793 to early 1794, when festivals routinely lionized ordinary men and women, the destitution of the poor became for Jacobins a scandal that could no longer be allowed.

Initial Jacobin approaches to poverty in 1790 had focused on charity or self-help. Many Jacobins figured prominently in the Committee of Mendicity, set up by the National Assembly in January 1790. Gradually, however, Jacobins began to think about more interventionist practices, some of them akin to "Medicare." In May 1794, at Barère's prompting, the Convention also adopted a program of pensions for the poorest 1 percent of the population. War victims were especially favored.

The issue of economic change crystallized with the decrees of Ventôse in the spring of 1794, a proposed scheme to redistribute the property of convicted "suspects." "How could a sovereign state survive," pondered Saint-Just,

> if civil relations have a logic that runs against the form of government . . . Yes: the nature of things has perhaps led us to results we had not imagined. Many of the enemies of the Revolution live in opulence; needs make the people dependent on their enemies . . . Half-hearted revolutionaries will find they have dug their own grave. The Revolution has brought us to recognize this one principle, namely, that whoever has been an enemy of his country cannot own property in that place. The nature of government has been revolutionized; but civil society has not been affected. The principle of our Government is liberty. The principle of our civil society is aristocracy.[82]

On May 11, 1794 (22 Floréal, Year II), Barère gave a report on the extirpation of mendicity in the countryside. Suspects' properties were to be seized, and lists of suitable indigent recipients were to be drawn up. Together, these rolls would make up a "book of national welfare." In a more modest way, the Jacobins of Toucy, in the Yonne, likewise proposed to outlaw extensive leaseholding, often used as a vehicle for modernizing economic individualism in the countryside: "it would be wise to set a limit to the number of farms that any one might own."[83]

Progressive taxation was yet another avenue. In 1789 Sieyès had already tried to insert a clause in the Declaration of the Rights of Man suggesting that state levies be used for income redistribution. Robespierre proposed something similar in April 1793.[84]

Jacobins hoped that civil society, with some small nudge, would reform itself. Partible inheritance and the division of estates equally among many heirs, they liked to think, would soon bring about the democratization of property that equal citizenship required. The argument was attractive because it enhanced individual becoming, but its more general effect on social structure was also obvious to all Jacobins.

Already, in 1789 Lanthenas had urged legislation on the issue. The question was widely discussed in the fall of 1790 after the club at Toulouse looked into bastards' rights to inherit as well.[85] Later, in February 1791, the Parisian Jacobins responded warmly to a widely circularized statement along these lines from the Carcassonne club. In December 1790 a *clubbiste*, while advocating the rights of children to inherit equally, asked:

> Whence this strange inequality, if not from the absurd laws that make it possible to doom to misery many legitimate heirs in order to benefit a single person? . . . The closer we come to an equality of wealth, the more we will tend toward that happiness whose highest point will be in an exact division of property among the members of society who, from then on, would be one vast family.[86]

And yet, of course, the Jacobins did not in the end transform French civil society. They sought to raise the poor to their level rather than to lower the rich to some draconian average. Hegel's message does highlight a basic tension with Jacobinism, even if we choose to disregard his hasty judgment on the automaticity of a link between ideological tension and the enactment of political terrorism.

Indeed, many doubts have been raised about the sincerity of their social engineering, especially as regards their planned sequestration and redistribution of goods in Ventôse. The Marxist historian Albert Soboul, for example, thought the law was not meant seriously and was principally designed to appease veterans or the Parisian sans-culottes, who were at that moment being pushed aside.[87] That judgment is too strong, but it is not wholly wrong, and it is certainly buttressed by the Convention's decision of March 18, 1793, taken at Barère's prompting, to decree the death penalty against any one who might support the communistic and confiscatory redistribution of land, a measure known, from Roman models, as the "agrarian law." It is striking also that on April 24, 1793, while courting the Parisian poor, Robespierre dared nonetheless to say that "the equality of material possessions" was a "chimera."[88] It was pointless to speak of peasants at all, decided the president of the Guéret Jacobins in November of 1793: "since there are no more seigneurs, there are no more peasants."[89]

What was Jacobinism's goal, asked Jeanbon Saint-André, the former Protestant minister who had become a strikingly upright Montagnard *Conventionnel* and a member of the CPS: to reestablish "a proper balance among citizens without threatening property, contrary to the accusations leveled against us by absurd malice. Far from our mind, far from the mind of any legislator, the horrible idea of wanting to cement the happiness of the people on a basis of injustice."[90]

The Jacobins' sincerity and their devotion to civil society are difficult to gauge given their drift to illiberalism and terror. It is no doubt symbolic that on the same day, in February 1793, the club at Tulle rejected and the club at Laval accepted the idea that veterans be routinely assigned confiscated properties.[91]

For some historians, the answers lie in a broad sociological or philosophical interpretation of the epoch. Others will be satisfied only by the specific historical context of individual events and of every Jacobin's thoughts and deeds.

The unavailability of relevant documents further complicates the issue. The relationship of the Jacobins to their immediate surroundings has always been a neglected archival facet in the history of the French Revolution. Although the public deliberations of hundreds of clubs have been either reprinted *in toto* or described in detail, no correspondence of any Jacobin society has ever been published in its entirety, though hundreds of such collections exist, many of them (at Poitiers or Reims, for example) ideally sited to become instances of "microhistory."[92]

On the basis of published speeches and programmatic statements (much favored by the Jacobins, who as a rule were neither shy nor withdrawn), it is tempting to side with Hegel and to grant his argument on the origins of Robespierre's defense of terror.

But we might have an altered view of the case if we had a better archival record of the Jacobins' involvement in civil society, taken town by town and person by person. Our image of the Jacobins would be quite different if we were able to focus less on the speeches they made for national or public consumption and more on their answers to the pleas of the weak and the destitute in their hometowns.

The Limitless Claims
of the Public Sphere

I cannot reconcile myself to the idea of an immoral patriot, or to
that [separation] of private from public virtue, which some think to be
possible.

Richard Price, *A Discourse on the Love of Our Country in 1788*

𝒥acobinism was an unfolding *projet*, a politicized explanation of the
human condition. It wanted to make men and women happier by improv-
ing the relations of nature (which was good), human nature (which was
ambiguous), and society (which was often bad). Jacobins were not metaphysical, but neither were they superficial or introverted. Although ordinarily uninterested and sometimes blind to many tragic aspects of man's
fate (the fear of death and unhappiness, loneliness, anguish), they did reflect profoundly on the larger meaning of many fundamental problems
whose nature still puzzles us, specifically, the social context of the self and
the meaning of "nation" for that nation's socially disadvantaged citizens.

The Jacobins sought to balance private conscience and public good. The
two had to be fused somehow, into a twinned purpose that defined *esprit
révolutionnaire*, of which Jacobinism was the purest essence. The Jacobins
envisioned a self that blossomed through a sympathetic understanding of
the Other. They seized on public opinion and on the cult of nation as the
means toward this end.[1]

The Jacobins considered public opinion a kind of collective conscience;
Barère described it, in November 1792, as "our guard of honor."[2] Jacobin

orators never spoke for themselves. They invariably claimed to speak for some more general opinion, a term the Jacobins used ceaselessly and broadly. Grégoire, for example, invoked public opinion as he reminded mothers of their obligation to breastfeed their newborns.[3] "Only public opinion has the right to rule the nation," explained Barère on the day of Robespierre's execution.[4]

In retrospect, of course, eighteenth-century public opinion appears less self-determined than citizens supposed at the time. It could be arbitrarily defined and manipulated. But for the Jacobins public opinion was an immanent source of truth that had been gathering momentum over time— since the fifteenth century, in fact, with Gutenberg's invention of the printing press.

Persecuted by *"l'infâme"* and emasculated by the censorship of church and state, public opinion in the past had necessarily been tentative and secretive. But in their own times it had become, they thought, a clear force, openly arrived at. Its dictates, perhaps slow in coming, were eventually irresistible and irrefutable. "Anyone must be suspect who has public opinion against him."[5]

The Jacobins regarded public opinion as the voice not just of the nation's popular sovereignty but of the nation's general will as Rousseau might have defined it. "Experience has proved," explained Robespierre on November 5, 1792, "in spite of Louis XVI and his allies that the opinion of the Jacobins and the popular societies were those of the French nation. No citizen created it or dominated it, and I did no more than to share it."[6] Legitimacy rested with those who were morally right rather than with majorities that might well be wrong, either in the nation at large or in the nation's elected assemblies in the capital. Public opinion was to the regenerated nation as private conscience was to upright individuals—not always heeded, alas, but always present.[7] It was the Incorruptible's greatest crime, explained his erstwhile colleagues after July 1794, that he had gradually become "the dominator of public opinion."[8]

How could this national opinion be heard? By listening to many voices, assumed the Jacobins at first. All citizens would be consulted and informed. And all instructed citizens, they presumed, would easily agree. In 1790–91 the Jacobins naturally assumed that all well-informed men and women of good will would soon be of one regenerated mind.

Consequently, the Jacobins understood that it might at times prove to be their self-imposed duty to comply—momentarily—with erroneous but democratically established opinion. In the summer of 1791, for example, after the nation's representatives had decided to restore Louis to his throne, many clubs (including those that had spoken against the king) outlawed further discussions of republicanism. Public opinion, they decided at that point, had spoken through the agency of the people's elected deputies; patriotism demanded compliance.

But when the enemies of the Revolution steadfastly refused either to be informed or, though informed, to change their minds, the Jacobins came to question their first stance of patient toleration. The flawed dictates of manipulated opinion, they reasoned, had to be scrutinized closely. When the ousted Girondins managed to rally some local support, Couthon concluded on June 24, 1793, that "a corrupt majority had corrupted opinion."[9]

The Jacobins gradually sharpened their understanding of legitimate opinion and began to speak instead of a moralized "public spirit." They also became more impatient. In 1790 they had had the time to wait for the uninitiated to see the light; by 1793 these voluntarists no longer had any time to lose. Deviants who refused to mind opinion's voice as the Jacobins had defined it would henceforth be forced to listen. "I understand the injury done to the Convention," wrote a Jacobin from Besançon after the purge of the Girondins, "but I believe that in these circumstances, we have to forgive the despair of a people that believed it was being refused justice and that it had no other way of saving the *patrie*."[10]

So it was that by late 1792 opinion had in fact become little more than the echo of their own sectarian voice. A Jacobin Conventionnel of 1793 who had failed to convince his hearers complained that in his district public opinion was as yet unformed. In the same way, a Jacobin might write that the tax he had imposed on the rich and the *aristocrates* had "given courage to public opinion and encouraged the patriots."[11] By 1793 opinion had become for the Jacobins a collective political consciousness that only men of truly good will (themselves) could readily understand.[12]

Jacobins did grasp one of the two great political messages of late-eighteenth- and early-nineteenth-century politics. They understood that sovereignty came from the people. But unlike their British and especially their American cousins—who had learned from a full century of acrimonious politicking that representative institutions were the scenes of bitter conflict—the Jacobins were not prepared by their past to see that honest men might differ on how popular sovereignty is best expressed.

As they moved from polite recommendation and observation to forceful control and exertion of themselves as ideologized agents of the centralized state, the Jacobins slipped from a benign belief in the exchange of varied opinions in 1790–91 to constraining censorship in 1793–94.

As confirmed individualists, the Jacobins initially preferred the idea of tolerated dissent, both in the nation's assemblies and in their own clubs. Despite their eventual drift to terror, Jacobins understood completely that their zeal for humanitarian goals implied (Kantian) agreement and not (Rousseauean) coercion. A frank and open exchange of views was, they thought, self-evidently, desirable.

But discussion soon lost its specificity and gradually became a mere first step toward communitarian decision making. A choice that had been settled in the club or the nation had to be accepted by every citizen, without reservations. The "democratic centralism" of modern Leninist and communist parties was not without precedent, even if its immediate antecedents were particular to itself. Jacobins had long since stumbled on this conclusion: "when some resolution has been passed, every individual then present will be obliged to sign it once the majority will have spoken, even if its decision went against the will of the minority."[13] Although Jacobins often and astutely intrigued in the unofficial meetings that preceded official voting, they explicitly forbade disagreement in the public electoral assemblies whose task, they said, was to choose—unanimously if possible—men of proven probity, reasonableness, and universal feeling.

In May 1791 Robespierre explained that the patriots faced a choice: "the end of liberty" or the "infinite liberty of the press"; but in March 1793 he warned that "the interest of the Revolution may demand certain measures to repress a conspiracy founded on the freedom of the press."[14] At the Paris Jacobin club in November 1793 Chabot, a defrocked and corrupt Jacobin, framed the issue nicely in his comparison of the French and the British press: "In the composite government of England, as under our former royalist constitution, the freedom of the press against the government is necessary to counterbalance despotism, to prevent governors from oppressing the governed. But under French Republican government, I maintain that . . . the author . . . who curses democracy should be crushed."[15]

The Jacobins never went so far as to ask for a government-directed press. They feared that the end of a private press would soon lead to outright dictatorship.[16] Nevertheless, nearly 10 percent of counterrevolutionary offenses tried before the Revolutionary Tribunals were "délits d'opin-ion,"[17] that is, offenses of speech and not of deed. In one way or another, many full- or part-time journalists came to a violent end: Simon Linguet, Desmoulins, Brissot, Carra, Robespierre, Hébert, Babeuf, and Marat.

Jacobin voting procedures reflected their ambivalent attitude to free speech. In the clubs, the Paris *sections,* and, at times, the Convention, the Jacobins preferred open voting, either by rising and standing or by voice vote. They questioned the need for secret ballots, partly because they did not like "factionalism" and wanted to intimidate their opponents and partly because they simply did not see the point. They held that the con-junction of private wills and a self-standing public good produced true opinion. Since public opinion could not err, what was to be gained by al-lowing dissenters to speak ill of it?

*T*ogether with public opinion, the legal and representative systems were imperative public frameworks for private action. Jacobins believed in what has since their rule become a hallowed French tradition, namely, that most disputes would lapse in a society governed by clear and rational laws.[18]

The Jacobins initially thought that good came from law, just as law came from man's sense of what was good and just. In a representative episode described in a "plowman's manual" of the Marseillais Jacobins, a group of Republican peasants has just caught some counterrevolutionary priests and prepares to lynch them on the spot. Anselme, the model Ja-cobin, rushes toward them, and shouts: "Stop! Stop! There's no justice without forms. The law, the law: you swore to be faithful to it." Anselme's voice, the narrative continues, "his presence, the respect they all feel for him, suddenly appease the plowmen whom overwhelming indignation was about to lead astray."[19]

At the same time, however, Jacobins felt that practical necessity might require laws to be waived from time to time. Bad institutions, bad judges, and bad precedents could justify abrupt violence. Force was part of poli-tics. Had not the Revolution of 1789 been itself illegal by the (false) stan-dards of the previous (unnatural) and monarchic order? The fall of the Bastille in July 1789 and the murder soon after of two highly unpopular royal officials—Foulon and Bertier—had been one such instance of legal il-legality.

The overthrow of the monarchy was another illegal but moral act. Although the constitutional monarchy at least had some revolutionary legitimacy because it been created in 1789, by August 1792 its violent overthrow had come to seem necessary to Jacobins in and out of the Convention. The same acceptance of necessity explains in part why the Jacobins responded passively to the September massacres of 1792 and to the purge of the legally elected Girondin deputies who were pushed out of the Convention in May and June of 1793.

An ongoing suspicion of impending conspiracies against liberty was particularly relevant to their quasi-constitutional justification of popular force. In July 1789, for example, when a constitutional monarchist deputy moved that the National Assembly condemn all political violence, Robespierre objected: "is there anything more legitimate," he argued, "than to rise up against a horrible conspiracy formed to destroy the nation?" And Buzot, who would in late 1792 become a leader of the Gironde and an arch-enemy of the Incorruptible, concurred fully at this point with his enemy-to-be: "who will be the guarantor of [despotism's] complete destruction?" he asked. If despotism "once again assembles its forces to bring us down, which citizens then will arm themselves in time to save the *patrie*?"[20]

Yet, it would be highly tendentious to describe the Jacobins as men of the blood, driven by an anarchic or sadistic impulse that aimed to liberate some socially imprisoned human spirit. The purpose of violence, according to the Jacobins, was to institutionalize the principles and rules demanded by the public good and expressed through the voice of opinion.

They totally rejected gratuitous violence perpetrated for no ideological purpose. Gilbert Romme, for example, a radical Jacobin and, later, a highly principled and suicidal Prairial martyr, initially approved the lynching of Bertier and Foulon, as Barnave had done in mid-July 1789, only to change his mind three days later when he described the assassins as "worse than Nero and Caligula."[21] From one moment to the next, Romme's overall view of the relationship of force to politics in revolutionary times remained unaltered, but his appreciation of relevant circumstances changed and led him to new conclusions.

Even at the height of the Revolution, Jacobin men of violence were few. In a city of 700,000, the September massacres of 1792 were the handiwork of smallish bands, most of them not Jacobins. Indeed, a tolerance for direct violence separated the Jacobins from the sans-culottes. Robespierre chose never to witness an execution.[22]

In a related vein, Jacobins despised dueling, for them *the* classic form of violent self-indulgence. In early 1790 a Jacobin named Grouvelle published a piece entitled *Point de duel ou point de Constitution* (Choose: Either Dueling or the Constitution). At Vannes members had to swear to forsake the activity.[23] Jacobins congratulated themselves on its disappearance from the armed forces, and they were shocked in 1790 when two of their leaders, Barnave and Lameth, were challenged by notorious noble rightists. When a crowd then ravaged the house of Lameth's antagonist, the Paris Jacobins boasted on *not* having incited them to this act of vengeful but deserved violence.[24]

Jacobins were ordinarily honest men of order, often lawyers, who had dedicated themselves to the application of universal rules of decency and common sense. They despised arbitrary acts, which they took to be the essence of the monarchic absolutism they had overthrown. Even their illegality had to have a legal look. After the summer of 1793, the Jacobins felt strongly that their tyrannical, anti-individualist, and illegal behavior should be retroactively sanctified by law. The laws of Prairial on judicial procedure during the Great Terror of the spring of 1794 can be read as a legal suspension of the rule of law.

Likewise, when indicted counterrevolutionaries took to killing themselves before their trial and legal condemnation so as to die while still technically innocent (thereby shielding their families from material confiscations and destitution), the Jacobins did not respond by extralegal confiscation. They decided instead to define legally the suicide of an accused person as a tacit and punishable confession of guilt. Revealingly, Robespierre, on the night of 9 Thermidor, after he had been rescued from the power of the Convention, whose legality he never ceased to recognize, was unable to react against this now hostile but still legal authority. Contemporaries quite appropriately thought it plausible that he had attempted suicide physically, since he had already done so politically.

In theory, then, the Jacobins never lost their respect for rules. From time to time, even in 1793, an accused person might escape on a technicality. Thus, a mayor accused of stealing grain who had replied that the law required he be caught *flagrante delicto,* which, he pointed out, had not been the case, was let off.[25]

It was the Jacobins' sad privilege to invent the show trials of political suspects, but they did so, as it were, on their own terms. Unlike twentieth-century totalitarians, they did not aim to bamboozle public or world opinion.

After two centuries of principled and murderous politics, our modern impulse is to question the sincerity of the Jacobins' views on moralization of public life through force. After 1794, the revolutionaries themselves raised such questions. Some were required to do so by the courts.

Arguments on the banality of evil spring to mind, but it is wholly implausible to suppose that the Jacobins of 1794 did not think hard about the rights and wrongs of executing their enemies by the cart load. Unlike modern fascists and Bolsheviks, Jacobins, consciously at least, were driven more by frustrated love than by hate, envy, or indifference. In Hannah Arendt's words, unforgiving rage is the proper response to modern horrors generally and to those of the German National Socialists in particular; but that can seldom be our unalloyed response to Jacobin misdeeds, however horrible they seem and actually were.

We remember Jacobins as ruthless politicians determined to carry out a revolutionary project regardless of its costs or legality. Lenin in our own century admired them for that very reason. But we should remember also that, from day to day, at least until 1793—when they became the unbending quasi-functionaries of the revolutionary state—the Jacobins strained not to force but to convince.

The true Jacobin knew what public morality and law should be, even when—from supposed necessity—he most egregiously violated its precepts. This pragmatic legalism, it may be added, deeply offended Immanuel Kant, who could easily accept that the Revolution should kill the king so that it might live, but not that the Jacobin deputies should act as both judge and jury, and use legal forms to carry out a gesture that was quintessentially political.

The Jacobins' response to him in turn, had they been apprised of his views, would surely have been—in the words of the poet Friedrich Hölderlin (1770–1843)—that Germans were rich in words but poor in deeds.

*A*lthough the Jacobins hailed individualism, they realized that no one existed in a void. They deemed the ideal Republican both disciplined and engaged, moral in his or her private life and involved in the moralized, public life of the polity. In any free state, explained Robespierre to his fellow Jacobins in May 1791, citizens were the sentinels of liberty: "You to whom liberty, to whom *patrie* is dear, you alone are charged with the care of saving it. The guarantee of the rights [of citizens] must be placed in their own strength."[26]

Thus, Jacobins enthusiastically participated in elections and in civic rituals. They read newspapers. They were eager to spread the word. They identified with the nation and tried to live model private and public lives. They supported the cause of the Revolution abroad. They also believed in friendship, charity, self-sacrifice, and goodness both within and outside the four walls of their homes.

A Jacobin always fought on two fronts, as a private achiever and as a custodian of public mores, careful to put community before private gain. At her trial, Mme. Roland thought of killing herself as a gesture of defiance against a judgment she knew was false. But on reflection, she decided not to challenge her jurors and resolved to accept her fate with resigned but exemplary Republican dignity. Many Jacobins with a strong personal sense of honor nonetheless thought it necessary to confess their errors publicly.

In private matters, Jacobins thought it noble to turn the other cheek: a visiting Conventionnel at Auch, who had had a brick thrown at him, refused to respond because a personal insult, he explained, was best left unanswered. But Jacobins were unforgiving when they dealt with the enemies of the common good.

Militarism was the extreme form of the Jacobins' involvement in civic matters. As early as December 1789 Edmond Dubois-Crancé reminded the National Assembly that "every citizen must be a soldier, and every soldier a citizen."[27] Under the Old Regime soldiers had often been despised by their aristocratic officers and by the self-absorbed civilian subjects of the king. (In Britain, the duke of Wellington's contempt for his own drunken soldiery would soon be legendary.) But after 1789 Jacobins worked hard to change these ancient ways. They proclaimed military service to be the highest form of the citizen's involvement in the state. At Dijon the club suggested in 1793 that all balls be shut down and that young men learn military exercises instead of dance.[28] Indeed, the prestige of militarized and sacrificial involvement was such that dozens of women cross-dressed to take part in revolutionary soldiering. (Many decades later, Napoleon III honored one such survivor with the cross of the Legion of Honor.) Local *clubbistes* never hesitated to welcome visiting officers.

Citizenship encompassed both private and public life. But who was a citizen? Instinctively, Jacobins would say "everyman" and, in lesser measure, "everywoman," though this view evolved only gradually (as with their attitude toward slavery, which they did not abolish until February 1794).

In the fall of 1789 the deputies in Paris did not at first agree. They developed divergent definitions of "passive" and "active" citizens. They defined as active citizens those of French nationality over the age of twenty-five who had fulfilled certain requirements: they had taken a civic oath to maintain the Constitution at any cost; they had enrolled in the National Guard; and, most important, they had paid an annual tax that amounted to three times the daily local wage for unskilled labor, the effect of the last measure being to exclude many unpropertied laborers in the cities especially. In addition to these 4.3 million people, 40 percent of adult men—another 3 million—were designated passive citizens, a larger number than had been excluded from the elections to the Third Estate in 1789.

The Jacobins did not comply with this distinction for long. Citizenship for them could be no more rationed by wealth than by birth. In Paris Robespierre and Grégoire soon objected. Desmoulins likewise exclaimed that the trust active citizens of all were those who had stormed the Bastille. Élisée Loustalot denounced the rule of the "pure aristocracy of the rich."[29] In July 1790 the club at Béthune became the first to follow these Parisian examples. That fall important clubs at Limoges, Aix, and Marseilles concurred. At Brest the *clubbistes* suggested that excluding passive citizens from the National Guard was particularly unfair. By the spring of 1791 this trickle of complaints had widened to a flood. In April and May of 1791 Robespierre, Pétion, and Brissot all attacked this cramping measure. In June 1791 the club of Bourbourg admitted citizens without regard to their categorization.[30]

After the Feuillant split, in the fall of 1791, all orthodox left Jacobins rallied to the idea of universal manhood suffrage; and to their approval and relief, the issue vanished when equal rights of citizenship were extended on August 11, 1792. (The voting age was also lowered from twenty-five to twenty-one.)

Jacobins, one might add, though eager to enfranchise the poor, were also insistent that everyone, including the very poor, should pay some taxes, because these were a proof of civic involvement. Some clubs required evidence of tax payment as a requirement for membership. Before 1789 taxes, they cheerfully admitted, had been a tribute surrendered to a despotic state. But now paying them had become a civic obligation. At Autun, where the *clubbistes* aggressively pursued this issue, 109 taxpayers were obliged to contribute over 430,000 francs. At Tulle the club sent messengers out to the countryside urging peasants to settle their accounts.

Money could not be a civic criterion for the Jacobin. But it was harder for the Jacobins to make up their minds about the social frontiers of citizenship. Where did the rights of civil society stop and the claims of citizenship begin? How porous were the borders between private life and public life? Where did individualism cease and moralized public life begin?

For Adam Smith (1723–1790), in some part at least, the common weal emerged spontaneously from private gain and competition. Thanks to the working of an invisible hand, private motive and perhaps private vice might yield some public good. But what the Jacobins wanted instead was to improve politics so as to expand private autonomy, which in turn would enable regenerated citizens better to understand the beauty of wider public life. As citizens, men would become better fathers and producers, which would in turn help them to become better citizens.

For Kant, in these same years, virtue was not essential to an improved public realm. Intelligent demons, mindful of the Hobbesian need to maintain public order, might learn to live in peace and perhaps to work together and share. But Jacobins could never accept a relativist notion of this kind. For them, as for Rousseau, private or public happiness without private and public morality was not possible. Citizens could not hope to behave as moral human beings in civil life without some supportive public context. Robinson Crusoe—however productive and Christian in his isolation—was an English, individualist fantasy that was beyond, or beneath, the imagination of the Jacobins. Individualism could thrive only in a universally shared context of moralized politics. Even women, whose first realm was the home, were nonetheless expected to add a public dimension to their lives: "Republicans are frank in their speech and faithful to their promises," explained a Jacobin at Ruffec. "You [women] will not be coquettish with us . . . You can continue the club in the heart of your home."[31] In this respect, at least, Jacobins were (unknowing) Kantians, promoting universally acceptable behavior for every man and woman.[32] Individual and communitarian values, like freedom and happiness, were as two sides of a single coin.

From 1789 to 1790 when nearly all of France moved in unison (miraculously!), it seemed that this synergy had already or nearly been achieved through the instantaneous regeneration of civic life. Dawn and rebirth were dominant themes.[33] "You breathed on remains that seemed inanimate," wrote Mirabeau. "Suddenly, a constitution was organized, and already, it is giving off an active force. The cadaver that has been touched by liberty has risen and received new life."[34]

Far from worrying about the limits of the civil and the political, Jacobins in these early days insisted on how much had already been achieved to make social relations fair, with free justice, equitably apportioned taxes, and the end of censorship. They celebrated the demise of corporatist and feudal constraints. They hailed the destruction of the hierarchies of status and nobility, which, they sincerely believed, had made daily life so oppressive under the Old Regime.

All these successes made it feasible to accept society as it was: individual nobles who had acceded to the end of the Old Regime were invariably given pride of place in both the clubs and the National Assembly. In these first months, Jacobins went out of their way to defer to the church and the king.

But as political consensus ebbed and then collapsed after the flight of the king to Varennes in June 1791 and the fall of the monarchy in August 1792, Jacobins increasingly rethought the relationship between civil and political, and they did so in what proved to be the worst way.

They sharpened, moralized, masculinized, and made more abstract their definition of public life. In so doing, they gradually lost sight of the separation of civil society and public morality: "to be an *honnête homme*," explains the Frenchman to a citizen of Philadelphia in a revolutionary pamphlet, "one has to be a good son, a good husband, and a good father, and . . . bring together every private and public virtue . . . That is where you will find the true definition of patriotism."

As familiar limits dissolved in 1794, the Jacobins' entire purpose began to waver. Unable to give up their demanding vision of citizenship, unable also to transform French social life, the remaining Jacobins, as Hegel explained, turned their attention to human nature itself. For Thucydides, human passions were unchanging. History's annals revealed the constancy of human responses to the great and immutable problems of private and public life. By contrast, Jacobin ideologues of 1794 make the case for the opposite conclusion. For them infinitely more than for us (or for Thucydides, obviously) the changing life of the spirit, the improvable essence of *esprit public,* mattered more than either human nature or its material envelopes. Regenerated, Jacobin man, now more virtuous, could and would rise above himself. Among the threats to normal, healthy lives, argued Grégoire in 1794, were "immorality, ignorance, (and) imprudence"; were these to be pushed back, he explained, "we might then reconstitute human nature [*reconstituons la nature humaine*],"[35] a view that was not far from that of the Girondin Jacobin La Revellière-Lépeaux, who wrote in 1798 that it was important, during the celebrations of national holidays, "to employ every means that might, so to speak, modify the substance of man, in order to have it overlap with [our] form of government and in order to make the love of liberty the dominant passion of man."[36]

*T*he Jacobins' growing cult of the revolutionary public good fed their disdain for recent history, and especially for the history of their own country as it had existed in its "unregenerated" prerevolutionary form. Jacobins might well choose to honor "old age" in the assemblies and the clubs, where they often chose the oldest member as honorary president. But they did so less from a respect for elderly wisdom as such than from a sense of humanity and a desire to mix the aged with the young.

If France and the world could be reshaped at will, what did it matter what the past had been? In a celebrated letter of September 1789, which he wrote in Paris to James Madison, Thomas Jefferson explained that "*the earth belongs in usufruct to the living* (and) . . . the dead have neither powers or rights over it.*" Jacobins concurred. They had some use for history. Before the Revolution, the trajectory of the newly created United States was often cited in France as a possible precedent. Cromwell was also exemplary. In March 1794 the far-leftist Cordeliers labeled Robespierre and his fellow Jacobin Collot *cromwellistes* on account of their propertied denial of popular goals. Likewise, after his fall in Thermidor, Year II, when opinion had become more conservative, Robespierre was also said to have been *unlike* the Lord Protector, then portrayed as having saved rather than destroyed the British Revolution.

But during Jacobinism's higher moments, specific historical events, including recent ones, seemed dubiously relevant. The painter David spoke of "erasing from our chronology those many centuries of error."[37] Clearly, the thousand-year history of the French monarchy had been an interruption more than a progression. Jacobins spoke about the "re-greening" of French liberty. Jacobin references to French history were often ghoulish and ironical, as when the terrorist Stanislas Fréron puckishly suggested that the king be decapitated (as had been a common mode of execution under the Old Regime) rather than guillotined, or that Marie Antoinette be dragged through Paris tied to the tail of a galloping horse, as a Frankish king had done to the captured queen Brunehilde in the seventh century.

The examples that seemed most germane to the Jacobins were drawn from the histories of ancient Greece and Rome.[38] In a comment on the city of Lyons, many of whose rebellious inhabitants had been silk weavers involved in the luxury trade, Jeanbon Saint-André commented, for example, that the Lyonese were notorious cowards and that "Sybarites cannot become Spartans." To a provincial club Carnot described Jacobins as "the heroes of Thermopylae. We shall be the Spartans of the Revolution."[39] And Louvet, in praise of fellow Girondist Jacobin Roland, said that his threatening message to the court had been couched in a style "worthy of Rome and Sparta."[40]

Jacobins felt emphatically that classical figures had prefigured the great men of their own times. They took Socrates, Brutus, Cato, and the mythical citizen soldiers of ancient city-states as their models, and often named their children for such ancient warriors. Some of them even renamed themselves accordingly. Jean-Baptiste Clootz became Anacharsis Clootz, after an Enlightenment travelogue of the 1780s that had ancient Greece as its theme; François Noël Babeuf metamorphosed into Gracchus Babeuf, after the populist Roman tribune. (He had at first chosen Camille but decided to improve on that choice.) Napoleon's brother, Lucien, an ardent Jacobin, is said to have called himself Brutus. It was the good fortune of Robespierre and his brother to have Romanized names to begin with—Augustine and Maximilian.

Symptomatically, the Jacobins often rewrote history altogether, as did Collot d'Herbois when staging Socrates' rescue from death by a revolutionary crowd. Similarly, in a remake of Molière's *Misanthrope*, the misanthropic Alceste was turned into a Jacobinical philanthropist instead.

*W*hen it came to aesthetics, Jacobins would have been decidedly hostile to theories of art for art's sake—had they been apprised of them.

Quite predictably, Jacobins often reacted passively to instances of cultural vandalism, a term now used in every language, and coined in January 1794 by Grégoire (who opposed it: "I coined the word," he later explained, "to kill the thing").[41] They did not invariably condemn dismal and destructive acts like smashing statues, burning books, or defacing paintings and religious objects. In Strasbourg local Jacobins urged the destruction of the cathedral's tower, a "pyramid erected in honor of superstition."[42] At Fontainebleau the club organized the public burning of royal portraits, some of them by Leonardo da Vinci, Giovanni Rosso, and Philippe de Champaigne. Statues of saints and monarchs in Paris, Reims, Nancy, Montpellier,[43] and many other places were destroyed or melted down.[44] At Poitiers a registry of the club's membership was carefully bound with parchment copies of Gregorian chants.[45] Jacobin artists like Antoine Chaudet and J. B. Wicar argued for the wholesale destruction of the books and manuscripts confiscated from private or public enemies of the Revolution like émigrés and monks. In November 1793 David ennobled this destructive yearning in a speech to his fellow deputies in the French Convention. Their task, he explained, was to liberate "the present, the future, and even the past, by planting liberty trees on the graves of our forebears, and by immolating in dedication to their souls the representations of our oppressors."[46] In Paris, in August 1793, François Hanriot, the more or less sans-culotte commander of the Paris National Guard went on record in favor of burning down libraries![47]

Not all Jacobins concurred, however. As men and women of learning and taste, many and perhaps most Jacobins privately found vandalism distasteful. In January 1791 Mirabeau warned against a "revolution of the Goths and the Vandals," and this point of view persisted to some degree. Unlike the popular revolutionaries, especially those of the *armées révolutionnaires,* which destroyed religious works of art, many Jacobin clubs were more circumspect: at Rodez, Coutances, and Tréguier, local Jacobins did what they could to stop such depredations. Most confiscated books were not burnt but distributed among libraries, especially in Paris.[48]

Similarly, many prominent Jacobins argued that it would make more sense to abhor pictorial representations of the past than merely to destroy them. Hence their decision on July 27, 1793, to set up a fine arts museum in the Palace of the Louvre, and their strategy of exhibition also: the newly created repository, they decided, would not be organized by artists or schools of paintings but politically, with collected representations of aristocratic selfishness, clerical hypocrisy, or monarchic despotism. Room by room, the new national museum would offer to the public an expurgated version of French history.

*T*he Jacobins' indifference to a French past, together with their ideologized espousal of a new and inspiring collective and civic good, found expression in their efforts to restructure time and space.

Nearly from the first, many clubs informally dated their deliberations from an informal reckoning that took 1789 to be the "first year of liberty." After November 1793 they also eagerly adopted the newly voted revolutionary calendar, which took as its starting point the proclamation of the republic on September 22, 1792; that day by good fortune coincided with the fall equinox, when day and night symbolically balance each other.

The new revolutionary year was divided into twelve equal months. Named for phases of the weather, each month had three "decades" of ten days, named for plants; five *sans-culottides* fell at the end of the year; and every fourth year had a supplementary *jour de la révolution*. Every cycle of four years was dubbed a *franciade*. Some revolutionary timepieces with a twenty-hour day, much prized by collectors today, were also manufactured.

To promote the new calendar, local Jacobins encouraged merchants to open on Sundays by holding their meetings on that day or by making it illegal for tavern keepers to sell wine to locals then.[49] They staged "*fêtes décadaires* as rival holidays."[50]

Space, too, was reappropriated by the nation. As a result of the great Festival of the Federation of July 14, 1790, tens of thousands of ordinary French people—many of them Jacobins—crisscrossed France (now truly their own nation) on their way to and from Paris. Thousands of French towns and cities were renamed: Grenoble became Grelibre and Saint-Denis, La Franciade.

Many of these new Jacobin rites (marked by bonfires, parades, floats, or "queen-for-a-day contests") merely echoed local folklore. Nonetheless, Jacobins made a conscious effort not just to rename but also to reclaim space for revolutionary consciousness. They quickly rehistoricized inhabited urban areas by celebrating revolutionary events on the very sites where they had occurred, and preferably on sites that had had an inverse significance in former and monarchic times.

In countless commemorations of the captured Bastille, hundreds of provincial mockups were stormed by ardent Jacobins. The original fortress, however, was destroyed stone by stone, many of them sold for profit by an enterprising Parisian named Pierre Palloy (1755–1835), who contrary to revolutionary legend went bankrupt. Others were used to build a new and still extant bridge across the Seine between the Place de la Révolution and the Left Bank.

*A*s Jacobinism and its new customs waxed, and as the prestige of an autonomous civil society contemporaneously declined, Jacobins also developed a more pronounced stand on the merits of luxury and frugality.

Some prerevolutionary philosophes had suggested that luxury was bad because it wasted scarce resources. Why allow a rich man to eat expensive oysters if the same amount of money could feed entire families? But others suggested that luxury was both a stimulant of economic growth and a remedy against banality and boredom.

After 1789 Jacobins eagerly joined in this debate. Here they found a field where they might defend private property (which was necessary) while striking a progressive stance against (Parisian) superfluities. Some Jacobins renounced sugar and coffee to underscore their disapproval not just of conspicuous consumption but also of colonial trade. Romme, when he discovered that his wife had bought goods on the black market, indignantly forced her to return her purchases. The Jacobin critique of luxury was ordinarily innocent enough, but at Lyons, where the livelihood of the poor depended on the production of expensive silk cloths, the Jacobins' dislike of *inutile élégance* had a highly deleterious effect.[51]

No less destructive were the views of an extreme, naturalizing, and primitivist Jacobin minority that dared to deny, first, the usefulness of industry and refinement and, second, that of science. Jacobins generally approved of scientific knowledge as an expression of enlightened modernity. Knowledge unlocked the underlying order of the universe. Newton was a significant figure for them, and one of Robespierre's first briefs as a young lawyer supported a man who had been ordered to remove a lightning rod from his house. Likewise, Marat was an aspiring savant who had been asked to organize an Academy of Sciences in Madrid.

Indeed, Jacobins were ideologically committed to approve not just of science but of industrialism as well. How could they reject ennobling, Promethean assertions of man's ability to master nature through reason? Mainstream Jacobins were—in theory—practical and modern-minded men.

Nevertheless, the Jacobins' lack of enthusiasm for applied science in manufacturing was quite plain. Most Jacobins, regardless of their walk of life, believed that agriculture, now individuated and made more rational, should remain the pivot of social life. Only the land could, nationwide, inculcate "science, experience, and diligence." Only agriculture would "moralize commerce, obviate the need for luxurious and costly imports, and wipe out mendicity."[52] Agriculture was a civic field. Industry was not.

The Jacobinical preference for nature over reason and for agriculture over industry had many causes. Most simply, Jacobins had little personal contact with applied science and technology. But their skepticism toward manufacturing also had a quasi-political motivation. Nature and the countryside, in their idealized vision, brought men together, while cities, luxury, and manufacturers divided them. In the long run, by destroying the anti-individualist corporatist structures of the Old Regime, Jacobin economics paved the way for capitalism. But revolutionary upheaval initially cut industrial production by 1800 to 60 percent of prerevolutionary levels.

*I*n 1789 the Jacobins asserted their civic goals gently, basing their thought on individualism, civil society, and also goodness. "La République," Roland explained in September 1792 to the newly arrived Conventionnels, "est une seule et même chose que la fraternité" (the republic is the one and the same thing as fraternity).[53]

Although their basic worldview did not change, by 1793–94 untoward circumstance and the weight of the past had gradually brought out an ideologized ferocity in the Jacobins' character. As many historians from Michelet's time in the 1840s to our own have observed, the *clubbistes,* to their own amazement, became quite fierce in hunting down the enemies of the nation. In the Jacobin view of life, man was not mysterious to himself; and when the Jacobins concluded that the enemies of the civic good would not change, they also decided that such foes were clearly evil and deserving of no mercy. In his novel of the Revolution, *1793,* Victor Hugo rightly compared the Jacobins' good conscience to "the blind certitude of the arrow that sees nothing but its target."

According to the Marxist critic Walter Benjamin, Klee's *Novus Angelus* anticipated man's eventual redemption as it might emerge from future and inevitable catastrophes.

Our own sensibility is even more lugubrious. For us, today's catastrophe is little more than the preface to yet other catastrophes, accidental or deserved.

Convinced that all catastrophes were behind them, the Jacobins firmly believed that the Angel of History had borne them to the promised land.

5

The Indisputable Claims of the Nation

Clearly, the love of homeland has engendered the most extraordinary feats of virtue: self-love, when furthered by this sentiment at once sharp and gentle, energizes our self-esteem without disfiguring it, and makes of it the most heroic of all passions.

Jean-Jacques Rousseau, *Sur l'Economie politique*

Although individualistic-minded and enamored of private property, the Jacobins were also ardent universalists. For them, the quasi-sacred public sphere deserved precedence over the pressing but profane claims of daily life. They lived in a world of property; but their dreams were elsewhere, and their reverie was often more real to them than the world of things.

Like the public sphere, the collective will of the nation was an ontological absolute, an undeniable origin.[1] Sovereignty was in the people. The *patrie* was every Jacobin's mother.[2] The *nation,* which embodied the political will of the *patrie,* was the font of sovereignty, politics, and truth. "The love of one's *patrie,*" wrote Grégoire on the occasion of the *fête* for Simoneau, was "almost innate."

The Jacobins had a complex imagination of the world. They often weighed humanity's oneness against the diversity of continents, of races, and of the ages. Likewise, as heirs of French economic thinking and occasional—if critical—readers of Adam Smith, many of them saw the inchoate events of their daily financial and economic life as facets of a single, invisible, but systemic market. The laws of supply and demand were palpable to them.

But humanity, economics, and the immanence of civil society did not structure their thinking as profoundly as the idea of Nation, their premier mental matrix. They often felt that everything else, including humanity, should be made subservient to the fact of nationhood. Slavery, for example, was inadmissible because France was a nation of free men. Conversely, the Jacobins, over time ceased to treat foreign military prisoners with any humanity because as enemies of the revolutionary Grande Nation, they deserved no mercy.

The "nationalization" of "middle-class" sensibility has been closely scrutinized in the history of Britain, Germany, and North America. Historians of the eighteenth century have traced a growing concern for the imagined community of nation in all of these North Atlantic communities.[3] But Nation was far more pronounced for the French Jacobins than for their neighbors to the north, east, or west.

Many Frenchmen, especially those living in border areas, may have been hard put to say what the nation was and where it began or ended. But the Jacobins had no such problem. They were first and foremost patriots. They were the citizens of a great republic. Civically and nationally oriented, they addressed one another in the clubs as Citizen Dupont rather than Monsieur Dupont, or by title as an informal official of Republican opinion, such as secretary, president, or "the previous speaker."

Their nationalized sensibility was no doubt embedded in an essential "Frenchness," in a shared and historicized sense of what life should be like. But the politicization of that Frenchness was as important to them as the thing itself. Jacobins cared deeply about other entities ranging from their hometowns to the whole of humanity, and a favored oratorical device of theirs was to come forward as the (self-appointed) spokesman of some larger group. They soon concluded, however, that other human groupings could only fully come into their own when they coincided with the interests of the Grande Nation, of the French Republic and its *esprit public*. God, it appeared, had created nations and peoples rather than mere individuals. Jacobins used expressions like "Dieu de la patrie" or "Dieu des Français." "O déité de ma patrie," ran François Gossec's patriotic hymn of 1794. Though not precisely divinely sanctioned, the Grande Nation certainly enjoyed divine protection: "The God of the French looked favorably on his beloved people and gave them the courage to struggle against its tyrants and to conquer its liberty."[4] The will of the Almighty, the fate of the nation, and the political cause that was theirs were like the many sides of a single truth.

In the political theory of the Old Regime, the French nation had realized itself in the king's one body. Hence the monarchic fiction that the king could not die. But in a debate on the royal prerogative, Robespierre turned that traditional image around completely. For him, the inviolability of the king was itself a legal fiction. Only the people were immortal and inviolable because their legal rights were founded "on the sacred right of nature."[5]

The Jacobins felt the claims of the nation deserved precedence over the rights of its many members. They evinced this view when discussing, in late 1791 and early 1792, the right of private persons to leave the country. In both Enlightenment principle and in the law as it stood, these nostalgic or, as a rule, fearful monarchists had a clear legal right to leave. But Jacobins denied them that advantage. The Jacobins did in principle accept every person's right to move about. That had been one of the grounds for abolishing hated serfdom, which in 1789 still existed vestigially in eastern France. And yet, in 1791 irate Jacobins searched high and low for reasons to deny would-be émigrés that legal option. They reasoned, for example, that by leaving their nation in the lurch, the émigrés had forfeited their rights of nationality and, with that, their full humanity. It would soon become legal to shoot them on sight, should they be apprehended upon returning.

Had the French formed a nation under the monarchy? The Jacobins, as has been said, were not sure. The regenerating Revolution of 1789 had so transformed the French that only then had they truly become themselves. Before 1789 Frenchmen had had no *patrie,* according to the Jacobins.[6] Nineteenth-century nationalists (French, English, or German) embraced the various traditions of their homelands. The Victorians had Cromwell and the martyred Charles I for legendary and inspiring heroes; Michelet had Joan of Arc and the atheistic soldiers of the Revolution. Indeed, Michelet aimed to show that French and universalist values always overlapped, and that in modern historical times universalism had invariably traveled in the baggage train of the French nation, be it monarchic or Republican. But Jacobins were largely foreign to this romantic, historicized, and nationalized view of public life.

The Jacobins did not see the antecedents of nationhood in a material context. They preferred to see their reborn nation as a new moralized entity, fashioned by "la sainte Révolution" from the wreckage of the Old Regime, and they saw the effects of that transformation everywhere.

They held up national borders, national sovereignty, and a national language as truths (or even things) that were self-evidently fated to exist. They naturally assumed that the nation was the proper matrix for institutions of all kinds, from politics and legal codes to weights and measures, *opinion publique,* currency, tariffs, trade, uniforms, a national musical canon,[7] ice cream,[8] decorations,[9] and the prospective bride of the king's son, the newly styled "prince royal." Many Jacobin societies warmed to the suggestions made by the club at Provins that the heir to the French throne (who was born in 1785 and died in jail at the age of ten) should not marry a foreign princess. He should be required instead to choose a French-born wife: "the kings of Sparta did not find their wives in Persia." Saint-Just wrote that although animals existed in a state of "amicable coexistence,"[10] human sociability depended on more structure, set as it was within the framework of nations.

Jacobins knew that the French nation was not uniform. It was common knowledge, for example, that northerners were taller than southerners. Jacobins also assumed as a matter of course that northern Frenchmen were more phlegmatic than their compatriots in the *midi.* They sensed the mix of sentimental lethargy and vengeful ferocity that distinguished the Mediterranean culture of southeastern France. But they saw such variants either as gradations within a single national model or as of no particular significance at all. They did not develop racialist theories of regional politics.[11]

They did not like the idea of free trade with other, rival nations. In 1786 the French monarchy, largely for reasons of international expediency, had signed a treaty for freer trade with Britain; French wine exports to England were less heavily taxed, as were imports of English textiles in France. The *clubbistes* of Bordeaux, a seaport, liked this treaty because it favored the sale of their local claret. In France as a whole, however, and nearly from the first, Jacobins complained about the accord, which a Strasbourg *clubbiste* described as the fruit of "the arrogant ineptitude of the [king's] minister."[12] Many clubs argued for a change in the treaty or, if that could not be secured, for the voluntary boycott of foreign (English) goods, as the Paris club did on June 3, 1790.

The Jacobins did not act merely from fear of competition, as it appears from their immediate acceptance of an internal national customs union. When France became a single trade zone in 1789, many inefficacious local interests stood to lose, since they had been protected by internal customs duties from the competition of more efficient French producers. But not a single club protested about that national economic bond. What the bureaucracy of the French monarchy had vainly labored to do since Colbert in the seventeenth century revolutionary national feeling effortlessly achieved. Competition from other Frenchmen was acceptable. Foreign rivalry was not.

Although solidly ensconced in regional civil society as landlords and as local notables, Jacobins were the diehard partisans of national solutions everywhere. They rationalized their self-interests and invariably argued that their local demands coincided completely with the common good. A club might be reluctant to see its hometown give up surplus food but it would couch that refusal differently. To export food, the local Jacobins might argue, would be to act as a cat's-paw for local *aristocrates* because a food shortage would turn local crowds against the Revolution. The Jacobins of Saverne fought the relocation of the civil tribunal from their city to Haguenau on the grounds that Saverne was a more patriotic city.[13] When they proposed a new road, bridge, or canal, Jacobins liked to reason that such public works would clearly benefit the national economy.

It is a tribute to the emotional force of Jacobin principle in the years 1792–1794 that this vision—one is tempted to say, political fantasy—actually transformed perceptions of local groups and events. Before 1789, the Jews of Bayonne, for example, had practiced in their synagogue as tolerated foreigners whose relationship to the French king was governed by renewable covenant.[14] But once emancipated by the Revolution, although it had turned on their religion, these patriotic Jews continued to meet, and in the same building, as regenerated citizens of the new French nation.[15] Their day-to-day existence may not have much been altered, but their perception of themselves, and of France as a nation, was completely transformed. Historically, it is hard to say where the greater transformation lay: in the belief of Christian and heretofore uninterested or anti-Semitic Frenchmen that regenerated Jews could be their fellow citizens, or in the Jews of Bayonne's belief that they could and should completely Frenchify themselves.

Jacobins were wholly unable to accept the pluricultural idea that nations are a kind of collage, "a civil association" of communities entitled to self-expression. For the Jacobins, national and political sentiments had to overlap completely. Every party must be criminal, explained Saint-Just in March 1794, "because parties isolate the people and the popular societies and are independent of the government."[16] Jacobins had no sympathy for dissidents, whether political enemies (Girondins) or regionalist-minded rebels (in southern France). They invariably linked their local and national political animosities, in assuming, for example, that speakers of particularist dialects had of necessity to have counterrevolutionary sympathies, despite evidence to the contrary. Like Randolph of Roanoke, an eccentric Republican senator from Virginia during Jeffersonian times, the Jacobins assumed that the sovereignty of the national state could no more be divided than the chastity of a woman.

In an inverted but related mode, Jacobins found it difficult to see that revolutionary principle could ever really run against national objectives. It never occurred to them, for instance, that the abolition of slavery might lead to the definitive breakup of the French colonial empire. They wished the slaves of Haiti to be free, but they did not foresee that freed slaves might spurn association with a French homeland and prefer to form their own and independent Haitian Republic.[17]

When the Revolution unfolded with its disharmonies and contradictions, nationalist-minded Jacobins were deeply puzzled. Private quarrels were surely bad enough: at Nay, after some difficult confrontations, the club announced that all could now come home. "All the members who had left the Society because of personal quarrels or misunderstandings will be able to rejoin the faithful members of said society."[18]

But public quarrels that set Frenchman against Frenchman on grounds of principle were wholly scandalous, so much so, that the end of a dispute on any terms was a hopeful sign. At Besançon a resigned and disabused Jacobin journalist thus opined that the coup of May 31, 1793, against the Girondins might prove a blessing in disguise, regardless of its rights and wrongs. It had at least ended an open quarrel: "its effect will be fortunate for the republic because it ends the struggle of the two parties . . . and the constitution will be better made."[19] The Carcassonne *clubbistes* in a letter to the Paris Jacobins similarly expressed their indignation at seeing the divisions that racked the National Assembly: "Will this party of the right and party of the left forever subsist amongst men whom we have brought together for the same goal and to the same end?"[20] In late 1792 the Marseillais Jacobins argued that the assassins responsible for the September massacres should *not* be hunted down because an investigation would "foment dissension among Conventionnels and among the *people*."[21]

The fate of the Montagnard federalist movement in the fall of 1793 (which culminated in a meeting of Montagnard *clubbistes* from hundreds of societies in Marseilles from October 3 to November 21) exemplifies the Jacobins' attitude to nationalist unity and divisive, pluralist politics. It was no surprise that the Montagnards of 1793 should have condemned the provincial Girondins' earlier recourse to federalist rhetoric. Everyone understood at that point that the purpose of regional opposition was only to create a political force outside the capital that the Gironde might use to counter the Montagnards, who then dominated the National Convention with the help of the Parisian poor. But the Montagnards' subsequent stance toward pro-Montagnard regionalism was more revealing. So keen were the Jacobins in Paris on national unity that they outlawed even those provincial political movements whose stated (and true) aim was to support them without reservation. Jacobins perceived any regional political activity, however orthodox, as potentially factional.

One is reminded of the response of an early-nineteenth-century Austrian emperor to the fulsome dedication of a monarchist musician: "But who *asked* you to write these songs?"

*A*ll Jacobins saw the nation as the font and justification of life, both social and political. But how could the nation's will best be ascertained? What institutions might best embody it: the national assemblies in Paris? the primary assemblies that elected them in the provinces?[22] a plebiscite?[23] an uncensored press, which Brissot dubbed the agency of "universal communication"? the clubs? the so-called federated volunteers who marched to Paris in July 1792 and helped overthrow the monarchy? the crowd?

These awesome questions the Jacobins never answered clearly. Indeed, as François Furet has perspicaciously observed, precisely because he was able to meet many varied tests of representativity (in the Convention, the clubs, and the popular *sections* of Paris) Robespierre succeeded in becoming the incarnation of what would otherwise have been an impossibly fluid revolutionary political sovereignty.[24]

The state should serve the nation. But what did the people want and how should the state be structured?

Although the Jacobins gave ever more convoluted answers to these questions, they initially and sensibly proposed that both the Jacobin clubs and the state's political agencies (ranging from municipal administrations to the National Convention) should simply listen to the people. At first, Jacobins considered the claims of any popular movement, including violent ones, worth pondering. They thought it normal that spectators should be allowed to comment noisily and sometimes aggressively on the decisions the nation's deputies might be deliberating at that very moment.[25] They set great importance on whatever petitions might be sent to them; and the clubs themselves often chose to petition elected or appointed authorities. Delegations were frequently invited to their halls. For some minutes and, at times, hours, self-sponsored emissaries would sit among delegates or club members so that all might deliberate together. On June 19, 1790, in an unconscious parody of this genre, the ex-Prussian baron von Clootz—now renamed Anacharsis, who also called himself "the orator of mankind"—led to the assembly a delegation of more or less disguised foreigners who were supposed to represent the many but now Jacobinically united nations and races of man. At the same time, the Jacobins obviously listened to some petitioners more than they did to others. At Robespierre's behest, they expelled Clootz from the Paris Jacobin club on December 12, 1793, and executed him on March 22 of the following year.

The polls, Jacobin instinct suggested, were a place where the voice of the assembled people might be heard. A nationwide election or referendum was the simplest and truest way to ascertain the will of the sovereign nation. Of course, the purpose of the nation's assemblies in Paris was to act for the nation as a whole, but potentially, the people remained forever sovereign. In July 1791, for example, after the king's flight to Varennes, the club at Clermont-Ferrand first asserted that a republic should be proclaimed and the National Assembly allowed fifteen days to do so, and then decided—when they were disappointed in their hopes—that the assembly should be dissolved and new elections held.[26]

The issue of unscheduled popular consultation climaxed during the trial of the king in January 1793, when the Girondins, who wanted to stop the progression of the Revolution, gradually lost control of the Convention. Although they had been the first to call for its convening in July 1791, they now reasoned with equally impeccable Jacobin logic that the execution of the king was too great a matter to be settled by the Conventionnels without consulting the whole of the French nation. The people, said the Girondins, should decide this issue for themselves. But this democratic proposal was rejected out of hand by the more leftist Montagnards, who suspected (as the Girondins also did, of course) that the likely outcome of such a plebiscite would run against them. France, argued the leftist Jacobins in the club at Marseilles, was a "representative government." An appeal to the people would "rip apart our unity and indivisibility." Direct democracy might be good in theory, but its effect would be to destabilize the Convention, which was "the center of our sovereignty."[27]

Moreover, arguing one side of this question (on behalf of the parliamentarians' right to judge, and against a popular appeal) did not preclude using an inverse argument when the need arose. Shortly after the death of the king the Jacobins of Marseilles on February 22, 1793, once again reversed themselves and asked that the Convention order the recall of all the deputies who had voted against the king's death. Sensibly enough, in this new context, the Brissotins responded by wrapping themselves in the mantle of the parliamentary inviolability and supremacy they had just denied. Even the Convention, they argued, could not rescind their mandates. They had received them from the people, and once that vote had been taken, nothing could supersede it. No assembly, not even one empowered to draft a constitution, could force them to resign.

A similar *chassé croisé* took place a few weeks later in April 1793 when the Montagnard Conventionnels rejected Condorcet's radically democratic constitution, which not only granted electoral rights to foreigners but included also a Girondin-inspired provision for the citizen's right to insurrection.[28] The radicalizing Montagnards—especially dependent on the support of the Paris crowd—understood that to ratify that constitution was ipso facto to vote for new elections, which they feared losing nationwide. The Montagnards, though in practice the most radical wing of the Jacobin club, then decided to reject the Girondin ultrademocratic plan, which, in theory, should have appealed to them.

Because a credible, Jacobinically correct argument could be mounted both for or against direct democracy, ways of deciding what the nation's will really was had to be at once stable and unsteady. "Amidst this universal agitation of both hearts and spirits," explained the far left Aixois Jacobins, "civic feeling must learn to constrain itself, to withdraw from time to time so that the influence of virtue [the scribe had written in and then crossed out *Vérité* (truth) instead of virtue!] will not be lost when it defends the interests of the fatherland."[29]

Ascertaining the nation's true will was a first (and difficult) step. Institutionalizing this apprehension of the nation's will was yet more difficult. A first and (momentarily) obvious answer seemed to be that the will of the nation was embodied in the Constitution, in the harmonized cooperation of "King, Law, and Nation" (Le roi, la loi, la nation). Jacobins—legalistic and eager, as was often said, "to conform to the laws"—fully expected that the successive revolutionary constitutions would become for the French what the Constitution had for Americans, a fetishist document through which the will of the nation was visible at all times. The Jacobin clubs, we should remember, were first known as the "Sociétés des amis de la constitution" (Societies of the Friends of the Constitution).

At the moment of its inception, therefore, many of them hailed the Constitution of September 3, 1791, as a perfect national monument—indeed, as "the most perfect masterpiece that had ever been created by the hand of man."[30] Molding this document had been a cathartic experience. "From the sanctity of this act" of drafting the Constitution, explained a friend of the publicist Bonneville, "comes civil religion, this cult of the law that uplifts the soul, advances thought, gives burning love for the fatherland, conserves and supports the superb edifice of the state."[31] The club at Bergerac, in January 1792, when revolutionaries were already much divided, decided that the *clubbistes* "would rather die than change any part of the Constitution."[32] Diffident citizens would soon be won over, and the Jacobins of Vitry-le-François expected that "the Constitution would be better loved when it was better known."[33] In the spring of 1793, appalled by the conflict of the Montagne and the Gironde, many clubs reminded their friends in Paris that constitutions were like a sacred ark. Much later, the slogan "Bread and the Constitution of 1793" also became a rallying cry for the far left, bespeaking some unspecified devotion to the idea if not the fact of constitutionality.

And yet, in practice, constitutionalism never acquired durable specificity for the Jacobins. In America, by contrast, the debate between federalists and antifederalists was warmly argued, and the public then ratified the Constitution (however lamely) at the polls. But in France constitution making was protracted, and the definitive adoption of the nation's charter occurred anticlimactically in the fall of 1791, when the revolutionary consensus on the monarch's role had been sadly eroded by the king's flight to Varennes earlier in the year. Moreover, the succession of one constitution-mongering assembly after another severely damaged the prestige of any basic text.

A self-proclaimed Constituent Assembly, self-empowered to establish its own ground rules (though not formed for that purpose), emerged from the Estates General on June 20, 1789. And this was only the beginning of a drawn-out pattern. Starting in August 1791, prominent Jacobins in and out of the Jacobin club in Paris (Condorcet, Pétion, and Brissot) urged the election of a Convention empowered to rewrite the nation's charter. They succeeded all too well: this assembly, which sat from September 1792 to

October 1795, drew up not just one but two constitutions—a text in 1793, which was never applied, and another constitution in 1795, which lasted until Bonaparte's military coup of 18 Brumaire (November 9, 1799).

The one national assembly that did not have constitution-making powers (the Legislative Assembly, which sat from October 1, 1791, to September 20, 1792) became discredited to the point of powerlessness and proved unable to control either the executive branch of the government before the fall of the monarchy or the Paris Commune afterward.

A comparison of legal innovation in the French and American republics also reveals the feebleness of the Jacobins' respect for constitutionalism and accepted law. Americans not only accepted their new Constitution as a fact, they were also quite reluctant to change their older civil laws. In the recently constituted United States even the most adamant revolutionaries (like Samuel Adams) unthinkingly accepted as legitimate British common law traditions, which were to remain unchanged—and restraining—until well after 1800.

By contrast, the Jacobin conception of law (as of the Constitution) was far more abstract and easily swayed by theories of jurisprudence. Before the French Revolution, modernizing but still conservative lawyers had struggled to reshape rather than replace older and feudal habit into a current, coherent, and abstractly acceptable code of law, just as Lord Mansfield had adapted English common law to commercial business needs a few decades before. But after 1789 French national assemblies focused on making new law, both civil and criminal, so as to fit a new jurisprudence into the changing spirit of the Revolution.

In the renewed debate of August 1791 on individual rights, many Jacobins insisted once again that rights came first, and the law or the Constitution second. "The true constitution," wrote Rousseau, "is not graven in bronze or marble . . . It is in the habits, customs, above all, opinion, that is in the heart of all citizens."[34]

Gradually, for the Jacobins, in 1792 and 1793, the fate of revolutionary sovereignty became far more important than the scraps of paper on which they had, at first, set much store. And some of them did continue to see that "a coming together of people is not the people" (un attroupement n'est pas le peuple).[35] But more and more Jacobins habitually took to theoretical justifications of illegality.

From both Locke and Rousseau, as well as from the commonplaces of Enlightenment rhetoric, Jacobins understood the idea of a binding contract between subject and king, or between citizen and constitution. Ultimately, however, they treated written political compacts as ad hoc arrangements that, in exceptional circumstances, true believers had the right to change at will for the sake of a higher good, namely, the progress of the Revolution.[36]

Repentant and newly conservative ex-Jacobins who had come to fear a revolution spinning out of their control did of course argue for the nation's Constitution above all else. But their sudden espousal of legalism merely confirmed the anticonstitutionalist suspicions of orthodox, hard-core Montagnards still intent on the progression of the Revolution. As the ranks of disabused Jacobins grew with every revolutionary hiccup, the opposing Jacobin radicals became more and more casual in their defense of written charters. As their Marseilles opponents put it, orthodox Jacobins "always spoke of Revolutions, and never of the Constitution."[37]

For those determined Jacobins who wanted to carry the politics ever further because they feared that Jacobinism would collapse if the Revolution faltered, what came to matter was the spirit not the letter of the law. In his praise of convulsive sexual creativity, the Jacobinical Marquis de Sade (1740–1814) touched a vital nerve when he exalted the "sages législateurs" of antiquity who had understood, he said, that insurrection was the permanent state of a republic.

Jefferson once suggested that a complete governmental and legislative overhaul should be made in every generation. This theory was not realized in America, but it was idealized by his French revolutionary counterparts, with a predictable effect on the prestige of constitutions as the limiting expressions of the nation's higher will.

As faith in the nation's Constitution waned, so did, a fortiori, its first practical embodiment—the belief in the sacrosanct attributes of the national representative assemblies the Constitution authorized. In time, even those Jacobins who approved of charters in principle came to question the legitimacy of constitutionally mandated deliberative assemblies.

Initially, Jacobins praised these bodies to the sky. In 1789 and again in 1792, the National Assembly and the Convention enjoyed great prestige as the obvious counterweight to the discredited monarchy. At first, any criticism of the Constituent Assembly seemed unthinkable, so unanimously accepted was the Third Estate's decision to proclaim itself a constitution-making body. In these early months, all Jacobins agreed that politics should function in a "representative" rather than a "democratic" system.

In September 1790 Barnave explained to the club in Paris that it would be unseemly for the *clubbistes* to censure as erroneous a judgment which had been submitted to the assembly and on which it had not yet ruled.[38] In later years, after 1792, when the assembly's monarchic foil had vanished, even Robespierre acknowledged that "a democracy is not a state where the people alone settle all public business."[39] In the typically glib wording of Barère, the republic was indivisible, but its government was representative. Assemblies could not be written off as ciphers. Electoral procedures were sacrosanct, and Jacobins as a rule did not criticize established methods of indirect elections (voting for electors who elected delegates), which were used in 1791, and again after 1794, as they were also, of course, in the American system of presidential choice.

True Jacobins never seriously considered a dictatorial or military political solution to their political problems. Tactically—because of the struggle against the king—and theoretically also, given the Jacobins' enlightened principles, the national assemblies from 1789 to 1792 garnered much good will. In the early months of the Revolution some clubs (whose members had not quite understood the implications of the universalist Revolution) addressed their petitions to "nos seigneurs [lordships] de l'Assemblée Nationale."[40] Jacobins in 1789 and 1790 willingly entrusted the nation's fate to the deputies' sense of "public felicity." Sieyès justified their autonomy in an ingenious way that brought together Adam Smith and Rousseau. In a large country, as in an economically efficient world, participation had to be specialized. Just as different workers made different parts of a single nail, so would political men (deputies) represent the nation, which would not cease to be a single, larger, Rousseauean, and organic entity.

Jacobins were confirmed partisans of a single assembly. The idea of second house on the model of the United States Senate was discussed in Paris in September 1789 and overwhelmingly voted down. The specter of the British House of Lords and, more important, Rousseauean assumptions about the indivisibility of the national will, vitiated a solution of this kind. "Liberty, equality, but never two chambers," read a sign on the walls of the club at Argentan, expressing a concern for the nation's single will that also made it impossible for Jacobins to accept the notion of a thoroughly independent judicial system.[41]

In their speeches and in their laws, then, Jacobins paid lip service not just to these single assemblies but to the notion of the separation of powers also, a concept which they equated, vaguely, with limitations of monarchic power. Nonetheless, their craving for unity dramatically affected what they thought of the rights and functions of not just assemblies but of bureaucracies as well. In the high theory of Jacobinism, pragmatically speaking, the role of any state institution was of necessity circumscribed. Of what practical use was the state if all citizens lived simple and harmonious lives? In his speech of March 13, 1794, to the Convention, Saint-Just criticized a polity that had almost been "unsurped by functionaries [*la cité est presque unsurpée*]" who monopolized state jobs and dominated "l'opinion dans les sociétés populaires." "Le Gouvernement est révolutionnaire," he went on, "mais les autorités ne le sont pas intrinsèquement."[42] In the end, the Jacobins' attitudes to both assemblies and bureaucracies resembled their feelings about the Constitution: they were legitimate only to the extent that they manifested the people's true and united will.

Indignant doubts about representatives' indifference to the wishes of the clubs soon rose to the surface. Especially galling was the deputies' decision to distinguish between fully enfranchised, active citizens and partially unenfranchised, passive citizens. Many Jacobins deemed this distinction so invidious, and so contrary to the Rights of Man, as to void the claim to representation of the assembly that had approved it.

Another wave of doubt about the assembly's right to rule assailed the *clubbistes* with the king's flight to Varennes and calls for the creation of a republic. In September 1791 Jacobin anxieties arose again when the Constituent Assembly forbade the clubs to file collective petitions. By the early summer of 1792 most clubs were overtly critical of the (now Legislative) Assembly. François Chabot, in a famous speech of June 28, 1792, for the first time railed against the assembly, powerless, as he saw it, because "strangled by the [monarchic] Constitution." And one month later (two weeks before the overthrow of the monarchy in August 1792) a Parisian Jacobin explained that the people "might be forced to recapture its sovereignty." The gap between clubs and legislature yawned ever larger, and was shut only in the summer of 1793 when Montagnard Jacobins came to dominate both the National Convention and the clubs.

After 1791 the many provincial Jacobins who wished to discredit the assembly fell back on various arguments, some of them anticonstitutional and populist (*vox populi, vox dei*), some of them legalistic. Since the issues that had divided the nation flowed from decisions taken by the National Assembly, did it not make sense, asked these Jacobins, that it should submit to a popular vote? How could the assembly itself decide an issue where its own sovereignty had been questioned? That would have made it at once judge and jury, and that could not be (an argument, incidentally, the Jacobins vigorously rejected when in January 1793 they found themselves having to prosecute the king and pass judgment on him).

In stages of disbelief, in late 1791 Jacobins distanced themselves from the Constitution, from the national assemblies, and from the deputies that sat in them; many Jacobins decided in early 1792, as one of them phrased it, that "le titre de député ne désaristocratise pas les aristocrates" (the title of deputy does not disaristocratize aristocrats). When monarchic anti-Jacobin deputies became obdurately conservative after the flight to Varennes, many Jacobin clubs denounced them as unfit to continue as members of the assembly. In Robespierre's logic, the will of deputies could not be denied when they "isolated themselves from their own work,"[43] but they lost that prerogative when they represented either sectarian interests or merely themselves. In early August 1792 he denounced "representative despotism."[44] Clubs stripped of membership deputies to the National Assembly who had voted the wrong way. At Châtelleraut, on August 1, 1792, a *clubbiste* suggested that the primary assemblies be convoked to elect new deputies who would help those already sitting so that the downfall of the monarchy might then be decreed.[45] Robespierre decried the "conspiracy of the deputies of the people against the people." Lists were published of monarchic deputies in the fall of 1791, as were in 1793 the names of Conventionnels who had voted for Louis's death, holding up all to public disgrace. On June 16, 1793, in the Paris club, Louis Dufourny argued that he "did not think that deputies can allow themselves to direct public opinion, because they themselves must be guided by it. Their task is to pass decrees and not to create the public spirit. To do so would be to act aristocratically."[46] It did not matter that some constituents might agree with some deputies: in the theory of Jacobinism, because the elected mandatories of the nation represented a fraction of the general will rather than some particular provincial place, a shift in the nation's (general) will implied that deputies should change their minds as well or be removed. Barbaroux, on October 9, 1792, thus suggested that a new Convention be convened at Bourges, to be made up of the *suppléants* of the then sitting Conventionnels, that is to say, of the men who had been elected in September to replace Conventionnels who might die or resign.

Just as the Jacobins argued that public opinion (whenever it turned against them) had been corrupted, so did the leaders of excluding groups within the assemblies turn on excluded deputies, calling them corrupt, conspiratorial, hypocritical, and malevolent. The Feuillants and the Girondins, Barnave in 1791, Brissot in 1793, and Robespierre in late 1794 (all of them leading Jacobins at one time or another) were damned by surviving Jacobins with the same epithets they had once hurled against their predecessors.

*I*n a political context where no laws or deputies could count on unswerving Jacobin loyalties, the situation of the king was clearly desperate.

In June and July 1789 Louis XVI, who had seemingly and selflessly accepted popular sovereignty, was wildly popular. As "the restorer of French liberties" he had generously placed the nation above his own powers. He had shown that he understood his place not just in relation to the assembly as the embodiment of the nation's will but in relation to revolutionary goodness as well. It thus made practical sense for soon-to-be Jacobins to want to associate the king with the business of government, and he was assigned a suspensive veto on September 7, 1789. This choice did not after all categorically deny the people's will. In theory, it made the king the common denominator of the nation's past, present, and future wills.

But even in 1789 many future Jacobins felt ambivalent about his role. Given their political principles, members of the Constituent Assembly could not assign to the king any true law-making powers. No Jacobin could have accepted that. Even diplomacy and the ability to make war and peace were in essence removed from the king's control. In the words of the abbé Grégoire, the king was like a priest; his function (and that of his bureaucracy) was not to rule but to serve the nation. Nor in the end was there much room for the king in their cultural system. Any sans-culotte could be expected to be good and civic-minded; but in the Jacobin scheme of things, kings were inherently suspect. As Saint-Just said on November 13, 1792, during the king's trial, in a short speech that instantly made him famous, "on ne peut régner innocemment" (no man can reign innocently).

Therefore, reasoned the Jacobins of 1791 and 1792, the king's veto, if it ran against the manifest and permanent will of the nation, could not really be applied. Though constitutional in the strict sense of the word, the monarch's veto seemed to them unconstitutional in the true sense of the word. "Now that the French have declared themselves to be the terror of tyrants," wrote a *clubbiste* at Apt, "it is incumbent on their king either to tremble or to prove he is their father."[47]

In June 1791, when the king ran away from the Revolution and thereby renounced the conciliatory views that had been attributed to him in the late summer of 1789, Jacobins all over France were shocked. They had sincerely believed the king had accepted his new symbolic role. They also sincerely believed that it was he and not they who had broken the constitutional compact of 1789. Had they not remained steadfast in their acceptance of laws they did not like, such as the distinction of passive and active citizens? They had been docile, respectful, nonfactional, and apolitical. The Jacobins of Aix, for example, who were among the most radical and violent of Jacobins, explicitly described themselves as apolitical, as "hommes vrois [*sic*], justes, et utiles à la patrie" (true men, just, and useful to the fatherland). But in the summer of 1791, Jacobins concluded that the king and *aristocrates* were leading France to civil war. As the club of Tulle put in a letter to the district's administrators, the *clubbistes* had "perhaps respected laws too much."[48]

Between Louis's restoration in mid-July 1791 and the fall of the monarchy on August 10, 1792, the monarch's prestige decayed inexorably. Every one of Louis's fitful assertions of his presence, especially when he vetoed legislation, brought about a flood of warnings from the clubs, reminding him to heed the nation's will. By February of 1792, clubs were making overt Republican noises once again.

Unable to accept the Constitution, the king, the assemblies, or the deputies as the unquestioned expressions of the nation's single purpose, the Jacobins gradually realized—and rather to their own surprise—that they themselves, assembled in their clubs, were the best spokespeople for the nation's elusive will. As a Dijon *clubbiste* wrote in an address to the Convention, "the popular society is nothing . . . but the nation itself."[49] At Beauvais, when joined by a delegation of the sans-culotte militia (the *armée révolutionnaire*), the *clubbistes* decided that they were now the people. The club, they explained, "had ceased to be a society and would now exercise the rights of an assembled people in order to weigh judgment on the [region's] administrators and their clerks."[50] Jacobins had at first intended (in

1790–91) to be no more than the mirrors that made clear for every citizen the shape of his or her own soul. But they gradually decided (in 1791–92) that they should also be the nation's lanterns and finally (in 1793–94) the republic's unforgiving sword as well.

Serving a representative function had not been part of the Jacobins' original purpose at all. To the contrary, as has been seen, in 1789 and early 1790 still, the *clubbistes* had set as their task the mere interpretation to the nation of the expressions of the nation's will that had been formulated by the National Assembly and the king of the French, as Louis XVI was then styled. Institutionally, the idea that the clubs should have more than an advisory function, and a limited one at that, was at first denied by many prominent Jacobins themselves. In a debate with Desmoulins, Brissot, who dominated the Paris club, argued that the Paris Jacobins could hardly claim to represent opinion, much less shape events, since the clubs were of their nature elitist. How many members have the opportunity to speak? he asked. And of these, he went on, how many of them were passive citizens, that is to say, of those plain people who had made the Revolution?[51] In late June 1792, when a Paris *clubbiste* suggested that Jacobins all over France should put pressure on the nation's elected deputies, militant Jacobins balked. "Without a doubt," replied an influential member, Pierre Robert, "there should be an impelling center, but I do not think that this center, this impulsion, should be in our society."[52]

Nonetheless, the Jacobins' collective sense of self grew ever stronger. After having seen themselves first as educators of the nation, then as advisers to the nation's elected officials, and finally as mentors,[53] the Jacobins imagined themselves to be the nation's censors, as men empowered by opinion to confirm the right choices of the deputies.

In time, the Jacobins also came to see themselves as constitutionally sovereign, or at least cosovereign, with the nation's assemblies. When the early compromise between the king (the "Premier fonctionnaire public"—or first public servant—as many *clubbistes* liked to call him)[54] and the National Assembly broke down, many Jacobins felt as the *clubbistes* at Montpellier did that "we would have to ask if it was not a mistake to say that everything should be given to the representatives and nothing held back for the people who must work together with the representatives."[55] After the summer of 1793, if asked what the nation's opinion was, many Jacobins would have responded brutally: "whatever is being thought in the clubs." At times, the *clubbistes* obliged the elected public authorities to take revolutionary oaths in the clubs—in the words of the Bourgoin *clubbistes*, "en face du peuple souverain" (face to face with the sovereign people).[56] At Limoges the *clubbistes* suggested that only members of the popular societies be allowed to vote in coming elections.

When dissenting opinions and events proved more stubborn than expected, Jacobins could not help but think that they should act for the nation directly. To save the nation's true will, they were prepared to struggle against its falsely institutionalized and merely apparent will.

On March 12, 1793, when the sans-culotte leader Jean Varlet urged the Jacobins to purge the Convention, he was shouted down and told that the law-abiding Jacobin club was not like the more radical and populist Cordelier club. But two months later, as Varlet had suggested, the Jacobins did purge the Convention. (Prudently, Barère, on behalf of the Committee of Public Safety, initially suggested that the deputies who had been removed resign. A few actually did so to maintain the fiction of an unsullied national representation, even if it had been achieved at their personal expense.)

Spurred by a new determination and anxiety, Jacobins worked hard to shut down rival societies. Like soldiers who destroy villages to save them, Jacobins preserved liberty by silencing its enemies. In December 1790, at Aix-en-Provence, the Jacobins forced the municipality to shut down the Society of the Friends of Religion, of Peace, and of the King, a mere three weeks after its founding. Many other examples of this prophylactic censorship could be cited.

Jacobins had no scruples about silencing their enemies and "conspiring for liberty." Just as diplomats are honest men sent abroad to lie for their country, the Jacobins were honest men who were at times "forced" to engage in excesses or untruthfulness for the sake of a higher message. They certainly believed that truth, eventually, would free all men; but they also knew that the "Machiavellianism of the people," like censorship, was fully justified, for some short time at least. Not everyone, they thought, deserved all of the truth all of the time: in the words of Condorcet (a rather gentle Jacobin) "the word 'revolutionary' only applies to those revolutions whose object is liberty."[57]

To assert their ideological and self-imposed purpose, the clubs soon took to purging themselves, just as they had purged other associations before.

The *clubbistes* of Courthézon, a small southern town, put it quite well: their aim was not to exclude but to reinforce harmony. If dissent could not be brought over to some right opinion, where a right opinion was known to exist, then disenfranchisement was the only solution at once sensible and democratic. It was time to consider, they concluded in the summer of 1794, "whether in our popular society there might be some members who were not in the spirit of the Revolution or [not] in conformity with the laws of our Constitution [and whether] we ought not to reject him from our society so as not to be in the situation of daily disaccord with one another."[58]

The mechanisms of self-purging varied. Sometimes, a visiting Conventionnel would eliminate most or, for that matter, all of a club's members. Sometimes, the *clubbistes* would entrust to the most pure of their members the choice of those who would remain.

Inevitably, however, such bloodlettings fed two different but mutually reinforcing and destructive trends. Jacobins, as they became more truculent, also cut themselves off from the broader public. And as the Jacobins' political base narrowed, their ability to rule the nation by example or consent also shrank, a wholly unforeseen development that furthered their exasperated determination to rule by all or any means.

By the summer of 1794 the purges had drastically thinned Jacobinism's ranks. A famous cartoon of late 1794 portrayed Robespierre, standing amid a sea of deserted guillotines, and about to execute the executioner. Another and more thoughtful rendition showed him surrounded by skulls and bones, about to guillotine himself!

Many clubs urged members to attend—all citizens had an obligation to be involved—and then purged some of the ones who had complied. At Orléans, of 800 Jacobins, only 150 were left in the club by July 1794. Though the number of clubs rose dramatically in the countryside in late 1793 and 1794 (on paper in any case), Jacobinism's hold over the nation became ever more tenuous.

Some Jacobins did not mind being in a minority because they assumed they would eventually become a majority, and then a community. They did not divide the political spectrum into a right, a left, and a center (although these terms were invented at the time). They saw instead a left (namely, themselves), which represented the nation's higher will; a corrupted *aristocrate* faction; and a *plaine* or *marais* (swamp) made up of pusillanimous people who were as yet uncommitted to the Jacobins' view of things. Centrists were men of good faith but small energy, timid people who cared about the nation but whose ideas had not yet gelled.

When the moderate but Jacobin-minded Republican Marseilles *sections* rose up against the local left-Hébertist Marseillais Jacobins, some of the moderates' sympathizers in an outlying Provençal town neatly expressed the Jacobins' belief in the reality of politically transformative epiphany. All that had been needed was for their partisans to rise, and "cet empire magique d'une minorité sanguinaire fut détruit par leur réveil" (from their coming awake, the magical empire of a bloody minority was destroyed).[59]

Jacobins were wily in the pursuit of their varied goals. Robespierre, for example, was an especially crafty leader, a fluid ideologue who managed over time to assert with unwavering aplomb contradictory opinions and, as Mirabeau once quipped, believed everything he said. The plotters who overthrew Robespierre often congratulated themselves on having been particularly successful conspirators.[60] For the sake of a higher truth had they lied so successfully.

It is the privilege of the pure at heart that they can, in good conscience, be wholly devious.

6

Jacobins as the Free Citizens
of a One-Party State

Although Abraham arouses my admiration, he also appalls me. The person who denies himself and sacrifices himself because of duty gives up the finite in order to grasp the infinite and is adequately assured . . . But the person who gives up the universal in order to grasp something even higher that is not the universal—what does he do? Is it possible that this can be anything but a spiritual trial? And if it is possible, but the individual makes a mistake, what salvation is there for him?

Søren Kierkegaard, *Fear and Trembling*

In the first one and a half years of Revolution, from the summer of 1789 to the winter of 1790, the Jacobins wished to be the devoted interpreters of the revolutionary state *and* the free agents of libertarian principle. French men and women, regenerated by liberty, they thought, were bound to accept revolutionary citizenship as well as their settled place in daily life. The Jacobins did not see the need to use the state to make that happen. Sylvain Maréchal's play of October 1793, *Le Jugement dernier des rois, prophétie en un acte en prose* (The Last Judgment of All Kings: A Prose Prophecy in One Act), often performed in both Paris and the provinces, depicted a desert island where liberated sans-culottes spoke a language of transparent truth and where politics had ceased to exist.[1]

To their tragic dismay, the Jacobins found that many people refused the Revolution's definition of their rights. Even worse, when libertarian Jacobins continued to serve the revolutionary state long after it had become tyrannical, they did so to dreadful effect because not the least of the many historical ironies which bore down upon the Jacobins was that their hopes of libertarian reconciliation proved to be historically counterproductive. Jacobins wanted to promote citizenship and deny divisive lines of class not just for France in their own time but for the entire world and forever. Yet, the long-range course of their tyranny had the opposite effect.

The "bourgeoisie" did not make the French Revolution, but the Revolution did make a bourgeoisie. No one in 1789 even began to foresee the extent to which the events would give the lie to the Revolution's civic vision of classless harmony.

Jacobinism during the years 1792–1794 can of course be seen as a drive to power rather than a passage into progressive degeneracy from an earlier state of historical innocence. Readers of Michel Foucault, for example, whose work is associated with Western culture's relentless emphasis on domination, could certainly conclude that Jacobins were from the first obsessed by discipline and self-discipline. Early conciliatory steps—like their endorsement of existing civil society—can be read as calculating gestures.

This view of a Jacobin thirst for power has added plausibility today because it dovetails with current historiographical sensibilities. A broad literature on imperialism and sexual domination reinforces our postmodern sense that "culture wars" are not just about culture but about control.

But Jacobins would have found such an explanation of their actions disconcerting and bizarre, insulting even. They would have pointed out that their initial stance in the period 1789–1791 was of genuine tolerance, that in these early days, they had sincerely been the politically neutral agents of universally accepted opinion and authority. Were they not the Friends of the Constitution, whose purpose was merely to explain the national charter to those of their fellow citizens who did not understand it as well as they? The Jacobins saw themselves as ecumenical uniters, and not as a factional party at all.

*B*ut not for long, of course. In January and February of 1790, for example, Jacobins did little electioneering despite the importance of many of the posts at stake. They assumed that their candidates would prevail because common sense always did so. In the municipal elections of July 1790 and of late 1790 into 1791, however, their electoral involvement grew exponentially. Though the great turning points of the Revolution did not hinge on election results, these contests were important to Jacobins as proof of their democratic ways.[2] Many prominent Jacobins were elected to local office, notably in Marseilles, Grenoble, and Toulon, all of which would prove to be Jacobin strongholds throughout the Revolution. To guide the electorate, Brissot in 1790 organized a Society of Patriotic Candidates that was widely copied in 1791 and 1792. Many clubs drew up lists of politically suitable candidates. In August 1792 Roland, the minister of the interior, actually used state funds to subsidize sectarian Girondin electioneering. Jacobins also influenced the promotion of Catholic clerics who had accepted the Civil Constitution of the Clergy.

Hereafter passionate Jacobin involvement in all elections became and remained the rule. (By contrast, nationwide, seldom did one person in five or so bother to go to the polls.) When some six thousand primary assemblies convened on August 26, 1792, for the elections to the postmonarchic Convention, the Jacobins tried to monopolize the field. In 1793 the Jacobins of Grenoble and Draguignan made it their business to keep antipatriots away from the polls.[3]

The staging of elections was only the most visible way in which Jacobins tried to influence the political system. They also acted more covertly to concert the action of patriots within legislative or administrative bodies they did not yet dominate. Indeed, the first important instance of this pattern came in 1789. In the Breton club of Versailles future Jacobins carefully prepared the theatrical and ostensibly spontaneous renunciation of feudal privileges that took place in the National Assembly on the night of August 4. Similarly, in France as a whole but especially in Paris, patriotic orators routinely used the clubs to rehearse the speeches they would make elsewhere as officials and as deputies.

The trending of the Jacobins toward ever tighter methods can be traced in many ways. The elaboration of ideological orthodoxy and the purging of dissidents, as will be seen, mattered most; but Jacobins also paid close attention to mundane organizational strategy. After 1791 they were eager to keep in touch with one another, and to proselytize.

Much energy was spent finding suitable locales. Ordinarily, Jacobins rented their premises. Eventually, many clubs chose to own a building of their own, often a former church or school. Seeing them comfortably ensconced in a confiscated clerical building that had been nationalized and put up for auction must have riled many an anti-Jacobin.

Money was another constant worry. Initially, the clubs charged fees, as social organizations generally had to.[4] Quickly, however, their rationale was altered. No longer called club dues, the fees were cast as badly needed cash for good works, rent, light, heat, and postage. Costs were high. Some clubs sponsored (unsuccessful) newspapers, which became another financial drain. Clubs delegated representatives and propagandists to the countryside, to other clubs, to Paris, or to regional meetings, all of which required money, a difficult problem since many clubs, especially in 1793–94, lowered or waived their fees altogether to attract a broader membership. Some societies suggested that *clubbistes* pay whatever they could afford. And unsurprisingly, being always short of money, the clubs tried to find the odd franc or livre. They urged members of other clubs to buy their propaganda. They tried to send their club mail through the good offices of elected officials who enjoyed franking privileges. They pursued arrangements with post office officials for bulk mail rates. Exasperated club treasurers sometimes threatened to haul delinquent members before the justices of the peace.

Rule making for the clubs similarly shifted from loosely defined procedures of sociability to more deliberately organized political activities. Although forceful personalities often dominated the clubs, in Paris especially, the Jacobins were communitarians who instinctively preferred direction by committee. The Paris club was run by a twelve-member body that managed the club's finances, a thirty-man committee that filtered applications, and a committee of correspondence, which soon overshadowed the other two. When the time came to purge the clubs, exclusions were decided by specially convoked committees that had been appointed by yet other committees. (France itself, of course, was ruled by a Committee of Public Safety delegated by the Convention to exercise executive power.) Presidents of local clubs were elected monthly; secretaries sat for longer terms, the aim of these rotating arrangements being to guarantee democratic fluidity.

Meetings remained formal. The tone of club life had to reflect the Republican dignity of their proceedings. Clubs insisted on sobriety and excluded inebriated members, who alas were all too numerous: "this is a misfortune common to many sans-culottes who are otherwise excellent patriots."[5] It was not enough to claim, as a member did in Dijon, "that wine had never caused him to change his public character."[6] At Vitry-le-François inebriated members were suspended for one week; a third offense led to exclusion.[7] The *clubbistes* at Pau petitioned the Convention to penalize drinkers.[8] When they were able, Jacobins—much like priests who struggled against drinking during services—ordered neighboring bars shut during their meeting times.[9]

Dogs were not allowed on club grounds. Accounts of debates underlined the occasionally "indecent" behavior of some members and their subsequent exclusion. The Jacobins of Peyrolas decided to punish members who had relieved themselves in the passage ways of the club's building. A first offense would lead to a reprimand; repeaters would be barred.[10] Insulting language was also grounds for disbarment. At Nay a member asked that the society be "preserved" from having to hear the words *bougre* (bugger) and *foutre,* which the "traitor" Hébert had so consistently used.[11] Jacobins had a strong sense of mission and of the dignity of public life. They insisted on the maintenance of decorum. Counterrevolutionary propaganda, after the fall of Robespierre especially, portrayed Jacobins as illiterate drunkards and their meetings as chaotic brawls. Nothing could have been further from the truth.

The timing of club meetings was at first haphazard, but this too was standardized. Clubs that had begun as reading societies were sometimes open round the clock. Members might at any time drop in to read newspapers, chat, or play billiards. But when the tempo of events quickened, club meetings became more purposeful and intense. At the Society of Merck at Bordeaux, whose records have been studied in detail, members met every three or four days. At Bernay, in the Eure, for which complete records survive, the *clubbistes* met about ten times a month.

The nature of debates also changed as the logic of Jacobinism became more clear. In October 1793,[12] clubs were required by law to make their sessions public.

In 1790 *clubbistes* had used passwords and secret codes to communicate confidentially in public places, but when Jacobins revived that habit during the Terror, it was because they feared that *aristocrates* might try to use the clubs to forge false identities.

In these many ways, the Jacobins inched toward becoming a modern, nationwide political party (of a kind). In the eyes of Albert Soboul, the clubs simultaneously became the armature of one-party state ("l'armature d'un parti unique").[13] Jacobins organized cross-club political actions. They wrote letters, and their mail, whose tone is far less formulaic than the better-known accounts and orations of the *clubbistes,* forms the larger part of many Jacobin archives today. They read and wrote newspaper articles. They feted visiting Jacobins. They circularized one another, as they also did the public authorities. At Tulle the club received letters from nineteen other clubs on the occasion of the Feuillant split. At Le Havre, in about five months during the spring and summer of 1794, 113 guests from twenty-nine other societies came to visit.[14] Nor did clubs hesitate to chastise one another when the need arose, as happened during the Feuillant-Jacobin split in the fall of 1791 and the Girondin-Montagnard conflict of the period 1792–93.

Paris was the heart of Jacobinism's ideological mission, and matriarchal terms naturally came to mind to provincial *clubbistes* when they conjured the image of the Paris club. The president of the club at Vitry-le-François, in his inaugural address, described the Parisian society as "this matrix club."[15] At Artonne the *clubbistes* referred to the Paris society as "our common mother."[16] In November 1790 the club at Riom proposed that all clubs send materials to the Paris club, so that it could distribute a news sheet to the provinces conveying the feelings of the network as a whole. In that same year the Jacobins of Lille suggested that clubs from all over France delegate representatives to Paris, as if the club were a kind of national revolutionary paraparliament. Desmoulins in the tenth issue of his paper, the *Révolutions de France et de Brabant*, compared the Paris club to a tree whose roots spread all over France;[17] many provincial clubs were founded, as Lameth claimed in December 1789,[18] by visitors who had seen the Parisians at work.

Strasbourg in January 1790 and Montpellier three weeks later were the first to affiliate themselves with the Paris club, which began in March to send out formal certificates of affiliation. In August 1790, 90 societies were thus connected to the Paris club, a number that rose steadily to 200 in March 1791, 400 in July, and a peak of about 800 in early 1794.

In many places (at Toulouse and Montauban, for example) provincial clubs simply took the Paris society's rules of order as their own. When delegates of southeastern clubs met in the course of a short-lived pro-Parisian federation of clubs held at Marseilles, their insignias were eloquently shaped: "the members of the societies are distinguished by having a card. Those from Paris have a large card."[19] Paris was the heart of the republic, explained a Girondin who had been expelled from the capital, and "wounds to the heart were always fatal."[20]

Over the years, many observers—such as Arthur Young in 1789 and Tocqueville in 1856—have remarked on the passivity of the revolutionized provinces in the face of Parisian fiat. Indeed, for Louis de Cardenal in the

1930s, the ensuing and artificial commonality of local Jacobin options in different parts of France was proof of Jacobinism's superficial hold. How could provincial Jacobins, he asked, who were so different in their unendingly varied local situations, be sincere when they proclaimed identical (Paris-based) principles? "For most of the members of these assemblies," he concluded (wrongly), "the Revolution was more a means than a goal."[21]

Some evidence, of course, supports this view of Jacobins as Paris-dominated country bumpkins. Many provincial Jacobins (and in October 1792 many newly elected Jacobin Conventionnels) were puzzled at first by the ideological quarrels that divided their Parisian brethren. In an injunction to their Parisian peers, who seemed bogged down in personal details, the confused and exasperated *clubbistes* of Strasbourg exclaimed about the Girondins' attack on Marat, "You have decreed his arrest, let him perish on the scaffold if he is a traitor. We don't know either Brissot or Marat. The republic is what we know and it is the only thing we want to know."[22]

Nonetheless, we can conclude that most of the provincial clubs, most of the time, were neither coerced nor deluded. Provincial *sociétaires* were quite able to understand the issues debated in Paris, even if they found the ins and outs of day-to-day politics hard to follow. Ideology mattered a great deal to them. Moreover, the flow of influence was often reciprocated. Parisian word and deed certainly drove provincials to become more bitter and unforgiving; but the mimetic admiration of the provinces likewise steeled the Parisians' resolve. François Xavier Audouin, the secretary of the Paris Jacobins, once wrote to the Jacobins of Limoges, "Why does the republic not see you? Why are the Convention and the Committee of Public Safety not informed of your successes? You do not realize how influential are the statements that are read to the Convention. They are like a signaling light that everyone looks to, and whenever a good example is presented there, it is close to being adopted."[23] If Paris was the heart of the Revolution, the messages from the clubs were the "regenerated blood" that kept the heart alive. Significantly, unlike most of the regional Jacobin clubs, the Paris club never created local branches directly.

Indeed, in parts of France where social or political tensions were running at fever pitch, many local clubs outstripped the "commune centrale du globe" in their radical demands. The local clubs agitated for the distinction between active and passive citizens in 1790, for the enactment of the *maximum* on prices in the summer of 1793, and for the formation of Committees of Surveillance, derived from the societies' own "committees of research," which had been designed to deal with the club's confidential correspondence. At Pontarlier and Limoges the clubs enforced procedures that antedated the law of suspects of September 14, 1793. At times, not just isolated clubs but entire regional Jacobin associations developed a national purpose that preceded the hardening of views of the capital: in July 1791 the activist club of Valence, the new *chef-lieu* or capital of the radical Drôme department, convened a federation of the clubs of the entire department in order to radicalize Jacobinism nationwide; and in the summer of 1793 the supposed need to officialize the use of terror likewise flowed to Paris from below.

*I*deologically and institutionally, provincial Jacobins found themselves traveling much further than they had ever dreamed possible in their early days. In 1790 they had begun as local worthies aiming to elucidate the decisions of the National Assembly to their fellow citizens: in January 1791 Antonelle, a rich noble who had become the Jacobin mayor of Arles and who would later preside over the Paris Jacobins, explained that the newly created Jacobin club of his city would soon become "the eye and the arm of this wise and gentle, firm and fraternal administration that henceforth can only act in concert with the public's will, which we must enlighten so that it can help us."[24]

In 1792 and early 1793 they became the ideologized members of a national "quasi-party" of opposition. And in a third mutation, in mid- and late 1793, they became the state.

A number of practical issues triggered the Jacobins' move from tolerance to state service and repression. The ideological connection between Jacobinism and militarism was especially important, and this link found practical embodiment in the relationship of the clubs to the National Guard, a shifting relationship that clearly facilitated their move from spectator to participatory politics.

Jacobins were deeply committed to civilian government. One of Robespierre's prophetic motives for opposing a French declaration of war against Austria in 1792 was his fear that military involvement would eventually lead to military rule.[25] *Quis custodiet ipsos custodes?*

The creation of a new and civilian army, the National Guard, spoke both to their cult of militarized citizenship and to their fear that an unrepentant, royalist military might stifle the new revolutionary state. Launched on July 13, 1789, the new institution had two advantages. It involved the citizen in the life of the nation, and it short-circuited the regular army, which in the years 1790–1792 was still dominated by noble-born, often counterrevolutionary officers.

The clubs were close to the guardsmen. In some towns, belonging to the National Guard was a prerequisite for club membership.[26] At Vesoul the club itself had spun off from the guard.[27] At Lille the club combined its antecedent Patriotic Union of the City and Castle Bailiwick of Lille with the Club of Fabricators, Manufacturers, and Artists and the Salon of the National Guard. Club meetings were often scheduled to enable members to participate in guard activities. Invitations were traded between the clubs and the guardsmen, who at times appeared en masse in the clubs with flags, fife, and drum. Near Marseilles, which had a club of guardsmen, *clubbistes* and guardsmen proselytized together in the backcountry.

Moreover, with the nation at war and the regular army becoming both more radical and more important, the Jacobin clubs increasingly participated in the Revolution's direct military effort, as patriotic onlookers at first and as government official later on.

At first, in September 1790, the National Assembly took umbrage at this politicization of the regular army. It declared illegal the creation of soldiers' and sailors' clubs and specifically barred garrisoned officers and soldiers from attending club meetings. The clubs reacted vigorously to this interdict. In January 1791 the Dunkirk *clubbistes* took it upon themselves to invite members of the local garrison regardless, and on April 29, 1791, the ministry of war rescinded its earlier order. Within weeks, soldiers from many regiments were attending meetings. At Nice half of the club members were military men, and in 1793 some all-military clubs came into being. At the other end of France, in some parts of Normandy, soldiers who were guarding against a British invasion were among the region's most radical members.[28]

Clubs followed military matters closely and looked after the welfare of individual soldiers. At Lille the club discussed ways of entertaining young recruits who were away from home for the first time.[29] The clubs regularly staged banquets in honor of volunteers. Jacobins welcomed returning soldiers, the wounded especially, whose mangled bodies became icons of the republic. Traveling volunteers were sure to find not just praise but food, shelter, and a helping hand along their way. Letters from the front were often read from the podium. Clubs also raised money for French prisoners abroad and visited wounded soldiers at home.[30]

Jacobins had an Orphic view of death and rebirth. True patriots could never really die because they lived in the memory of a harmonious nation. The clubs strove to memorialize the fallen soldiers of the Revolution as examples of patriotic selflessness. At Montauban in April 1791, when church officials refused to officiate at the burial of a guardsman, the local club took the matter in hand. Chabot, soon to be executed for corruption, then gave an oration that recalled the names of all the region's fallen victims.[31] At Reims, as in many other places, the club had prominently displayed a memorial list of heroes and then went one step further by awarding their heroic names to selected members who had done "works that were transcendent and genuinely Republican."[32]

Symbolically, many a club resolved to equip a cavalryman *(le cavalier Jacobin)* on the nationally adopted model that had been launched in August 1792 in Paris by the *section* of the Arcis quarter. That example was soon taken up in the capital's suburbs by the club of La Franciade, formerly known as Saint-Denis. The club at Morlaix boasted that its cavalryman Pierre Bian was in part of African origin, a fact whose universalist meaning did not escape its members.[33] The Strasbourg club suggested that clubs all over the nation raise funds to launch a three-decker man-of-war (the largest kind of vessel then afloat) that would be called *Le Jacobin;* and at the departmental level, many clubs joined together to pay for an entire vessel.[34]

The Jacobins made significant material contributions to the war effort. In the first years of the Revolution, Jacobins probably hastened the decomposition of the royal army,[35] but in later years they did all they could to maintain the morale and equipment of the nation's armed forces on both land and sea. Between May and June 1792 alone, the National Assembly received 650,000 livres from 114 clubs.[36] By 1794 the *clubbistes* had handed over to the army hundreds of thousands of shirts, trousers, and shoes. On April 12, 1794, the club at Lunéville reckoned that it alone had contributed 108,667 francs and 8 sous, 365 pairs of shoes, 64 pairs of boots, 397 pairs of stockings, 181 pairs of pants, 43 overcoats, 73 vests, 25 coats, 671 shirts, 19 hats, 168 pairs of gaiters, 3 crates of bandages, 7 rifles, 17 sabers, 46 breastplates, 55 cartridge boxes, 2 saddles, 50 yards of cloth, and 77 blankets.[37] Women also participated in these matters; in Besançon the women's Jacobin club (named the Friends of Truth and Equality) started as an association of women who had come together to sew clothes for soldiers.

In 1794 the clubs even took it upon themselves to designate the young men and future soldiers who would attend the new Ecole de Mars in Paris, a school intended to shape the militarized cadres of the young republic.

*A*nother concern that led the clubs from observation to administrative involvement and eventually to dictatorship was their desire to support the national currency. The monarchy's deficit had propelled it to its doom, and many of the revolutionary government's day-to-day problems had money as their primary cause.

Because the revolutionaries respected property and because bondholders were, as it happens, close to many of the most prominent revolutionaries (like Mirabeau, a Jacobin and a friend of Parisian capitalists, as they were already called), the Revolution did not repudiate the prerevolutionary debts of the French Crown. Besides, only a respected government—which paid its debts—could borrow. But when financial matters went from bad to worse, and when the assembly voted to create paper money or *assignats* in December 1789, many clubs wrote to Paris to congratulate the deputies on the inception of this monetary instrument, whose creation Desmoulins hailed as a triumph for the Revolution.

The Jacobins approached issues of finance and currency both practically and from a moral point of view. They understood that the value of the *assignats* depended not just on faith in the Revolution but—in part at least—on supply and demand, and also on the expectation of where the curves of supply and demand were likely to meet in the future. They used forced loans, for example, to decrease the amount of circulating currency and lower price increases.

Nonetheless, the Jacobins also wanted to believe in the connections between money, morality, and politics. Saint-Just was hostile to inflation because it weakened the citizen's love of work. Jacobins decried the selfishness of those who rejected revolutionary currency and preferred gold (in itself, they reminded their fellow citizens, a useless metal). The clubs often attributed higher prices and unexpected shortages to conspiratorial plotting. Food was costly, they argued, because it was being shipped out of France;[38] and their fears sharpened with the declaration of war in the spring of 1792, when many clubs suggested that national stocks should be built up with an eye to guaranteeing supplies and driving prices down.

Jacobins were convinced—not wrongly, in the short run—that force could be used to drive up the value of paper money. (The *assignats* rose a bit in value in early 1793, as Jacobins came ever closer to wielding power, and then rapidly became worthless after the fall of Robespierre.) The clubs did what they could to prop them up. Indeed, since paper money was initially issued in large denominations, they organized *caisses patriotiques* (patriotic banks), which issued smaller bills backed by their own credit and which in 1792 were taken over by the municipalities. They denounced speculators who tried to change paper money into gold, an exchange allowed by law until April 1793, when paper became the only legal tender. At Saint-Jean-de-Luz, near Spain, the club asked the Convention to treat metallic money as if it were counterfeit currency.[39] Rather improbably, the *clubbistes* of Lorient pledged never to assign different prices in *assignat* and silver for the same object.[40]

The clubs also took seriously their role in supporting the *maximum*, a key element of the revolutionary government's plan for a guided war economy. Provincial Jacobins strongly approved of the *maximum*, which many provincial clubs had been enforcing de facto before the national law was passed.

In retrospect, we can conclude that the law was profoundly destructive. Although contemporaries did not see it in these terms, this coercive legislation sacrificed long-term economic stability to short-run advantage.[41] Its principal if unintended momentary effect was to enable the state to requisition goods at a fraction of their real costs, a shift that Jacobins perceived in terms of public morality and social fairness rather than of predictable material consequence.

Pressured by the need to act in order to secure popular support and feed the army, Jacobins chose to forget that economic individualism was basic to their purpose. Instead, they reasoned (as others in France had for centuries) that everyone was entitled to eat and that the opponents of the *maximum* were selfish. *Clubbistes* kept a sharp eye on the price of goods, food, and rents.[42]

The clubs dealt with food shortages directly. At home, they oversaw local bakers closely, monitoring the quality of the bread. At Marseilles the club actually took over the business of baking bread in the ovens of the city's fortresses. At Rennes the club asked the municipality to subsidize bakers who could not make ends meet if they were to abide by the rates of the *maximum*.[43] At Bordeaux some bread was sold for a quarter of its market value. In a similar and practical vein, other clubs sang the praises of the potato, advocated the extermination of pets, and urged an interdict on brewing beer (which used hops) or making hair powders that had a flour base. They supported the decree of November 17, 1793, which imposed the dilution of wheat with oats, hops, or chestnuts, now declared to be the ingredients of a new "Republican bread."

To secure these economic goals, the clubs at first used moral pressure to resolve what they took to be an ethical issue. But the Jacobins soon decided to use more efficacious means. Clubs excluded members who overcharged. After the summer of 1793 they took public matters into their own hands, by identifying merchants who were violating the law and by arranging for their immediate arrest. In the spring of 1793 the club at Bourbourg decided to meet daily until it ensured that the *maximum* was everywhere respected.

Jacobins carried out many other police functions. They brought their enemies to the attention of judges and prosecutors. They tracked down draft dodgers and "suspects," a term that was loosely defined in September 1793 when the clubs were authorized to draw up lists of such people.

Early in the summer of 1792 many clubs spontaneously formed departmental "central committees" to gather, in the words of a club at Bordeaux, "intelligence, transmit it to other central committees, and recommend appropriate action."[44]

Inevitably, the clubs and the Revolutionary Tribunals, both in the provinces and in Paris, grew ever closer. In the spring of 1793 many clubs pushed for the creation of tribunals. The clubs frequently acted as informal preliminary bodies that might decide to forward cases to the official courts. At Amiens the local Revolutionary Tribunal actually met on the club's premises. At Lunéville a person who had been acquitted in Paris was reincarcerated when he decided to come home.

An important responsibility involved the *certificat de civisme* (certificate of civic virtue), a kind of political passport without which life could become not just nasty but quite short. (In September 1793, citizens unable to produce these certificates were declared subject to immediate arrest.)

In many places, Paris especially, the clubs, or popular societies as they were called after the summer of 1793, arrogated the right to give out—or withhold—certificates. Initially, in late 1792, this prerogative had been entrusted to the police, to elected authorities, and to the more or less self-started but legally sanctioned Committees of Surveillance, some of which had their origin in the spontaneous creations of local clubs the years before.[45] At Vervins, symbolically, the city hall or *maison commune* also housed the club and the Committee of Surveillance.[46] But in time, particularly after March 1793 when the Convention decided that every municipality should have such a committee, individual Jacobins infiltrated the committees.

This supervision of police action gave great power to the *clubbistes,* to such a degree that in January 1794 an anxious Convention ordered the societies to stop demanding that public officials be able to produce the certificates,[47] whose use was gradually abolished after the summer of 1794.

Jacobins also stepped up their control of elected officials who were not Jacobins. In 1790 they had begun by amicably criticizing local officials, but after 1791 they increasingly aimed to supplant them. The problem, explained Brissot to the Paris club in April 1792, was not that some officials were Jacobins. It was instead that all officials were not yet Jacobins: "would it please heaven that everyone be a Jacobin, from the public servant who sits on the throne to the most humble clerk in the ministerial offices!"[48] After June 1793, when Brissot had been excluded from the club, Jacobins did in fact take over countless important governmental posts. On September 13, 1793, they were entrusted with the supervision of local officials. In November 1793 the Convention decided to circularize them routinely so that they might know what was expected of them by the state. On November 13 clubs were authorized to filter candidates for office. This change of affairs made it difficult for them to go on as critics, a function the clubs never formally abandoned, however. As late as August 1793 the Jacobins of Breteuil, for example, persisted in defining their task as surveillance, not administration.[49]

Jacobin *clubbistes* were now required to look for saltpeter, direct road repairs, pave streets, hunt down wild animals, set the time for local markets, supervise prices, oversee harvesting and threshing, recommend suitable candidates for local office, inspect birth and death records, check mail deliveries, and so on. In April 1793 the war ministry directly asked the clubs for opinions on the reliability of army officers. They were used also to publicize laws and, if need be, to translate them into local dialect.

In brief, Jacobins were very busy. Not unjustly, at Marseilles in the summer of 1793 a conservative Republican faction that had briefly overthrown the more radical group which had previously taken over the local club labeled these left Jacobins as "intriguers and anarchists . . . (who) disposed of everything, pronounced on everything, and arrogated to [themselves] universal power."[50]

*T*he Jacobins' fevered pace reminds us also of the makeshift nature of the revolutionary state. Conventionnels often accepted the clubs as partners because they had no alternative. The First Republic had few officials, and fewer established routines. In a way, the revolutionary government's reliance on terror, on military repression, and on the clubs as well all speak to the inadequate institutional development of the French revolutionary state and to the relative inefficiency of its police. However feared, the revolutionary police was far less efficient than the royal police had been before 1789, or than Napoleon's imperial police would be after 1800.

In any instance, the connection between the clubs and the national assemblies, kept purposefully loose at first, had tightened by mid-1793. In 1791 Jacobins had determined that the Legislative Assembly could do no right. But in 1793 the Convention could do no wrong. Why were the Poles holding out against the Russians? Because, explained the *Nouvelles politiques,* the patriot Tadeusz Kosciusko had of late stayed for some months in Paris and seen the nation's deliberative assembly at work. "It's in the National Convention that he found this sacred fire of liberty, this hatred of tyranny and this love of the people, without which an insurrectionary chief is nothing but a tyrant."[51] Before 1789 publicists had argued that public opinion was above the king. But in 1793 Jacobins concluded that public opinion was not above but within the National Convention. True, admitted a Jacobin journalist at Besançon, the news of Robespierre's conspiracy in August 1794 was shocking, but his errors proved only that all should stick with the Convention through thick and thin: "Let us bless . . . the supreme being who has guided the hand of our representatives . . . who has enlightened the people about their true interests, and who has rallied it around our national representatives."[52]

The Conventionnels *en mission,* who radiated out from Paris to the provinces, also had a close connection to the clubs. These deputies relied on the clubs and, to make them more secure, often purged their membership. Their visits were triumphal and carefully orchestrated events with fireworks, bells, banquets, bonnets, and trees of liberty. Conventionnels like Carnot, who in Paris stayed away from the club, attended and joined the provincial clubs when on tour. Particularly gratifying was the appearance of a local hero who had made good and returned as a living expression of national sovereignty.[53] After June 1793 the Jacobins' devotion to whatever the Convention wanted rose to unprecedented heights. More than seven thousand congratulatory addresses were sent to the Convention by the clubs between August 1793 and August 1794.

Indeed, so reliable had the clubs become to the state that the state sometimes took them for granted. In late 1793 and early 1794, mindful of this devotion, the Conventionnels and the army could and did bypass the clubs at will. Maure, on his mission to Auxerre, complained in the early summer of 1794 that small clubs often got in his way: "You can hardly imagine, citizen colleagues, how the committees in the small communes and the societies that have been set up there recently annoy the constituted authorities and obstruct the march of government . . . Their misdeeds must constantly be set right."[54] Likewise, Carnot, in Paris, "organized" the Revolution's military victory not primarily through the clubs but through the state's tentatively reconstituted system, which, ironically, had been seriously disrupted by Jacobin purges of lukewarm but experienced officials in the fall of 1793, in western France especially, where it seemed from Paris that experienced civil servants had often been replaced by inefficient revolutionaries.

So it was that Robespierre on 26 Ventôse, Year II, warned the clubs no longer to purge state employees at will. The government would lose control of the nation if they did, and the clubs would succumb to "ambition and intrigue" if that power were granted to them.[55] Agents of the centralized state did not hesitate to threaten the clubs just as they threatened everyone: "if you do not act on my request within twenty-four hours," wrote an *agent national* to the club at Carcassone, "I will instruct the Committee of Public Safety of your silence."[56] At Bouzigues, near Montpellier, an annoyed official wrote to the *sociétaires* that he was surprised by their passivity. Zeal and patriotism should have pushed them along. "Your interminable delays force me to demand [your payment]."[57]

*S*ome critics of Jacobinism have explained its drift to repression and bloodshed citing the perennial (and therefore ahistorical) urges of men to kill their fathers, marry their mothers, and commit other sins. One can point, for example, to the Jacobins' supposedly Oedipal desire to kill their father-king-priest in January 1793 in order to possess or repossess their mother-nation.[58]

Arguments of this psychiatric type have plausibility today, given our current frame of mind; and French Jacobins did use a psychiatrically curious, neoclassical language of martyrdom and sacrifice. But so did many other eighteenth-century revolutionaries, from Boston to Geneva, with quite different effect. But in terms of this book's objectives, not much is to be gained from juxtaposing a political statement like Jacobinism to ahistorical generalities regarding mankind's psychiatric structures. Indeed, the mechanical application of "psychosocial" or Freudian analysis in the 1990s is no more fruitful than were the mechanical applications of crude Marxist analysis in the 1950s.

A better point to be made about the Jacobins' supposed blood lust is to remember, again, that most Jacobins as private persons disliked, or indeed despised, the Terror. Robespierre was in principle opposed to the death penalty, which Grégoire described in November 1792 as a "barbaric residue [*ce reste de barbarie*]."[59] Jacobins grieved over the division of their country and their clubs. Although purges were a necessity, they compared the exclusion of any Republican to a wake.[60] The guillotine seemed to them a horrifying object which was restlessly shifted from place to place in Paris, as every chosen site unexpectedly proved to be inadequate or embarrassing. The Jacobins' instinctive reaction to the Terror was less apparent in Saint-Just (who himself eventually perceived its frozen uselessness) than in Camille Desmoulins, who in December 1793 quoted Machiavelli on the subject: terror, he thought, was the characteristic tool of despots because, as the Italian had explained, it engendered an equality of fear. How revealing was the unknown Jacobin of Metz who rose in his club in the spring of 1794 to say that "if Terror is the order of the day for patriots as well, that would be the end of liberty. Then the republic would have been a dream and despotism would have risen once again, more awesome and hideous than ever."[61]

For the Jacobins, terror was neither a ruse of history, as materialist historians have argued, nor an inevitable response to materially ascertainable dangers. Nor was it the realization of innermost, sadistic desires, as some would have it today, or the work of perverse men suddenly empowered by bizarre circumstance.

Jacobins fell back on repression and terrorism less because of their problems and their principles (on sovereignty in particular) than because of the inherited social atavisms that structured their sensibility and that ran directly against the grain of their Enlightenment ideas. "Terror," writes Antoine de Baecque, an exceptionally lucid historian of this period, "[set] itself up as a last judgment and [became] politics taken as religion."[62]

Historiographic opinions on Jacobin terrorism have differed and always will differ broadly. For some, as in the judgment of a contemporary and distinguished historian, consciously understood envy drove the Revolution to extremes: "it was from . . . visceral hatred, not from the refined abstractions of the contented cultural elite, that the extreme Jacobin revolution found its authentic voice."[63] For others, excessively universalist, Rousseauean principles were at stake. In this second view, any program of "critical rationality" will evolve into statist abuse.

Finally, the Terror of 1793–94 has been defended as a reasonable and Jacobin alternative, as a reaction of "coactive energy" galvanized by foreign and domestic threat, but it is equally unsatisfactory to see Jacobins as fated to tyrannous abuse.

In these pages, the Terror is seen instead as a brutalized, backward-looking gesture of despair, as in this unwittingly comic proposal of some Jacobins in a small town not far from Paris:

> That on the days of our meetings and especially when they fall on a *décadi* . . . some of our members will betake themselves to the above mentioned drinking places, will study the mind of the drinkers, will make known to them the happiness and felicity which are felt by all the citizens of a free government and the incalculable advantages promised to us by our holy Revolution. And if by chance, some citizens allowed themselves to speak too belittlingly of the Revolution, they would be ordered arrested with the most stringent rigor.[64]

The Jacobins' decision to fall back on terror was for them a bitter and horrifying irony, as it must also seem to us today.

7

Social Reconciliation: Fraternity

> The moral condition of a nation results less from the absolute state of its members than from their relationships to each other.
>
> Jean-Jacques Rousseau, *Fragments politiques*

*J*acobin ideology strove for unity. Its starkly polarized constituent parts were intended to be reciprocative and complementary: civil society and the public good; public man and private woman; nationalism and internationalism. The Jacobins hoped that the disciplined self and the nurturing nation would soon be fitted together and remain so always, two parts, as it were, of a single doctrine of "National Individualism."

For the Jacobins, freedom was both a promise of becoming and a contract of harmonious and accepted obligation. Consider the words of *clubbistes* at Louhans during a *fête décadaire* in honor of Rousseau. From the top of an artificial mountain, they preached "the Rights of Man, the sacrifice of the Passions, and the Duties we have to one another . . . O! such a lovely morality. Everyone cordially embraced his and her neighbor."[1] "All citizens," explained Barère on August 23, 1793, "are in the debt of Liberty . . . Men, women, children, in the name of liberty and equality . . . the Motherland calls you all to help the armies of the Republic . . . Here we are united [*nous somme tous solidaires*] the metallurgist like the legislator, the physicist and the blacksmith, the savant and the day worker . . . the impoverished artisan and the rich landlords, the inhabitant of the country and the city dweller. Everything is reunited. They are all brothers. They are all useful. They will all be honored."[2] At Aigues Mortes the local Jacobins (whose club was officially named the Society of the School of Patriotism Established at Aigue Vives) basked in contentment when they observed young and old, sisters and brothers, magistrates and soldiers, all dancing the farandole. Everything was in harmony, even the birds, "who joining their song to those of all these Frenchmen and women, filled the air with their melodious sounds, and seemed to pay tribute to the regenerators of liberty."[3] Jacobins liked patriotic songs that were sung in unison. They did not like bawdy tunes. They did not make clever, cruel jokes.[4] At Toul the club's charter explicitly ruled out malicious pleasantries since these were "humiliating, embittering, gave birth to hatred, and destroyed the spirit of fraternity that should rule in our meetings."[5] In the words of Octavio Paz, humor creates ambiguity, and the Jacobins were unambiguously fraternal.

They cherished harmony. Patriotism, explained a Jacobin orator at Montpellier, required "l'union parfaite des corps administratifs, militaires, judiciaires, et religieux."[6] Dissent not just in politics but in any significant cultural or civil domain was *prima facie* unacceptable: "it is not from the womb of discord and public disorder that happiness can be born."[7] "The common interest," wrote Sieyès, "is to consider and treat one another reciprocally as the means, and not as the obstacles, to our happiness . . . The exercise of force dislocates all social relationships and those of humanity."[8] Jacobins opposed the death penalty for civil, nonpolitical crimes and corporal punishment in schools.

In their quest for more perfect unions, Jacobins looked forward to find operative instruments of togetherness, and backward to postulate a unifying view of man. They adopted negative strategies—derived from age-old cultural atavisms—such as the pursuit of common enemies and the artifices of rhetoric. But they also had a positive sense of the underlying unity of social and moral life.

Central to the Jacobins' unifying sensibility was the classically enlightened belief that all forms of life made ordered, balanced sense. The cosmos, history, public life, and the duties of the citizens formed interlocking rings of concentric truths.

Most Jacobins had probably not heard of the high theories used to justify this view of life, like the Great Chain of Being, which since ancient Greece was said to unite the cosmos. Nor did they know of the Swiss biologist-philosopher Charles Bonnet (1720–1793), who proved—to his own satisfaction at least—that all moral truths overlapped.[9] But they shared Bonnet's sensibility. They were fascinated by the wholeness of God's creation. "Microscopic discoveries," wrote Mirabeau's philo-Jacobin doctor, Georges Cabanis, "have taught us that life is everywhere . . . [In] the very organization of our fibers, there may exist innumerable causes of different forms of life, whose correspondence and harmony with the system taken as a whole . . . makes up our self . . . All forms of life in order to be entire and whole must be set within the totality of a single life endowed with every major organ."[10] "Nature," explained Saint-Just in his description of the king as an antisocial being, "creates life from a union of elements."[11] "Liberty," said a Jacobin in a remote city of central France, was like "a great electric chain of which the society at Tulle is the last ring and whose first link is in the hands Robespierre, of Pétion, of Grégoire, of the immortal Mirabeau."[12]

Nation and political unity overlapped, of course, but Jacobins did not stop there. Any manifestation of social discontinuity—in the nation as a whole or in any private context—disconcerted them. In the next generation many Romantic writers would hold to a truncated vision of social life, which posited that some chosen private (and poetic) lives might thrive amid public ruinations. Jacobins denied that view.

There was, for example, no room in their schemes of togetherness for deviance, antisocial excess, or criminality. They felt harsh toward civil as well as political criminals. "It has to be," explained Couthon in May 1794, "that these domestic crimes [cohabitation out of wedlock] should disappear as public crimes will disappear; and for that to happen, [public] opinion has to speak clearly, and crush in its execration all those who practice [them]."[13] At Coutances the club decreed a "state of permanent surveillance of morality," a task it decided to entrust to the "sexe modeste."[14]

Jacobins instinctively resisted conflict. In handling civil excesses and disputes, they invariably inclined to reconciliation, arbitration, and juries. Marriage, they thought, should be a freely consensual, mutually binding contract. Divorce, when they legislated it into being in September 1792, was essentially arranged by mutual consent, especially when children were not involved. Their penal code provided for local "tribunals of conciliations" to settle petty quarrels.

The theory of the absolutist Old Regime had assumed that only state and monarch stood between chaos and civil order. In the monarchy's Christian scheme of things, man was a fallen, predatory creature. By contrast, the Jacobins believed in the underlying immanence of community. The state served to allow the emergence of natural, immanent harmonies, rather than to reshape civil society. Couthon, when organizing in early 1794 a monthly burning of feudal documents in his home department, explained that he aimed "to bring back peace and concord" ("ramener la paix et la concorde").[15] Significantly, he did not say that such a step would *create* harmony. Social peace, in his mind, had existed latently all along.

Jacobinism optimistically wove together private and collective self-improvement. For the Jacobins, the Revolution had made it possible to bring personal purpose into accord with political goals, and these in turn expanded the citizen's sense of private space.

The idea of regeneration made this vision of self and public responsibility more accessible. In the revolutionary words of Choderlos de Laclos, the sometime adviser of Philippe Égalité (the Jacobin cousin of the king) and the author of a scandalous novel entitled *Liaisons dangereuses* (a prerevolutionary manual of sexual conquest and duplicitous manipulation), the Revolution had "regenerated the virtues and the happiness of the people." According to the Jacobin view, after many centuries of obscurantist darkness, the French had blessedly recovered the proud character and the masculine, vigorous, and conciliatory virtues that had prevailed in the country's simpler past.[16] Should a club exclude a man who had lied before he had joined the club but who had not lied since? Here was a regenerative question the Jacobins of Courthézon considered earnestly.[17]

Jacobins had a lively understanding of the many registers that modern Western culture offers for self-construction, but they had a strong preference for integrative values. Though certainly committed to self-becoming, Jacobins despised the idea of individualism taken as self-conscious, aestheticized, and solipsistic artifact. The Jacobin, for example, was clean and neatly dressed (unlike the sans-culotte) but he was no self-displaying dandy. Jacobins did use clothing as a quasi-theatrical prop, but they looked less to the fashion of the day than to historically or culturally sanctioned signs of civic virtue. Brissot, for example, chose to dress in black like a Quaker, a sartorial pose given credibility by a recent visit to America.

Jacobins discounted visions of the self defined by the acquisition of arcane learning, scholarship, or manipulative Foucaldian control. "The speculative sciences," explained the Montagnard Bouquier in December 1793, "detach those who cultivate them from society." The Jacobins considered knowledge merely the handmaiden of reigning goodness. They admired Jacobin mathematicians and scientists (like Condorcet or the chemist Hassenfratz) more for their politics than for their science. In a debate on the promotion of naval officers, Le Chapelier denied the usefulness of competitive examination (which favored those who had had the time to acquire book learning) and stressed character and experience instead: "I want to see brothers-in-arms who can usefully serve the nation."[18]

They were also unimpressed by wealth and acquisition as a standard of self-assertion. They conditionally approved of man as producer, but only if his economic strivings coincided with the public good.

They saved their enthusiasm for selflessly and even suicidally heroic individuals. They idealized those moral souls who chose or accepted a patriotic death that transformed individualism into communitarian wholeness. Robespierre, in late 1791, explained that he would gladly sacrifice his life to the nation and the future. "Should I be the victim of some miserable cabal, I will at least die with a name that will be dear to posterity."[19]

Sociability in its most affective forms—that is, sacrificial fraternity and unbounded friendship—were critical themes for them. They agreed with Saint-John's judgment, "Greater love hath no man than . . . [he should] lay down his life for his friends." "Je t'aime plus que jamais et jusqu'à la mort" (I love you more than ever, and unto death), Robespierre wrote to the widowed Danton in February of 1793. In his *Institutions républicaines*, Saint-Just went so far as to suggest that Jacobins should periodically take it upon themselves to explain to their fellow citizens why they had broken with former friends, if such had been their sad fate. This obligation the Jacobins never set into law(!), but friendship they valued till the end. (At Alençon the Girondin-dominated club was called the Society of Assembled Friends.) The illness of a fellow Jacobin always caused concern. Clubs often delegated members to visit sick colleagues and bring them food and newspapers.[20] They attended the funerals of deceased colleagues and wore mourning for them; on one particularly important occasion, the club at Aix bought four yards of black ribbon to distribute. To underscore their friendliness, the *clubbistes* took up age-old rituals of sociability: a member at Auch reminded his peers that in olden times, when a "frère compagnon" (a member of the century-old guilds) had left the city, his friends would walk with him a ways, carrying his bag; Jacobins, he thought, should do the same with departing volunteers.[21] In his lament on the death of Chalier, who had been executed by anti-Jacobins at Lyons, Collot d'Herbois explained that his friend's despair was born not of weakness, or fear, but from the "cruel idea of having been abandoned by the Jacobins."[22]

Friendship opened the private into the public. Domestically, friendship brought together individuals of different age and gender. Publicly, amity stood as a sign that material differences of wealth and rank could be transcended by men of good will. In October 1793 Parisian Jacobins spearheaded the use of the revolutionary and informal pronoun *tu* instead of the more formal *vous*, just as they had also dropped the use of the word *Monsieur*.[23] Jacobins praised sacrificial military courage and were especially taken with courageous assertions of defiant loyalty.

Some clubs required that *clubbistes* in their speeches call each other "brother." Jacobins continuously purged their ranks, but often for the sake of fraternity. By eliminating unworthy brethren, orthodox Jacobins made brotherly affection more feasible for those who remained.

Even sodomy, incest, rape, and other acts proposed by the Marquis de Sade were presented as fraternal (or sororal) gestures. It was only by realizing all of their varied sexual impulses, explained this opportunistic Jacobin, that men—by their nature at war with themselves, with women, and with one another—could perceive their underlying and Republican sameness. Sade's bizarre ideas were wholly unrepresentative; and yet, his Republic of Evil was a (grotesque) elaboration rather than a plain denial of Robespierre's tyrannical Republic of Virtue, where applied goodness rather than transcended evil enabled men to be at one with their fellow revolutionaries.

The Jacobin ideal of fraternity was most clearly expressed in the joyful and participatory revolutionary *fête*. Both Diderot and Rousseau had criticized the celebrations of the Old Regime as too ritualized, artificial, and lacking in public grandeur. But the Revolution gave their heirs and disciples a chance to transform these public holidays, after 1792 especially. Revolutionaries took to commemorating the great moments of the Revolution. The taking of the Bastille was a favorite landmark.

The celebrations of such revolutionary holy days were coterminous with the life of the clubs. The *fêtes* were the "cornerstones of liberty"; and the committee in charge of preparing them often was—after the Committees of Correspondence—one of the most important agencies of the societies. All over France, clubs actively staged revolutionary *fêtes*, which were understood to be both festive and political events. In Paris, for example, David's staging on April 15, 1792, of the rehabilitation of the Swiss guards of Chateauvieux provided a radical Jacobin response to a conservative *fête* that the National Assembly had ordered to commemorate the death of Mayor Simoneau. In 1794 Robespierre proposed that the republic set up twenty-three universalist celebrations, the most famous of which—the Festival of the Supreme Being—took place on June 8, when tens of thousands of citizens assembled in Paris and all over France to celebrate this pastoral commemoration of nature's productive goodness.

The *clubbistes* placed constant emphasis on the unifying purpose of the *fête* and of the revolutionary celebrations. In Paris, wrote a revolutionary journalist on the occasion of Mirabeau's funeral, which was attended by "nearly all the deputies," it seemed that "all of the French People from the [nation's] eighty-three departments" were present there.[24] "Every estate, all ages, all sexes [*sic*]," wrote a Jacobin from Montauban about a *fête* staged there in the summer of 1791, "formed a ravishing spectacle . . . [it was like] a charm that swept up even those who were most indifferent to this kind of pleasure."[25] To underscore its holistic purpose, a *fête* might pair men and women; civilians and soldiers; mothers and daughters; soldiers and officers; boys and girls who were reciting alternate verses of the Declaration of the Rights of Man in contrapuntal rhythm; the healthy and the sick or wounded; the youthful and the aged. Pregnant women (representing continuity) might carry sheaves of wheat, fruits, vegetables. At Metz the club involved a company of sexagenarians carrying pikes and preceded by a sign that read, "a citizen is born, lives, and dies for the fatherland."[26] In "Bourg-régénéré" (Bourg-en-Bresse) the local club's commemoration of the abolition of slavery was particularly expressive: twenty youths dressed as warriors surrounded by as many women preceded a float with a young citizeness representing equality. On another float perched young white women breastfeeding black babies and young black women breastfeeding white babies. Two more citizenesses on horseback, one representing virtue and the other liberty, accompanied liberty's chariot.[27]

Ideally, all of the villagers would take part in their town's celebration, and where that was not possible, unity and transparency were expressed indirectly. The widely celebrated *fêtes de la Victoire* (like the ones held in January and February 1794 to celebrate the victory of Toulon) went one step further by associating the cult of the victorious dead to the cult of living heroes.

Though choirs and singers each had their role in the *fêtes*, the music of these events subordinated orchestras to collective voices. Harmonic variety was reduced to make the music of these celebrations more accessible to all, and in the autumn of 1793 polyphonic music (which implied a divided social body) virtually disappeared, replaced by "homophonic, choral writing, predictable harmonies, and eminently singable melodies,"[28] like "La Marseillaise." Across Europe, these revolutionary cantatas, with their "massed choruses and martial airs," later became important sources for nineteenth-century opera, whose subjects were often political (persecuted Huguenots, Sicilian rebels, Roman revolutionaries, and the like).[29]

Of necessity, the ostensible motives for staging a *fête* changed radically as the Revolution progressed: the installation of a bishop in 1791; republicanism in the summer of 1793; and dechristianization in the fall of 1793. (The club at Fontainebleau staged thirty-seven different kinds of celebrations.)[30] But the need for Jacobinism to celebrate its existence as an inclusive doctrine did not change.

The Jacobins favored charity as another theme of reconciliation. As private persons, they certainly did not disdain either respectability or property, which they took to be a guarantee of individualism and personal independence, as it had also been for the Radical Whigs and John Locke in both Britain and America. On March 2, 1793, for example, in a report that dealt with the desirability of selling confiscated property in large or small lots, the Conventionnel Delacroix, who wished to increase the number of landowning peasants, assumed as a matter of course that it is "above all else among those who own land that the homeland can hope to find that the courage which is needed to defend it is united to the love of order and the respect for laws."[31]

But poverty had a certain aura for Jacobins nonetheless. Bad luck, thought these contented owners of property, entitled the unfortunate to the solicitude of the fortunate. Jacobins also sensed that in daily life, property was just as likely to be a sign of prideful vice as it was of virtuous generosity, perhaps even more so. They were relieved when able to be kind, to invite local indigents gratis to their fraternal banquets. For them, as for Rousseau, human nature was defined by both self-assertion *(amour-propre)* and compassion *(pitié)*. Robespierre spoke of every man's right to subsist, and he praised "that imperious impulse which attracted all Jacobins" toward "enfeebled men." In Paris, in May 1794, at Robespierre's prompting, the Convention provided for a *fête du malheur,* and at Périgueux the *clubbistes* dedicated it to Marat.[32] Jacobins felt an especially strong impulse to be charitable with fellow Jacobins and soldiers, their children, companions, and widows. Many clubs had a Committee of Benevolence,[33] a counterpart to the better known Committees of Surveillance. Jacobins admired a fellow *clubbiste* who had selflessly and quietly disrobed in a corridor to give his shirt to a deserving person. They sympathized with the victims of any great misfortune, however distant. When a major fire at Limoges made three thousand people homeless, the local *clubbistes* appealed to Jacobins all over France for help: "as human beings, as Frenchmen, as friends of the constitution, we address ourselves to you, to beg you to come to the succor of our dear and unfortunate fellow citizens."[34] Jacobins raised funds for the civilian victims of the Austrians' bombardment of Lille, and for the families of volunteers from the department of the Gard who had drowned in the Rhône. Many Jacobins understood the need for free legal advice, free medical care (many clubs had a Health Committee), and old age homes or, as at Valognes, "asylums" where the sick and elderly might find shelter and company.[35]

Jacobins apprehended that generosity, citizenship, and the sustained tolerance of destitution were ultimately incompatible. Although censorious of workers who placed their pay before the needs of the public good, Jacobins also took note of "the dangers to which misery might expose the Constitution";[36] and any scheme that could increase the ranks of owners of property was welcome to them. They warmed to the idea of redistribution through confiscation, especially of émigré properties; and in the spring of 1794 some of them at least gave thought to generalizing these confiscatory practices. A Jacobin of Loudun even mused in late 1792 that Harrington's *Oceana* was "un excellent plan pour la communauté des biens" (an excellent plan for the community of goods).[37]

Patriotism, in the words of the president of a Normandy club in January 1791, was not just about sacrificing one's blood for the nation: "it is also about turning the enemies of the Revolution into the zealous partisans of our liberty." Suppressing abuses, they knew, meant sacrifice and perhaps even coerced sacrifice; but their primordial goal, they also knew, was to make brotherly proselytes, not martyrs: "The intolerance of priests nearly destroyed Catholicism. Let this great danger be an example for the priests of liberty."[38] Jacobins believed in patience and compassion: "those men who are the enemies of our principles need to be understood: because they are the victims of habit and prejudice, it is hard for them to accept ideas that are beyond their strength."[39] Many clubs had Committees of Conciliation: at Toulon the committee worked "to dry up every source of internal division."[40] The club thought highly of this institution and threatened to disenfranchise associated clubs that did not have one.

Typical of the Jacobins' desire to please and to reconcile their fellow citizens was the decision of the Marseilles club to send out three professional arbitrators as commissioners to the neighboring department of the Vaucluse in 1792. (One of them, named Monbrion, charged one hundred livres a day for his work, and his yearly income of 10,000 livres surpassed the dreams of avaricious sans-culottes. He liked his work, which he had taken on, he said, because "a lack of instruction" lay behind all disagreements.)[41]

A favorite time in the life of the clubs and of the National Assemblies was those moments when members, heretofore divided by some quarrel, suddenly fell into each other's arms. The best-known such instance, the "baiser de Lamourette," occurred in Paris on July 7, 1792, when in response to a call by a Girondin bishop of that name, all deputies embraced. Lamourette had sought to reconcile those who yearned for a second chamber—which was anathema to the left—and those who yearned for a republic, which was anathema to the right. (Lamourette, alas, was executed shortly afterward.) Priests who abjured their vows on the floor of the clubs were ritually entitled to a public embrace.

The Jacobins considered the ability to forgive as important as the ability to defend their principles. Jacobins were expected to be "inflexibles et inexorables," but they also thought of themselves as "justes et humains." They deemed it appropriate to extend amnesties on the anniversaries of great events. Many of the *fêtes* the Jacobins orchestrated had reconciliation as a theme, forgiveness being the natural complement of (lapsed) togetherness. At Aigues Vives (formerly Aigues Mortes) the ceremonies inaugurating the club involved a contrapuntally performed *Te Deum,* with Catholics and Protestants singing alternating verses.[42] Clubs were ashamed of quarreling, and the Strasbourg Jacobins decided to leave blank pages in their minutes of stormy meetings, until such time as peace had been restored.[43] In June 1791, after the disputes occasioned by the king's flight to Varennes, the ultraradical Jacobins of Aix (who styled themselves the *anti-politiques,* since politics were necessarily divisive) promised to forget all private quarrels and to banish from their bosom anyone who made an allusion to the king's flight. Even at the Terror's high point, the Aixois *clubbistes* argued that the Convention could not encourage anticlericalism because ensuing quarrels would be humiliatingly derisory. The Revolution's aim, they went on, was "to banish from the breasts of men all causes of grief, all seeds of hate."[44]

The Feuillant schism in the fall of 1791 instituted exclusion, soon to be followed by execution in the fall of 1793. But the initial response of over two hundred shocked and provincial clubs was to urge the Parisian Jacobins of the right and of the left to mend their ways together. The club at Bergues reminded the friends of Barnave and Robespierre that they were but two parts of a single "mother society."[45] Two years later, the response of the Aurillac club to the Montagnard-Girondin schism was similarly ecumenical: "we know nothing about a right side or a left side, or about mountains and valleys, or about any of these labels, which would be both ridiculous and insignificant, if they were not dangerous . . . Here all patriots are united to defend their liberty."[46]

In short, dissensions of all kinds were unpleasant to the Jacobins, even small and familial ones, since they knew that great oaks of public strife might grow from the small acorns of private unhappiness. "Arguments and discord, stirred on by fanaticism, are racking this city," concluded the Jacobins of Auch, in the Pyrénées. A private quarrel could at any moment become the signal for civil war. "Rivers of blood might flow."[47] Jacobin clubs liked to stage the forgiveness of old quarrels, as at Lunéville, where a local noble burnt his letters of nobility before his fellow *clubbistes* and forgave a *curé* with whom he had been quarreling for half a decade.[48]

*J*udith Schlanger has written, rightly, that the "great, irreplaceable" advantage of the body as an organic metaphor is its simultaneous ability to describe and to make understandable.[49] For the Jacobins, it was the image of the family that played this all-important role. The Paris Jacobins were the "mother society." Marseilles was "the eldest son." Many provincial centers wrote of regional clubs as their children. Jacobins were completely devoted to the theme of the nuclear family, as a symbol and as unifying fact in political and social life. Ideally, the Republican family was to be a perfect microcosm of the larger nation, an instrument of socialization that prepared the child to become a participating member in the political community. Not surprisingly, clubs presented themselves sometimes as "the mothers of all citizens" and as families, or "second families," to their members. In his complaint of mid-July 1794 against populist *assemblées sectionnaires,* Couthon likened them to "denatured children who wanted to stifle their mother." *Clubbistes* were brothers, fraternally united. One Montagnard Jacobin, while railing against the Girondins in the Paris club, explained that his enemies were like ungrateful children "tearing the bosom . . . of their tender mother."⁵⁰ Le Carpentier, a rather ferocious Conventionnel, was welcomed by the club at Saint-Malo to the popular song "Where Can One Be Happier Than in the Bosom of One's Own Family?" a tune written by André Grétry and much praised by Diderot years before. One club turned away a visitor so that it might deliberate "en famille," which even in a literal sense was not untrue, since many Jacobins signed themselves onto membership roles with familial tags, as in Dupont *fils*, or Durand *père* (junior, senior, uncle, nephew, and so on). At Strasbourg the founding charter authorized fathers to bring their sons to the meetings. At Gaillac the city fathers readily granted a *certificat de civisme* to Jean-Antoine Courtaud because, *inter alia*, "he belongs to a family that has always provided proof of pure and enlightened patriotism."⁵¹ The abbé Grégoire expressed relief at the thought that prosperous villagers, who used to marry only within their class (or, what was even worse, their extended and physiologically degenerate families), would now marry beyond these limits "because we have in France today only one family."⁵²

Familial and political values overlapped, and the Grenoble Jacobins in the spring of 1794 looked forward to nurturing in the souls of youthful citizens "the love of the *patrie*, of liberty, of equality, and of filial piety, the respect of old age and misfortune, the hatred of tyrants."⁵³ Jacobinism helped mothers and fathers to rethink even their most mundane familial tasks: in the days of the Old Regime, swaddling had been enchainment; but now, these clothes, designed to conserve and strengthen the child, had become so many "tendres maillots" (sweet swaddling clothes).⁵⁴ An important aspect of revolutionary regeneration was precisely that the Old Regime had fragmented French society, and that 1789 had as it were "refamiliarized" it: "after these Gothic institutions comes a simple legislation whose unity embraces an immense people, and creates a single and numerous family, inspired by the same feelings, concurring in the same views."⁵⁵

Marriage, like friendship, was a great symbol of unity, a chance to bring together the private and the public, the real and the symbolic. In Vinay the club decided to stage yearly a wedding to unite "the most virtuous and patriotic young woman of the district" and some "valorous soldier, distinguished by his Republican character and his military exploits."⁵⁶ Many clubs provided dowries for poor and politically deserving brides. A (widowed) Danton—though the perfect, hard-living, and sensual foil to dried-up and, in Carlyle's phrase, "sea-green" Robespierre (who probably died a virgin)—took a wife and not a mistress. Jacobins thought poorly of celibacy, which they considered a form of egoism. In the Constitution of 1795, membership in the Council of Ancients was restricted to married men and widowers.

Like marriage, divorce was endorsed by the *clubbistes* in whose view the two institutions were not at all incompatible. The recognition of marital disunion did not license adultery but laid the groundwork for another, better-suited, and more productive union. (Jacobins liked large families and seemed oblivious to French society's increasingly indulgent attitude to birth control.) The point of divorce was not merely to separate unhappily yoked individuals. Its deeper purpose was to enable them to recombine in new, different, and happier familial units. Besides, like the family, marriage and divorce were not ends in themselves but means to higher and integrative private and public permutations. When he suggested that childless couples be required to adopt a child, Saint-Just, as usual, went further than most Jacobins would dare to go; but in this matter, at least, he did so along familiar lines. No Jacobin, it may be added, ever endorsed abortion. Doctrinally, that stand would have made no sense to them. As the moderate Jacobin Rabaut Saint-Étienne explained in the context of the nation's educational responsibilities, it was the Jacobin state's obligation to take the child in hand even in the cradle: "the unborn child already belongs to the nation."[57]

Family and citizenship went hand in hand. In a letter of congratulation to the local juring bishop, who had just married a priest and a nun, the *clubbistes* of Périgueux remarked that many of his now married priests were at last able to "practice the most useful virtues . . . For a real patriot, the only good priest is the one who binds himself to the public good by the sweet ties of marriage and of fatherhood."[58] The curé of Lavardens, who announced that he had married "a shepherdess," was roundly cheered. Clubs censured priests who refused to marry divorced people. "Presbyterial celibacy" was unnatural. Its practice was a "sterile virtue" at best, and at worst a breeding ground for vice.

Jacobins did not hesitate to interfere in the family life of their fellow *clubbistes*. The Jacobins of Nantes gravely considered the admonitions of their brethren from Albi about an adolescent who had deserted "la maison paternelle." Many clubs sternly reminded members of their familial duties, of the obligations of the young to support aged and indigent parents especially.[59] At Béziers the club passed a judgment worthy of King Solomon in a conflict involving a noble-born young man named Nattes, his beloved, and her father, Estagnol, who had invoked the exclusion of the noble-born Jacobin radical Le Peletier, brother of the well-known martyr, from the Paris Jacobins in order to reject the young nobleman's proposal of marriage. The club vouched for this *ci-devant* (ex-noble): "his republicanism has entirely purged him of his birth stain: the sans-culottes have adopted him as a brother"; it ruled that Nattes could marry Mlle. Estagnol at some later time, after she had turned twenty-one.[60] Half-jokingly, a Jacobin at Brive suggested that patriots who were celibate and wanted to divorce should have their pick of aristocratic women.[61] Noble women who had secured a divorce from their émigré husbands and who were suspected of having done so to preserve family properties were strongly urged to remarry.

Nevertheless, families were not always an unmixed blessing, and Jacobins endorsed familial life only insofar as it was the means to larger Republican togetherness. Jacobins were quite aware that families might become tyrannical or, even worse, the instruments of collective selfishness. They prized Brutus, who had murdered Caesar, his adopted father. The family was not an end in itself but—like the clubs and the Revolution—an institution that enabled individuals to become their true selves. Families taken as particular units—that is, families (like those of the Parlementaires under the Old Regime) which served either to thwart individual members or to yoke their varied egoisms so as to thwart the public good—were not just bad but perverse and unnatural. In consequence, Jacobins took many steps to deny nepotism in the management of clubs. They did not tolerate family intrigues, which had been the warp and woof of life under the Old Regime. Arranged marriages were not to their liking. They were uninterested in the continuity of families and of family patrimonies, and thus set the rights of heirs, whether male or female, above familial prerogative. "Children," said Barère on June 1, 1794, "belong to the general family, to the republic, before they belong to particular families. Without this principle, there can be no Republican education."[62]

Jacobins also favored adoption, another indication that while devoted to the theme of family, they had no interest in blood ties, or race, familially or collectively defined. On routinely humanitarian grounds, the clubs supported the creation of orphanages, but their interest in the parentless had deeper causes. Clubs acted as godparents to children, gave them Republican names (Cato, Portia), and at times even adopted orphaned children directly. The clubs acted toward these children as the state did to the clubs, and as the clubs did to one another: as members of a single family. At Nérac, the *clubbistes* urged the National Assembly to advise municipalities all over France to adopt the children of fallen soldiers: "by more energetically electrifying the patriotism of . . . families, [adoption] would perpetuate from generation to generation a hotbed of soldiers of liberty and heroes of the fatherland."[63] Agree to be affiliated with us, wrote the society of Agde to the Paris Jacobins: "we would be pleased to be your adoptive children."[64]

*T*he inner peace and familial harmony Jacobins sought implied a particular perception of the self's relation to its own desires. Here again, Rousseau, who so eerily expressed Jacobin sensibility long before Jacobinism existed, was a model Jacobins could easily understand. A conscientious individual had to exercise extreme self-control. By limiting his ambitions and his needs, by requiring less, every citizen could give more and thereby secure greater spiritual fullness. As one Jacobin put it, "to live frugally is to diminish our needs and to guarantee our independence."[65] In Paris Louvet (who was notoriously fond of sweets) made the same point in a supporting speech at a Jacobin meeting on a motion to boycott the consumption of sugar: "the most dangerous enemies of a people that wishes to be free," he warned, "are soft and effeminate habits: if you wish to pulverize your enemies, accustom yourself to diminishing the sum of your needs."[66]

Jacobins were not Rabelaisian. Their laughter was measured, communitarian, and politically engaged.[67] They could not accept even the balanced, skeptical traditions of Montaigne. For the Jacobins were closer in their sensibility to the self-denying message of Pascal, Racine, and Rousseau (an avid reader of these two predecessors), that is, of writers who had been fascinated (and horrified) by man's propensity to selfish evil and who were obsessed by man's need to compensate for his self-seeking turn of mind.

Jacobins tried to be puritanical in their daily life. At Bergerac self-indulgent members did huddle around a stove in wintertime, but the *clubbistes* of Avallon were closer to the mark when they refused to heat their building. More heat would only serve to attract the weak.

Jacobins contemptuously disapproved of tippling and gluttony. Their banquets were frugal, fraternal exchanges: "It is our desire to come together that makes for the great pleasure of the table."[68] At the absolutist court, food had been ostentatiously displayed; in the next century, the preparation, presentation, and consumption of food was to be for the rich an important weapon of social exclusion in the bourgeoisie's repertory of class distinctions. By contrast, in 1793–94, for the revolutionary poor, food was a necessity. But for the Jacobins, ideally, food—like sex—was the occasion of shared, fraternal, transcendence. The Jacobins, who categorically rejected the eighteenth century's cultivation of elegant self-indulgence in the form of domestic comforts, stoves, and tubs, also disdained exotic food and drink, like chocolate and sugar. At Beauvais they asked the municipality to keep cafés from serving "bavaroises au lait."[69] (Some of them, however, did make an exception for coffee, which was then associated with intellectual endeavor.) At Thann the *clubbistes* organized a "frugal and patriotic" meal, which ended with "fraternal embraces," as did the Jacobins of Exmes, in the Orne, where a "promenade civique" followed a "repas frugal" accompanied by hymns.[70] In the neighboring town of Vire, they organized a "banquet civique où règne la frugalité des Spartiates" (a civic banquet where Spartan simplicity ruled). No one could spend more than fifteen sous. Extra meat was given to the poor.[71] At Besançon, where the men's Jacobin club denounced "the scandalous scenes" that had taken place in the women's club, the women retorted that the men had wasted funds collected on behalf of volunteers to stage a patriotic banquet.[72] Couthon, one of the most powerful men in France, was happy to report in February 1794 that, though quite sick, he received meat for bouillon only once a day: "il faut que les républicains soient sobres" (Republicans must be sober).[73] Half a century before, Montesquieu had congratulated the French for having avoided the excesses of both north and south: "we often eat in company, and we do not drink to excess."[74] Jacobins followed those two rules religiously.

As they seized on brotherhood and abstemiousness as key virtues, they censured counterrevolutionary *aristocratie,* gluttony, and self-indulgent, abusive corpulence. (Much was made in Jacobin caricature of the king's appetite and excessive girth.) Jacobins expected of themselves—as others expected of them—a lean and hungry look. They did not think that living well was the best revenge.

Being intensely mindful of community norms, the Jacobins were—or wished to be—intensely honest. They were shocked by evidence of Danton's corruption: it was a sign of Robespierre's political acumen that he was able to associate the fate of the Dantonists with the peculation of

Chabot and Fabre during the dissolution of the French East India Company. It was also proof of the Jacobins' moral collapse after 1794 that many of them (Barras, Tallien, Lecointre) took legal or illegal advantage of their political prominence and grew quite rich. Jacobins rewarded officials who refused to be bribed. They criticized gambling and especially lotteries, which they wished to make illegal. In March 1793, on behalf of the Committee of Public Instruction, Jean Dusaulx, a Parisian Jacobin, reminded his fellow Conventionnels of Cato's view that patriotism and games of chance could not coexist. As soon as lotteries became popular in modern Europe, he added, "virtue had become more rare, public spirit took on a different shape."[75]

Jacobins also had strong feelings about sexuality. Sensuality was a natural quality. As such, it could therefore be seen as proof of the natural and moralized complementarity of the sexes, a thought which Mme. de Bellegarde, the noble-born, émigré mistress of the noble-born Montagnard Conventionnel Hérault de Séchelles, amusingly derided when she puckishly explained that the more she made love, the more she loved the Revolution; and the more she loved the Revolution, the more she made love. (Hérault was executed in early April 1794.) Jacobins, however, took a dim view of the "plaisirs impurs (de) Priape." Saint-Just did write in praise of incest, but even this self-conscious and preposterous text can be read as paean to primal harmony refound. In a celebrated remark, Baudelaire wrote that the Revolution had been "faite par des voluptueux." That was not so. It was doubly appropriate that the Semurois Jacobins should ask that male and female prisoners be strictly kept apart. *Aristocrates* should be deprived of pleasure and were in any case incapable of true union.[76]

Sex was a relation of sublimation between a mundane thing (the human body) and an elevated principle (unity), a mode of transcendental thinking that Jacobins, of course, applied in many domains, ranging from the purpose of the family to the difference between naive patriotism and politicized nationalism. Much can be read in David's celebrated if unfinished painting of the androgynous youth Bara, who had given his life for his country, and whose sexless body, without breasts or genitalia, neither male nor female but both simultaneously, was at once intensely sexual and utterly devoid of carnal implication.[77]

Jacobins were not at all repelled by the specifics of female physicality. They wrote lyrically about breastfeeding. But bodies for them were no joking matter. Arthur Young, who knew France well, claimed that French attitudes to bodily functions were generally less genteel than those of his own compatriots. Yet at Besançon the club unanimously voted to ask the *agent national* to punish men guilty of urinating in full view of the public.[78] An aspect of the Montagne's coup against the Gironde in June 1793 that most distressed the journalist of the *Mercure universel* was that the encircled deputies had been unable to relieve themselves in private, a state of affairs he described as a "chose bien humiliante."[79] David did pen drawings at once political and scatological, but these were out of character and penned with an eye to attract the attention—or so we can presume—of uneducated citizens. A reason given to justify a preference for French over local dialects was its supposed purity.[80] Jacobins rejected an apostate priest who used "expressions that presented obscene ideas," which they deemed particularly offensive to the "virtuous women" present in their hall.

The Périgueux Jacobins understood the place of revolutionary sex perfectly when they contrasted the "liaisons légitimes" of the married priests to the "liaisons libidineuses" of the unmarried clerics: if such "a vile being" dared to make public his "sensual and corrupted" ways, he would be "jeered, and driven from our bosom."[81] For the errant Marquis de Sade, prostitutes were "the children of nature," but Jacobins had a dark view of such women, whom they perceived not as victims of hard times but as corrupters of the nation's morals. In many places, prostitutes were denied entry to the clubs.

Much has recently been made of the supposed homosocial dimension of the Jacobins' emphasis on heroism, in Jacobin painting especially. And undeniably, David, like many of the young painters who were bound to him by close friendships, did have a fondness for vast canvases prominently displaying naked, entwined, and beautiful masculinized bodies (their private parts barely concealed by phallic objects of all kinds: swords, sabers, lances, scabbards).

In all likelihood, however, our impulse to see this hypothetical homosexuality as a significant part of the Jacobins' thinking would have been distressing to them and should probably be discounted, even if our own modern frame of mind makes it difficult for us not to think of them in this way. Jacobins, though they did not choose to criminalize homosexuality, nonetheless disapproved of the practice when they bothered to think about it explicitly, which was seldom. Pierre Chaumette, a populist Jacobin suspected of having a homosexual past, "redeemed" himself by actively perse-

cuting Parisian prostitutes. Cambacérès, the most prominent of Jacobin ho-
mosexuals, did achieve high office, but definitely in spite of his sexual preference rather than because of it. Condorcet called homosexuality "a disgusting vice."[82]

In a way, Jacobin definitions of morality and sexual normalcy prefigured
Victorian principles, the difference being that Victorian gentlemen, however kind, considered the world through the cruel and exclusive lens of
reputation, wealth, gender, nationality, class, education, speech, and race;
whereas the Jacobins, however cruel and terroristic, passionately believed
that their inclusive values of self-respect, decency, sacrifice, and sexual
virtue could, would, and above all else should become the birthright of
every man and woman.

These may be unexciting principles. And it cannot be denied that Jacobin
prose often seems flat and even tiresome, the expression of an impoverished view of human nature; but that first impression must be put aside.
True enough, the Jacobins had little interest in the two great themes of
eighteenth- and nineteenth-century European prose, the psychological ar-
cana of sexual relations and the intricacies of social stratification. But that
is because their minds were elsewhere, and in any case it is largely in the
realm of words that good repels and evil fascinates. Indeed, what holds our
attention as readers often disgusts us as active participants in the business
of daily life, which is what the Jacobins aimed to be.

*E*ntranced by sublime individuals who loved the nation completely, the
Jacobins sought to commune with society through heroism. At Montpellier
the *clubbistes* decided to erect on the city's main promenade a column of
liberty, with a marble plaque on which would be engraved, first, the Declaration of the Rights of Man and, next to that, the names "of great men."[83]
This gesture reflected their view that great figures achieved the progress of
mankind. In ancient Greece heroes had stood between heaven and earth,
with parents both human and divine. Jacobin heroes, by contrast, were all
too human, but they too were giants who bridged different worlds: the private and the public, the future and the present, the self and the community.
(Counterrevolutionary, antiheroic *aristocrates* were by comparison often
described as pygmies.) For the Jacobins, heroic deeds towered over both
past and present and, fittingly, it was they who invented the war memorial,
to carry into the future the memory of fallen and revolutionary warriors.

Jacobin heroes, it should be added, were definitely masculine. Although women figured prominently—and anonymously—in Jacobin iconography as nurturing goddesses of reason, liberty, or justice, most of the politicized women that Jacobins perceived by name were the quasi-demonic enemies of their cause, like Marie Antoinette and Charlotte Corday.[84]

Jacobins sincerely believed in heroic passion. It was only *misguided* zeal that threatened private and public harmonies. When properly politicized and reconstructed, heroic passion could nurture private love and public friendship. "Hypocritical priests say, know how to overcome your passions, and they call that morality," wrote a sensitive Jacobin, "a hot and active Republican must say: let men be passionate, but know how to rule your passions. Passions give men energy. A passionless man is nothing but a federalist and a moderate, or a hypocritical Feuillant, incapable of great things."[85]

In Western culture, heroism and democracy have generally been dissociated. The modern hero—especially in his fascistic incarnations—defines himself against the masses. In Jacobin culture, however, heroism and democracy cohabited perfectly. The Roman poet Horace (a favored writer in prerevolutionary French secondary schools) had escaped from others so that he might find himself: the Jacobin hero did precisely the reverse.

Indeed, heroism was for the Jacobins compatible not just with sacrifice but with mediocrity as well because those two conditions had one vast thing in common: a concern for others. Jacobins also found a place in their heart for the averageness and modesty of ordinary men and women who from their essential and unexciting nature unthinkingly fitted their modest sense of self into the social whole. "Is it not a demonstrable fact," asked a Jacobin at Semur, "that great talents and sublime virtue are often the handmaidens of mediocrity and are often incompatible with opulence?"[86] In its description of the *fête* for Bara and Viala, the Besançon club insisted that there had been nothing "supernatural" about the life and death of these two young people. To the contrary, it was precisely their transcended ordinariness that struck the Jacobins' imagination. The heroic fate of these (banal) adolescents proved that the revolutionary spirit could enable even ordinary children to act like men, just as ordinary men might strive to be heroic. Jacobins warmed to the fate of plain men and women who had raised themselves to spiritual greatness by some unexpected gesture. When a *clubbiste* jumped in a river to rescue a drowning child, the club at Tulle asked that he be made a gendarme, as a reward perhaps, but also, no doubt, because those who had excelled in the private sphere could also be expected to excel in a public role.[87]

It follows that the Jacobins were simultaneously attracted to and wary of extraordinary and charismatic leaders. Instinctively, they trusted leaders who resembled themselves. Shared ideology mattered more to them than individual prowess. They identified most closely with Robespierre, a moderately gifted and modestly heroic small-town lawyer. They were ill at ease with Mirabeau, a talented, stentorian, extravagant, and incestuous aristocrat.[88]

Jacobins did assume that history was about Great Men, about Great Legislators especially, but it was clear to them that true genius lay in the ability to understand the unspoken, unformulated needs of the community as whole. A legislator, wrote a Marseillais pamphleteer, "is a man whose talents and virtues have earned him the esteem and confidence of his fellow citizens, who has been delegated by them to form the Constitution, and who is like one of the Gods each time he gives a just law to his fatherland."[89]

Everyone valued selflessness, but this quality was particularly relevant to the truly great. Lycurgus, for example, had abdicated after giving Sparta the laws that it needed. On his return in 1794 from the victory of Fleurus, which he had triumphantly orchestrated, the young Saint-Just refused all praise: "we have to praise the victories and forget about our own selves . . . If everybody had been modest and not been enviously eager to hear others being praised more than himself, we would be more at ease with one another."[90] His friend Robespierre concurred: "to be good [*pour être bon*], a magistrate must immolate himself for the people."[91]

The Jacobins saw modern politics as marked by the appearance and disappearance of such heroes. Mirabeau was the first of their great votive figures: "his head, stronger than all the tyrants' satellites, can overthrow every throne and break every scepter."[92] Though deputies in Paris had been suspicious of him while he lived, this liberal aristocrat had been popular in the provincial clubs; and his death marked the first massive Jacobin outpouring for a fallen warrior. The *clubbistes* at Aix made available a lachrymatory vase for his mourners.[93] At Sens the local *clubbistes* attended a performance of Brutus en masse, because this was the Roman whom Mirabeau most closely resembled. Many societies ordered his bust. A Jacobin of Bordeaux explained that Mirabeau was greater even than Rousseau.[94]

Marat, though more beloved than Mirabeau, also drew more criticism. Indeed, no prominent revolutionary had such a mixed reputation. Marat's sympathy for the poor was widely understood and admired. (David's painting of the man is his only truly profound canvas.) In 1791—albeit mainly for political reasons—Marat had denounced the abolition of professional guilds and corporations, which had afforded artisans a measure of protection. He also elicited the deep sympathy of female Parisian *patriotes*. But Marat was not kind. He was perceived as the most sanguinary of all the revolutionary leaders and was only partly trusted, given his regard for the populist Parisian crowd.

At first, few clubs subscribed to his newspapers and many of them demanded his arrest. Orléans and Coutance in November 1792 urged legal action against "the infamous sect and the monster who leads it."[95] Cherbourg ordered the burning of his newspaper, *L'Ami du peuple*.[96] In early 1793, after the February food riots in Paris (an apparent attack on property that occurred before Robespierre and the Jacobin leadership decided to mobilize the poor against their Girondin enemies), a wave of anti-Maratisme swept the clubs. Pézenas inverted one of Marat's favored invocations to say that his head must fall to save two hundred thousand others. Cognac also wanted to do away with the "eternal provoker of murder and pillage."[97]

But Charlotte Corday's murder of Marat in the early afternoon of July 13, 1793, suddenly made of him the premier Jacobin martyr. At Rouen the club wanted to replace the statue of Joan of Arc with a bust of Marat. At Montpellier, in the fall, the *clubbistes* read the "apologia of the incorruptible Marat . . . [This] reading excited the sensibility and applause of the assembly." At their meetings a few weeks later there broke out the "redoubled cries of 'Long Live Marat, long live the National Convention.'"[98] At Courthézon the club made plans to assemble on a forthcoming *décadi*, together with the local officials and National Guard, to weep at the mausoleum "of one of the greatest defenders of liberty, one of the most tender friends of the people, and the most intrepid enemy of *aristocratie*, cruelly murdered by a fury sent forth by this same *aristocratie* and fanaticism."[99] The seaport of Le Havre became Havre Marat. The club of Saint-Pierre-d'Autils renamed itself the Society of the Friends of Marat.[100] At Breteuil-sur-Hon, in the Eure, the rue Au Loup was rather dubiously renamed in his honor.[101]

By the winter of 1793, Jacobins commonly invoked his memory along with Le Peletier's and Chalier's. (Of the three, two of them had been murdered, and one executed.) A brisk trade for their varied busts developed, much as had happened in 1789 with the stones of the Bastille. The Courthézon *clubbistes* in early 1794 considered purchasing a set of busts at Avignon, at one hundred francs apiece. Upon reflection, however, buying prints of the three men was judged more sensible: one could find such portraits in Carpentras, they noted, "at a reasonable price."[102]

The Jacobins' thirst for harmonizing sacrifice ran deep. Every citizen was a potential hero, but every hero had to accept the idea that death might be the price of victory. Grégoire in 1800 reminded his fellow (defeated) Jacobins that "great men, who have almost always been persecuted, like to live in the future: their genius sets them ahead of their times, and they carry their appeal to the tribunal of posterity: the future, which has inherited their virtues, their talents, will acquit the debts of the present. Who could regret having been vilified, if that is the price to pay to spare the tears of humanity?"[103]

Marat once threatened on the Convention floor to shoot himself if his words were not heeded. Ironically, his murderess, Charlotte Corday, a confirmed Plutarchian Republican, was no less ready than he to give up her life for the republic. Though noble-born and convent-educated, this young woman was neither a royalist nor a Catholic, but a Girondin Jacobin, and in the summer of 1793 her sympathies corresponded to the Jacobin thinking of western and northwestern France. She wanted to kill Marat so as to reconcile all Republican Frenchmen, at the cost of her own life. As Saint-Just had explained, "if Brutus does not kill his enemies, he will have to kill himself . . . I have chosen my course."[104] And Corday's gesture was understood precisely in that sacrificial sense by another would-be suicide, Adam Lux. This young German disciple of Rousseau was a friend of the Girondins. Enraptured by Corday, whom he glimpsed on her way to the guillotine, Lux suicidally denounced her judges in a placard that he managed to have printed and posted on the walls of the capital. Arrested, he then demanded the death penalty, so as to inspire all true Republicans.

Jacobins took fraternal liberty seriously. They ritually swore to kill the first of their numbers to betray the cause, or to die with the Revolution if worse came to worst: "I swore to live free or find my grave beneath the ruinations of my fatherland."[105] "All of our thoughts, our entire existence," wrote Collot d'Herbois from Lyons, which had been ravaged, "are fixated on ruins, on graves, where death threatens to engulf us also. And yet, we feel a secret satisfaction . . . It seems to us that humanity has been avenged . . . and the fatherland, made more strong."[106]

So great was the Jacobins' thirst for communitarian sacrifice that in 1792–93, many Jacobins on the way up accepted suicide as a test of their commitment, just as they welcomed it as a way out in 1794–95.

Death was an appropriate punishment for those who rejected Republican fraternity, and self-inflicted death was an answer for those who had failed to make fraternity attractive to the nation. In Paris Robespierre's friend Philippe Lebas took his life on the night of 9 Thermidor; and Robespierre may have tried to shoot himself to avoid arrest. His last speeches do far more than merely hint at suicide as a redemption of failure: "Let them prepare the hemlock for me. I will await them on these sacred seats. At least, I will leave for my fatherland the example of my constant effort. To the enemies of humanity, I will leave opprobrium and death."[107] Those who sought the public good had often perished: "Phocion had had to drink hemlock. So had Socrates on the day of whose death Athenians had crowned themselves with flowers."

Many provincial Jacobins also chose suicide. On 19 Thermidor, during a discussion at the Jacobin club of Nîmes of Robespierre's execution, one of his local supporters suddenly pulled out a pistol, shouted "I am dying for the fatherland," and fired a bullet at himself.[108] One of the fourteen Nîmois Jacobins arrested at the time—of whom five were to be lynched in jail—killed himself. At Marseilles, in these same days, when troops loyal to the Convention surrounded the radical Jacobin club of the city, the club's president jumped off the roof to his death.[109] At Rouen one of Robespierre's local allies, a surgeon and a municipal official named Guyet, killed himself on 12 Thermidor with a razor.[110]

"Liberty or death" was the motto of the heroic Jacobins in the years of their triumph. "Fraternity or death" was the theme of their despair when their dreams of unanimity collapsed.

Together with the cult of sacrifice, education was another key element in the construction of Republican unanimity. Examples of the Jacobins' concern for education abound, from David's didactic canvases and *fêtes*, to the opinions of the smallest clubs, as at Artonne in central France where political education and "philosophy" were assumed to be one and the same thing.[111] At Courthézon the *clubbistes* concluded that "the people can never be too instructed, because it is instruction that develops sentiments [and] renders them worthy and capable of being some day useful to the fatherland and to the nation."[112] In Paris, Ducos, a leading Girondin Jacobin, expressed the same thought more grandly in a speech of 18 December 1792 to the Convention: "It is the task of public education to rectify erroneous notions, occasioned perhaps by habits born of oppression, and even from our resistance to it; education will soften our mores, forestall their ferocity [and] sow in our souls those principles of humanity . . . on which [all] popular governments will henceforth rest."

Education furthered rather than countered nature's work: "le peuple est bon," thought the *sociétaires* of Provins, "mais il a besoin d'instruction" (the people are good but need instruction).[113] Education brought out the happier side of the human condition. "If the theory and practice of education were carried to the point of perfection of which they are capable," reasoned Grégoire, "a criminal code would be almost useless." The clubs themselves, in the words of Lanthenas, were like a branch of public instruction,[114] "schools of civic virtue."[115] At Louhans schoolchildren were required to come to the club every fortnight to show what progress they had made in their studies. At times, the *clubbistes* subsidized schoolteachers' salaries from their own pocket.[116] At Bergerac, at the prompting of visiting Conventionnel Josephe Lakanal, a former priest and schoolteacher, the club decided to levy a tax on the rich to create four local primary schools.[117]

Many Jacobins vacillated between defining education as neutral, apolitical instruction (a Voltairean view) and taking it as moral guidance or a means to spiritual rebirth (a Rousseauean view). They understood that a state which was mindful of civil society's autonomy ought to have a limited sense of its task as educator. But they could not resist the temptation to wrest education from the hands of the church and to make it a vehicle of Republican unanimity. Lanthenas, for example, proposed a system of centralized state education whose purpose would be to teach a "universal morality" that might serve as the basis of the social compact. Education in his scheme would be compulsory for both girls and boys to the age of thirteen. In deference to the simultaneously egalitarian and meritocratic nature of Jacobin ideology, particularly deserving students would receive scholarships and go on to higher study.

It was a mistake, wrote Grégoire, to think with "Diderot and a few others like him that nature creates wicked men. The effect of this discouraging fatalism is to stifle emulation, to cheapen virtue."[118] Education corrected the vagaries of nature and made people whole, a critical advantage, argued Condorcet, in an age newly characterized by the division of labor and the routinization of labor for the poor.

So keen were the Jacobins on education as a key to Republican morality that some of them lost sight of instruction altogether. Because they focused on nature rather than reason, these left-wing iconoclasts dared to attack all higher learning. A citizen who knew many complicated things, they thought, was separated by his knowledge from his fellow men. His strength was a weakness. Some far-fetched Jacobins wanted to abolish not just academies and universities (all of which were either terminated or completely reshaped) but secondary schools as well. In December 1793 Bouquier argued that "aristocratic pedagogy" was a threat to democracy and that the republic should allow only those scientific schools that were basically vocational.[119]

But Romme, a mathematician, rationalist, and confirmed Jacobin, violently (and representatively) disagreed with this obscurantist stand. It was, he asserted, a "profoundly perfidious opinion" to insinuate that "in a state founded on Equality, instruction might be useless; and philosophy, dangerous." That had been the argument of "nobles and some priests." Only a system of national education could "regenerate our customs, and give to the Constitution an unshakable foundation."[120] Jacobins did rank goodness above knowledge, but in their overwhelming majority, they found it hard to imagine that these two values could really strain at each other. Many existing French institutions of higher learning—the celebrated Grandes Écoles like the École Normale, the École Polytechnique, the École Centrale, and the Conservatoire de Musique—were created by Jacobins and neo-Jacobins between 1795 and 1799, as was the modern Institut de France, which replaced the academies, especially the Académie Française, which had been suppressed in August 1793.

The redirection of individual self-love toward the public and communitarian Republican good, was the Jacobins' fondest hope: "see how [Le Peletier's] features are serene," wrote David of the portrait he had just painted of this sacrificial victim. "The man who dies for one's country has nothing to reproach himself."[121] Anyone who doubted that the two goals could coincide completely ceased ipso facto to be a patriot and lapsed into *aristocratie*. Jacobin exegesis even distinguished genuine (and truly communitarian) heroes from the false courtiers of facile popularity who seemed selfless but were in fact intensely selfish.

In his triumph, Robespierre had been hailed as virtue incarnate, a perfect example of sacrifice. But after his fall, the terms of the equation were necessarily inverted; it was now his complete indifference to or even detestation of the public weal that was often mentioned. According to the *clubbistes* of Mayenne after 9 Thermidor, Robespierre "had borrowed the words of justice and probity in order to make himself popular, though his heart was full of vices."[122] Four days after the death of the Incorruptible, the *Vedette de Besançon* likewise denounced him as "a hateful conspirator who needed to sacrifice everything to appease his pride and ambition," the proof being that he had even tried "to dominate public opinion."[123]

A true hero had to be truly representative and fraternal.

Spreading the Word: Rhetorics of Harmony

Who summons each one to common dedication where each will sound in masterly accord? Who makes the storms become like passions? Who weaves pointless green leaves into honored laurels of every kind? Who guards Olympus and unites the Gods? Man's power in the poet incarnate.

Goethe, *Faust*

*J*acobins had a truth, and since they hoped everyone would accept their message, they were born to propagandize. As disciples of Rousseau, the Jacobins could neither understand nor accept faction and division; but as disciples of Voltaire as well, they did not want to coerce. They wanted to convince; and to do this, they worked in every aesthetic register, from elegant allegory to scatological print and song. This political stance up to a point implied a certain conventionality of style. Fascist and Soviet artists of the 1920s worked to find the new aesthetic tropes that would underscore the political novelty of their times. But Jacobin artists, who wanted to convince plain people more than they wished to dazzle their peers or superiors, generally made themselves work within established styles and genres. Still, what Jacobins lacked in creativity they more than made up for by the relentlessness of their search to represent their goal of togetherness.

To that unifying end, the clubs soon moved from excluding visitors to including as many of them as they could. Then, to attract wider audiences yet, the clubs diversified their appeal. They gave public readings. At Honfleur the *clubbistes* had a different subject every day: on Sunday, the "duties of a Republican"; on Saturday, "readings from the best passages of ancient and modern history, especially the crimes of French Kings."[1] Some clubs also organized lectures on such important subjects as "Man's nature and his duties to his fellow men" (at Riom); "Signs that distinguish false patriots" (at Saint-Flour); or "Virtues are the order of the day" (at Agen).[2] Thoughtful revolutionaries who understood that the power of the church depended heavily on its social role in society instinctively responded by turning the clubs into rival social centers. In Burgundy one deputy even suggested club dances as a remedy for counterrevolutionary idolatry.[3] At Reims a card-making Jacobin offered seven thousand cards to the club. Many clubs seriously considered a proposal made by the Poitiers *clubbistes* to launch a balloon designed to scatter over foreign soil thousands of copies "of the French constitution, the catechism of the Rights of Man, and the best works relating to liberty." So that important French aeronautical secrets would not fall into enemy hands, they planned to make the aerial machine self-destruct at the end of its mission.[4] More important perhaps to the Jacobins' propaganda efforts was the Parisian Bureau d'Esprit Public, set up by Roland and the Girondins in late 1792 to systematize the diffusion of Jacobin principles through print. Condorcet argued that thought, word, and debate were inextricably bound to print: "it is through the printing process alone that discussion among a great people can truly be one."[5]

Rousseau's ideal citizens met to think and act. France, alas, was no small Swiss canton where all citizens might know one another. Nevertheless, all French citizens could meet metaphorically by reading the daily or weekly press. The *clubbistes* at Pau reasoned that "it is only from knowing the whole news that truth can be found."[6] Barère urged his readers to read the British press so as to know what the infamous Pitt was thinking.[7]

Of course, long before 1789, newspapers had already become a fixture of social life in France.[8] But the French Revolution gave a vast and democratic push to that trend. Jacobins were obsessed by the power of this particular form of the printed word. Louvet declared a journal that could be sent through the mail to be "the easiest, most prompt, and least costly way to spread the truth."[9] Brissot, who had had a long prerevolutionary career as a publicist, deemed newspapers even more important than the clubs.[10] At Vitry-le-François Jacobins identified three sources of information: the decrees of the National Assemblies, instructions sent by the "mother club" in Paris, and the collective reading of *papiers politiques* on the club's premises.[11] Sensibly enough, some clubs then demanded—unsuccessfully— free franking privileges.

For the Jacobins—as in the enlightened, "feminized" salons of eigh- teenth-century France—reading, speaking, and thinking were cumulative rather than competing activities. Listeners who had heard a writer read his subversive work aloud to the mixed audience of a prerevolutionary salon would have been at home in a revolutionary club.

Many clubs tried to create a newspaper of their own: in Grenoble in De- cember 1789; in Angers, Versailles, Arras, and Aurillac in 1791; in Castres, Nancy, and Caen in the first half of 1792. A few more were launched in 1792, by the Paris club especially, with another handful in 1794 at Reims, Marseilles, Sedan, Chalons-sur-Marne, and Bordeaux.[12]

The societies' assembled members made decisions about the terms, size, and contents of posters. They also promoted almanacs: in September 1791 the Paris Jacobins awarded a prize to Collot for having assembled with the *Almanach du Père Gérard* the text "best adapted to explain to the people the spirit and principles of the French Constitution." They hoped that it would provide "instructive parts" on the history of the Revolution, on the history of kings, and on the themes of duty, Rome, and Sparta. A number of clubs took it upon themselves to reprint this text for local consumption. The Conventionnel Jacques Coupé urged the clubs to distribute it to the peasantry, as part of a five-part program that included newspapers, dance, song, and theatricals. Printing costs were often a club's major expense.

Clubs routinely subscribed to newspapers (as many as twenty at a time). Their favorite in 1792–93 was the relatively inexpensive *Annales patrio- tiques et littéraires de la France* of Mercier and Carra, which tended to downplay social conflict: three hundred clubs subscribed to this sheet. Later, after Carra had opted for Girondism (and was executed in October 1793), many clubs fell back on the *Journal de la Montagne*, which was the Paris club's official journal from June 2, 1793, to November 18, 1794. It had nearly six thousand subscribers—most of them Jacobin appa- ratchiks—and it received a large governmental subsidy.[13] Newspapers were a critical weapon in the Jacobins' armory, whether directed against their avowed enemies or one another: the Paris Montagnard Jacobins did not get around to launching their newspaper until the summer of 1793, when they began their battle with the Girondin Jacobins for control of the provincial clubs.[14]

Journalists like Louis Keralio in the spring of 1790, and Barère and Carra afterward, circularized the clubs to secure subscribers;[15] to attract an audience, Laclos, in his *Journal des amis de la Constitution,* founded in 1790, had a special rubric entitled "Correspondance hebdomadaire" (Weekly Correspondence) to describe the goings-on of the provincial clubs. Cleverly, Carra went one step further and inserted eulogistic references in his columns to this club or that, to secure more paying readers. In fact, we only know of the existence of some women's Jacobin clubs around Dijon because of their being mentioned in the press. Clubs traded their own newspaper with other clubs in order to keep in touch. Private letters carrying public news reinforced a current fed by the newspapermen who published and solicited letters from their public.

Newspapers were read singly and collectively. The literate subscribers of the *Feuille villageoise* were specifically urged to read the paper aloud to their less learned fellow citizens.[16] In many clubs the rules of order specified that newspapers would be read aloud if a number of members requested it. Hours of opening were often set by the arrival of the stagecoach with the latest newspapers (*papiers publics* or *papiers nouvelles*) from Paris. Many club secretaries complained that members took the newspapers home. At Moret many members left "as soon as the news sheet had been read, a considerable number of members left even before the session's end."[17]

We read newspapers desultorily, if at all, bombarded as we are by information of all kinds; but Jacobins read them carefully. The format of their newspapers was plain, small and, in a word, unattractive to the eye. But that did not matter to them. One can easily conjure some *clubbistes,* huddled and enthused over a sheet like a group of Parisian washerwomen whose husbands were away at the front, who met periodically to read Bourdon's *Le Créole Patriote* and ended one such reading with enthusiastic cries of "Long live the Convention! Long live the Jacobins!"[18]

Clearly, then, Jacobins were fascinated by the presentation, consumption, and manufacture of news: journalists, for the Jacobins, were like the poets of Romanticism, the self-proclaimed "hierophants" of modernity. Yet, in the end, Jacobin newspapers were a failure.

True enough, some Jacobin-inspired newspapers did quite well. (To succeed financially, a newspaper had to secure about 500 subscribers.) Readers were of course more numerous, though we have no way of ascertaining precise figures. During the Revolution the *Feuille villageoise,* which from September 1790 onward aimed to find a peasant audience,[19] had a readership of 15,000. Brissot's *Le Patriote français* had 8,000 subscribers and was at times printed in runs of 20,000. By comparison, the most famous of the prerevolutionary French-language newspapers, the *Gazette de Leyde,* had between 4,000 and 9,000 readers.

Generally, however, the Jacobins were unable to make their press durable. Of all the newspapers they founded between 1789 and 1792, only ten proved truly viable and only two survived beyond July 1794. Most did not last for more than a few months. Six hundred clubs subscribed to the Parisian *Journal de la Montagne* after June 1793, but only because they were more or less required to do so. In the Seine-et-Marne, only 13 of the department's 79 clubs signed on.[20] The *Journal patriotique* of the Angers Jacobins had a mere 129 subscribers.

Newspapers inspired by a single brilliant figure like Marat, who wrote his paper from start to finish, including the letters to the editor, did succeed. But many provincial club newspapers were collectively and boringly directed. Clubs created formulaic and tiresomely repetitive sheets: "impassioned, dull-droning, Patriotic eloquence; implacable, unfertile," wrote Carlyle of the revolutionary press in one of his most insightful pages.[21]

From the spring of 1790 on long-winded speeches began to crowd out plain news, which was in any case reported unrealistically and quite predictably, reverses being invariably presented as unforeseen but ultimately useful steps in the eventual unfolding of final victory. As both readers and publicists, the Jacobins were unfruitfully entranced by the echoes of their own voices and disputes. Revealingly, clubs took only the papers that shared their doctrinal angle and ordinarily dropped their subscription to them when opinions diverged. Besides, newspapers were not cheap: a yearly subscription to the *Feuille villageoise* cost nine livres, about four times a worker's daily wage.

Newspapers and club meetings were the Jacobins' principal propagandistic efforts, but because the Jacobins, like the early Christians, believed it their obligation to carry forth the word everywhere and in person (a quasi-religious duty often mentioned in their founding charters), their desire to convert and preach spread to other realms as well. As the political horizon darkened, as enemies arose, propaganda became more and more important to the Jacobins, after late 1791 especially. In October 1792 the Savoyard Jacobins at Chambéry, whose club had come into being only three weeks before, decided to send one hundred of their twelve hundred members "armed with the torch of Liberty and Reason" to both town and country.

Their mission was to instruct their compatriots (whose province had just been annexed to France) about regeneration and the "recovery of their inalienable rights."[22] Regional centers, with close ties to neighboring areas, were especially active in this respect, in the southeast particularly. At Lourmarin a Jacobin who described himself as a "missionnaire du patriotisme" single-handedly created a number of clubs in the Vaucluse, as did Isoard from Marseilles in the Basses Alpes.[23] Constitutional priests, or priests who had abjured their vows, were often chosen by the clubs as the messengers of the new word, perhaps because of their "hands-on" experience.

The Jacobins propagandized the army for moral as well as political reasons. They wanted to secure the army's loyalty but also to encourage soldiers to be heroic citizens. From December 1792 onward many Jacobin—or near-Jacobin—newspapers (those of Marat and Hébert especially) were assigned government subsidies, ostensibly so that they might reach the nation's soldiery. Ironically, since officers frequently disapproved, many of the papers went unread.

Carrying the word, winning friends, and influencing people were critical aspects of Jacobin life. But as to which "word" and how it should be spoken Jacobins were of two minds. As practical men, rooted in their communities, they wanted to speak plainly. But as confirmed idealists, they often preferred abstraction, allegory, metaphor, and imagination to mere description or factual narration. Jacobins cared more about family than they did about homes. Robespierre in early 1793 disdained the "chétives marchandises" (flimsy merchandise) that mattered so much to the poor. Jacobins loved words, particularly lofty words. An accused person might miraculously be let off (even by the perpetrators of the September massacres) if he or she found the right thoughts or gestures to sway a jury or a crowd.

Jacobins were imaginative people. Time and again, one feels, the mind of these successful, practical, highly efficient, and down-to-earth administrators, soldiers, and officials was elsewhere. Their few jokes tended to play on the inconsequentiality of the concrete: "Everything is fine," wrote Baille (who would later kill himself) from Toulon. "There's no bread."[24] From their enemies' point of view, however, Jacobins were unusually prone to (self-serving) "double-thinking."

Of course, many Jacobin goals, such as the abolition of feudal dues, a more just apportionment of taxation, and equality before the law, were substantive issues that everyone understood. But even then, a wide gap separated the abolition of feudal dues as it was understood by peasants and by Jacobins. For the latter, the night of August 4 represented an end to an intolerable system of contempt. (Robespierre characterized the Old Regime as a "cascade of disdain.") Dues mattered in their own right, but the image mattered just as much as the thing itself. Peasants saw things differently. Even those Jacobins who favored working hand in hand with the poor were marching to a different and more distant drum.

Jacobins managed simultaneously to live reality and interpret it as they wished it to be. They saw one thing and thought another, a discrepancy that spilled into many of Jacobinism's seemingly inexplicable contradictions. They could terrorize their neighbors in the name of universal love, or want to make the individual the first pivot of modern social life while continuing to live in the day-to-day context of inherited, familial, clientelistic, and traditionally gendered manners set by regulated custom and corporatized economics. Robespierre once voted against the death penalty; and one of the last acts of this innovating individualist in his hometown of Arras was to draft a statement on behalf of a local, tradition-bound craft guild.

François Furet has eloquently described this abstracted side of Jacobin ways of thinking: the French Revolution, he writes, was a burst of ideas "whose meaning society was hard put to keep within bounds . . . [The Revolution] fuelled the competition for power through an ever escalating egalitarian rhetoric . . . Revolutionary ideology (became) the arena *par excellence* of the struggle for power among groups."[25]

Not surprisingly, the Jacobins pondered not just which words should be spoken but "the sublime art of speaking" itself. They searched high and low to find the signs and symbols that their audience could accept. More particularly, they hesitated between rational and emotional strategies.

Unknowing pre-Romantics, Jacobins thrived on that melodic emotivity which the French Enlightenment had associated with primitive, prelinguistic, "ossianic" times.[26] Isnard, a Girondin Jacobin from Marseilles, once reproved his colleague for not having "respected his enthusiasm." Emotion was a sacred and positive value, which the Jacobins underscored by great sweeping gestures, ably pictorialized by David in his painting *The Oath of the Tennis Court,* where members of the Third Estate are shown baring their breasts in poses that strike us as hopelessly artificial but that these theatergoers found lyrically appropriate. At Lyons the "martyred" Chalier gesticulated, wept, rolled his eyes, and leapt onto tables. Jacobins were known for "giving way to the impetuous movements of their heart." At Courthézon the abrupt appearance in the club of a "défenseur de la Patrie" caused "a sudden moment of ecstasy, admiration, and tenderness" to sweep through the assembled townspeople.[27] In a stylistic burst, Camille Desmoulins wrote that to render "the human race free and happy is a sublime experience."[28] The Jacobins of Vaulry celebrated the feast of Reason with "all the fire and zeal that such an important matter demanded."[29] To paraphrase Carlyle, Jacobin orators did not disdain the finely hewn obelisk; but oftentimes, their instinctive preference was for the sublime Alpine peak.

Jacobin oratory depended on energy and exaggeration. Its practitioners always depicted the nation as on the edge of a precipice or on the verge of doom. *Aristocrates* were intolerably villainous; *patriotes*, dazzlingly courageous. Marat, alternatively praised to the heavens or sincerely loathed, was himself a perfervid author of novelistic and hyperbolic prose, all of which is hardly surprising if we remember that Jacobins lived in an age that saw the birth of literary genres like the Gothic novel, the *roman noir*, and the newly invented melodrama.[30] The Jacobins of Versailles, when they described the king during his trial as a "tiger athirst for blood" and his courtiers as "satellites who lit and stoked his rage,"[31] were speaking as many Frenchmen did at the time, on the stage at least and perhaps in real life.

Jacobin orators relied on a mix of sublime and natural images, at once fascinating and frightening. The abbé Grégoire urged the Paris Jacobins to be "like immobile cliffs, at whose foot the ocean's waves bellow and are shattered."[32] Crises were compared to storms, and the Convention's edicts to bolts of thunder. Dorfeuille, the actor, described the mass executions of Lyonese rebels as the "fire of a thunderbolt."[33] Jacobin orators were fond of such naturalist metaphors: at Abbeville a *clubbiste* likened the eradication of the Catholic Church to the "extirpation by the roots of a poisoned tree that shaded the entire universe."[34] The abbé Grégoire said the hereditary nobility was to a well-managed state what "moss was to vegetables and rust to metals."[35]

Jacobins loved lapidary and melodramatic formulas: "Liberty, Equality, and Fraternity or death"; "Lyons warred on Liberty, Lyons no longer exists"; "virtue without terror is weakness"; "death is an eternal sleep" (a slogan Robespierre did not like); and so on. These aphorisms, we can once again surmise, came naturally to men who saw life abstractly and in black and white.

Jacobins liked to reason a fortiori. They did not argue by building slowly and deliberately from the ground up. They began instead by establishing a hyperbolic, emotionally valid truth and then proceeded to make their more mundane argument, as a footnote to their larger point.

Jacobin orators were careful observers of pantomime. (David gave thought to staging the events of the Revolution in this genre for a *fête*.) They were fascinated by sign language because this silent speech was—or so they thought—not merely pure but preverbal also, and as such a natural tool of regeneration.[36] Jacobins consulted actors on both declamation and gesture,[37] and many people connected with the stage worked closely with the clubs: Talma, who revolutionized the stage by playing Romans in Roman costumes, had ties to both David and the Girondins. Dorfeuille traveled from club to club with his set speeches. Other Jacobins (Collot d'Herbois, Fabre, and the more populist Hébert) had eked out their prerevolutionary living near the stage as authors and impresarios.

At the same time, however, mindful perhaps of a sustained tradition that had been fed by Rousseau—who had criticized conversation, salons, and the *abus des mots*—the Jacobins favored a completely different, unemotional, cold, and rational oratory. Robespierre, a lackluster speaker with a squeaky voice, whose style was quite precise, despised theatricality; and his charisma depended wholly on his audience's sense that he could speak nothing but the truth. "Let us be calm," he advocated, "let us deploy reason in all of its majesty."[38] Saint-Just, after complaining that the mass of paper produced by the bureaucracy was proof of its tendency to inertia, concluded that "it is impossible to govern without being laconic."[39] Condorcet went one step further by emphasizing silent reflection as the means to rise from the private sphere to the universal world of shared ideas.[40]

Jacobins knew full well that the prerevolutionary Parisian art of conversation had too often been the vehicle of dissimulation and insincerity. Plain speech (the preferred mode of many Jansenist linguists) seemed to them superior to embellished prose, especially when aimed at simple people. Cambon, in charge of the nation's finances in early 1794, was often praised for his "briefness and patriotic force." "Do not look for eloquence in my speech," wrote a Jacobin geometer of Loudun to his friends at Poitiers, "I only care about self-evident truths that can ward off the evils and dangers with which fanaticism and ignorance forever surround us."[41] After the king's flight to Varennes, Brissot, one of the first avowed Republicans and a man who liked to eat and dress simply, explained with condescension that he was weary of listening to vague and therefore miserable pro-monarchic objections. He looked forward instead, in both the clubs and the press, to a "cold" discussion—cold but impassioned, no doubt. Ja-cobins distinguished between their calm but energized deliberation and the Machiavellian coldness so characteristic of the icily evil (or ragingly de-spairing) *aristocrates*.

Jacobins also favored scientific metaphors. An orator at Vitry-le-François condemned *aristocrates* who vainly used specious arguments to "divert this column of philosophic fluid, of this vegetable milk of liberty, which is for them what water is to hydrophobes."[42] The Girondin Jacobin journalist Carra announced that he had geometric, mathematical, and geo-graphic proof of the queen's treachery.[43] In one of the most famous images of the day, Grégoire said of kings "that they were in the moral order what monsters were in the physical order of things."[44] Antoine Momoro, a Cordelier, spoke of a "moral saltpeter whose explosions have already so often served the cause of liberty and equality."[45] Electric images were highly prized: in his musings on the function of the clubs, a citizen of Aix reflected that the "friction of ideas [had] electrified the souls of Republi-cans."[46] In Paris a deputy-physicist suggested that the mother society "had electrified the ardent friends of the Revolution" in the capital, who would in turn electrify the provinces.[47] A Jacobin from Caen urged his Parisian brethren to "electrify yourselves . . . We bring you back the sacred fire that you have sent us."[48] Many orators likened the Constitution or even society as a whole to a machine, man-made or celestial. Billaud-Varennes com-pared government to mechanics: features that had not been combined "with precision, both as regards their numbers and their size, will yield un-even motions, and will occasion endless breakage."[49] The Paris society was the sun to the province's moons and planets. And the guillotine, of course, was the most notorious machine of its time.

In short, Jacobins left no oratorical avenue unexplored in order to con-vince. They evinced an eloquence at once "laconic and paroxysmal."[50] Every rhetorical device that brought men together was worthwhile. At Aix a visitor was welcomed by the club's president "with that frankness, that eloquence, and that firmness which alone can serve to propagate the patri-otism that inspires them," to which the visitor responded, we are told, "with much vehemence."[51] Thibaudeau bluntly explained that Jacobin speakers should avoid two shoals: giving dry lists of "unconnected, iso-lated facts, with no connection to one another, without chronology," that would not hold the listeners' attention, elevate the soul, or produce grand effects"; and drowning "heroic actions in a wealth of words, in irrelevant reflections, or gigantic phrase [whereby] one saw the historian's tale rather than the hero."[52]

Emotivity, hyperbole, science, metaphors, and fine words were acceptable, because all of them, singly and together, could become useful paths to a shared truth. "It is very hard to be united by opinions," a Jacobin grammarian explained in a speech to the Robespierrist Paris Commune, "when you are separated by language . . . As children of the same family, we must have the same thought and be moved by the same sentiment."[53] Although many of their myths, symbols, and principles were in fact ambiguously charged (Lucius-Junius Brutus might be seen as an unnatural father or a dedicated patriot; denunciators could be seen as either duplicitous or civic-minded), they abhorred obfuscation.[54] Clearly, the clubs' place was to publicize the assembly's decrees, but how should it be done? asked the *clubbistes* of Castres. By giving "clear and easy explanations," they replied.

The eagerness of Jacobins to carry their message to the nation gives a particular twist to their growing hostility to rural and regional dialects, which were spoken by nearly half of France's inhabitants—Bretons in the west, Basques, Alsatians, Flemings in the north, and speakers of "langue d'oc" patois in the south.[55]

It was a truism of the late eighteenth century that national languages were profoundly expressive of national character; and French—the language of a regenerated, free people—deserved the national and international place of honor it enjoyed. Some of its prestige came from the existence of the exiled diaspora of French Protestants, themselves victims of monarchist tyranny.

Clearly, other systems of communication (like the sign language of the deaf) also had their universalist appeal. But as a rule, Jacobins considered French the most universal of all spoken languages. Accordingly, for their own good, peasants who did not speak the language of Rousseau should be made to learn it. How else could they become the self-governing citizens of a universalist republic? Barère, in a speech of January 27, 1794 (8 Pluviôse, Year II), associated all regional forms of speech with counterrevolution, and the Convention voted to send French language teachers to its border areas. "The two sciences that are the most neglected and the most useful to man," stated the abbé Grégoire, a correspondent of Jefferson who had lived in France for many years but had not learned the language, "are the cultivation of man and the cultivation of the land. No one has better understood this than our brothers in America, where everyone knows how to read, write, and speak his national language."[56]

Though basically committed to the use of French, the Jacobins at first (in 1790) tolerated the local idioms, which were spoken by plain people and which many linguists thought to be more emotionally expressive than French. Many clubs went out of their way to accommodate non-French speakers: they held some of their meetings in dialect, used it for some of their publications, and allowed those who knew no French to speak as they would.

In 1793, however, when they set as their goal the enforcement of their universalist point of view, they rejected dialects. On June 4, 1794, Grégoire spoke of the "needs and means to wipe [dialects] out." "France has received from America," wrote Antoine Tournon, a Jacobin grammarian, "the example of legislative regeneration. Let us give to all nations the example of linguistic regeneration."[59]

To that end, Jacobin linguists brought forth schemes to make French more accessible by simplifying French grammar and making French spelling more phonetic. In 1791 Jacobins of all hues, from Condorcet and Brissot to Anacharsis Clootz and Robespierre, supported a Society of Amateurs of the French Language.

Persecution of dialect speakers was a simpler path, and by 1794, Saint-Just had come to entertain visions of linguistic if not ethnic cleansing. German speakers from Alsace would be resettled in central France, while Alsace would be Frenchified. Alsatian villages should be renamed for soldiers who had died at the front, he proposed.

In part this approach reflected the exasperation of Frenchmen in the capital with the hostility of southern *fédérés* in Provence and the frustration of royalist peasants in the west as well. But the evolution of the Jacobins' thinking on language followed the overall trajectory of their political and linguistic situation.

At first, the Jacobins' innovative use of language and of themes, their "discourse," gave real substance to their new thoughts. In this phase, ideas and social context, politics and culture, words and things, all reinforced one another. For example, by presenting the attackers of the Bastille not as a rebellious mob but as inspired citizens overthrowing despotism, journalists who dealt with the event made it what it has been ever since: a landmark in historical time, the precise moment at which the thousand-year-old Old Regime ceased to be.[58] Stylistically innovative, Jacobin journalists used direct prose, often of the "you-are-there" variety. The Jacobin journalist was himself a transforming hero whose personal descriptions transcended his immediate concerns. His choice of words and syntax underscored the universality of the events he described and marked their relevance to the lives of his regenerated readers. The subject of these early Jacobin sentences might indifferently be the individualistic "I" of the journalist or the collective "we" of the readers.

But this enriching exchange of words, things, and events soon ceased. In 1789 new or renewed words of citizenship and popular sovereignty had enabled Jacobins to formulate their project of universalist fraternity. By 1793 these same words had lost their libertarian meaning. They became instead a weapon of politics, a kind of thought control that enabled the few to exclude and tyrannize the many. As the young Benjamin Constant was to write in 1797, "the perfidious friend, the faithless debtor, the obscure denouncer, the mendacious judge all found ready-made excuses in a set language [*dans la langue convenue*]. Patriotism," he went on, "became the banal and expected excuse for every misdeed. Great sacrifices, selfless acts, and the victories of an austere republicanism born of antiquity became the pretext for the unleashing of selfish passions."[59]

In brief, by 1793, Jacobin rhetoric had become self-referential, stilted, and falsely enthusiastic.[60] Many commentators remarked on the woodenness of late Jacobin oratory. Their "politically correct" circumlocutions became ever more numerous and artificial: nuns were "jeunes anachorètes," soldiers were "guerriers intrépides," bishops were "bipèdes mitrophores," nobles were the "ci-devant aristocratie équestre," and so on. As Thomas Crow has acutely observed of David, "the more coercive and conformist the political moment, the more abstractly beatific [his] images had to be."[61]

This trend calls to mind, once again, Hegel's notion of absolute freedom. In the first months of the Revolution (and of the prerevolution, in 1788–89) the Jacobins' use of new words (nation, *civisme*, citizenship) was vital and socially creative: new words created new ways of feeling. Sensibly, Jacobins at this point were hostile to representations of *fêtes* on the stage (Plato's mimesis of mimesis) because they wanted *fêtes* to be associated in the public mind with spontaneity and transparency rather than thespian artifice. Going further Barère even urged revolutionaries to "reform spectacles where people go for money" and asked that they be completely transformed and "turned into fêtes that are given for the people."[62]

But as the Jacobins moved toward abstraction, and lost touch with French society, their *fêtes* became dryly and artificially allegorical and their words calcified. When the French Revolution became "a discursive event" *only*, rather than a cultural and social revolution that shaped and was shaped by new words and concepts, its days were numbered.

Michelet first commented on this critical shift, which also gives visual expression to Hegel's notion of "absolute freedom," defined as a flight toward abstraction that was born of an inability to give citizenship true meaning in a society unexpectedly divided by nascent class divisions.

*T*o sway their fellow citizens, Jacobins relied principally on the spoken and the written word. Instinctively, Jacobin authors adapted the telling of their revolutionary story to the requirements of the literary genres that were popular at the time, just as contemporaneous Methodists used popular tunes to express a renewed religious spirituality. In 1789 alone, more than a hundred texts adapted politics to either English romances or French *contes*, the likes of which Voltaire had made so popular.[63]

But Jacobins were vitally interested in other mediums also. Singing was an especially important part of Jacobin ritual, as appears from the testimonial of the Conventionnel *en mission* Pierre Dubouchet, who wrote that "nothing is more suitable than hymns and patriotic songs to electrify Republican souls. I have witnessed their prodigious effect during my mission in the departments. We always ended the meetings of both clubs and official sessions by singing hymns, and their invariable effect was the enthusiasm of members and spectators."[64] It was the Jacobins' role in the diffusion of "La Marseillaise" as a revolutionary anthem in 1792 that ensured its success. (At Metz a revolutionary Jewish enthusiast penned a Hebrew version of the hymn.) In the south especially, public dancing of the farandole was a ritualized part of the Jacobin *fête*, a pan-artistic, cross-class happening, with dance, costumes, statuary, instrumental music, song, and declamation. "We ended by dancing and singing the Carmagnole," wrote the *clubbistes* of Laval, "with a musical accompaniment; in a word, we had an opera, a ballet, and an orchestra, and above all else, a frank gaiety that left the most delicious sensations in the souls of the spectators."[65] Indeed, singing was so much of a good thing that at Provins, the abstemious, self-denying *clubbistes* decided to allow it only on the *decadi*.

Unlike Rousseau, in this respect at least—since Jean-Jacques had been a confirmed enemy of the corrupting Genevan stage—the Jacobins encouraged every art form, provided that it be politicized: seldom has any group of people been so massively adverse to Kant's description of high art as purposiveness without a purpose. "I consider artists to be very fortunate," wrote a Jacobin poet at Rouen, "when they dedicate their genius to the public spirit, to the benefit of their brothers, in a word, to the republic."[66] In Paris, on March 10, 1794, the Committee of Public Safety opened a new Théâtre du Peuple to further the regeneration of the dramatic arts. In Paris and the provinces, Jacobins attended plays and sponsored benefit performances for the army and for war victims. They thought it right that actors donate their time as Jacobins had donated their zeal. The highlight of any show came when, on both sides of the stage, enthralled spectators and actors joined in singing or recitation, a conjunction of purposes which proved that the artificial stage was a true representation of current politics, and therefore no artifice at all.

Jacobins, one must add, also censored plays. François de Neufchâteau, once blessed by Voltaire and himself an erstwhile Jacobin, was imprisoned for his staging of Richardson's *Pamela*. So was Gingené, the editor in the spring of 1794 of a publication which had mildly suggested that apolitical, creative artists might also have a place in the Revolution.[67]

Nevertheless, Jacobins were intent patrons of the arts. In many ways, moreover, they were themselves everyday artists who created or revived innumerable symbols and allegories. They assumed that art's first function was to represent mimetically, but they also understood the captivating value of symbols like the tricolor flag; the revolutionary pike, a (masculine and Freudian?) symbol of direct action; and the living and fruitful trees of liberty, "le signe chéri des français" (the dearest sign of the French, a distant echo of festive maypoles and pre-Christian folk customs).[68] In June 1792 the Jacobins of Mazargues, a village next to Périgueux, proudly offered to their urban brethren a "crown of pines" borne by their own tree. They chose their symbols with care: at Montignac the *clubbistes* hesitated; elms did grow more quickly, but oaks were a more forceful symbol. They selected the oak.[69]

In fact, Jacobins obsessed about signs. Just as Condillac had thought that words could express essences, so Jacobins believed that signs might perfectly express "the signified," as did, for example, the physical appearance of their foes. The true Jacobin wore his heart on his sleeve and could be immediately recognized as virtuous by his fellow Jacobins, just as *aristocrates* could be judged by their conspiratorial physiognomy.

Baroque obfuscation was completely foreign to the Jacobins' way of thinking. They prized immediate comprehensibility and created or appropriated many images of light, transparence, and all-seeing (Masonic) eyes. Bernard Poyet, who described himself as an "architecte Jacobin," despaired at being denounced as a counterrevolutionary because the classical motifs he had set on a canon foundry of his design were misunderstood and taken (wrongly) to represent monarchic crowns. Wiser than he, many Jacobin architects relied on *architecture parlante,* in which the shape of a building or its architectural details spoke quite literally to its functions (chains on a prison gate, flowing water on a fountain, and so on). Indeed, even before the Revolution, the architect Claude-Nicolas Ledoux—no Jacobin, to be sure; but an artist whose style expressed the feelings of the age—had proposed a bordello in the shape of an erect phallus. This type of thinking was often replicated after 1789, if only in the sense that a plain style was meant to express plain feelings. Many Jacobin monuments that employed classical or Christian motifs (Cato or Hercules; martyrs or grieving mothers) came complete with an explicative legend, written emphatically not in Latin but in French. Jacobins in charge of staging parades weighed the advantages of live models for dead heroes rather than plaster statues. Which would be the more convincing—an exact look-alike or a more suggestive image?[70] They preferred song to orchestral music, whose message they found too general.[71]

Of course, when pressed, Jacobins agreed that external signs might well be irrelevant: "remember above all else," said the president of the club at Vitry-le-François, "that you can judge men only by their habitual actions. The feelings they display externally when confronted by circumstances they did not expect are nearly always the image of their innermost sentiments."[72] Why should Jacobins *not* be forced to wear a phrygian bonnet? Because, as a spokesman for the Jacobin majority explained, clothes are neither here nor there: "It is by his actions that a patriot is judged."[73] In Paris Saint-Just concurred: "Let us not always judge men by their speech and appearance. Those who today say and act differently from the way they spoke and acted yesterday are guilty, in our eyes, of dissimulation."[74]

Still, on balance, it was only for the enemies of the Revolution that outward sign might be no proof of inner grace. One Conventionnel surmised that the enemy's heart had renounced what his hand was signing, something that could never have happened to this Conventionnel since his own heart, word, and pen were always in complete accord.

Jacobins pitied fellow Jacobins who had been deceived. Any honest man, after all, might be duped once. In fact, to have been fooled by the false sign of a hypocritical *aristocrate* was roundabout proof of one's own honesty. At the same time, of course, as Billaud threateningly said to Danton upon the arrest of his crooked friend Fabre, one must not be too misguided for too long.

In this context of overlapping signs and symbols, conforming to the established rituals of the Revolution was an acid test of political rectitude. Clubs festooned their meeting halls with a rich variety of symbols that asserted their revolutionary commitments: busts of votive figures; models of the Bastille; French, American, English, and Polish flags; portraits; honor rolls; allegories of virtue; tablets of the Rights of Man; and revolutionary mottoes, the most common of them being "Liberty, equality, fraternity, or death."[75] At meetings members were careful to stick tell-tale cards into their hats.

Needless to say, given the tempo of revolutionary politics, many charts, banners, and busts appeared and then suddenly disappeared. The remains of Mirabeau, which had been placed in the Pantheon, were removed therefrom in November 1793. Likewise, Marat's corpse, though eulogized in July 1793, was "de-Pantheonized" in November 1795, and his ashes thrown into the public sewer.[76] Initially, the Paris Jacobins were pleased to own the bust of the materialist philosopher Helvetius, a hero of anti-Catholicism; but Robespierre, who sponsored the cult of the Supreme Being and did not like the "atheistic" Encylopedists, arranged for its removal.[77] The rise and fall of revolutionary symbols serves as an excellent barometer of revolutionary politics.

Clothing also became a symbol to the Jacobins: rare was the bourgeois Jacobin (like Thibaudeau, a notorious opportunist) who dared to imitate the dress of the Parisian sans-culottes. Jacobins ordinarily recognized that people were free to dress as they pleased. On October 29, 1793, the Convention had formally confirmed that right. But they expected citizens, women especially, to dress respectably and in a civic manner. At Reims a drummer was reprimanded for wearing "unconstitutional clothing." Goddesses of liberty or nature might in print and painting display their nurturing breasts (a statue erected in 1793 had ninety-three of them, one for each department), but ordinary citizenesses were expected to be more chaste. Much was expected also of priests or former priests. Should Jacobins wear hats, bonnets, or no headgear whatever? Should Alsatians be allowed to wear Germanic folk costumes? Should members wear their hair short ("à la républicaine") or long?[78] Complicated arrangements were worked out from place to place and time to time. At Bénévent the rule was that hair could be no longer than eight inches. In the Paris *sections*, wearing the red phrygian cap (which had been associated with convicts) was made mandatory in December 1792.[79] The Jacobins of Reims decided that the president, irrespective of his wishes, would be required to wear the now popular red phrygian cap and that ordinary members might do so if they wished. At Montaigut, however, the *clubbistes* ordered six bonnets "to decorate the [club's] president, secretaries, and censors when carrying out their duties."[80]

Wearing the national (blue, white, and red) cockade became an affair of state. Some clubs required it; the club at Montauban decided to expel from the city all strangers who did not wear it. But others wanted to deny suspects and nobles the right to wear this revolutionarily ennobling sign. In any instance, on July 8, 1792, men were required by national law to wear it, as were women on September 21, 1793. At Carcassone the *clubbistes* urged that this law be "vigorously enforced."[81] Robespierre himself was always impeccably dressed and peruked in the manner of prerevolutionary times. Thus, the Jacobins made conflicting fashion statements, but all spoke to a fund of shared concerns.

More expressive than clothes were the very bodies of the Jacobins, both male and female, and of their enemies as well.[82] Naked Jacobin masculine bodies expressed the myth of the warrior citizen, and were the nation's own. The nurturing bodies of women, by contrast, belonged both to their children, who had a natural right to breastfeed, and to their warriorhusbands.

When intact, Republican bodies represented triumphant nature: although David's private portraits were intensely realistic—consider his self-portrait with a prominently displayed facial disfigurement—his official likenesses of revolutionary heroes like Marat or Robespierre were either plainly inaccurate or highly stylized. David's Jacobin bodies betokened a perfect, transcendental truth.

Even injured or impaired masculine bodies had value as representations of the sacrificial commitment to the Grande Nation: Marat's corpse, though decomposing rapidly in the summer heat, with one arm stitched to its trunk, was triumphantly paraded through Paris. It was a common practice of visiting soldiers in the clubs to bare their wounded bodies so as to underscore their spoken words.

One can also read the morbid appeal of the guillotine as an inverted sign: there the body of the anti-Jacobin was deprived not merely of life but of wholeness. Whereas Jacobins were heroes fated to immortality, the rejected, guillotined, disjointed bodies of anti-Jacobin conspirators and *aristocrates* were bloody proof of their moral as well as physical annihilation. For good measure, Louis's and Marie Antoinette's royal and decapitated remains were thrown into a lime pit.

The executions of the Old Regime had contrapuntally opposed the brutally disjointed bodies of criminals to the wholeness of the king's body: the gruesome dismemberment in 1757 of the failed regicide Damiens, who had struck the king's sacred body with a knife, was an eloquent reminder of that bond. In imitative contradistinction to these hallowed precedents, revolutionary punishment inverted this rite. As the bodies of counterrevolutionaries were mauled and severed publicly, the revolutionary's body became immortal.

*J*acobins loved to sing the praises of selfless men and heroes, but they needed also to deride the profane meanness of their enemies. Punishment involved shaming. Clubs kept not just rolls of honor but rolls of dishonor as well. A constitutional bishop suggested that the aristocrat François, marquis de Bouillé, who was to have helped Louis XVI on his flight to Varennes, should have his name written up in red letters, so that passersby might disdain it; and the names of right-wing deputies were indeed put up in such colors on a black background at the club in Montpellier. At Largentière the club considered issuing yellow cartridges to cowardly National Guards.[83] The club at Tulle, where the pursued Girondin Bernard Lidon had killed himself, placed his ashes in "an urn of shame."[84] A somewhat deranged Conventionnel named Jean Debry even proposed that dissident priests found guilty of organizing resistance to the Revolution be branded.

Jacobins believed in the close fit between fact and symbol and fetishistically inverted them in terms of cause and effect. Destroying the sign would help somehow to solve the problem expressed in the sign: General Dumouriez, for example, who had betrayed the nation in April 1793, was often burnt in effigy, as was Buzot in his hometown. At Marseilles Mirabeau's bust was veiled. At Chartres the bust of Petion was decapitated. Many clubs organized the burning of medieval parchments, papal bulls, feudal records, and university diplomas. At Lauris the Jacobins decided to erect and set on fire a tree of feudalism with documents pinned to it in lieu of leaves.[85] When supporters of the king circulated a petition in June 1792 to protest the action of the Parisian crowd that had broken into the royal palace, the club at Lons-le-Saulnier ordered it burnt on the public square. The practical result of these auto-da-fés was, of course, to make impossible some future recourse to the courts; but the more important and quasi-magical effect was to annihilate a monarchic past or an obnoxious present. The *clubbistes* of Saverne wished to burn some remaining royal portraits "so that the fact of their existence would be completely destroyed in the memory of right-thinking people."[86] Vandalism (already discussed in the context of the Jacobins' indifference to the past) was not by any means common to all Jacobins. But it did exist and have obvious relevance to the Jacobins' desire to give their own symbols a freer field of play.

An absurd version of the Jacobins' attention to hostile signs came with the execution at Bordeaux in early 1794 of the actor Arouch, who was found guilty of having too strongly declaimed, while on the stage, "Long live our noble King!" In vain did he exclaim at his trial and on the way to the guillotine: "But it was in my part!"[87]

Jacobins took pains to destroy rival signs and to enforce the Convention's decree on the destruction of coats of arms and royal fleurs-de-lis. The secretary of the club of Carcassonne ripped a cross from a woman's neck because she should have been wearing "un coeur de Marat."[88] Alternative symbols were not just destroyed but transmogrified or displaced by a new, revolutionary version. A republic, explained Saint-Just in 1793, is constituted by the "complete destruction of its opposite"; on the day of Bailly's execution in late 1793, the guillotine was moved to the Champ de Mars, the site of the massacre he had ordered in July 1791. At Montpellier, in September 1793, the club decided that on a coming Sunday the British flag together with a mannequin of the "infâme Pitt" would be burnt on the city's main square, and that a liberty tree would be planted on that square, "at the very spot where had stood the statue of the tyrant," Louis XIV in this instance.[89] At Aix the club distributed food on Christmas Day, an obviously preemptive step. The Jacobins of Courthézon put a red bonnet on the statue of Saint-John. The Montaigut Jacobins staged a *fête* where the tricolor flag overthrew the monarchy's white standard. At Louhans, Mirabeau's bust was smashed on the occasion of a countervailing *fête* in honor of Marat.[90] In February 1793 a Parisian Jacobin said of Claude Deseine (a deaf sculptor) that he had "used his chisel to reproduce the traits of the most immoral of men" (a reference to Mirabeau, who had died in 1791), but that he would soon "purify that chisel by making the bust of Michel Peletier."[91] At Auch, the Jacobins decried the use of black cloth in funerals: a tricolor cloth would be more appropriate, they thought.[92] The Parisian Jacobins agreed. A report to the Paris Commune on 21 Nivôse, Year II, called for the edging of cloths in various hues: white for those who died prematurely (with the legend "They were growing for the fatherland"); red for adults ("They were living for the *patrie*"); and blue for the aged ("They lived for the *patrie*"). At Gaillac the *clubbistes* instructed the municipal councillors to participate in new funerary rites. It was necessary, they explained, "to carry out for citizens those duties which humanity demands," and since Catholic rituals had been abolished, a new ceremony should be elaborated. Councillors would be involved sequentially in this "fonction importante," wearing the signs of liberty.[93] The General Council of the town concurred, though it also chose to remind the *clubbistes* that the estates of dead private persons should continue to pay for these new rites.

Fragments or ruins of older symbols were often recycled as part of new monuments. The painter David urged that some statues of the Old Regime be melted down so that "posterity might learn that the republic's first . . . monuments were built with the debris of the last five monarchs' luxury."[94] Renaming towns and streets was an easy way to achieve this goal of signalized rebirth as when a "rue Duchesse" became "Benevolent Street." In the Bourbonnais, somewhat bizarrely, the town of Lurcy-Lévis (named after a great noble family) became Lurcy-le-Sauvage. The paths of Jacobin *fêtes* were carefully planned to include former clerical or monarchic sites (like the Tuileries Palace or the Church of Sainte Geneviève—now the Pantheon—so that royal or ancient buildings might acquire a new and revolutionary image.

Jacobins did at times keep some older symbols, but only to degrade them morally. Do not destroy the house of Dumouriez, said the Jacobins at

Toul. It would be much better to preserve Dumouriez's childhood home as a "monument to infamy."[95] Let us keep Richelieu's tomb, proposed Grégoire: "seeing such monuments reinforces our hatred of tyrants by dooming them . . . to be perpetually pilloried."[96]

Logically enough, Jacobins were exasperated by the destruction of their own signs: they were shocked when spectators ripped up their posters or ignored the anniversaries of such great revolutionary events as the execution of the monarch and the fall of the Bastille, which all regenerated citizens knew as "the time of their birth."[97] Jacobins were aghast when their enemies desecrated or chopped down liberty trees, those ubiquitous and arboreal symbols.

And inevitably, after 9 Thermidor, the Jacobins turned upon many of their own, now discarded signs with as much vigor as their enemies had done. At Courthézon the *clubbistes* waited for the arrival of a visiting Conventionnel to stage a parade through town ending at the foot of the tree of liberty, where they burned the effigy of Marat waiting on "the tail of Robespierre" (an obscene pun that referred to die-hard Montagnards). For good and exculpating measure, they also threw into the blaze their own society's diploma inscribed "Terror is the order of the day."[98]

*J*acobin aesthetics were complex. Although they used plain and immediately comprehensible signs, Jacobin artists also relied heavily on allegory (perhaps showing an angel blowing in a trumpet that represented fame, or truth as an unveiled woman). This allegorical concern was in some sense surprising because tropes of this kind had been decried before 1789 by enlightened art critics, then more intent (as the Jacobins also were) on spontaneity and unspoiled nature. But from a Jacobin point of view, allegory, which the Jacobin architect Quatremère de Quincy described as "an imitation that is to some extent non-imitative," had its merits nonetheless because it too could help to clarify and dignify the more complicated mechanisms of mundane social life. Allegory reminded Jacobins that reality was to be transcended, that society should be transparent, that man should rise above himself, that what was seen could stand for what was as yet unseen.

The entire range of Jacobin aesthetics, symbol, and oratory came together in the decor and speeches of the civic *fête*. Reminiscent in their purpose and their method of ancient Greek and civic theater, the *fêtes* were complex communitarian performances. To bring their message home, the organizers of these public feasts (whose political purpose has already been described) mobilized every possible aesthetic avenue, suitably revolutionized.

Often staged outdoors and in commemoration of fallen martyrs, the *fête* ritually moved as a procession from one hallowed historical site to another or, in small towns where no such sites existed, from one public square to another.

The Old Regime *fêtes* had been spectacles where the faithful observed more than participated. In the Roman service, moreover, officiants in their robes resembled actors in disguise. The Jacobin *fête* inverted these relationships completely, or tried to do so. When Jacobin participants wore allegorical costumes, they assumed natural, unaffected symbols, as when Robespierre carried a sheaf of wheat at the celebration of the cult of the Supreme Being in May 1794, or young women dressed in white as goddesses of Reason in October 1793.[99] Like the imposition of French over dialects, the style of the *fêtes* evolved in ways that paralleled the overall evolution of Jacobinism's purpose. Many of the earlier *fêtes* of the Revolution had been spontaneous and quite wild, in the late fall of 1793 especially. By contrast, the late Jacobin *fête* was highly structured. The Festival of the Supreme Being in the spring of 1794, for example, was pacific and orderly, in striking opposition to previous festivals, like the *fêtes de la raison* that had been celebrated in the previous winter and had involved ribald and feminized scenes of symbolic destruction.[100] Because it focused on the destruction of the Old Regime and on placating the popular movement, Jacobinism had at first gravitated toward theatrical and even operatic rituals of cathartic violence. But later festivals were more transcendental in their purpose. Michelet was not wrong to see in that stylistic shift a sign of the Jacobins' removal from the cordial unanimity of 1790 to the sectarian ideology of Robespierrism.

Jacobin poetics and ritual, as Crane Brinton insightfully understood half a century ago, bring to the fore another critical element of Jacobinism, namely, its connection to religion. Was Jacobinism truly an expression of Enlightenment ideas? Or should we see it instead as a religion, as Hegel and even Tocqueville did? "The French Revolution," wrote Tocqueville, "is a political revolution which worked like and then took on the appearance of a religious revolution."[101] The archreactionary Louis de Bonald, who likened Jacobins to Mohammedans, argued that both groups despised the one true religion. Bonald also pointed out that these "sects" sought to destroy the family, the one through divorce, the other through polygamy![102]

Jacobins resolutely denied that theirs was a religion at all. Jacobinism, they thought, was a secular ideology and set of attendant practices—a symbolically rich but earthbound "political culture" in today's parlance—that could fruitfully coexist with and perhaps complement any existing religion. When a Jacobin at Castres suggested that both Protestant and Catholic women be invited to participate in the celebration of Bastille Day in 1791, a fellow member remarked that "there could be no question of religion when patriotism was at stake."[103] The idea, he went on, was to invite not these or those persons but "everyone in general." Specific forms of worship did not matter to them: Protestant children, explained a Jacobin at Niort, should be admitted to the local Catholic secondary school, where they might learn "this universal moral sense, which makes for worthy men and good citizens regardless of the nature of the cult they worship."[104] Peace, declared the *Patriote français* in February 1790, can only reign where all cults cherish and interweave one another, as was true in Philadelphia, where seventeen different religions cohabitated peacefully.

For many months, the clubs maintained close ties to the dominant Catholic Church. Six percent of all Jacobins whose profession is known to us were priests (who accounted for a mere 0.5 percent of the French population, so that priests may well have been the most overrepresented profession in the clubs). Even Dom Gerle—whose (defeated) motion of April 1790 aimed to make Catholicism the religion of the state, was a member of the Paris club. At Ligny-en-Barrois in the Meuse, twenty-nine of the ninety-two founding members were priests.[105]

The warmth Jacobins might feel toward religion in general came out in September and October 1790, when the clubs enthusiastically accepted the Civil Constitution of the Clergy. In early 1791 many clubs were heavily involved in the choices of the new priests and bishops. The abbé Fauchet, for example, was elected president of the Paris Jacobins in November 1791. In 1789, he had taken part in the attack on the Bastille; and in April 1791, thanks to the *clubbistes*, he had been elected constitutional bishop of the Calvados department.

According to the Jacobins, the constitutional church and the clubs were destined to agree. After all, were they not both "noninstitutions" of a kind, since neither juring priests nor Jacobins had any selfish goals? "Qu'est-ce que l'Église? c'est la réunion des fidèles" (What is the church? the coming together of the faithful).[106] The same definition applied to the clubs, which assembled citizens who spoke not for themselves but for the entire nation. "If the principles of the purest, most unadulterated Christianity were ever forgotten," explained a nonconstitutional and episcopal vicar to the Jacobins of Lauris, whose first president had been a priest, "we could recover them painlessly. The French Constitution itself finds in [those Christian principles] its strength and a renewed vigor. It is by marrying religious and civic duties," he wrote, "that men can be made religious without being uncivic, and patriotic without being irreligious."[107] "It is not God who needs religion, it is man," wrote Camille Desmoulins. "God has no need for incense, professions, and prayers; but we need to have hope, consolation, and a rewarder."[108] As late as 1793 many Jacobins pointed to the early Christians' cult of equality as a living model. Jesus had been "the first sansculotte." In April 1794 Gobel, the more or less Hébertist constitutional archbishop of Paris, was charged with atheism as well as conspiracy.

But despite their quasi-metaphysical affinities, Jacobins and Catholics rapidly parted ways as the nonconstitutional, orthodox, and papal church moved ever further from the Revolution. Religion and "refractory" priests—clerics who had refused to accept the Civil Constitution—became a major subject of club discussion in the spring of 1791 and 1792.

When hundreds of priests renounced their vows, the clubs welcomed these apostates, particularly when the new members evinced a desire to marry. Some of their conversions were announced on club floors; others took place in churches where a priest might enter a confessional in his clerical robes and emerge, regenerated (like Superman from his phone booth!), in the uniform of a National Guardsman. Eventually, many clubs asked that nonjuring priests be rounded up. In April 1792 the Jacobins of Nantes discussed having them arrested or deported; and on August 26, 1792, two weeks after the fall of the monarchy, their expulsion was indeed decided.

Religious matters quickly went from bad to worse. The influence of refractory priests on women was a particularly sore point for many Jacobins. The priests were said to be the "secret perturbators of familial tranquility; they cause women to distance themselves from their husbands, which runs counter to the unambiguous words of Christ, who never ceased to urge women to remain united to their spouses."[109] Soon, even the prorevolutionary juring priests who had accepted the Civil Constitution of the

Clergy lost favor with the Jacobins. The club at Aix—clearly a radical society—had begun to side against them as early as May 1791. By late 1791 a number of southern clubs were physically humiliating them. In April 1792, when the National Assembly decided in principle that priests should be forbidden to wear clerical garb in public, only one club protested; and in early June 1793, at the height of the struggle with the Gironde, Chabot, himself a defrocked priest, argued (absurdly) that the constitutional clergy were the Jacobins' worst enemies.

To be sure, in 1793, Montagnard Jacobins disliked the constitutional clergy more than the Girondin Jacobins did, though some of these "Brissotins" (like Isnard) were fanatically anticlerical as well.[110] But the supposed connection of the Gironde to the constitutional clergy, symbolized by the abbé Fauchet (who was executed in late October 1793), did neither the Girondins nor the juring priests much good. Eventually, most constitutional priests were pushed out of the clubs, though some of them were readmitted after the fall of Robespierre in the winter of 1794.

Revolutionary anticlericalism climaxed in the fall of 1793 with dechristianization, which was marked by the shutting of churches, the taking down of church bells, the confiscation of valuable ritual objects, and the forced conversions of priests. True enough, this movement was not as a rule initiated by the clubs: it was more often the tool of deputies from Paris (like Albitte, Fouché, and Javogues and his assistant Dorfeuille) and of the sans-culotte militias (the *armées révolutionnaires*) that radiated out of Paris and some provincial cities. Nonetheless, many clubs were involved not just in the staging of anticlerical revolutionary *fêtes*, but in the humiliation of priests and in their forced conversion and marriage.

Jacobinism's relationship to Protestantism and Judaism also moved from tolerance to rivalry and persecution. In the south especially, Protestants were among the warmest supporters of the Revolution, and some Calvinist ministers, like Jeanbon Saint-André and the Rabaut brothers, not only joined the clubs but became national political figures of the first rank. (One of the Rabauts was executed, but Jeanbon Saint-André survived and later became a Napoleonic prefect.) At Montauban, a southern city on the Tarn river whose population was heavily Catholic, most of the *clubbistes* were Protestants,[111] and the driving force of anti-Jacobinism in many parts of the southern Languedoc region was anti-Protestantism in disguise, although Protestant Jacobins were careful to present their own revolutionary involvement as a nonreligious, secular, and universalist preference.

In the mid-1790s Catholic polemicists liked to present Jacobinism as the historical successor to the Reformation, which may not be untrue metahistorically but was certainly not so in the shorter run: the Jacobin-dominated Convention just as intently shut down Protestant temples as it closed the churches of the Catholics. (In the Gard fifty-one out of seventy Protestant ministers resigned their post.) Protestants who were Jacobins did not complain. What was fair for the Catholic clergy had to be acceptable all around.

The situation of France's forty thousand Jews, though not dissimilar, was more complicated. In 1789–99 the underlying Frenchness of Protestants was never questioned, even by those who deplored their foreign ties. But in prerevolutionary years, even the most vocal defenders of Jews like the abbé Grégoire imagined Jews as quasi-foreigners. The emancipation of Jews was important but only as a step toward their Frenchification and eventual conversion. Jews simply were not yet French.

After 1789, however, many regenerated Jacobins came to understand the logic of including Jews as citizens; and hundreds of Jews responded by becoming enthusiastic Jacobins. Though many Alsatians (like Jean-François Reubell) were notorious anti-Semites, the Jacobins of Strasbourg, when asked in January 1790 by their Parisian brethren what they thought about the granting of citizenship to southern Jews, responded that Alsatian Jews should be citizens as well. "The Jewish sect," wrote a *clubbiste* at Nîmes of Jews who had voluntarily contributed to the war effort, "has been worthy of our revolutionary circumstances; it is the first sect of the department to offer to us its ritual vessels."[112] At Carpentras Jewish Jacobins, after transforming their synagogue into a Temple of Reason, went one step further in February 1794 and made it the site of a Jacobin club. As individuals, Jews joined Jacobin societies at Avignon, Bordeaux, and Nîmes, poorer Jews tending to be more radical than the richer ones.

By 1794 Jacobin opinion on Jews was split. Apolitical Jews were an object of derision and persecution. Tallien, a Jacobin terrorist who ruled at Bordeaux, lumped together Old Regime judges and Jewish merchants as "more than suspect." Baudot, a friend of Danton, disliked all Jews: they more than anyone, he wrote, should have welcomed the Revolution since they had been "beasts of burden" under the Old Regime. But in every town, he wrote, "they set their cupidity higher than their love of the fatherland, and keep to their ridiculous superstitions in the place of reason. I wonder if it wouldn't be worthwhile to think about regenerating them through the guillotine," a joking reference, perhaps, to Grégoire's prerevolutionary plan for the regeneration of Jews through freedom. Many Jacobins in eastern France gave Jews a hard time, denying them *certificats de civisme*, expelling them from the National Guard, and trying to exclude them from the clubs. At Thann all Jews were placed under surveillance, and the club at Toul wanted to deport "suspect Jews."[113]

As a rule, Jacobin thinking on Jews and Jewishness developed along one of two lines. At times, Judaism was condemned along with other faiths. Synagogues were shut down. At Dijon the club demanded that the ritual Jewish slaughter of animals be suspended. "All citizens without distinction" should eat the same meat.[114] At Besançon a Jacobin denounced Jews for their particularist desire "to make [their] people distinct from a generous nation that has sundered their shackles."[115]

But more often Jews were considered as members of this or that political faction rather than as Jews per se. Conventionnels promoted Jews who were politically reliable. Conversely, at Nîmes after Thermidor, victorious rightists purged all Jews from the club. Overall, two Jews were executed there, one as a Jacobin moderate and the other as a Jacobin extremist. Without exception, those Jews who were prosecuted either by Jacobins or by anti-Jacobins at Lyons, Nîmes, or Paris were put to death for their politics and not for their religion or supposed race. The Paris Jacobins were doctrinally on target in their view of the problem when they concluded that Jewishness was a nonissue: "The republic does not know the meaning of the word Jew," explained a *clubbiste* on 6 Brumaire, Year II (October 27, 1793), "because this term no longer refers to a people but to a sect. The republic has no interests in sects and deports its votaries only when they disturb the social order."[116]

Jacobinism's anguished relationship of rivalry to all religious institutions including the constitutional clergy, which was its own creation, brings us back to Tocqueville's view of Jacobinism as religion. In many aspects, ranging from ritual to theology or principle, Jacobinism, as it moved from sensibility to ideology, was—or rather, *became*—a kind of religion that necessarily competed with other religions for the loyalty of men's minds and feelings.

Some roots of Jacobinism's neoreligious intolerance have already been described. Numerous other links can be made between Jacobinism and religious passion, especially as regards rites and symbols.[117] Jacobins did not precisely pray to the Lord as Louis XVI's subjects had prayed to their

Christian God; but they did "implore" their "deity" to look favorably on the designs of the Grande Nation. Moreover, many Jacobin ways, words, and means were clearly borrowed from Roman Catholic ritual. Contemporaries took notice when, in late July 1789, processions of white-robed penitents marched religiously from one end of Paris to the other in thanks for the Revolution's "deliverance" two weeks before. Likewise, in September 1789, a religious parade featured a wooden replica of the Bastille in the place of the Holy Sacrament.[118] The rapport between speakers and audience in the clubs was reminiscent of responsive reading in a church. The revolutionary themes of regeneration and adoption[119] had clear religious antecedents. Nor is it coincidence that the campaign for linguistic unity after 1791 most occupied pro-Jacobin priests and former priests who had been keenly interested in dialect long before the Revolution. Before, it had mattered to them that the gospel should come to the people. Now they wanted to make universalism accessible to all citizens, including those who did not yet speak the language of the Grande Nation.[120]

Club meetings recalled the Roman mass. Parallels could be drawn as well between hymn singing and the ritual intonation of "La Marseillaise," or between reading from the latest Jacobin newspapers and readings from the Bible. Jacobin rhetoric (often spoken from purchased or confiscated pulpits) clearly derived from Christian rhetoric. The luminous tone of revolutionary ceremonies can be read as neoreligious statements.

Another point of similarity was the "civic baptisms" invented by the *clubbistes* of Strasbourg in June 1790, which became commonplace in 1793–94, when thousands of children were renamed for heroes of antiquity, for martyrs of the Revolution, or from dates taken from the revolutionary calendar. (One policeman is on record as having had his child baptized as Robespierre, and changing it on 12 Thermidor.)

Like the Catholic Church, Jacobinism had its saints (Marat, Chalier, Le Peletier) and its relics. When Cambon (vainly) proposed in November 1792 to disestablish all churches, the tone of the one club that supported his idea was revealing. "A good farmer," wrote the Jacobins of La Souterraine, "a brave soldier, a virtuous citizen, these are the saints whose memories we will honor."[121] Symbolically, many clubs met in former churches, and the vandalistic destructions were sometimes imagined as forms of purification and expiation that would appease the shades of fallen revolutionary heroes.[122] The inauguration of a club or its move from one locale to another was a quasi-religious occasion, with processions and the display of busts and banners. Many clubs collected donations for the poor. Delegates of the clubs went around as apostles or "civic missionaries" to teach "the catechism of the Revolution" or the "catechism of liberty." The Declaration of the Rights of Man was "a gospel." At Bar-le-duc local Jacobins praised the "mission apostolique" of the Paris club.[123] At Saint-Flour all meetings began with a reading of the "Revolutionary Commandments of the Mountain" and the "Republican Decalogue." The Convention was "le Sinaï des Français." Lafayette, said Robespierre, was the Cain of the Revolution.

In many ways, Jacobin "theology" differed sharply from Christian belief. Jacobins had no explicit sympathy for dark Augustinian or Calvinist views of predestination, or even for the doctrine of original sin. Religiously inclined observers will also note that the response of these revolutionary technicians to the misery of life's victims—many of whom, of course, were the victims of their own frenzy—was all too often an impatient or even mocking silence. Indeed, some might suppose that Jacobinism could not be sustained in 1794 precisely because it was only mimetically religious.

Jacobin art and politics, though obviously thoughtful and reflective, did not provide coherent answers to man's deepest anxieties, whose weight on the human spirit the Jacobins were in any case reluctant to recognize. Their greatest artist, David, is a less profound painter than his pre-Romantic contemporaries, Turner (1775–1851) and Goya (1745–1820) especially. Jacobinism's concerns were too worldly; its solutions, too rational. Jacobinism, though it yearned for transcendence, was too "unmetaphysical."

But Jacobinism's failure to become a religion has a silver lining. If Jacobinism had merely been a modern version of traditionalist religion, it would now be less relevant to our own modern or postmodern lives. Jacobinism continues to hold our attention because its aim was to mold citizens, not angels.

Secular-minded admirers of Jacobin principle will also note with relief that Jacobinism was at its most sterile when closest in its spirit to institutionalized religion.

9

Unifying Enmities at Home and Abroad

> To feel pity for the wicked is a great cruelty toward men.
>
> Jean-Jacques Rousseau

𝒥acobins yearned for togetherness. With universalist goals and the rhetoric of truthful friendship, they took politicized fraternity as their lodestar.

At first, Jacobins expected easily to bridge the antitheses of their thinking. Their descent into terror was perhaps a fated historical tragedy, but it was some months before Jacobins suspected that they might either fail or fail to convince. In the small Normand village of Cany, in the summer of 1794, a few weeks before the fall of Robespierre, the *clubbistes* still voted to disseminate a proclamation on the iniquities of religion because "enlightening and guiding the simplicity of agricultural citizens is only a matter of more of us spreading [knowledge] in the countryside."[1]

Initially, Jacobins had such confidence in their self-evident message that they did not believe they could have durable enemies. As Desmoulins put it to the assembly's deputies in the first issue of his newspaper, in November 1789: "as of now, you have no more enemies . . . all that is left for you to do is to govern France, to make her happy."[2]

Jacobins were intensely puzzled by the spectacle of "fanaticism forever struck down but forever reborn."[3] They were convinced that the next exclusion—or the next—would be the last. "Lafayette alone has divided us," wrote Robespierre in early July 1792. "Ah! punish Lafayette and the first bonds of our union will once more be tightened. A new federation will bring us back to our first sentiments."[4] "The agony of aristocracy has begun," explained Leclerc on June 1, 1793, to the Paris Jacobins as the crowd prepared to purge the Convention of its Girondin deputies, "the people are going to the Convention. You are of the people. You must be there."[5]

And yet, despite—or perhaps because of—these expectations of total success, seldom has any political group been so steadfast and so acrimonious in denouncing its assembled enemies, nationwide and in the clubs. The dark side of human nature may be less than dark than most of us like to think, but the moralizing Jacobins insisted, first, that they had no dark side at all and, second, that their enemies were very dark indeed. Like many sincere people, the Jacobins, in their heart of hearts, were suspicious of men and women who did not see the world as they did. What *clubbiste* did not know that the souls of refractory priests were the breeding grounds for "les serpens de l'envie, les fureurs de l'intérêt personnel" (the snakes of envy, the furors of personal interest)?[6]

Jacobins could not resist labeling everyone as either manifestly good or bad. And this moralizing drive, when conjoined to their inherited inability to distinguish heresy from dissent, propelled them to the detestation and dehumanization of their enemies, to the murder of the prisoners their armies had captured in the field, and, in a word, to Terror. A saddening similarity links the Jacobin description of the noble-born during the Revolution to the image of the Jew in National Socialist propaganda: incapable of hard work, Jews (in 1933) and nobles (in 1794) were parasitical, oversexed and unmanly, cowardly and prone to political extremes—royalist/capitalist for the former; *enragé*/communist, selfish, and cosmopolitan for the latter: "L'Égoiste . . . n'a point de patrie" (A selfish person has no homeland), declared the Jacobins of Semur.[7]

In the debate within Western culture on the nature of the Other, the Jacobins' view of life corresponds quite well to Freud's description of otherness as not truly foreign, but as a projection outward of a repressed and mirrored self. *Aristocrates* were the darkness Jacobins feared to find in themselves. Contemporary historians find it difficult to define what "counterrevolution" was because the French Revolution was itself volatile and changing.[8] But Jacobins had no such problem. Aristocrats inverted the values of Jacobinism. They were selfish, covert, mean, and dishonest. What is an *aristocrate*? a model deaf-mute student was asked in sign language. He responded, "An *aristocrate* is someone who does not like good laws and who desires to be a sovereign master, and to be very rich. My name is Massieu."[9] In brief, everyone was potentially aristocratic, and many were soon labeled as such. In the long run, this pattern of accumulated enmities and denunciations was fatal to the fortunes of the Jacobin ideal. But in the short run, purges did unite those Jacobins who had remained faithful to the cause. As Brissot once explained, the Revolution needed to be betrayed.

Their enemies, the *aristocrates*, were lurking all about. No deed was too dark for them, from rape and rapine to their inexplicably successful prayers for rain on the occasion of some revolutionary *fête*.[10] Edmond Dubois-Crancé said of Pitt, the British prime minister, that he was like "an evil deity, invisible to us. Pitt is everywhere." The specifics of these betrayals were sometimes hard to secure, but it was a cardinal principle of Jacobin thinking that although *they* worked in plain daylight (had they not opened the doors of their clubs to the public?), their *aristocrate* enemies conspired against them, ceaselessly, in the dark. Themes of light, dawn, flares, and darkness permeated Jacobin rituals. The trajectory of revolutionary *fêtes* favored broad vistas where even distant spectators might see clearly. Their funeral rites required that the face of the deceased not be covered during the attendant civic ceremonies. In a letter to the *clubbistes* of Villecroze, Minister of the Interior Roland declared that "one more popular society in the republic is a torch that is lit to dissipate the shadows of ignorance and superstition."[11] Jacobins were figuratively and literally enlightened. *Aristocrates*, by contrast, liked to meet at night, calling up images of a witches' sabbat.

The guilt of the Revolution's enemies was less to be proved than to be inferred. Rousseau, a paranoiac genius, had complained to Hume—as many a Jacobin prosecutor was to argue in 1794—that it was in the nature of intelligent conspirators not to leave inculpating evidence behind. The absence of proof was, he thought, proof most eloquent. As Desmoulins explained in May 1793, "as regards conspiracies, it is absurd to ask for positive facts; violent indications must suffice."[12] Even calumny might be useful evidence because experience showed false accusations to be invariably inefficacious "if directed against individuals whose conduct offers daily proofs of civic-mindedness and probity."[13]

Revealingly, in 1794, Jacobins were especially concerned with the conspiratorial plans of people already in jail, a preposterous idea to us, but one that made great sense in the context of Jacobin thinking on the nature of guilt and on the relationship of signs to truth. Incarceration in itself was cause for suspicion, they reasoned, since the prisoner had to have transgressed some public mores to begin with. Moreover, once in jail, convicted conspirators had nothing further to lose, and might therefore be assumed to be conspiring yet again. From a Jacobin point of view the only difference between their imprisoned conspirators and free suspects was that those in jail were likely to be even more desperate and dangerous.

Every sharp-eyed Jacobin was on the lookout for enemies of the cause, and ever more so as the Revolution progressed. Even in 1791, at the time of the king's flight to Varennes, when feelings overall were still relatively tranquil, the Jacobins were convinced (quite wrongly) that war, at best, and a bloodbath (their own especially), at worst, would surely have occurred had the king succeeded in escaping. After his fall, Robespierre himself was suddenly revealed to have been an unusually successful plotter. Retrospectively, the Jacobins of Tulle grudgingly admired "the great skill with which all the different parts of [his] horrid system were bound together."[14]

With so many conspiratorial enemies, the ever more alert and strident Jacobins turned to denunciation of their foes. Originally, that term had meant bringing cases of glaring and abusive injustice to the attention of public opinion. As such, it was endorsed by the municipal law of December 1789, which explained how active citizens could "denounce" bad municipal administrators. In the fall of 1789, Desmoulins likewise hailed "l'innovation hardie de la délation" (the bold innovation of denunciation),[15] which Mirabeau had also praised by this time.[16]

But the idea of denunciation soon took on an even darker, more punitive meaning, which Brissot praised in September 1791. In November of that year Marat presented this dark practice as a civic obligation,[17] and after his death in 1793, Hébert prided himself on the centrality of denunciation to the Revolution's new purpose. The Paris club, and in turn nearly all the provincial clubs, came to require a "serment de délation" (an oath of denunciation), which at Artonne became a "duty." The club at Toul urged all patriots to denounce violators of the new economic laws to "public opinion and to the police";[18] and in February 1793 the Convention made this duty into a lucrative occupation by offering a reward of one hundred livres to anyone who turned in either an émigré or a draft dodger.

The Jacobins' obsessive desire to ferret out enemies from under every bed was so characteristic that it was often satirized, at least until it became fatal for anti-Jacobins to make fun of their successful rivals. One witty counterrevolutionary polemicist imagined a Jacobite sabbat whose gyrating members hurled absurd denunciations of all kinds:

> Je dénonce l'Allemagne
> Le Portugal et l'Espagne
> Le Mexique et la Champagne
> La Limagne et le Pérou.
> Je dénonce l'Italie
> L'Afrique et la Barbarie
> L'Angleterre et la Russie
> Sans même excepter Moscou.[19]

Ironically, this Jacobin habit was so pervasive that even anti-Jacobin Republicans who had accused Jacobins of being tyrannical lapsed into a mimetic and denunciatory mode whenever fortune favored their own cause. "You have to understand," explained a Lyonese non-Jacobin revolutionary as he denounced the denouncing Jacobins, "that a denunciator is the most honorable of men if our homeland is in danger."[20]

Denunciation, it should be added, was not a covert, anonymous, or cowardly act. "Dénonciations particulières" (private denunciations) were still seen as shameful and many clubs struggled to discredit them.[21] Indeed, some troubled *clubbistes* debated the wisdom of denouncing not just public officials but politically unreliable private persons as well. A few clubs refused to read unsigned letters, even if others, like the Venetian Senate, had a box where members might let drop unsigned accusations. Individual Jacobins were expected to sign their denunciations, which took a great deal of courage since public accusations invited revenge, as many a pursued—and murdered—Jacobin was to discover after Thermidor.[22] Militant revolutionaries who had been denounced by other Jacobins indignantly rejected accusations they knew to be false, unless these accusations related to an opinion that had suddenly become incorrect: "I thank my Jacobin brothers for their surveillance," said Chabot in November 1793, "and should I fail [again], I would thank them for denouncing me to the Convention, and for sending me to the scaffold." (Chabot was executed in April of the next year).[23]

Along with this drive to denounce, hunt, and destroy came a tendency to dehumanize, a drift of thought that, in the historical perspective of our own inhuman century, may well be Jacobinism's most dismal legacy. The

Jacobins saw anti-Jacobins as lacking humanity's essential moral character-istic, the ability to tell right from wrong. But were their enemies unable to act morally from choice or from their intrinsic nature? Answers varied from time to time, but it was clear to the Jacobins that their enemies knew themselves to be perverse: a Montagnard Conventionnel thus reasoned that "we must destroy the evil-minded ones who in any case expect to be the victims of their evil impulses."[24]

Aristocrates were associated with dirt,[25] disease, and madness. For some weeks in late 1791 Louis XVI was rumored to have gone mad and to be roaming about the Tuileries smashing the palace furniture. In July 1792 a number of clubs[26] suggested that the assembly set up a regency and depose the king on grounds of insanity, a politically advantageous move that would have had the added advantage of being thoroughly constitutional. At Marseilles, in May 1791, after the abbé Raynal (1713–1796) had re-tracted the enlightened anticolonial principles of the prerevolutionary works he had written in collaboration with Diderot, the *clubbistes* sol-emnly escorted his bust to the lunatic asylum. *Aristocrates* were shown grinding their teeth, raging, throwing up, excreting, and foaming at the mouth. For Saint-Just, sweat was to the body what *aristocratie* was to the body politic. In a circular of late 1792, threatening to break with Paris over its tolerance of Marat, the club at Angers denounced the self-styled *Ami du peuple* as the source of a "pestilential miasma."[27] Nonjuring priests were compared to lepers, fit to be quarantined in some faraway place, in papal Rome perhaps.

Accusations of cannibalism were a favored trope: *aristocrates* were called "antropophages royalistes." The English, declared Barère, were a "peuple cannibale."[28] The king, said the Conventionnel Bouquier, was a "carnivorous monster."[29] Dynasties, explained Grégoire at the king's trial, "have always been voracious breeds that live off human flesh." "All the monuments of history," he concluded in November 1792, "testify that this class of purulent beings was always the leprosy of governments and the scum of humanity."[30]

Jacobins also associated *aristocrates* with impure femininity, idleness, petulance, irresponsibility, and pessimism.[31] By contrast, the Jacobins saw themselves as optimistic, responsible, pure, and virile.[32] Charlotte Corday, Marat's murderess, was immediately and universally decried as an unnat-ural harpy. The queen was another common target. By dwelling on her physicality—at times in the most explicit manner—Jacobins killed many birds with a single stone. They emphasized the weakness and sexual incompetence of her husband. They reminded their audience of the foreign-born queen's supposedly unnatural and oversexed character. They reasserted the antithetical masculinity of the regenerated nation's public space. And they devalued monarchic rule by reasserting their own claims to moral hegemony.[33]

Jacobin caricature relied heavily on animal imagery. Enemies were presented as vampires and hyenas, monstrous apparitions who savored the blood of the *patriotes:* theirs were "the claws of a harpy, the tongue of a bloodsucker, the heart of a vulture, and the cruelty of a tiger."[34] At Lyons a king dressed in a tiger's skin received the homages of a wolf-noble and a fox-priest. Louis XVI was often portrayed as a pig, Marie Antoinette as a panther or a tigress.[35] The royal family was shown scurrying ratlike through the sewers.[36]

Jacobins seldom took up the vocabulary of race as such. Indeed, they ordinarily struggled against it. Africans were black, explained the *clubbistes* of Alençon, not because of their race but because of "the climate of the country they inhabited." In the Jacobin perspective, nobles were not born wicked, even if they almost invariably became so in the end. Jacobin theatricals often depicted the adoption of a noble baby by worthy non-noble sans-culottes.

Nonetheless, the Jacobins' hatreds were so strongly felt that at times they did come close to spilling into racist theory, and in the fall of 1793 all nobles, in virtue of their birth alone and regardless of their opinions, were excluded from the clubs. The Dijon society had proposed such a step in the early spring of 1793, and the exclusion of the noble-born (which ran against the basic Jacobin principle of individual equality regardless of birth and race) was taken up by the Paris society with the approval of Robespierre. On 28 Germinal, Year II, all nobles were barred from joining both the clubs and the Committees of surveillance. Many sincerely Jacobin nobles (like the marquis de Soubrany and the brother of the martyred Le Peletier) were seriously disconcerted by this move, as were many clubs.

The Jacobins' penchant for exclusion and wild accusation was of course noticed at the time, and anti-Jacobins at Lyons were able to predict with remarkable accuracy what Jacobins would say about them: "they will tell you that we are a triumphant aristocracy, they will tell you that the sans-culottes have been murdered by the rich . . . that the rich of Lyons are Brissotins, Rolandins, moderates and *aristocrates,* counterrevolutionaries, that the white cockade of royalism is their emblem; they will tell you that [we] want the return of tyranny, of feudalism, of despotism."[37] Unfortunately, this insight did them little good.

*J*acobins had two kinds of foes—their former friends and their ancient enemies. Of these, the less important were the few die-hard counterrevolutionaries who rejected the message of 1789 *in toto* and from the start.

Why Jacobins initially had so few enemies on the right is easily understood. The Old Regime was not overthrown in 1789. It collapsed instead. Its demise, still unthinkable when the Estates General opened on May 5, 1789, was in essence consummated six weeks later, on June 17; and by the late summer of 1789, most nobles were probably resigned to the more basic principles of the Revolution, namely, equality before the law and individuated social forms. Hundreds of noble-born aristocrats joined the clubs, and many more bought up confiscated religious property, a clear if muted endorsement of the new order of things. In time, many nobles even became Republicans, like the king's cousin, the duc d'Orléans, and his son, the future king Louis-Philippe d'Orléans, who reigned from 1830 to 1848 and was a Republican general in 1792 and early 1793. Fear and not a desire to conspire drove most émigrés to leave.

Popular Catholicism was admittedly much stronger in 1789 than the Jacobins suspected. But pre-Romantic, Catholic, and reactionary organicism, though already consciously articulated in Germany and England, was unknown in France at the time. In 1789 the only organized group that argued in France for inequality and hierarchy from anti-Enlightenment premises was the short-lived Club of Massiac, formed by Paris-based, slave-owning planters. Even after Thermidor, between 1795 and 1799, anti-Jacobin royalist newspapers made reference not to traditionalist Catholic principles of family, authority, and hierarchy, but to Montesquieu's far more moderate idea of intermediary bodies and limited government.

Once abroad, many émigrés did gradually become politically reactionary and, at times, sincerely Christian. (The future Charles X, youngest brother of the king, a political émigré in July 1789, converted to Catholic rigorism at the deathbed of his lifelong mistress, Mme. de Polastron, in 1804.) Nonetheless, even Vendéen peasants, at first, had specifically material and nonideological grievances, like the military draft or being shut out from the apportionment of the lands that had been confiscated from the church. It was because the Revolution unfolded in such an excluding way, and not because they believed in some counterrevolutionary principle, that these peasants moved into active opposition.

Thus, the Jacobins' most hated enemies were not noble or counterrevolutionary outsiders at all, but former Jacobins, people who had once been sympathetic to Jacobinism's larger goals but had recoiled from its consequences or evolution for one reason or another. As one Marseilles *section* put it, the seemingly Republican "intrigants" (or intriguers) were much worse than the counterrevolutionary *aristocrates*, who were more easily detected and whose absurd, outdated ideas made them politically insignificant.

The first revolutionaries to drop out of the Revolution and to incur the enduring wrath of the Jacobins were the Monarchiens—most of them members of the Third Estate, some of them liberal nobles. The mixed and neo-aristocratic constitutionalism of Montesquieu was dearer to their hearts than was the general will of the Jacobins' Rousseau. Indeed, Mousnier, their spokesman, was at loggerheads with the Jacobin club in his hometown, Grenoble, as early as the spring of 1790.

In some key respects Mousnier's sensibility remained close to that of mainstream Jacobins (he too believed in popular sovereignty), but even the early institutionalization of Jacobinical ideas often offended him. The assertion of man's natural rights in the Declaration of the Rights of Man in early August 1789 seemed to him dangerous; the disestablishment of Catholicism, unadvisable; the diminution of the monarch's rights, excessive. The popular insurrections of the countryside in July 1789, and in Paris on October 5 and 6, struck him as ominous. By his defense of the king's right to veto legislation in the fall of 1789, Mousnier and the Monarchiens pushed themselves out of the *parti patriote,* now honing its intellectual armory in the Paris club.

As the Monarchiens were the first partisans of the Revolution to give up on its progression and to emigrate, they were ironically, of all Jacobinism's enemies, the ones that most often survived. Like his three main associates—Gérard de Lally-Tollendal, Nicolas Bergasse, and Pierre Malouet (who was also a friend of Necker)—Mousnier managed to flee abroad. He later secured employment under Napoleon. Had he remained in France, Mousnier would surely have shared the fate of Virieu and Stanislas de

Clermont-Tonnerre, two of his political friends, who were shot after the siege of Lyons in 1793.

The next two waves of *aristocrate* former revolutionaries involved the Feuillants in 1791–92 (as already discussed) and the Girondins in 1792–93. Girondism, though more difficult to define historically, was wonderfully easy to manipulate as an accusation. The hopelessly imprecise doctrinal line that divided Girondin suspects from other Jacobins allowed any Jacobin whom other, dominant Jacobins did not like for whatever reason to be plausibly arrested for having somehow been a Girondin all along.

Since most provincial Jacobins had sided with the Girondins in early 1793, it was not practical to accuse them all in 1794. To have done so would have reduced many clubs to nothing. But henceforth, thousands of Jacobins lived in the shadow of this accusation, and with it, of the guillotine. In June and July of 1794, to come to the notice of the authorities in any way was to invite a deadly fate, as happened in July 1794 to the imprisoned poet André Chénier, once a close friend of the painter David. Knowing him to be innocent, his father foolishly brought his son's case to the attention of Barère, who obligingly arranged for the poet to come to trial, with the result that Chénier, who would otherwise surely have survived, died within a few days of the Terror's end for no particular reason.

The last great ex-Jacobin to become an enemy of the remaining Jacobins was none other than Robespierre, whose reputation completely changed in the space of days, even hours.

From early 1791 onward, the star of the Incorruptible One had risen irresistibly. At Chartres the club put up his statue. The Jacobins of Strasbourg sent him a civic crown as evidence of their "undying affection." But in late July and early August 1794, time and time again, accounts of Robespierre's fall elicited spontaneous cheers in the provincial clubs. After Danton's fall, 170 societies had sent formulaic congratulations to the Committee of Public Safety for having unmasked this traitor. But 361 addresses—more genuine in their tone—were sent by the clubs to Paris after Robespierre's death, albeit fewer of them from the south than the north.

Eager not just to end but in a way to forget the Terror, the Jacobins in late 1794 turned against the memory of Robespierre all of the psychological and rhetorical weapons that had been theirs since 1791 and that, of course, Robespierre had also employed in his day. The *clubbistes* at Mayenne wondered if he had purposefully encouraged the royalist Chouan guerrillas.[38] It was also said that he had intended to marry the king's daughter and become king himself. Collot d'Herbois, a left Jacobin, explained on 12 Vendémiaire that "to understand his motives, one would have had to be as he was. To compute the depth and atrocity of his perfidiousness, one's soul would have had to be as perfidious, as atrocious as his had been."[39] Robespierre and his closest friends, some opined, had obviously conspired against the Revolution and were probably in the pay of foreign governments. The tyrant's guilt proved his accusers' innocence: because they were not just blameless but wholly without guile he had managed to dupe them for so long.

Beset with enemies at home, the Jacobins also had enemies abroad. Initially, the Jacobins were filled with good will for France's neighbors. They believed in a politics of virtue at home, and in virtuous international politics as well. For these patriotic votaries of a universalist Enlightenment who had taken a vow of perpetual peace, nation and internationalism overlapped: "Let us be united to one another as Frenchmen," wrote the leading Girondin Jacobin Lanthenas in early March 1792, "and we will have taken a great step toward our union with other peoples."[40]

In 1790–91 Jacobins were overwhelmingly antimilitaristic and pacifistic. The Limoges club contacted the London Corresponding Society to "establish in concert with it the means to realize that sublime plan of a perpetual peace that has been for so long considered chimerical."[41] Just as domestic injustice had its root cause in the absolutist state's monopoly of public life, so did the Jacobins assume that war had heretofore been the natural desire of corrupted monarchies. Peoples were not enemies; their rulers were. God intended nations to coexist harmoniously. In a prefiguration of the young Europe of the 1830s and 1840s, Jacobins envisaged a humanity united by moralized, national consciousness: "O! God of all nations! Bring together all the inhabitants [of the world], let them be united by the sacred links of liberty and equality: may hospitality be like a religion, may succor and exchange chain them as if they were a nation of brothers, a single family! Let envy, hatred, and discord, and the very words of war and politics seem meaningless to them."[42]

They hoped for peace at any cost. "Today," wrote a Jacobin at Aix in October 1791, "the torch of philosophy has lit up the world . . . Nothing would be more worthy of France than to . . . invoke peace with the same ardor with which others seek war. Let us instruct peoples! . . . Appeal to them as brothers . . . Let us renounce war!"[43] On January 20, 1792, the abbé Fauchet, a prominent Girondin Jacobin, suggested that France symbolically give up its embassies and ambassadors.

Just as Jacobins wished for domestic public life to be transparent, and unimpeded by bureaucratic regulation, so did they think that the citizens of different nations ought not to be cleft asunder by the amoral states hemming them in. Jacobins were careful to distinguish between foreign leaders (whose hostility was no surprise) and their duped followers, secretly sympathetic to the Revolution. In July 1792 the *Manuel du laboureur et de l'artisan* ran an article in which Anselme the Jacobin gathered rural workers to explain the Constitution and the rights of man. A woman asks: "Are these rights for us too?" Anselme replies: "Yes. They are for all in general, and even for foreigners."[44]

Jacobins especially warmed to foreign nationals who hoped to regenerate their own country in imitation of the French. They assumed that the principles of the new French Constitution, perfect and universal, would sooner or later be taken up everywhere. The smallest evidence of pro-French leanings anywhere was celebrated as a portent. It was encouraging, wrote the Marseillais Jacobins on March 23, 1793, that the sultan of Turkey, "as a sign of alliance, adorns himself with our colors and considers with interest the sacred tree of liberty."[45] Some Jacobins in 1792 actually expected that Britain would intervene militarily on their side. Later, news of an uprising by London sans-culottes was eagerly awaited. The Montpazier Jacobins in February 1794, for example, still thought that most Englishmen were covert Francophiles, eager, like them, to execute King George and Pitt. Two hundred thousand Frenchmen should conquer Britain so as to "fraternally embrace Charles James Fox and all the friends of liberty," they suggested.[46]

But the Jacobins' avuncular moralization of international relations, like their tolerance of dissenting opinion at home, soon eroded. When Catholics in France refused to join the constitutional church, Jacobins passed rapidly from tolerance to blame and, then, to ideological persecution. A similar pattern of growing intolerance structured their understanding of France's place in the world.

Should Jacobins agree to live in peace with unregenerated foreign rulers, or should they interfere in their neighbors' politics to overthrow unworthy foreign monarchs? The Jacobins declared peace to the peasants' huts but war on lordly castles. On November 5, 1792, Chaumette concluded that the whole of Europe should be "Jacobinized"; and in April 1793 Robespierre argued that "different peoples must come to one another's assistance according to their ability, like the citizens of the same State. He who oppresses a single nation declares himself the enemy of all."[47] Jacobins were particularly eager to help the Belgians and the Dutch, who had tried to emancipate themselves even before 1789. Poland ("the France of the North") was another favorite. They also (selectively) praised foreign republics. Many clubs flew the flags of both the United States and Geneva. The inauguration of a display of French, British, and American flags in the Paris Jacobin club in November 1790 was the occasion of one of its biggest *fêtes*, and was echoed in many parts of France. By contrast, Venice and Genoa, two ancient but aristocratic republics, were never mentioned. Indeed, in May 1792, a Jacobin of Semur objected to the planting of an Italian poplar in lieu of a French oak.[48]

The next turn of the screw made the Revolution a servant of French nationalism, an imperialist shift softened by ideological and neophilosophical flummery since France was said merely to be reaching for its "natural" frontiers. External political surrogates made up for ideological bankruptcy at home. By mid-1793 only the *Bostoniens* and the *Philadelphes* were left as friends of the French Republic.

Necessarily, the shifts of Jacobin policy toward exploitation plain and simple did not endear the French Revolution even to its most progressive neighbors. Initially, French armies had found supporters in every country. But in 1793–94 the French also found much resistance. At Aachen, in the conquered Rhineland, only 26 of the city's 23,000 inhabitants agreed to join the newly founded Jacobin club.

The Jacobins' anguished relationship to England best exemplified the Jacobins' trajectory from cosmopolitan openness to nationalist hatred. By 1789 the French and the English had intermittently been at war for a century. Nonetheless, what the Jacobins chose to remember was the admiration of the philosophes for British politics and culture (quite tepid in Rousseau, but exuberant in Montesquieu and Voltaire). Brissot had stayed in Britain and had then thought of London as the capital of world freedom. Danton read English quite well. Jean-Paul Marat had lived for many years in England and his *Chains of Slavery* was first published in England, in English, in 1774. It was in an English translation that Desmoulins, in March 1794, found the quotations from Tacitus that he used in his attack on Robespierrist terror; and his newspaper, *Les Révolutions de France et de Brabant,* was replete with references to Harrington, Sidney, Toland, Gordon, and Trenchard.[49] From 1789 to 1791, when focused on opposing the resurgence of the Old Regime, the Jacobins had genuinely admired British ways, like habeas corpus. They were impressed by the weight of an elected Parliament in the machine of British government.

Jacobins also followed the Anglo-American Radical Whig tradition, whose most famous apologist the world over, Tom Paine, arrived in Paris in November 1789. (He was elected to the Convention in September 1792, arrested in the fall of 1793, and nearly guillotined in July 1794.)

Jacobin personal contacts with English radicals found their first public embodiment when the London Corresponding Society and the Paris Jacobins exchanged messages in the fall of 1789. In London Richard Price proposed a Franco–British–Dutch alliance, Holland being commonly thought at the time to be the world's most advanced society socially and economically. At Nantes the *clubbistes* directed not one but two delegations to London, the second one arriving in time on November 4, 1790, to celebrate the anniversary of the Glorious Revolution. Dozens of other clubs followed suit. The visit of Pétion, the future mayor of the French capital, to the English capital in November 1791 was widely hailed in France. In their eulogy of the London Society of Constitutional Whigs, which had praised the French Constitution, the *clubbistes* of Brest hailed "the worthy descendants of those intrepid Whigs of the seventeenth century who had defended the rights of man and to whom the English of today owe their economic prosperity and political stability."[50]

But as the Jacobins veered to the assertion of virtue and community at the expense of individual rights, their view of Britain changed completely. They thought less about Parliament and more about who it really represented. In 1789 the Monarchiens had often been known as the *anglomanes,* but this more or less amiable nickname was soon perceived as violently insulting.

Where they had interpreted the rigid borders protecting British civil society from the state as a defense of free individuals against encroaching monarchic abuse, they came to see instead a selfish, acquisitive society that an even more selfish monarchic state made no effort to reform. By 1794 England had become for the Jacobins a shorthand notation for the rejection of universalist values and the defense of particularist selfishness. Quatremère de Quincy, an architect and art historian, compared the French national museum, which made great art accessible to all, with the ways of Britain, where great paintings were tucked away in the private country homes of the rural rich. By 1793 British liberties, no longer an apparent guarantee of freedom, were seen as the bulwark of social egoism and even cruelty. Saint-Just defended the Terror by pointing to the hundreds of death sentences that the British assizes routinely decreed. On October 9, 1793, the sale of British-made goods was forbidden (a prefiguration of Napoleon's Continental blockade), and the next day English civilians residing in France were ordered arrested, a break with international law as it was then known. Clubs furled their British flags. Foreigners who had once been welcomed in the clubs were expelled or interned.

In May 1792 Robespierre had still been conditionally praising the English in comparison to the French; but in mid-January 1794, at the Jacobin club, he initiated in Paris a long debate on the wickedness of British ways. In the last days of January he denounced the "crimes" of the English cabinet, crimes that all too many ordinary Englishmen were willing to accept. As a representative of the French nation, he explained, "I proclaim that I hate the English as a people."[51] Jacobin dislike of Britain ran wide and deep: in the spring of 1794, the Jacobins of Luxeuil urged that London be conquered so that slavery could be abolished from the city that was its spiritual center: "Legislators," it concluded, "order that London be destroyed."[52] Richard Cobb has reminded us of a Jacobin at Lille who suggested that wolves be set loose in Britain where they had long since been extinct. "May our victorious battalions carry onto territories where kings rule death and devastation," wrote the *clubbistes* at Bergerac. "May slave peoples learn by counting our victories how great is the might of a people that fights for liberty."[53] In short, Jacobins' perceptions of England mirrored their evolution at home from the praise of individualist liberty to the acceptance of universalist dictatorship.

"We would be horrified at a Prince who would order his prisoners massacred":[54] so wrote Rousseau in the 1750s, a sign that warring states were expected to pay some attention at least to those rules of decency being increasingly applied in civil life. But on October 10, 1792, the president of the Rouen club advised local volunteers to show no mercy for tyrants and to spare only women and children who were the ignorant "instruments of despotism." And on May 26, 1794, the Jacobin-dominated Convention voted that British and Hanoverian prisoners would henceforth be executed on capture. Then, on July 4, 1794, it resolved that all foreign soldiers captured on French soil who had refused to surrender would be executed.

Many clubs went out of their way to praise this decision. On July 26, the day before his fall, Robespierre called for just such executions.

True enough, these laws were seldom applied, although the crew of a captured British vessel is on record as having been shot or made to walk the plank.[55] But captured French émigrés, who had likewise been doomed by a ruling of the Convention on October 9, 1792, were routinely put to death as traitors.

Jacobins loved to love their fellow human beings, but they also loved to hate their foes. "Citizens," said Barère on March 7, 1793, "one more enemy for France is one more triumph for the cause of liberty!" The life of the republic and the death of its enemies, especially if they had once been friends, were exaltedly and sacrificially entwined. Collot d'Herbois mused after the massacres at Lyons that "by killing all these scoundrels, we guarantee the life of many generations of free men."[56] The most personally decent Jacobins found it hard to condemn terrorists like Carrier or sadists like Lebon who murdered in their name. Even (utterly egregious) instances of cannibalism could find some Jacobin apologist.[57]

*M*eanwhile, the antipatriots hurled insults back at their Jacobinical enemies, beginning with the word "Jacobin" itself, a term of derision together with its many variants: Jacobites, Jacots, and Jacoquins (Jacoscoundrel). Like the terms "Whig" and "Tory" in Britain, or "Beggars" in Holland, the nickname was taken up in defiance, rather to the annoyance of Robespierre, as has been mentioned, who did not like its informal and particularist, nonuniversalist connotations.

The least interesting accusations raised against the Jacobins had to do with their supposed character as private persons. In this naive and wrongheaded view, the Jacobins were seen as common criminals: "Some seem to think that Jacobins are a sect particular to our own century, foreign creatures heretofore unknown in the human species, monsters unknown to previous ages. Open the records of history, you will find Jacobins everywhere."[58] Much was also made of them as lawyers without briefs, doctors without patients, embittered intellectuals of the fourth rank—accusations that proved useful material for conservative nineteenth-century historians of the Revolution.

Their enemies frequently turned the Jacobins' choice insults against them. Jacobins, for example, were said to be cannibals, an efficacious rhetorical charge because at least one such instance had actually been proved. Montgaillard in his memoirs wrote of an (apocryphal) tannery at Meudon, where breeches were made of male human skin, female skin being too soft and useless.[59] The journalist of the conservative *Petit Gautier* portrayed Jacobins as they had described the Monarchiens: part tiger, part bear. "Ses formes sont brutes, grossières, son maintien est lourd. Il a l'air taciturne, l'encolure hideuse, le poil ras. Féroce et carnassier, il égorge pour le plaisir d'égorger" (The shape of the Jacobin is rude and crude. His stance is heavy. His air is taciturn. His hairs are short, his frame is hideous. Carnivorous and fierce, he slits throats for the pleasure of the thing).[60]

More suggestive anti-Jacobin polemics gradually appeared, however. One connected politicized Jacobin criminality to the despised religious fanatics of yesteryear by referring to the deranged intransigently Catholic monk Jacques Clément, who had stabbed the relatively tolerant Henry III during the Wars of Religion.

Another innovative and "pre-Romantic" strategy, which only emerged during the course of the Revolution, and after 1800 especially, was to damn Jacobins as the neo-enlightened foes of a Christian, organicist society. In 1798 the abbé Barruel (1741–1820) linked Jacobinism to Freemasons and Jews, just as he had before the Revolution associated the Enlightenment with destructive godlessness and suicide in a popular book entitled *Les Helviennes*. In a variation on this theme, repentant Jacobins were depicted as driven by remorse to self-destruction. The voluntary death of the *enragé* Roux was presented in this way by the Catholic abbé Guillon.[61]

Unsurprisingly, the theme of Charles-Pierre Ducancel's *L'Intérieur des comités*, a great Thermidorian theatrical hit of the late 1790s, which aimed to expose Jacobin motivation, was that the terrorists had been not just illiterate but envious.

But more intelligent, modern-minded critics seized nearly immediately on Jacobins' two central and flawed arguments: that only Jacobins spoke the truth; and that only Jacobins understood the nation's will. The conservative, Swiss, and Protestant critic Jacques Mallet du Pan (1749–1800) keenly commented on the Jacobins' relentless belief in the rightness of their cause. Brissot, he said, was especially threatening since he took every complaint "as an attack on natural law."[62] "Be my brother, or I'll kill you," mocked the anti-Jacobin royalist journalist Antoine Rivarol.

Jacobins were also accused of denying their own first principles. In May 1791 Le Chapelier (one of the first deputies to join the Jacobin club in

1789) argued that if the clubs acted as a group without the unanimous support of their membership, they would end up denying the will of their dissident members. Collective club petitions, he explained, by definition trampled the rights of the individuals, a fundamental part of the Revolution's message.

As early as 1790 *clubbistes* were accused of being *aristocrates,* because they too were a particularist group outside the nation's will. This charge became commonplace during the debate that began in May 1791 and ended with the basically unenforced law of September 29, 1791, banning affiliation and correspondence among clubs, a measure that the Toulon club deplored as a "décret plébicide."[63]

Many anti-Jacobins attacked the clubs' pretensions to represent the nation: that was the task of the National Assemblies. The clubs were really "corporations." Sporadically brought forward in 1791–92, this charge was repeated after the fall of Robespierre. "In our opinion," wrote a Protestant friend of Sieyès, François Boissy d'Anglas, in 1795, "no society can declare itself to be 'popular' without challenging the rights of the people taken as a whole."[64] Bourdon de l'Oise, once a leading Jacobin, opined that they were "une aristocratie exclusive." Far from being the nation's conscience, the clubs were factions, "collections of men who, like the monks they resemble, had chosen one another. In the entire universe I do not know of an aristocracy that is more clearly formed . . . It is not the people who constituted these societies; the name of 'popular society' was of their own making."[65] Roederer, who had once been a militant Jacobin but who had been jolted into opposition by the execution of the king, penned a celebrated pamphlet on the issue, tellingly entitled *Des Sociétés particulières telles que clubs, réunions, etc.*[66] Dupont de Nemours wrote of a "noblesse clubbiste";[67] and in his attack on the newly Babouvist d'Antonelle, a right-wing journalist, cleverly linked the membership of this formerly Jacobin marquess in a prerevolutionary and exclusive club reserved for the noble-born, with his revolutionary membership in an "association de patriotes exclusifs," a "nouvelle noblesse" that thrived in the "ruins of France" and the "blood of Frenchmen."[68]

*T*he Jacobins had a relentless desire to strike down their enemies and to impose their mark and images on the nation. In fact, the intensity of their feelings puzzles us. Sensible, rational—and Apollonian—explanations of their animosities have great relevance to our understanding of their motivation, obviously. But so do, perhaps, dreamlike or nightmarish Dionysian speculations.

In the older justice of the monarchy, law-abiding, moral subjects had been reinforced in their positive sense of self by the monarch's exemplary justice, at once swift and awe inspiring. The occasional but spectacular cruelty of traditionalist punishment (quartering or breaking on the wheel) was not easily forgotten. In 1757, the point of brutalizing the king's would-be assassin, Damiens (who was later absurdly rumored to have been an uncle of Robespierre), was to restore harmonious social and political normalcy. But no series of punishments, however long and stringent, could ever calm the Jacobins' inner doubts. Before 1789 the king's subjects had relied on him to maintain cosmic moral order. The Jacobins had no such choice; and some dark unspoken fear, perhaps, fed their punitive extravagance.

Jacobinism began as a libertarian doctrine of individual freedom and becoming. But its fate in politics depended in large part on the happy balance and conflation in society of individualistic and universalist values. Where modernity was weakly felt, as in rural France generally, it did not thrive. Where modern lines of class were more sharply drawn, it would collapse. In minds and places where individualist values were feebly implanted, its drift toward communitarian excess could not be arrested. And in those hearts and spirits where the punitive habits of the Old Regime were deeply ingrained, Jacobinism seemed bound to resolve its difficulties by recourse to force and to anathema. In so doing, it became the very reverse of what it had hoped to be. How telling that the commissioners sent by the club of Tournan to "purge" the neighboring society of Ouzouer-la-Ferrière, a small town not far from Paris, should have commented that its membership could not be pure because it was too numerous.[69]

In this lugubrious drift from ingathering to exclusion, we find the measure of Jacobinism's terrorist decay.

10

Applied Jacobinism: The Social Ecologies of Jacobin Principle

> You have no idea of that part of the world: it's like nothing else. Everyone there is a royalist or a terrorist. There's no in between. In Dijon or in Poitiers, people are reasonable; they talk. In Marseilles, they start with the knife.
>
> Carnot (a Burgundian) in a letter to Thibeaudeau (a Poitevin)

*J*acobinism was an increasingly ideologized understanding of enlightened modernity that attempted to reconcile social harmony and individual transcendence. Given its internal contradictions, revisionist historians have moved along one of two paths to explain Jacobinism's terroristic drift.

Their first and plainest strategy is to argue that 1794 was the extension of the dark side of 1789. Regeneration, citizenship, and popular sovereignty were, in this view, from first to last the libertarian mask of Jacobin intolerance and exclusion.

As early as 1789 Sieyès wrote of the supposedly unproductive, selfish, and exclusive French nobles who claimed (imaginary) descent from the ancient and conquering Franks of the fifth century that now was the time for them to return to Franconia. Pessimistic historians can read this amusing injunction as a first step toward the fatal political exclusivism of 1794. Revolutionary discourse, they would say, has an inner logic; and the joking dare of Sieyès in the spring of 1789 inevitably became the murderous words of Robespierre in 1794. (Much to the dismay of Sieyès, incidentally.

When asked what he had done during the Terror, this pacific man sighed and replied, "I lived" [*J'ai vécu*].)

This emphasis on pretotalitarian continuity explains the illiberal activities of the Comité des Recherches (Committee of Inquests) set up in 1789 by the revolutionary Paris municipality to track down counterrevolutionary crimes. It also accounts for the National Assembly's Rousseauean definition, that same year, of the crime of *lèse nation* (activities injurious to the nation), the antecedent, it is said, of terrorist intolerance in 1793–94. It makes the illiberal definitions of sedition, complicity, and evidence contained in the "liberal" law code of 1791 an introduction to the notorious legislation on suspects in September 1793.[1]

In this straightforward revisionist view, then, the Great Terror of 1794 had antecedents in the ambiguities of the Jacobins' idea of freedom.[2]

Beyond this first line of thinking is, of course, the other and more convincing (but still uncertain) and condemnatory Hegelian route, which emphasizes instead the inevitability of terrorism as a solution to Jacobinism's ideological dilemmas. From their hopeless contradictions and inability to convince, willful Jacobins are said to have been inexorably driven forward to oppress people whom they could not sway.

But Jacobinism's decline into terrorism can be seen quite differently. Obviously, one can no longer argue (as many Marxist historians did in the middle decades of this century) that the Terror resulted from an exogenous and unforeseeable military setback. It cannot be our moral purpose to excuse the Terror. We cannot successfully argue today as Marxist historians once did that the victims of Jacobinism's cruel vindictiveness "deserved" or at least caused their fate, by inadvertently driving the Revolution to excess. It makes little historical sense to say that *aristocrates* had to die so that the Revolution might live. Today, the reverse seems true. Had fewer counterrevolutionaries been killed—and avenged—the Revolution would have been more widely accepted than it was.

We can neither lose sight of the Revolution's tens of thousands of hapless victims—most of them anonymous or nearly so—nor turn our back on the Jacobins' enlightened expectations. Universal reason was their guiding star, as it must still be ours. We must find a way both to pity Jacobinism's victims and to salvage the part of the Jacobins' universalist and democratic purpose that resonates today. How, then, can we secure our goal of conditional blame and exoneration?

We must set Jacobinism in different contexts: ideological and social; past, present, and future. Placing Jacobinism's trajectory in the context of France's antecedent and clerico-monarchic history of intolerance (as will be done in the next chapter) makes it possible to gauge the influence on the Jacobins of the intolerant assumptions common in the world they knew. But we must also consider Jacobinism's relationship to social divisions in different parts of France to gauge the weight of ideology in Jacobinism's drift to terror.

Jacobin ideology was not, in 1793–94, like the laws of the Medes and the Persians, a fixed and graven thing. How it evolved depended greatly on its context in space and time. Much is to be learned, for example, from the wild variations in rates of executions from place to place. Four of France's eighty-seven departments staged more than a thousand executions, but six had none and thirty-one had fewer than ten.[3]

True enough, the most successful Jacobins (Robespierre, Saint-Just, Couthon) were confirmed ideologues, often indifferent to the management of social life as it was, or even as it might be. They placed more importance on man's nature as it ideally could become. Indeed, for many of their enemies, precisely this way of thinking made the Jacobins dangerous. In the witty words of one royalist journalist, Jacobinism was to politics what philosophy was to daily life: "It is like a prospectus of that world which exists in the archives of the Eternal Geometer and which, according to the divine Plato, is far more beautiful than the world itself."[4] Many critics, Tocqueville among them, have also emphasized the abstract, "unrealistic" side of revolutionary and Jacobin politics.

But it is no less true that Jacobinism was a practical and eventually terrorizing governmental doctrine firmly set in many specific social situations. Here, nascent social class, whose lineaments will be traced from place to place, is the most important. But other contexts were also of consequence.

Of these the broadest was Europe. Jacobinism managed to survive in France in 1792 because in that year, and once again in 1795, the east European absolutist monarchies (Austria, Prussia, and Russia) were more intent on carving up Poland—a relatively trivial goal—than on destroying the French Revolution, which, as they should have known, was by far their most critical ideological assignment. The strength of Jacobinism has to be measured—*inter alia*—against the weakness or incompetence of its enemies. Had a young Frederick the Great been the ruler of the militarized Prussian kingdom in 1789, our sense of the Jacobins' determination and ability might be quite different from what it now is.

The timing of Jacobinism in the history of the North Atlantic world also mattered. On the one hand, Jacobinism came after the American Revolution, which legitimated its Republican aspirations. On the other hand, Jacobinism also came after Britain's "nonrevolution" of 1780. Had Britain's Old Corruption collapsed as it nearly did at that time under the pressure of domestic, Irish, and American events, French property owners, mindful of England's turmoil, would have been far more cautious in their universalist assertions.

If John Wilkes in London had still been in 1789 a successful and radical figure rather than "an extinct volcano," revolutionary Jacobinism in Paris would surely have had a much smaller audience. The French Revolution postponed Britain's age of reform by a generation, and a similar though inverted situation might well have prevailed across the English Channel if George III had persisted even further in his ill-fated American endeavors.

A comparison of Jacobinism and contemporary Anglo-American radicalism is also heuristically useful. Many links connected Jacobin sensibility in France and Radical Whig assumptions in England and America at the time.

When he spoke in late August 1792 of a "philosophical consanguinity" that linked French patriots to foreign reformers, the Jacobin bishop and deputy Lamourette probably had the Lockean Enlightenment in mind. But a better comparison would have been with the American Radical Whigs of the 1760s and 1770s.

There, similarities abounded. Some expressed a shared conservatism, as in the belief that property was a guarantee of liberty because it enabled ordinary citizens to resist a monarchic state.

Others, however, were potentially radicalizing. Both Anglo-American Whigs and French Jacobins had given up on the old notion of a society of estates. They believed in popular sovereignty, in a broad franchise, in unicameral legislatures, in a weak executive, and in the right of the people to censure their legislators. They also tended to assume that they represented truth manifest, and that their elitist enemies were conspiratorial and undeserving. Jefferson (like Barère) once wrote that from time to time, the tree of liberty should be watered with the blood of tyrants. And Benjamin Franklin's preference to his dying day was for a single-chamber parliament and a plural executive. But neither Jefferson nor Franklin was a terrorist.

More immediately, in France itself, Jacobinism in the period 1789–1794 was set in differing and specific urban and rural contexts, which have onto-logical relevance because they inform our sense of Jacobinism's relation-ship to social fact and class formation. It matters, for example, that the im-plantation of Jacobinism across the land was hardly uniform. Jacobin clubs were more numerous in southwestern and southeastern France, and to the north and northwest of Paris. Clubs were more sparse in the west. They were fewer in mountainous and newly annexed areas.

The fate of Jacobin ideas during the Revolution, like their implantation, also varied greatly from place to place. Social structure was essential here. In some areas, as in Lyons, Jacobinism sharpened lines of class and con-sequently collapsed. In others, in small towns especially, it erased them and thrived instead. In Marseilles, likewise, Jacobin ideas were (up to a point) a bridge that enabled the Jacobins to secure a wide and popular au-dience.

In brief, Jacobin ideology during the reign of Terror was recognizably the same in the capital and in the provinces; but its causes and effects var-ied widely. The link that runs from Rousseauean principle to Jacobin au-thoritarianism is not as clear as has often seemed to historians more con-cerned with ideas than with social circumstance.

Lyons, Saint-Étienne, and Nîmes: Jacobin Catastrophes

Jacobinism at Lyons was "a disastrous failure."[5] Its demise leads us to ask why, in this city, where a great gap separated rich and poor, did so many working people nonetheless join the wealthy in their insurrection against the Jacobin Republic?

The answer matters for the history of Jacobinism and for the history of European class formation as well. But it also matters in its own right: Lyons with its 150,000 inhabitants was one of the largest and most "pro-toindustrialized" of France's largest cities. Its population rose from 97,000 in 1700 to 146,000 in 1785.

If we define "class" as the modern consciousness of belonging to a social grouping that has particular economic and cultural strategies, the social structure of Lyons verged on modernity. In this densely packed, hilly place, squeezed between two rivers, social relations between the rich and the poor, though ostensibly harmonious, were in fact quite tense.

The 30,000 silk weavers owned their looms. They did not yet think of themselves as destitute, proletarian workers. At times, they made common cause with the larger merchants who controlled the silk trade. Up to a point, rich and poor alike at Lyons were similarly affected by a slump in the silk industry, by a rise in foreign competition, by a fall in French import tariffs, or by the emergence of new techniques of textile manufacturing.

Beneath this surface harmony, however, tensions rose in the late 1780s between the weavers and the masters. In 1786 a bitter, bloody strike pitted the artisans and journeymen against the 400 *marchands-fabricants* (merchant-manufacturers). Three strikers were hanged. Their leader, Denis Monnet, was imprisoned. He was to resurface after 1789 as one of the city's leading *patriotes*. For the silk industry, 1787 and 1788 were the two worst years of the entire eighteenth century. In the late 1780s perhaps half of its working population was on some kind of relief.

At the top of the social scale in Lyons, relations between the upper bourgeoisie and the nobility looked bad but were in fact quite close, essentially because all owners of property at Lyons, regardless of their status, had come to understand that the poor were potentially their common and worst enemy. Ostensibly, before 1789, the numerous and prominent Lyonese nobles were exclusive, a curious (though not unfamiliar) stand since many of them were of *parvenu* origins and derived their newly found noble status from ennobling municipal office rather than ancient lineage. (Lyons was largely administered by members of a "consulate." Consuls were elected or, better yet, co-opted, from a handful of bourgeois patrician families who acquired noble rank after a mere two years in office.)

In reality, the gap at Lyons between rich nobles and rich non-nobles was not as great as it first seemed. A shared cultural sensibility united nobles and rich bourgeois. The new Masonic lodges, which in Lyons had a mystical turn of mind, provided common ground for all of the city's elites. The Enlightenment had a broad following among nobles and non-nobles. Religious fervor was declining. Fewer religious books were sold in Lyons than heretofore. Fewer young women were deciding to take vows.

On the other shore, many rich and aspiring traders remained traditional corporatists in their worldview. Merchants might be eager to consider labor as a (modern) wage-valued commodity rather than a (medieval) contribution to the general welfare whose worth was set by custom. But they were still tradition-minded in wanting to have the right to limit access to their profession.

In short, the Lyonese elite was culturally amorphous. Politically, it was content to depend on the Crown. During the monarchy's last and fitful attempt to become a genuine absolutist monarchy in the early 1770s, the Lyonese had accepted the authoritarian abolition of the Parlements. In early 1789 the masters did support the national patriotic cause, but as followers rather than as leaders. The economic message of both the noble and bourgeois *cahiers de doléances* (the grievance books drawn up for the meeting of the Estates General) was essentially the same. Bizarrely, the city's delegates to the Third Estate were reminded by their peers that the deputies of the first two estates were entitled to "deference and respect" by virtue of their birth and status.[6]

True to this order of things nothing much happened in Lyons after the fall of the Bastille in Paris. The aristocratic *consulat* managed to hold on until February 1790. Although a new *corps de volontaires* did come into being, these citizen-soldiers continued to take orders from established authorities and, in late July 1789, they fanned out into the countryside to put down the peasant panic known as the Great Fear.

In the context of national politics, the conservative docility of these Lyonese volunteers was anomalous. But given the reality of Lyonese class solidarity at the top, their deference was not unpredictable. In patriotic circles, Lyons acquired the reputation of being a *ville aristocrate*.

In February 1790 a new election finally ended the era of the consulate. Like the new departmental administration, the new municipal officers, though patriotically inclined, were hardly militant Jacobins. A Jacobin club did come into being, and it affiliated with Paris in the spring of 1790. But its leadership was not bold. In late 1790 the Lyonese *clubbistes* rejected as slanderous the "accusation" that they had tried to influence the elections by circulating lists of suitable candidates. But even this initially moderate stand was too much for the Lyonese bourgeois. In March 1791 the club still counted only 224 members, or less than one-fifth of 1 percent of the city's population.

By contrast, however, the Revolution pushed preindustrial Lyonese artisans into political modernity. On September 10, 1790, working people organized a Club of the Friends of the Constitution. By January 1791 it counted 3,000 members and by April 1791, approximately 4,500. The society soon spawned twenty-eight clubs, each of them grounded in the popular life of the Lyonese *quartiers,* and all of them connected through a Central Club. Passive citizens were allowed membership. Ostensibly, these popular clubs shared the Jacobin ideal of law-abiding patriotism. Nonetheless, the local bourgeoisie could read between these ordered lines.

The bourgeois *patriotes* who had taken over city hall in the early winter of 1790–91 were doubly careful. They treated the indigent with deference and spent a great deal of money on food subsidies; but they also steered clear of the Jacobins, whose rhetoric they feared since it was visibly radicalizing the poor. Louis Vitet was the new mayor who embodied this two-pronged policy. So as to be politically correct, he crossed swords with the more conservative departmental authorities about nonjuring priests especially. But he was otherwise extremely cautious.

This schizophrenic arrangement might well have gone on, had not the king's flight to Varennes in June 1791 upset everyone's applecart. The event frightened and discredited the middle-of-the road Lyonese *patriotes,* who had welcomed the Revolution as the promise of institutional reforms that would have little social or cultural effect. On the far left, the popular revolutionaries became even more aggressive. In May 1792 an impoverished silk weaver was elected commander of the city's National Guard. The city now had 30,000 people out of work. During the winter of 1792, tempers frayed yet further.

Sandwiched between the cautious municipality and the radicalizing populists, the local Jacobins demagogically urged the poor to greater militancy. Chalier, their leader, a personally unstable man, had recently been to Paris and completely absorbed Robespierre's voluntarist universalism. Chalier shifted the terms of the Lyonese argument. The Revolution, he decided, was really a struggle of the poor (who were *patriotes*) against the rich (who were *aristocrates*). The Revolution would either go forward with the help of the poor, or falter and then die. This new mood was not without effect. On September 9, 1792, crowds armed with axes and crowbars broke into the local jail and murdered eleven Catholic priests and noble officers. Five days later, they assaulted food shops. A self-appointed "tribunal féminin" took it upon itself to set prices for confiscated goods. Chalier encouraged these moves. The Revolution's survival, he explained in the words of "La Marseillaise," called for the shedding of "impure blood."

On October 28, 1792, with the help of the working poor, Chalier's small Jacobin minority took over the municipality. Within weeks, however, the Jacobin-popular alliance that had brought him to power fell apart, an ominous prefiguration of Parisian politics in 1793–94.

During their brief stint in power, the Lyonese Jacobins did their best to reach out to the poor; but in the end the poor rejected them. In Paris this cross-class alliance succeeded, in 1793 at least. But in Lyons it failed. The difference was that in the capital, the Jacobins controlled the national government and were able to pass national legislation—on price controls, for example—demanded by the Parisian plebs. In Lyons, by contrast, the bourgeois Jacobins could not deliver. They had much less leverage. They did not control the regional administration, much less the nation as a whole. And in any case, even Chalier, for all his rhetorical Jacobinism, never thought of taxing the rich as more than a temporary solution to short-run problems. In consequence, in early 1793, the Lyonese poor began to drop out of Jacobinism just as the rich had done before them.

Local food prices shot up. Paper money lost its value. Local popular revolutionaries quickly realized that many of the Jacobins' wider goals (such as the mobilization of national resources—and men—for the war effort) could only be realized at their expense. They were shocked by the Jacobins' critique of luxury, which they took to be an indictment of the silk industry and a cause of their unemployment. By March of 1793, the working poor of Lyons had abandoned Chalier.

Though attacked from the left, the Lyonese Jacobins found few friends on the right. The *marchands-fabricants* despised Chalier as much in early 1793 as they had in 1790–91. The Lyonese Jacobins' only strength was their connection to the Paris Jacobins, which was not enough. On May 2, 1793, Lyonese Jacobinism collapsed. If imitation is the highest form of flattery, the Lyonese moderates can be said to have done their best: on July 15, they tried and executed Chalier on a trumped-up charge.

The victors who overthrew Chalier, the moderate *patriotes* of 1791–92, were, so to speak, "reformist revolutionaries," that is, insurrectionary partisans of the Revolution who nonetheless wanted to defend liberal and parliamentary forms of government. They were simultaneously Republicans and bourgeois liberals. From 1789 to 1791 their sensibility had been quite close to that of the Jacobins. They too had seen the need for institutional reform. But in 1793 they rejected not just Montagnard centralism but the Jacobins' moralizing, universalist ideology as well.

The Lyonese moderates were not federalists who wanted to wreck France's central government completely. And they were certainly not royalists, as was claimed by the Montagnards. They were in fact bourgeois democrats; and in any case, they had little choice but to take up that option. To organize resistance to Chalier's self-appointed Jacobin *clubbistes,* the moderates had to rely on the majorities of the legally sanctioned town meetings in the city's *sections.* Ironically, although the Jacobins of Lyons claimed to represent the people, the moderates actually did so.

Though four hundred people were killed when Chalier was overthrown, the moderate victors and their occasional Girondin Jacobin allies did not think the Parisians would assume that Lyons had been the site of a counterrevolutionary coup. (The regional authorities had sanctioned the overthrow of the Jacobin municipality.) The victorious rebels, though anti–Montagnard Jacobin, accepted the authority of the visiting Conventionnels *en mission.* They hoped that for the sake of efficiency and national defense, the Paris Jacobins would accept as their interlocutors at Lyons the victorious enemies of the Lyonese Jacobins.

But one by one snapped the links between the anti-Jacobins in Lyons who claimed to be obedient to the state and the Jacobins who dominated the state in Paris. Each side progressively drew back. François de Virieu, a *ci-devant* noble and a former Monarchien, was appointed head of the Lyonese departmental National Guard. By July 25, 1793, the Lyonese anti-Jacobin revolutionaries had broken with Paris.

Personal factors were important in the genesis of the break, as was the Parisian Jacobins' assumption that their Lyonese opponents—regardless of their stated desire for cooperation—had to be by definition counterrevolutionary putschists, immoral men who deserved to be pushed aside.

Precedents also mattered: in the Vendée, in March, a rural rebellion that had been allowed to get out of hand had almost cut short the Revolution. Now, in July, the Paris Jacobins were eager to make an example of an urban revolt that, they feared, might spread. As it happens, however, that did not occur. Peasants in the neighboring areas, convinced that the Lyonese were indeed royalists, helped the Jacobins to track them down.

In September and October 1793, at the order of the Jacobin-dominated government in Paris, the regular army converged on Lyons, whose three- to four-thousand-man soldiery, with some popular support, managed to hold out for some weeks. Nonetheless, Lyons's defeat was but a question of time; and when it occurred, fearful Jacobin terror surged. At first, the purpose of the punitive Military Commission, the Commission of Popular Justice, and the Temporary Commission of Republican Surveillance was to punish "les grands coupables" and to separate "le séducteur de l'homme séduit" (the seducer from the seduced). But in early November, the Temporary Commission decided to stage massive executions by cannon shot. Lyons was to be destroyed utterly. The name of the city was changed to "Commune Affranchie" (Emancipated Commune). Couthon suggested that the city's inhabitants be dispersed and new settlers brought in. On December 4, 1793, sixty men, chained together, were killed by artillery fire; two hundred and eleven more (including, accidentally, two policemen) were executed the next day. The wounded were sabered to death. The soldiers sickened, and on December 5 the commission decided to rely on firing squads and the guillotine instead.

Subsequent events are principally of local interest, but the social sequences that led to the fall of Lyons were revealingly representative, as appears from a comparison with Saint-Étienne and Nîmes, which like Lyons also had many preindustrial cloth-working inhabitants.

Saint-Étienne, close to Lyons, was important in wartime national politics because of the fifty thousand rifles it produced yearly. The city was also the modern center of a sizable textile industry. The local aristocracy was weak. Its unchallenged and busy middle class was intellectually apathetic and politically timorous. As in Lyons, many Stephanois property owners were afraid of the poor and were unlikely to be driven leftward either by antinobilism or by ideological Jacobin visions of a better world.

In the fall of 1792 local politics were nonetheless radicalized by the results of the municipal elections that had been decreed by the Convention for the nation as a whole on September 25, 1792. In the spring of 1793 Saint-Étienne workers, now better organized, developed embryonically socialistic claims. Predictably, at this point, the local notables, following the lead of the Lyonese rebels, arrested some leading sans-culottes and Jacobins.

But the Stephanois bourgeoisie was more cautious than the Lyonese had been vis-à-vis Paris. In June 1793, with the arrests of the Girondins in Paris, Lyons and Saint-Étienne diverged. The Jacobins' coup in Paris drove the moderate Republicans of Lyons to the right. The Stephanois were far more prudent. They carefully noted that many other provincial centers (like Toulouse and Montauban) had refused to side with the Lyonese rebels against the ruthless Parisian Jacobins.

The breakdown of politics at Saint-Étienne was thus less acute than it had been at Lyons. In July 1793 the rebellious anti-Jacobin National Guard of Lyons invaded Saint-Étienne, where it hoped to find both arms and allies. And some Stephanois workers did join the anti-Jacobins, as had happened at Lyons; but most of the Stephanois textile workers continued to believe that the local Jacobins were their class allies, and they refused the Lyonese invaders their support. Together with these committed artisans, the city's defeated Jacobins fled to the hills. But the wary local Stephanois moderates, though hostile to the Jacobins, did not do much to harass them. They remained tepid in their support of the occupying Lyonese, however much they may have sympathized with their cause.

Retribution at Saint-Étienne was consequently less fierce when the Convention's troops recaptured the city from the Lyonese on September 17, 1793. Inevitably, some of the Stephanois who had sided with the Lyonese were ordered executed by the Jacobins' man on the spot, the unbalanced Conventionnel Claude Javogues; but Saint-Étienne suffered much less than Lyons, where the gap between rich and poor was more sharply drawn and politics much more bitter.

Nîmes presents yet another variant on the theme of Jacobinism and class formation. In this modern city nascent class consciousness was quite strong even before the Revolution. Textile workers were numerous at Nîmes and soon organized a popular society with a populist profile quite distinct from the Club of the Friends of the Constitution, though that society was radical as well: Courbis, a lawyer and one of its leading members, railed against the supposed slavery of factory operatives at Nîmes.

Overall, however, in this class-conscious city rich and poor (or some of them at least) cohabited quite well because the Protestant bourgeoisie was more radical than in Lyons or Saint-Étienne. Many of Nîmes's prosperous Calvinists like the Rabaut brothers were reluctant to move to the right. Republicanism likewise satisfied many of the Nîmois populists. Jacobinism's message of fraternity and charity made the local bourgeoisie—already sensitized by its peculiar religious situation—more rather than less sympathetic to the claims of the poor. In Nîmes, as would also be true in Marseilles, Jacobinism provided an ideological bridge across a narrow social divide.

To be sure, local anti-Jacobins were also strong in this southern city (passions ran high in the Midi), briefly forcing Courbis into hiding in 1793. But with the intermittent help of Parisian Jacobins, Courbis and his friends managed to hang on until August 1794. (Courbis was mysteriously murdered in 1795.)

In Saint-Étienne caution had incited the local bourgeoisie not to side too openly against the Jacobins. In Nîmes Jacobinism also ruled, for a while at least, if for a different reason, namely, that religion mattered more than class.

The complex relation of social class to Jacobin loyalty also appeared in France's first Mediterranean naval base, Toulon. The large number of workers who labored in the state-owned naval dockyards there ought—in theory—to have generated a radical popular audience for left-leaning Jacobins. But that did not happen because the Toulonais arsenal workers were exasperated by the Jacobins' thirst for their ship-building labor. From a Jacobin point of view, the war effort came first and the conditions of workers, second. Laborers responded accordingly, and Toulonais Jacobinism collapsed.

Marseilles: Mediterranean Sociability and Jacobin Parthenogenesis

In Lyons class differences destroyed Jacobinism's prospects. In Marseilles social divisions were of a very different kind, and Jacobinism was a great success, albeit of a peculiar kind.

In France's fourth largest urban center (in 1789, the city had 110,000 inhabitants, 90,000 of them within the city walls)[7] Jacobin principles had an unusually wide resonance. Thus, when civil war broke out in this southern metropolis, the two camps were not really Jacobin and anti-Jacobin (as in Lyons) but two variants of a single Jacobin theme.

To the left were populist Jacobins who had secured a popular audience, and who then decided—with the help of the Parisian Jacobins—to give their Jacobin principles greater actuality. To the right were socially middling Jacobins with some popular support, who agreed with their enemies on matters of principle but differed from them on quotidian politics, especially as regarded the administrative autonomy of their city.

In Lyons Jacobins were few because Jacobinism was rejected by the propertied and *patriote* bourgeoisie, which accepted the events of 1789 if taken to be the promise of institutional reform, but which was not interested in the moralized program of Jacobinical regeneration pushed forward by Chalier. To make matters worse from a Jacobin point of view, after some initial hesitation, the Lyonese Jacobins were also rejected by the poor, for whom Jacobin words buttered no parsnips.

In Marseilles, by contrast, many hard-core middle-class Jacobins were ready to work with the urban poor. Moreover, the Marseillais poor, in turn, were quite willing to follow the lead of their Jacobin mentors. In an atmosphere of life-threatening civil war, more than six hundred Marseillais left Jacobins could be counted on to fight to the bitter end. In Marseilles, as in Nîmes, Jacobinism worked quite well because it served as the basis for a cross-class alliance on the left.

The Revolution began in Marseilles in March of 1789, well before the fall of the Bastille, when rioting occasioned the creation on March 26 of an emergency Council of the Three Estates, which struggled to restore law and order. Only in late May did the royal authorities and their docile Swiss mercenaries restore the king's writ in the city, and then for but a short while.

As in Lyons, the Marseillais old order managed at first to stagger intact through the events that had convulsed Paris in the summer of 1789. In the winter of 1789–90, however, the newly elected but still cautious municipal government was forced by the radical *patriotes,* first, to disband the conservative *garde bourgeoise* that had come into being as a compromise after the fall of the Bastille in July of the previous year and, second, to set up a new and more popularly recruited National Guard, along the lines of the assembly's decree of August 10, 1789.

Then, on April 11, 1790, the local Jacobin club came into being, and in the last days of that month the Jacobins and the National Guard captured the surrounding forts by stealth, an event immortalized in Jean Renoir's great film *La Marseillaise,* of 1938. On December 8, 1790, at Mirabeau's behest, the National Assembly broke the power of the last Marseillais royal official, the provost-marshal of Provence. By 1791 Marseillais radicals had achieved prominence at home and an enviable reputation for radicalism in the country at large.

The city's municipality also drifted steadily to the left. Radicalized by growing unemployment and by the meagerness of food subsidies, which the nearly bankrupt municipality could hardly afford, the poor became more vocal. The mayor of Marseilles, Jean Raymond Mouraille, though basically a moderate *patriote* rather than an ideologized Jacobin, sided with them. He ordered the inspection of all business correspondence so as to track down supposed conspirators.

Encouraged by these circumstances and by the leftward drift of national politics as well, the Marseillais Jacobins became steadily more aggressive. On February 26, 1792, eight thousand Marseillais disarmed a Swiss regiment garrisoned in the neighboring city of Aix. They forced a purge of the administrative board of their region, the newly created department of the Bouches-du-Rhône. In the summer of 1791 the club organized the first of its "pilgrimages" to the papal enclave of Avignon: hundreds of Marseillais National Guards marched off to lend the Avignonais radicals a helping hand. Then, in March 1792, the Marseillais went to Arles and overthrew the "chiffonistes" who had driven local Jacobins underground. Emboldened, the Marseillais *clubbistes* also invaded the neighboring department of the Vaucluse. Clearly, the Marseillais had a long history of marching when on the eve of the monarchy's collapse, in June 1792, five hundred of them (under Jacobin leadership) marched off to Paris to the tune of "La Marseillaise."

In the summer of 1792 the entire political spectrum of the city continued to drift leftward. Relations steadily worsened between the ever more powerful Jacobin club and the patriotic but non-Jacobin and socially conservative departmental administration, which had been forced to move from Aix to Marseilles. By April 1792 the Marseillais Jacobins and their fellow Aixois Jacobins had established a firm control of the region's club network. Their emboldened populist allies also became more aggressive. Between July 23, 1792, and September 8, 1792, a dozen "counterrevolutionaries" were murdered on the streets of Marseilles. On September 15, 1792, the left Jacobins seized control of the Marseilles club and threatened the departmental authorities. They charged their moderate enemies with misusing the newly constituted local Revolutionary Tribunal.

The conjunction of local events (higher bread prices) and national politics (the execution of the king) radicalized the Marseillais Jacobins yet again. In January 1793 pro-Montagnard Jacobins, led by Louis-François Isoard (1765–1795), decided that their future was to the left, in an alliance of Jacobinism and populism. On March 19, 1793, after proclaiming their complete allegiance to the Paris Jacobins and to the Montagnards, the Marseillais *clubbistes* secured the regional authorities' consent to the disarming of "suspects." (In Paris, the law of suspects was to be passed much later, in September 1793.) On March 27, 1793, the Marseillais Jacobins welcomed four visiting Conventionnels *en mission* to the club.

Locally, ideologically progressive but socially conservative ex-Jacobins worried about this steady leftward trend of the club. They decided to fight back, not inside the club (that could no longer be done) but in another forum, that of the thirty-two Marseillais *sections,* which were local deliberative assemblies recognized by law.

The first goal of these chastened, middling Jacobins was to maintain Marseilles's local independence vis-à-vis Paris. Their second aim was to resist what they took to be an excessive institutionalization of the very principles they shared with their populist opponents. They did not want to move from a rhetoric of equality to its concrete embodiment.

Disagreements sharpened. In April 1793 the radical Jacobin *clubbistes* persuaded the visiting Montagnard Conventionnels, Moïse Bayle and Joseph Boisset, to arrest and replace the patriotic but non-Jacobin mayor. On April 20 a *section* dominated by the right Jacobins accused the new left-Jacobin municipality of "despotism." The tenth *section* of the city claimed (in paradoxically typical Jacobin language) that the new pro-Montagnard municipality was run by intrigants "who borrow the language of patriotism the better to seduce." Boisset's and Bayle's response was that the sections (which were legally constituted but harbored their local allies' enemies) should only be allowed to meet sporadically. The *sectionnaires* refused. On April 28, 1793, the sixth *section* proclaimed the greater authenticity of its republicanism: "the *sections,* far from moving away from the spirit of the Revolution and from republicanism, have worked, on the contrary, to consecrate the principles of popular sovereignty and to apply that sovereign right."[8]

Without formally marking a break with Paris, the local *sections* overthrew the local Montagnard administration. Baille and Boisset left the city, as did the leading local radical Jacobin, Isoard, who fled to Paris, where he joined both the Jacobin club and the more leftist Cordelier club. The victorious Marseillais *sectionnaires* then proceeded to purge both the municipal administration and the club, a gesture that had national effect since it prompted the Girondins in Paris to make one last (and futile) effort to break the hold of the Montagne over the Convention.

But just as the Girondins were really ex-Jacobins who had merely lost their resolve, so in Marseilles were the momentarily victorious *section-*

naires, though hostile to the leadership of the Jacobin club as it had come to be, not at all opposed to basic Jacobin principles. (Many of the *sectionnaires* were quasi-proletarian dock workers.) Marseilles, once again, took after Nîmes, with its leftist Protestant, pro-Jacobin bourgeoisie, rather than Lyons, where Jacobins were few and where anti-Jacobin opposition was so heterogeneous as eventually to include both covert royalists and the poor. In Marseilles, where cross-class sociability was strong, all the players shared a more or less Jacobin frame of mind, even if opinions differed on the practical translation that Jacobin principles should have.

Unsurprisingly, the victorious Marseillais *sectionnaires* restored the Jacobins' Revolutionary Tribunal, if on their own terms. They arrested their leftist opponents in the name of the Revolution. They legalized searches without judicial warrants. In the last days of May 1793, in the nearby city of Salon, which they occupied, a moderate Marseillais Jacobin explained that although confiscations of property were illegal, so was selfishness: "The poor cannot molest the rich, and the rich cannot abandon the poor . . . And as far as I can see, the Republic is a great tree of which commerce and industry are the branches and of which agriculture is the trunk. If you cut that down, everything will collapse."[9]

The rebellious, right-Jacobin Marseillais legitimated their stand not by an appeal to violated royalist tradition but by reference to pure Jacobin principle: "Sovereignty does not allow for any absolute fractions. There is however a *relative sovereignty* that a citizen, or a part of the nation's citizens, can claim to exercise whenever those rights that have been transmitted and ceded by the social compact are violated. This is a prerogative granted to the citizen [as a right] of resistance to oppression."[10]

In short, if we look beyond the city's day-to-day politics, we can see that Jacobinism had completely swept the ideological field in Marseilles. In that city Jacobins who had sided with the militant poor struggled against other more socially conservative Jacobins, who bizarrely enjoyed their own measure of popular support, since in Marseilles many people—including the very poor—resented the local left Jacobins' habit of kowtowing to Paris and to Parisian emissaries. Paradoxically, the ability of the Marseillais to mount their "federalist revolt" (as the *sectionnaires*' rebellion was unfairly labeled by the Paris Jacobins) proved local Jacobinism's vigor, not its weakness, as was true at Lyons.

In Marseilles, then, anti-Jacobins were Jacobins of a kind, as appears from the career of Charles Barbaroux, whose sad trajectory also illustrates the interweaving of private choice and public fate. Born in Marseilles in 1767, this gifted young lawyer was active in local prerevolutionary literary societies. In 1788 he traveled to Paris, where he studied science under Marat's direction. One of the premier Marseillais patriots after the fall of the Bastille, Barbaroux was arrested by the royal authorities and on his release became one of the founders of the Marseillais Jacobin society. At the forefront of advanced populist politics, Barbaroux actively worked with his fellow radicals to undo the conservative municipality at Arles. In April 1792 he went so far as to request an amnesty for Jourdan, the organizer at Avignon in 1791 of the first large-scale massacres of the Revolution. ("Coupe-tête" Jourdan was forcibly released from jail by a patriot crowd. He was later rearrested and eventually executed in May 1794.)

Barbaroux's great misfortune was to be elected to the Convention. Had he stayed in Marseilles, this populist friend of Marat would surely have remained on the far left of Jacobinism. But in Paris Barbaroux fell in with the Girondins for personal reasons (he had become a close friend of Manon Roland); and when his Girondin patrons quarreled with the Paris Jacobins, the man foolishly chose the side of the Girondin Jacobins against the Montagnard Jacobins. Duly excluded from the Jacobin club of Marseilles and later, in June 1793, from the Convention as well, Barbaroux fled to Caen, where he met Charlotte Corday and where he vainly tried to organize an anti-Jacobin Girondin army. Defeated and pursued by Montagnards who might well have been his friends had he chosen otherwise, Barbaroux killed himself in June 1794.

Barbaroux's career has a kind of logic; but because it turned on happenstance more than principle, one can imagine for him other scenarios, as one also can for all the Marseillais Jacobins. Thus, if the right Jacobins of Marseilles had been accepted as valid partners by the Paris Jacobins, there might never have been a Marseillais rebellion.

Or, in a second and much more grand scenario, had locally stationed troops opted for the Jacobinism of the Marseillais *section*, had they rejected both the visiting Conventionnels and the Paris Jacobins who had illegally expelled the Girondins from the Convention, then the Marseillais right Jacobins might have won nationally. Marseilles might have triumphed over Paris, and the milder Marseillais version of Jacobin ideology might then have dominated nationwide. The alliance that had been struck in the capital between Robespierrist Montagnards and Parisian sans-culottes would have been overthrown from the outside in the summer of 1793 instead of succumbing from within in the winter of 1793–94. A milder, more rhetorical, and less ideologized Jacobinism would have prevailed nationally, for a while in any case. The Great Terror of 1794 might never have occurred.

But, as it happens, neither of these two alternate trajectories developed. On August 25, 1793, regular army units under General Jean-Baptiste Carteaux, on orders from Paris, overthrew the Marseillais federalists. Isoard was returned to power. The Jacobin club was restored. Montagnard terror battened down the city, as in Lyons and in the Vendée, its purpose being less to cow potential enemies than to punish vengefully. Buildings were ordered razed. Marseilles was renamed "The City without a Name." The re-Jacobinized Revolutionary Tribunal judged 975 individuals and sentenced 289 of them to death. Another 218 people came before a military commission; 123 were executed.

The Marseillais left Jacobins welcomed the vengeful terror that Paris demanded. Suggestively, however, they did not completely give up on the local independence they had accused their federalist enemies of asserting against the Paris Convention. They too were local patriots of a kind and soon decided to organize a regional Jacobin congress, with the purpose (quite different from that of the *sectionnaires* whom they had just defeated) of supporting Paris and even pushing it along toward the populist left. Isoard, who while in Paris had come into contact with the Parisian sans-culottes, advocated this policy of activist collaboration.

Since he had sided with Robespierre and against the Girondins in June 1792, and since he was also a member of the Paris club, it was hard in September 1793 for the Parisian Montagnards to disavow his actions from one day to the next, and Isoard's scheme was allowed to bloom. In early September 1793, 255 pro-Montagnard delegates from 71 Jacobin societies of southeastern France met at Valence, halfway between Lyons and Marseilles.

These hard-core provincial left Jacobins decided to hold another congress in Marseilles itself. They met on September 28, 1793. By October 7, 1793, 250 Jacobin societies were represented there; and by October 20 there were 400. Eventually, 1,500 pro-Montagnard delegates gathered in one or another of these regional congresses, representing one-half of all the clubs of southwestern France, the part of the nation where Jacobinism was most firmly implanted.

But after some hesitations, the Montagnard Conventionnel *en mission* Fréron decided with Parisian approval on November 21, 1793, to shut this congress down, despite its support for the Parisian cause. Isoard fled once more, pursued by his equally radical but more central-minded ex-friends, the very ones who had put him back in power in September 1793 when the socially conservative Jacobin *sectionnaires* had been defeated. Clearly, by late 1793, Parisian Jacobins were less interested in ideological cooperation than in plain and dumb obedience. Isoard, to finish this Marseillais story, was ironically to share the fate of the Parisian Montagnards who had found him too independent. Captured after the fall of Robespierre, the man was executed in September 1794. In June 1795, 127 other imprisoned Marseillais Jacobins were murdered by a mob with the passive consent of the local police.

Like that of Lyons, but in a wholly different register, the history of revolutionary Marseilles has a telling social message. In Marseilles, Jacobinism had a wide audience. The reasons for this remain to be studied in detail, but owe a great deal to the region's intense sociability, which tied the bourgeois to the plebs.

The Marseillais had a strong, cross-class sense of place. (In the first months of the Revolution, the Marseillais had tried to become their own department, as Paris had become the department of the Seine.)[11] The Conventionnel Fréron said of them that they behaved as if they were a nation unto themselves. Many Marseillais did not speak French but relied on their own local version of Provençal. The city was geographically isolated from the rest of France, oriented to the sea more than to Paris, which was over a week's distance away by stagecoach. It was united by its distinctiveness. Under the Old Regime, all of its inhabitants had shared certain privileges, and the city's entire economic life was dominated by 72 interlocking guilds. Marseilles had many charitable societies or confraternities, whose ties to the local militia were also close. The guidance of the city by its 700-odd merchant families was broadly accepted. Its feebly implanted noble families, which numbered less than 80 in a city of 110,000, did not play an important or divisive role. The city had a long experience of civic politics. And unlike Lyons, Marseilles was economically buoyant. One-fifth of France's foreign trade transited through its port. Overall, the Marseillais were by their social nature well situated to take to Jacobinism's assertion that a common political purpose could be shared by a socially variegated audience.

The ties that bound this organically structured city to the surrounding countryside also contributed to the local Jacobins' regional successes. The entire region breathed through the city's harbor. Moreover, regional habits of sociability broadened the success of Marseillais Jacobinism into the city's hinterland. Links between town and country were numerous and close: five thousand *bastides,* or country houses belonging to the Marseillais bourgeoisie, scattered around the city.

In the more conservative Vendée, peasants lived in isolated hamlets, their collective life limited to churchgoing. But in Provence, by radical contrast, the countryside was, as it were, informally urbanized. Much of the Provençal peasantry lived in large towns that had an urban feel, whose social life was highly structured and interconnected. Before 1789 the department of the Var, which was to have clubs in 135 communes, had counted 97 brotherhoods (or *confréries*); these played a role similar to that of the Masonic lodges for the urban bourgeoisie: within their compass, ordinary social distinctions were at least partly ignored. Long before 1789, the members of these quasi-rural religious societies were in the non-Catholic habit of deliberation and election, and they naturally looked to the Marseillais Jacobins (federalist or not) for guidance. (Ordinarily, Isoard's pilgrimages out of Marseilles and into the small outlying towns of the backcountry began with a request for help from local oppressed patriots.) Marseillais and Aixois Jacobins, it may be added, were particularly intent on using local dialects rather than French to make their point.

In short, peasants of this region were, in the words of Maurice Agulhon, "structurally fated" to democratic politics. When the Marseillais Jacobins formulated their political philosophy, the peasantry in the hinterland was ready for them. The club was affiliated with 62 societies in the local department of the Bouches-du-Rhône alone, and to scores more in the neighboring departments of the Vaucluse, Var, and Basses Alpes.

Once again, the basic message is that as an ideology, Jacobinism in 1793–94 worked quite well (as had Jacobin sensibility nationwide from 1789 to 1791) in situations where class lines were either muted or not resented and where ties of intra- and interregional sociability were strong.

The Colonies: Jacobin Black on Royal White

The nature and success of colonial Jacobinism can likewise be set in a social frame. Even in the Réunion, a distant island set in the Indian Ocean between India and South Africa, the social profile of local Jacobins had a familiar look. The fifty-seven founding members of the Jacobin club at Saint-Denis, the island's capital, were mostly artisans, small traders, soldiers, and employees. Above them were the island's wealthier inhabitants, who soon moved out of the Jacobin orbit altogether; and beneath them, the island's poorer inhabitants, who did not get involved initially. The picture resembled that in France, except that in the Réunion the rich were slave owners and the poor were not sans-culottes but slaves.[12]

France's richest Atlantic colony—Saint-Domingue as it was then called, Haiti as it was known after its revolution—had a more complex social structure, as did the neighboring islands (still French to this day) of Guadeloupe and Martinique. At the top of the hierarchy in these Caribbean islands were the planters, rich, white, and many of them nobles like Napoleon's future empress Josephine (by birth a Martiniquaise). These "grands blancs" cohabited uneasily with prerevolutionary government officials: the planters were vocal in the defense of their own interests; and, for their part, French royal officials were committed to enforcing the many restraining and mercantilist directives the "great whites" cordially disliked.

Below the white magnates were the "petit blancs" (small merchants, traders, shippers, often recent migrants), many of whom were instinctively drawn to Jacobin ideas after 1789; and next to them, were the Creoles of mixed French and African parentage, many of whom were free and some of whom owned slaves.

And supporting this entire arrangement were of course the slaves, of different African tribal origins and varyingly Frenchified. Rates of slave mortality and of compensatory slave importations were much higher in the islands than on the North American mainland. Many slaves were thus newcomers.

Events in revolutionary Haiti moved quickly. At first, and to forestall Paris, white slave owners took the law in their own hands and ordered the brutal execution in January 1791 of the elegant and wise mulatto leader Vincent Ogé, who had just returned from Paris. Then, on May 15, 1791, the National Assembly in Paris recognized some free men of color (but not black slaves or men of color born of a slave mother) as citizens. Planters were aghast: "No, we would rather die than accept this infamy . . . If France sends troops to enforce this decree, it may well be that we will resolve to abandon France."[13]

By wanting too much, the planters secured their own destruction, and a slave revolt erupted on the night of August 22, 1791. (News of it reached

Paris on October 27.) A three-way fight soon developed on the island among slaves, planters (who pinned their hopes on an English occupation), and free men of color, who were intermittently allied to government officials and to the planters. Matters became more complicated yet when news reached the island of a decree of April 4, 1792, granting full civic equality to all free men of color.

By 1793 the island's conflict had turned into a set of raging and intricate civil and international clashes involving French soldiers, English soldiers, local whites, French officials, Creoles of mixed European and African origins, and blacks. In the midst of rising anarchy and confusion, the French envoy Léger Félicité Sonthonax ordered the abolition of slavery in the northern part of the island on August 23, 1792, a decision sanctioned by the proclamation in Paris of the end of slavery on February 4, 1794.[14] But events were by then too far gone, and nothing could arrest either the decay of French authority or the murderous decomposition of the social fabric.

For a history of Jacobinism, however, what matters most in the study of Haitian Jacobinism is less the story of the breakdown of France's control over its colonies than the social background and ideological assumptions of the Caribbean *clubbistes*.

Initially and as might be expected, Caribbean Jacobins, all of them whites, had come from various walks of life. Some were rich, some were less rich. But in Haiti, as in the Réunion—and as in Lyons—when universalist ideology was translated into social fact (in this instance, when the issue of emancipation unexpectedly arose), most of the propertied whites dropped out of Jacobinism altogether.

More perhaps than any instance of domestic Jacobinism, the failure of colonial Jacobinism illustrates the extreme sensitivity of Jacobin ideology to underlying social cleavages. Where these tensions ran most high, Jacobinism failed most completely.

Paris: Ideology and Class Consciousness

Parisian Jacobinism was unique. Jacobins only loosely belonged to the human fabric of the capital, whose class structure was rather fluid, in its upper reaches at least. Paris was a far more complex place than either Lyons or Marseilles; and in any instance, most of the Jacobins residing in

Paris were not genuinely Parisian. Though we do not have a precise social and professional breakdown for the Paris *clubbistes*, we can surmise that their club more closely resembled that of cosmopolitan Nice, where most Jacobins were outsiders, than those of the Dordogne region, where in many places over 90 percent of the *clubbistes* were locals.[15]

Parisian Jacobinism had other distinctive traits as well. It was on the floor of the "mother society" on the rue Saint-Honoré that Jacobin principles found their clearest form. In addition, from their closeness to the nation's government, Jacobins in Paris were of necessity less focused than their provincial brethren on meeting the ordinary requirements of daily life. The capital's Jacobins naturally assumed instead that their first task was to guide the entire Revolution's fortunes, an awesome responsibility that pushed them forward to daring innovations like working with the urban poor in 1792 and early 1793 or crushing populist activists in the spring of 1794.

Institutionally, the great distinction of the Paris club was its quotidian role as a staging area for the ongoing critique of the National Assemblies' decisions. Indeed, the club had originated in Versailles in April 1789, when Breton deputies of the Third Estate decided to meet as a group to organize better their parliamentary strategy, as on the night of August 4, 1789. This connection of club to state solidified after May–June 1793, when the Montagnards excluded the Girondin deputies from the Convention and for the first time had control of both the club and the state.

The thrust of discussion in the club changed accordingly. Before May 1793 the society's debating floor had been the exciting site of conflict and criticism. History was made and unmade there every day. With the summer of 1793, however, the Paris club became little more than an instrument of the revolutionary government. The club's tribune still debated great issues but in a different and deferential way. In early 1794 Robespierre was the club's leading figure, but he was before that the spokesman for the Committee of Public Safety. He might choose to accuse his opponents in the club rather than in the Convention, but he did not expect to be contradicted in either place, a rule of statist domination that applied to provincial clubs as well, if less ostentatiously, as Louis de Cardenal pointed out long ago. After June 1793 the axis of local *clubbiste* thinking was everywhere readjusted. Members reacted less to the needs of the public than to the diktats of the state's representatives in the provinces (the Conventionnels *en mission*) and to the decrees, in Paris, of the great Committees of General Security and of Public Safety.

With this national shift from querulousness to passivity came a second problem. How would the Parisian Jacobins deal with the capital's sans-culottes, whom the revolutionary state both feared and needed?[16]

Considered sociologically—and with hindsight—as an imaginary and "ideal type," the Parisian Jacobin was quite distinct from his sans-culotte neighbor. Jacobins were often propertied and educated. Sans-culottes, though quite varied in their backgrounds—especially as regards their leadership experience—were often very poor. (In some parts of Paris, one in six of them was an indigent on relief.) Sans-culottes worked with their hands. They were obsessed by the price of food, of bread and wine especially. They were rough people. Drunkenness for them was no disgrace. Their speech, their manners, and their dress were instantly recognizable. Jacobins read books; sans-culottes told stories. Both types believed in hard work and private property, but they came to those concepts from different points. Sans-culottes were prone to violence and excess, both practical and rhetorical. They considered blood-letting, wife-beating, and quarrelsomeness normal aspects of daily life. Their jokes and humor were physical and gross. Sans-culottes were keen on direct action (or, to speak more plainly, on violence and murder). They held the guillotine in high regard and liked to carry pikes, no doubt the Freudian symbol of their virile cult of physical force. Their social instincts were communitarian. They feared that economic competition would proletarianize them.[17]

Institutional loyalties and political experience further sharpened these meaningful social and cultural differences. Especially important for the sans-culottes' sense of self were the assemblies of their sixty local Parisian districts, which were reshaped by law into forty-eight *sections* in June 1791. The *sections* controlled the local National Guards. They were bodies to be reckoned with. Sans-culottes took great pride in attending the *sections'* deliberative meetings and in serving as part-time soldiers in their paramilitary extensions. (The cannoneers of the Faubourg Saint-Antoine had a particularly strong esprit-de-corps.) It is estimated that about thirty thousand people attended at least some of the *sections'* meetings.[18]

The popular movement had other distinctive political characteristics. Women participated there more than elsewhere. Sans-culottes politics were often familial, cooperative affairs. Husbands and wives made up political teams, displaying a unity of emotional purpose that gave a sharp edge to their politics.

Accordingly, after 1791 the sans-culottes developed a battery of highly specific demands. They wanted price controls, progressive taxation, pensions for the wives and widows of soldiers, more schools, free hospital care, aid for pregnant women, and even socialized or at least subsidized medicine. They were hostile to the idea that the rich might somehow avoid serving in the army. Whether male or female, they did not want to work in large workshops, as government officials in charge of making army clothing hoped they would. They were eager to exclude all nobles from public life regardless of their personal commitment to the Revolution. They were ever more convinced that the use of state terror would resolve economic problems. A good case, then, can be made to show that Parisian sans-culottes and Jacobins differed widely.

And yet, the reverse is also true. In many ways, sans-culottes and Jacobins were quite close. In Paris many dedicated revolutionaries belonged to both the Cordelier and the Jacobin clubs.

Paris in 1789 was still a preindustrial city where tens of thousands of people were neither middle class nor working class, but both or, to be more precise, neither. Parisian workers were as a rule artisans who labored in small shops and often expected to rise socially with age. Most Parisian employers had fewer than ten employees.

Many sans-culottes were quite well off. Carlyle's view of "all-needing sans-culottisme" is only half true. Their populist leadership included many members of the professions, as well as some artisans who had been so successful that they could now afford not to work at all, like the celebrated master carpenter Maurice Duplay, in whose house Robespierre resided in 1794. Sans-culottes assumed that they "owned" both their skills and their guaranteed status, which meant that though unpropertied in a strict sense, they resembled Jacobin landlords and shop owners in their thinking on the critical issue of property rights.

Sans-culottes also shared many cultural preferences with their Jacobin neighbors. Their rules of morality were, by strict Jacobin standards, imperfect (many Parisian artisans did not bother to get married). But, like the Jacobins, they disliked vice, gambling, idleness, and prostitution. Both groups had a productivist rather than a commercial view of life. Sans-culottes instinctively believed that surpluses should be shared, but none of them wanted to confiscate the property of the rich outright and across the board. And just as the anticlericalism of Jacobins who yearned for quasi-religious transcendence can be read as a transposition of older Christian themes into more modern words, so can the sans-culottes' primitive sense of justice be seen as an adaptation of ancient ideals of social justice. The most famous lines of the sans-culottes' favorite and violently anticlerical song, "Ça ira" (All will be well), looked forward to the hanging and lynching of the Revolution's enemies ("les aristocrates à la lanterne, les aristocrates on les pendra"); but subsequent verses were filled with Christian images, of the Gospels being realized, of contented souls, of the mighty being humbled and the humbled, raised.

Jacobins and sans-culottes were often in rough political agreement. Both groups believed that sovereignty was in the people, and the Jacobins themselves were not above accepting force as an occasional means of asserting their right to represent that sovereignty. Both hated factions. They supported roll calls and open voting. They defined themselves in opposition to *aristocrates* (who were selfish, arrogant, and idle) rather than owners of property, not to speak of "capitalists."

It often happened that the terms "sans-culottes" and "Jacobins" were used interchangeably, by provincial Jacobins especially, for whom the former had an essentially political dimension, as in the wholly inappropriate usage "nos frères les sans-culottes des campagnes" (our bothers, the rural sans-culottes).

The sans-culottes' favorite news sheet, called the *Père Duchesne,* did rely on obscene language that was quite different from the Jacobins' often stilted prose. But the editor of the paper, Hébert, was a well-educated actor who had married a convent-schooled wife and whose revolutionary style was a pastiche of a traditional literary genre, the *langue poissarde,* a largely imaginary prerevolutionary dialect or code that bourgeois writers conventionally attributed to fictitious popular types. When shorn of its obscenities, Hébert's message had a distinctly Jacobinical profile, and the man can be described as a populist with Jacobin connections, just as Collot and Fabre were Jacobins with populist colorations.

Culturally, economically, and socially, then, Paris Jacobins were not far removed from those who became in the spring of 1794 their hostile rivals, if not their political enemies. The difference between them often was no more than the gap between those prone to see the present as it was and those inclined to think Jacobinically of what it might become.

Once again we see that Jacobinism and the shape of class structures were entwined, as both causes and effects. Where lines of class became more sharply drawn, Jacobinism stumbled. And in Paris, where Jacobin politics rose to fever pitch, class lines were correspondingly sharpened, so that Jacobinism eventually collapsed, a victim, as it were, of its own intensity.

In deciding whether the sans-culottes and the Paris Jacobins formed a single—if varied—group, or two quite distinct social entities, we must remember that politics from 1791 to 1793 often intensified social consciousness. In E. P. Thompson's celebrated phrase, classes are not things; and a good example of that aphorism is the rise and disappearance of the sans-culottes. Ephemeral (since they vanished from the political scene after 1795), they nonetheless flared and illumined the future social landscape of the entire nineteenth century.

Bonneville

In the history of Jacobinism, the case of an outstanding Parisian revolutionary ideologist close to the *sociétaires*, Nicolas Bonneville, also serves to illustrate the interplay of Jacobin ideas and practicalities. In brief, Bonneville's failure expresses quite well the growing irrelevance in the period 1789–1794 of those people who considered ideology without reference to national and practical politics.[19]

Born near Paris in 1760, Bonneville traveled extensively in Germany, where he was involved with Bavarian mystical freemasonry, and in Britain, where he lived for some time in the mid-1780s with Brissot. (He was also a friend of Tom Paine, who later adopted Bonneville's children. One of them became the director of the West Point Military Academy. The Bonneville salt flats in Utah are named for him.)

Many of Bonneville's ideas were typically Jacobinical. His *De L'Esprit des religions* of 1791, for example, was aggressively anticlerical. The people had been misled. Were they not the victims "of those incurable prejudices born of that sacerdotal hypocrisy . . . [which] degrades the human species and shears the people of all of nature's benefits?" Electors, he thought, should never lose the right to recall their deputies, whose first duty was to vote according to their electors' wishes. Bonneville, who much admired Rousseau, was an early convert to republicanism and joined the Cordelier club as well.

His own club, the Cercle Social, attracted many important Jacobins— or near-Jacobins—like Sieyès, Condorcet, Brissot, and Marie-Joseph Lequinio.[20] Bonneville welcomed feminists as well, among them, especially, Etta Palm d'Aelders. In late July 1791, after the king's flight to Varennes, Bonneville proposed to fuse his club with the Jacobins. The new society, he argued, would stand for "enlightenment, energy, and effective power, [and could] save liberty by a universal correspondence, at the center of which will be only truth, common to all."[21]

Bonneville's chief associate, the abbé Fauchet, took an even more progressive stance by advocating rural communism and the redistribution of property. (It was Fauchet, incidentally, who invented the terms sans-culotterie and sans-culottisme.)

Bonneville had a lively sense of the kind of ideas that appealed to "public opinion," and he was interested in the broad diffusion of his views. In 1791 the man published a polyglot translation of the Constitution and made it the aim of the Cercle Social to be the universal sounding board for the worldwide Republic of Letters. The new club, dedicated to equality and union, would become, he wrote, a "foyer de lumière et un corps de résistance" (a source of light and a body of resistance). Bonneville also chose to locate his Cercle on the rue Saint-Honoré in the Palais Royal, a worldly center of gambling, prostitution, and news hawking that had been the spiritual center of the Revolution since Desmoulins had harangued crowds there on July 12, 1789. (The Jacobin club on the rue Saint-Honoré was only a few blocks down the street.) Unlike the Jacobins, who hesitated to make their debates public, Bonneville's club had from the first an intensely public purpose. Its debates were printed in a house organ, the *Bouche de fer*, as Bonneville had also started a printing house. He in fact had a string of successes. The Friends of the Truth, created in October 1790 as an extended version of the Cercle Social, even offered affiliation to other societies like the Paris Jacobin club. In its time, it may well have been the largest club in France.

Yet, despite its ideological purity and regardless of Bonneville's sense of popularized communication, the Cercle Social never did fuse with the Jacobin club. In fact, it soon came to a dead end. Its leading figures either left or, like Fauchet, found themselves excluded from the Jacobin club. This failure is easily explained. Bonneville, in Michelet's words, was a dreamer, "trop souvent dans les nuages" (too often in the clouds), invariably disappointed in his many efforts to be elected to public office. Practical politics frightened him, as they did the Girondins, many of whom were his friends. The man was too reluctant to sacrifice his private likes and dislikes to public need. His failure can be read as the cost of sticking to a script that the more practical *clubbistes* gradually rejected.

Ideology certainly mattered to the Jacobins as well, but they, unlike him, were also men of action, whose tactics and at times principles fluctuated as political necessity required. Praxis, rather than obstinate prejudice or *parti pris,* was the magnetic north of their doctrinal compass.

Robespierre was at times an inflexible doctrinaire, far more so than the bumbling founder of the Cercle Social. But Robespierre was also a shrewd politician who managed to outwit—and destroy—any number of opponents. His mix of flexibility and inflexibility reminds us that Jacobinism was not just an ideological monolith but a complex sensibility whose varied configurations changed in time, space, and social circumstance. Applied Jacobinism was one thing in 1791 and another thing in 1793. At Lyons, it differed from what it was in Marseilles, Nîmes, or Paris. Each city and each club had its own character and problems whose unraveling depended in no small part on the varieties of class formation from one place to the next.

Beset by problems it often brought upon itself (war, inflation, the Civil Constitution of the Clergy), Jacobinism's inner dynamic drove revolutionary politics forward. One Jacobin group after another purged its weaker brothers. But when confronted by conservative opposition and newly formed class awareness, Jacobinism's suddenly narrowed appeal faltered and decayed. Its accentuated words of universalist reconciliation sounded empty. Its happy balance of communitarian and individualist principle broke down. Ensuing confrontation brought its darker, terrorist instincts to the fore. And in this wholly unexpected conflictual context, Jacobin republicanism fell apart.

11

Looking Backward: On the Origins of Jacobin Sensibility

The contradiction between our condition and our desires, our duties and our inclinations, between nature and social institutions, between man and citizen, is the source of human misery. Give him entirely to the state, or leave him entirely to himself, but if you divide his heart, you will break it.

Jean-Jacques Rousseau, *Fragments politiques*

*W*e can identify the phases of Jacobinism's moralizing trajectory, its difficulties and its palliatives, as it moved relentlessly from humanistic universalism in 1789–90 to terrorism in 1793–94. We can speculate on Jacobinism's ideological contradictions and divided nature. We can also see how class conflict elicited Jacobinism's atavistic responses to unprecedented problems.

But why did Jacobinism come into being in the first place? How did the contours of prerevolutionary French society and culture affect Jacobinism's shape and goals? And why consider this problem *after* rather than before looking at Jacobinism itself?

These questions raise complicated issues of ontology that are hard to resolve because our views of the Revolution's past and present are hopelessly circular. Different understandings of the Old Regime's collapse imply different views of Jacobinism's deeper purpose, just as different understandings of revolutionary politics after 1789 determine our varying sense of why the Old Regime decomposed.

A Marxist appreciation of the Revolution's purpose finds Jacobinism's prerevolutionary origins in "socioeconomic" change. An ideological explanation, like François Furet's, points to the antecedent collapse of the Old Regime's ideological substance. And my own perception of the Revolution as a cultural upheaval that centered on a new view of self, society, and politics, incites us to seek the many and varied cultural origins of this broad social and political transformation.

In the historiography of the French Revolution three specific explanations of the Old Regime's failure and of its relation to Jacobinism's future have emerged:

Tocqueville's, which focuses on the inability of the centralizing Crown in the late eighteenth century to resolve rising social conflict as it had in the past;

The social (ordinarily, Marxist) interpretation, which emphasizes the creation of new social formations and sees Jacobinism as the weapon of a nascent bourgeois class;

And the more recent "revisionist" interpretation, which treats Jacobinism as an autonomous, free-floating ideology that naturally (and terroristically) expanded in the vacuum caused by the decay of the monarchy's prestige.

Of these explanations, the one presented by Tocqueville in his *L'Ancien Régime* of 1856 is still the best known. In 1789, argued Alexis comte de Tocqueville, the exclusive nobility—which had paid no taxes since the fifteenth century—existed unchallenged. Nobles knew they were *born* to rule, socially at least. By the late eighteenth century, however, a humiliated but richer, better-educated, meritorious, and utilitarian-minded bourgeoisie existed as such also. It knew that it *deserved* to rule. A wide gap separated these two social groups. In England gentlemen were identifiable by their manners, irrespective of birth. But in France *gentilhommes* were distinguished by their birth, irrespective of their (often bad) manners. When the upstart, Enlightenment philosophes further poisoned the mind of the rising bourgeoisie with their impractical dreams and rabid anticlericalism, the center could not hold. Class openly clashed with class. And since France— unlike America—was a country where for centuries only the centralized, modernizing, and absolutist government had been able to accommodate warring social groups, society necessarily fell apart when the monarchy lost its ability to direct events.

Thus did Tocqueville arrive at the great paradox of modern European history, namely, that revolutionary Jacobinism erupted in the country where feudalism and absolutism were most senescent and mild. He defined Jacobinism as the ethic of an aggrieved bourgeois class that, unbeknownst to itself, was destined to carry France's bureaucratic, centralized, and oppressive monarchic past into a democratic future.

The "social interpretation" of the Revolution was quite different. From 1890 to 1990 five generations of Marxist historians labored to highlight the prerevolutionary economic and social background of 1789. In France this was the task of Jean Jaurès before 1900, Albert Mathiez in the 1920s, Georges Lefebvre in the 1930s and 1940s, Albert Soboul in the 1960s, and Michel Vovelle and Claude Mazauric after that. Abroad their work was amplified by many highly gifted social historians (George Rudé in Australia; Walter Markov and Anatolii Ado in Russia; Galante Garonne in Italy; Kare Tönnesson in Norway; Norman Hampson, Gwynn Lewis, and Colin Lucas in England), most of whom were only tangentially Marxist, or, as a rule, not Marxist at all.

Their first aim was to highlight the prerevolutionary material transformations of French life (more trade, the appearance of infant industries, the specialization of production, an incipiently capitalist conception of wage and profit, the beginnings of a national market, and so on). Their second and more ambitious goal was to speculate on class formation before 1789 so as to clear the ground for a class interpretation of Jacobinism after 1789.

Many dwelled on the decline before 1789 of tradition and culture-bound corporatism. They underscored the appearance of new economic animosities that, even before the Revolution's crystallizing drive, separated bourgeois employers from more class-conscious workers, as at Lyons, where strikes had become common in the 1780s.

Other social historians focused instead on the renewed tensions that pitted a rising middle class against a declining aristocracy that was at once envied and admired, imitated and detested. They emphasized the impact of a "feudal reaction," whose main ingredients were the recovery by greedy nobles of forgotten feudal dues; the emergence of the law courts as the newfound vehicle of aristocratic resistance to absolutist and rationalized government; and the excluding aristocratization after 1750 of the bureaucracy, the church, and the military. In this social or material vein, modern class distinctions were said to exist well before 1789. (This book, of course, denies that view.) Even before Jacobinism and the Revolution had come round to sharpen everyone's political sensibility, a prerevolutionary bourgeoisie—in the context of this social argument—was already fighting a two-front war.

Social historians imagined the Third Estate to have disdained the landowning and still feudal-minded aristocracy as frivolous, immoral, idle, parasitical, oversexed, and incapable of fighting successful wars. Only country nobles (who were fancifully supposed to be patriotic, poor, honest, and civic-minded) counted as exceptions to the bourgeois rules of resentment, envy, and self-satisfied sense of moral superiority.

These historians characterized the French bourgeoisie of the 1780s as increasingly repelled by the poor, now thought by those who owned property to be threatening, illiterate, ill-mannered, ill-kept, unfamilial, dirty, misshapen, and prone to violence. The postrevolutionary perception of the 1830s and 1840s, which turned the laboring classes into a subset of the dangerous criminal classes, was, we are told, foreshadowed in prerevolutionary times.

For the social historians of the Revolution, then, Jacobinism was first and foremost the expression of a rising bourgeois class consciousness. For them, it lacked even the meager specificity that it had had for Tocqueville. Its universalism was a transparent cipher, designed to discredit the falsely Christian, selfish, and particularist feudal class that was aped and detested. At heart it was a defense of bourgeois property. Indeed, when they looked forward from 1793–94 to their own day and society, many hard-core Marxist social historians, in the Soviet Union especially, found Jacobin terrorism to be the morally irrelevant price that the bourgeoisie had had to pay for asserting its domination over other doomed but stubbornly insistent social groups.

By contrast, the more recent revisionist explanation of the Revolution's origin focuses on the ideological antecedents of Jacobinism's terroristic fate. It is only incidentally concerned with its social origins. It asserts, as did Tocqueville, that the democratization of life had indeed made antecedent social and political arrangements irrelevant; but it does not dwell on Jacobinism's ambient social frame, which—as it supposes—French revolutionaries were in any case ideologically fated to ignore.

Revisionism assumes as a matter of course that on the eve of Revolution nobles and bourgeois had in the main become the like-minded members of a new and culturally uniform, socially mixed elite. It downplays the relevance of feudalism to prerevolutionary French social life and economics. It is not concerned with class formation.

Although it stylishly relies on linguistic theory, art history, and political science, the modern, cross-disciplinary, and revisionist view of the Revolution is largely an expanded restatement of much older views on the importance of the ideological origins of the French Revolution. (In Victor Hugo's words, "C'est la faute à Voltaire, c'est la faute à Rousseau.")

The revisionist view is flawed because it neglects the social context of Jacobinism and is reluctant to see Jacobinism as a broad cultural movement. But its understanding of Jacobin ideological specificity has merit.

The view of Jacobinism's origins presented in this chapter expands varyingly on these different ways of seeing. In a Tocquevillean manner, it too insists on the consequences for Revolutionary politics of the monarchy's place in French cultural life, though it does so in ways that would have disconcerted the author of *L'Ancien Régime*. In large part, it attributes the genesis of Jacobinism's moralizing stance to the interplay of prerevolutionary French politics and culture. From the social historians of the prerevolution it borrows the idea that economic change did indeed destroy the foundations of social traditionalism in prerevolutionary France. But it stops distinctly short of saying that a bourgeois class had come into being before 1789. Finally, like the revisionists, it stresses the importance and relative autonomy of ongoing ideological and cultural change.

Which is to say that this combined perspective identifies two prerevolutionary sources of Jacobinism: first, the *social* ramifications of the rapid movement of French society in the eighteenth century from traditionalist equilibrium to modernizing disequilibrium; and, second, the *political* and *cultural* effects of French absolutism.

The argument is not just, as Norbert Elias rightly thought, that new styles of behavior appropriate to absolutist court life became valid models for French society as a whole; or that the acceptance of some political principles by all, regardless of caste, held within themselves the implication of other universalist assumptions that would eventually be applied regardless of class: if all today were equal subjects of an absolutist king, they might all become tomorrow the equal citizens of a free republic. The point must also be that in the mid-seventeenth century, when the newly ludovician monarchy laid a claim to all of public space, many propertied persons readjusted their personal goals accordingly. Absolutism transformed not just the style but the moral substance of French social life.

When forced to withdraw from an independent public life, the elites of the French nation (whose economic foundations were left untouched) found themselves able to moralize their private lives, in theory at least; and they could do so because they had by and large chosen not to become involved in nascent capitalist ventures that required compromise, haggling, and profiteering.

This critical political and cultural arrangement was transformed once again after 1750 when the prestige of the monarchy began to wane. In the second half of the eighteenth century, propertied and educated Frenchmen increasingly decided that public life should become the playing field not just of the Crown, as had been true since the day of the sun king a hundred years before, but of the sovereign nation also, that is, of the people, best represented, as it happens, by themselves. But the elite of the French nation did not match these new claims with a renunciation of their previous and moralizing way of looking at the world. Rather, they hoped to carry over into the newly reclaimed public sphere the same principles of moralized private life that they had evolved a century before when the absolutist Crown had excluded them from immediate political influence. In Diderot's judgmental words (which the Jacobins of 1794 could have easily understood), "to raise the moral standards of a nation is to augment its capacity for both good and evil; it is, so to speak, to encourage a people to great crimes and great virtues."[1]

Jacobinism emerged from this doubled social and social-political situation. Its "socioeconomic" place "betwixt and between" gave feasibility to even its wildest schemes of universalist harmony and to its vision of a moral public space where the ancient Christian and Platonic dream of reconciling the rights of the one to the claims of the many might finally be realized.

In brief, voluntary Jacobinism vigorously rejected the idea that the living were doomed unwittingly to recreate or extend the past. Yet, that was indeed to be Jacobinism's fate.

Arrangements

In greater detail, then, what was the Old Regime whence Jacobinism sprang?

Our presentist response—and rightly so, for once—is to see early-eighteenth-century France as a kind of golden cultural and social time. In modern literature, theater, opera, and film, its imagined decor has taken on an air of harmonious fantasy. (Marie Antoinette—recently satirized by Madonna—is with Napoleon the most famous figure in the entire length and breadth of French history from Joan of Arc to Charles de Gaulle.) Talleyrand—first a prerevolutionary and noble-born bishop, then a tangential Jacobin, and finally the foreign minister of the Directory and of Napoleon—once sighed that those who had not known the Old Regime did not truly know "la douceur de vivre" (the ease of living).

The Jacobins of 1791 did not see (as would the Bolsheviks of 1917) their country's cultural history as a sequence of unredeemed disasters. Far from it, the Jacobins were convinced that France had been, or could easily have become, the world's most pleasant place. Thus, in the mid-eighteenth century, French society delicately balanced many (pleasing) contrasts, though these would soon become the contradictions that set the course of Jacobinism's rise and fall.

Jacobins in 1789 carried within themselves not just a sense that modern society and traditional state were now at odds with each other. They also felt nostalgia for a happier, more integrated past, which they were confident they could recreate and improve.

Of these earlier harmonies, or transcended differences, which Jacobins would want to recreate, if in a wholly new register, the most obvious involved the cultural integration of town and country, as well as of religion and enlightened modernity.

In 1750 (some historians, like Eugene Weber, would even say until 1900), France functioned as a heap of "immobile villages," turned in on themselves, uninvolved in the market, and without much contact with modern life or one another. In 1789 more than four out of five Frenchmen lived in villages or small towns.

French rural life, based on leaseholding in the north and sharecropping in the south, was organized around what might be puckishly described as "modernized traditionalism." In France 95 percent of peasants were free to move about, as compared to tsarist Russia, for example, where 90 percent of peasants were landbound serfs.

But these freely moving country dwellers were not modern farmers, eager to buy and sell. It was often next to impossible for them to find the coins to buy salt for their animals or to pay their taxes, which on average came to about one-fourth of the gross national product, and even more in some places. Many poorer peasants lived on the edge of destitution.

Surprisingly, however, this impoverished rural world was basically at peace with itself and with a distant state that did not severely impinge on it. (Taxes were high indeed, but universal military conscription was invented only in 1793 by the Jacobins.) In addition, eighteenth-century rural France was spared military invasion, an important point because the happiness of premodern peasantries largely derived from the absence of catastrophes, natural or man-made. As Tocqueville observed in 1856, in France more land was in the hands of peasants than in any other country of Europe, southwest Germany excepted. Not atypically, in the area near Paris, nobility and peasantry each owned about one-third of the land.

Significantly, rural insurrections were very rare in eighteenth-century France until the Revolution, when they cropped up nearly everywhere from 1789 to 1793. Jacobinism's happy relationship to the peasantry was in a sense an extension of these ancient equilibriums.

In prerevolutionary France country and town coexisted harmoniously. Urban life was itself quite tranquil, superficially agitated to be sure, but set in its ways nonetheless. Riots were formulaic in both the modesty of their claims and in the ephemeral nature of their achievements. Urban food shortages were less severe. (In the roadless past, prices had been low in one province and sky-high next door.) Most French cities changed little in the first half of the eighteenth century. In a few, like Valenciennes in the north, the population even declined.

Commercial capitalism flourished in ports along the Atlantic coast especially. Bordeaux, the capital after 1789 of the Gironde department, was Europe's second port, but overall, capitalism was not nearly as disruptive in France as it was in rapidly urbanizing England or in the ebullient thirteen colonies. Though France was the most advanced of the economically undeveloped nations of the Continent, it was also the least advanced of the capitalistically organized countries in the North Atlantic world.

Many eighteenth-century city dwellers were actually peasants who went out to their fields every day. Many urban dwellers had gardens. (Hospitals and religious houses invariably did so.) Prosperous people often lived in the country in the summer and moved back to the city in the colder and wetter seasons. City people and peasants alike knew time not from watches but by the sound of bells and the sight of sun and moon. In some places, the landless worked on the farm in the summer and in the city during the winter. Few and far between were city folk who had no personal experience of rural life. Even in Paris the city's center was no more than an hour's walk from rolling wheat fields. Jacobinism's rural fantasies seem less surprising when set in this context of cultural continuity.

This subdued tempo of urban change had other effects as well. Unlike the political elites of eighteenth-century transatlantic Anglo-America, who were deeply involved in innovating trade, the propertied class in prerevolutionary France was still uniformly based on land and the professions, law above all else. Looking forward from 1750, we can see why Jacobin industrialists were so rare in 1792.

A comparison of Paris and London highlights this contrast of urban commercial evolution in France and revolution in Britain. London was the world's first seaport and, after 1701, more populous than Paris. An engine of commerce, it drove forward not just trade and manufacture but the commercialization of English agriculture as well. By contrast, eighteenth-century Paris, despite its growth, remained primarily an administrative and artisanal center. The industries that thrived in the French capital—luxury and semiluxury goods, furniture, mirrors, rugs, watches, fashions—catered less to mass consumption than to the needs of the noble, the famous, and the rich.

The creation of the Bank of England in London in 1694 (with the help of enterprising French Huguenot refugees) antedates the postrevolutionary birth of the Bank of France in Paris by more than a century. Eighteenth-century French private and state finance was stunted, which explains the importance in French life of foreign-based or foreign-born Swiss bankers, like those two honest brokers, the intermittently intelligent Necker—Louis XVI's only bourgeois minister—and Clavière, also a Protestant, and in 1793 a suicidal Girondin. Their presence in the French capital before and after 1789 speaks loudly to the uncertain position of France (with Holland, Britain, and North America) in the concert of advanced, capitalist societies.

Town and country were not that far apart materially; and before midcentury, that sense of proximity also held sociologically. In the nineteenth century vast differences separated tightly knit rural communities from individuated urban social settings, where men and especially women were left to fend for themselves as best they could. To be "poor and pregnant" in the Paris of the Belle Époque was not an enviable fate. But—in theory, at least—that was not so in eighteenth-century France. In both town and country, only the unfortunate or the willfully marginal remained isolated from a web of interlocking guilds, families, clans, neighborhoods, vestries, brotherhoods, and the like.

In brief, France before 1750 prospered economically and remained stable socially. It had even found rough religious accord between town and country, where rates of church attendance were more or less identical.

This harmony was all the more deeply felt for being a striking departure from earlier times. From the beginning of the sixteenth century to the end of the seventeenth century, the country had been ripped apart by religious quarrels and religious civil wars. (It is estimated that at one point, in the 1560s, more than half of the French nobility had converted to Calvinism.)

But from royal force or social exhaustion, that travail had by 1700 been resolved. Public religious conformity had been harshly reimposed. When Catholicism was given pride of place and Protestantism declared illegal with the revocation of the century-old Edict of Nantes in 1685, more than one hundred thousand French Protestants left, a number of them for North America. Those who remained were required to convert, ostensibly in any case.

Quarrels within the Catholic Church also abated after the turn of the century. During the reign of Louis XIV, intra-Catholic rivalries had run high. On the right, so to speak, were the Jesuits, who represented the papalist wing of the church. In the center were the Gallicans, who claimed that the French Catholic Church, protected by the king, should not invariably defer to Rome, especially as regarded the material organization of the church.

On the left, as it were, and more eccentric yet were the Jansenists, whose curious variant of Calvinist doctrine subsisted within the church as a heresy of a kind and within French society as an expression of an unusually coherent way of life.[2] Because they believed man to be incorrigibly sinful and because they thought predestination more important than good works, Jansenists were not much interested in either public life or business. Aloof by choice from capitalism, and by necessity from absolutist politics, Jansenists preferred to be judges rather than administrators, landlords rather than entrepreneurs.

Uninvolved in the more tumultuous aspects of public life, they were able correspondingly to set high moral standards for their private lives. Their neo-Calvinist speculations on grace and free will struck a responsive chord among large parts of the French possessing class, both noble and non-noble. Pascal—a recluse of a kind, whose father had been a worldly tax collector—best expressed this Jansenist sensibility. His goal was not to transcend man's situation by good works but to withdraw from public life and to promote a self-humiliating (and ultimately self-enhancing) denunciation of humanity's sinful willfulness and insatiable physicality. With similar self-deprecation, La Rochefoucauld in his proverbs explained that most of man's virtues were vices in disguise.[3]

In the first decades of the eighteenth century Jansenists, Gallicans, and Jesuits were hardly supine. The first concern of the Jansenist publication, the *Nouvelles ecclésiastiques,* was to malign the Jesuitical *Journal de Trévoux.* Nevertheless, in the 1750s these quarrels were far milder than they had been in the last decades of the seventeenth century and early decades of the eighteenth. A truce generally prevailed, and the church at midcentury was a vigorous, reasonably harmonious, widely accepted, and ideologically dominant institution.

Catholicism's relation to the Enlightenment, soon to become the church's bitter enemy and Jacobinism's fountainhead, was likewise, in this earlier period, of suspended hostility rather than of hostility plain and simple. The anticlericalism and anti-absolutism of Jacobins and of the late Enlightenment have obvious antecedents in the thought of the seventeenth century: Bayle before Diderot, Locke before Hume, Descartes before Condorcet, and so on. But this filiation of radicalizing thought, though highly commendable as a framework for the history of ideas, does blur the fact that before 1750, contemporaries did *not* have a driving sense of a separation between the administratively modernized absolutist state and modern or enlightened ways of thinking.

In the seventeenth and eighteenth centuries, modern science and literature grew within Royal Academies and not against them. The members of the state-created Académie Française were proud of their kingly right to define French grammar.[4] In the raging quarrel of the Ancients and the Moderns, the modernizers—who praised the France of their day to the detriment of ancient Rome—were resolutely royalist. One of Voltaire's first major works in 1723 was an epic poem that glorified the king's ancestor five generations removed, Henry IV, whose beloved equestrian statue ennobled the Pont-Neuf, in the heart of popular Paris. In the middle decades of the eighteenth century, this most famous critic of world injustice in all its forms could still write that he "defied anyone to show me that any other monarchy on earth was less oppressive of laws, of distributive justice, and of the rights of humanity . . . and [more creative of] great things done for the public good than [the French Crown] during the fifty-five years of Louis XIV's personal reign."[5] Indeed, Voltaire, to his death in 1778, remained more favorable to reform from above than to reform from below. "We are entering a golden age," he wrote in 1776 of the young Louis XVI, "thanks to the [new] king and his ministers. I did not expect to die content; my hopes have been surpassed."[6]

Overwhelmingly, at midcentury, French men and women shared Voltaire's modulated optimism. In 1866 the Goncourt brothers, who invented late-nineteenth-century naturalism as a genre and renewed the historical study of French society before 1789, perspicaciously noted that unlike earlier Dutch or Italian still lifes, which had ordinarily represented exotic fruits and plants, the canvases of the archetypal prerevolutionary French painter Jean-Baptiste Chardin (1699–1779) were more modest. They were all about pears and apples. Eighteenth-century France, they wisely concluded, was content. It did not seek anything beyond itself.

French Absolutism

The essence of French social forms before 1750—that is, the bedrock from which Jacobinism sprang—was this social and ideological balance between old and new, a mix all the more remarkable for having found its mirror image in the nation's hybrid political institutions, themselves an amalgam of the very new and the very old.

French absolutism, rational, ordered, and bureaucratized (a word of French origin), became the model of modernity in central and eastern Europe. But in France it was layered onto a vital traditional society that it regulated and did not attempt to transform.

Even at its height, in the late seventeenth century, the might of the absolutist Crown in France was not constructed against the will of the nation's elites (a few thousand intermarrying families of great nobles, financiers, and prominent members of the professions, mainly law). French absolutism in the 1660s was, instead, accepted with no small relief by both nobles and non-nobles, all of them exhausted by a century of religious and civil wars.

A tacit bargain was struck after the civil wars of the 1650s. On one side, the possessing class suspended its secular opposition to the absolutist centralism that had been creeping forward for centuries; and on the other, the newly centralized state accepted and even revivified traditional social arrangements (but not strictly political ones, of course). Symbolically, although the monarchy did build new boulevards and royal squares in the nation's capital, it did so on the city's edges, and Paris's medieval heart survived untouched until the 1850s.

Indeed, in many *economic* ways at least, absolutism actually bolstered the traditional rankings of estates. The tax exemptions of nobles were largely maintained. The purpose of the court at Versailles (where bourgeois ministers faced off with lordly courtiers) was more to regulate and balance than to deny existing social instincts.[7] Provincial law codes were not standardized, and Voltaire observed that a voyager in France changed laws as often as he did horses. In Paris, in 1765, it was thought curious to be sure, but not absurd, that a judge could convict a usurer by arguing from a nearly thousand-year-old, Carolingian, religious, and communitarian text.[8]

Only in the realm of high politics did the Crown meaningfully innovate. The sun king did indeed claim to control all of society's public space; significantly, the heart of this new and bureaucratic state was not the old royal palace of the Louvre, in Paris, a city with which the traditionalist French monarchy had been closely associated for nearly one millennium. It was instead the absolutist king's new and majestic, neobaroque palace at Versailles, where the gifted royal impresario staged his spectacular politics with unprecedented flair. There, only ten miles from the older capital in space, but some distance from it in time, the leading artists of the day were hired to assure the staging of the monarch's power. The absolutist state dominated literature, music, painting, and architecture—now carefully structured and monitored in the newly created Academies of Letters, Arts, and Sciences.

Social traditionalism survived, but the administration of the kingdom was overhauled indeed. High officials belonging to a number of overlapping councils at Versailles filtered the reports of two thousand, increasingly important bureaucrats: in Paris the secretaries of state and counselors of state or "masters of requests"; in the provinces subdelegates and their superiors, the *intendants* who were after 1672 entrusted by Louis XIV and Colbert not just with the collection of information but with the supervision of regional administration in every province.[9]

In the fading and soon to be distant past, the lord chancellor, as the keeper of the king's justice, had been the prestigious pivot of royal governance. But now, that central role was in the hands of a comptroller general (Jacques Necker's title), who supervised not justice but finance. After 1660 the French state-machine—centralized, rational, productivist, statistical, and goal oriented—became a model for the modernizing monarchies of central, southern, and eastern Europe.

And yet, because it ordinarily respected vested interests, this innovative and absolutist state system was not thought at first to be tyrannical, or even despotic. Many subjects of Louis XIV and Louis XV were convinced that France, unlike Russia or Turkey, was a constitutional monarchy of a kind, not only because the king had to obey some rules (such as those that governed the line of succession to the throne), but also because the Crown was pledged to respect inherited privilege. Louis XV was, at first, a beloved and prestigious quasi-priest. (To this day, the names of those who murdered or tried to murder French kings—like Jacques Clément in 1589, Ravaillac in 1610, and Damiens in 1757—send shivers down the backs of French schoolchildren.) Many religious celebrations (Te Deums, especially) reminded ordinary people of the monarch's semidivine nature.)[10]

So it was that in the mid-eighteenth century not just French society but French politics as well (though conceptually contradictory) nonetheless seemed to be completely harmonious: "Sir," said in 1783 the younger Pitt, the Jacobins' future nemesis, to a French abbé during his one trip to France, "you do not have political liberty, but as regards civil liberty, you have more than you think."[11]

In some broad sense, Jacobin sensibility can be said to have begun embryonically when absolutism ceased to be an accepted model. Jacobinism was simultaneously a recycling of absolutist ways of thinking (the king had been sacred, the people now were instead) and an alternative to the strangely balanced system—at once traditionalist and absolutist—that had blossomed in the first half of the eighteenth century.

Unravelings

More important yet than these stabilizing legacies to an understanding of the Jacobins' innovating turn of mind was the gradual collapse of these earlier arrangements between 1750 and 1789. As historians ever since

1789 have endlessly discussed, Jacobinism's roots were in the seculariza-
tion and antireligious radicalization of French high culture.

At midcentury, the philosophes grew more bold. First, Montesquieu
published in 1748 his *Esprit des lois* (the favored reading of Saint-Just),
which in effect explained that kings were created for people, and not peoples for their kings. Montesquieu's text crystallized anti-absolutist libertarianism throughout the North Atlantic world and, more than any other writing, served to delegitimize the absolutist monarchy. Henceforth, even the
reactionary Parlements were more likely to justify their anti-absolutist
mumblings by reference to this quasi-English theorizing than to the traditions of pre-absolutist France.

Another landmark was Diderot's *Encyclopédie*, which chronicled mankind's—not God's—achievement, in the applied sciences especially. By this
time Voltaire's conciliatory theism was being challenged by materialist
atheism on its left. Newtonian science, astronomy, Buffon's anthropology,
Montesquieu's typology of laws, and the new discipline of geology were so
many scientistic pieces that combined to bring revealed religion into question.

Anticlericalism in its various forms, both external and internal to
Catholicism, surged throughout prerevolutionary France. Wills were less
likely to carry religious invocations. Young men and women were less
likely to join the church. Conceptions out of wedlock rose slightly. The
number of books dealing with religious topics dropped off precipitously.
Religious unease affected the church itself. French clerics were more divided institutionally and doctrinally in 1789 than at any time since the Reformation. A strong current of clerical opinion criticized the arrogance of
the bishops. And the Jacobins inherited this sensibility. Perhaps as many as
twenty thousand clerics abjured their priesthood in 1793–94; three thousand priests renounced their vows and chose to marry; and hundreds, as
has been said, joined or founded Jacobin clubs in 1790–91.

More pervasive than antireligious feeling was a new emphasis in French
social life on individualism as a core social value; and individualism, of
course, was soon to be one of Jacobinism's two cardinal principles. Economically, individualism meant a growing sympathy for entrepreneurialism
(a French word).[12] In criminal matters, it manifested itself as a desire "to
make the punishment fit the crime." Individualism also lay behind the
praise of meritocracy. It likewise structured the epoch's anguished discus-

sion of private happiness and boredom as well as its anxieties about death, suicide, immortality, and fame.

Individualism implied a reappraisal of the central traditionalist concept of social and political privilege. The ascription of certain rights to only some individuals came to be seen as an aristocratic abuse and a negation of public liberty. Previous cultural models, as in the mid-seventeenth-century plays of Corneille and Racine, had emphasized conformity to established norms of feudal or courtly honor; but after midcentury individual self-fulfillment became the more common standard.

Future Jacobins (and many others, to be sure) thrilled to the sincere account of private passions laid out in epistolary novels like *La Nouvelle Héloïse* or Léonard's *Les Amants de Lyon,* told through the private, highly sexual but highly exemplary letters of a blameless woman, made public as proof of private sincerity: "through letter writing the individual unfolded himself in his subjectivity."[13] After 1750, every aesthetic genre was affected by this deepening—and gendering—of individual sensibilities, as appeared in the semifrivolous painting of Fragonard and in lucrative pornographic pamphlets, many of them penned by writers of the first rank like Diderot. (The term *pornographe* was coined in Paris in 1769 by Restif de la Bretonne.)[14]

Midcentury audiences of Paris opera houses had still thought of musical performance as the occasion for social display. By the late 1770s and 1780s, however, they sought in opera aesthetic and emotional inspiration instead.[15] Mme. de Genlis, the companion of the Jacobin-minded Philippe Égalité, was said to faint at least twice a week from excessive sensibility, usually just after the arrival of her first guests.[16]

New individuated thoughts brought forward a need—both explicit and implicit—for new cultural institutions as well. Meritocratic scientific and provincial literary academies, lending libraries, Masonic lodges, and learned societies like the *sociétés de pensée, musées,* and *lycées*[17] were interconnected intellectual institutions[18] with a political future. Some of them would mutate into Jacobin clubs; all of them had a telling purpose. Their members worked to spread the word of tolerance and a faith in every human being's capacity to improve the structures of social life. At Versailles courtiers were of unequal rank; but in a Masonic lodge, all Masons were (more or less) equal, whether dukes or commoners. "As with other clubs," someone wrote of the membership of the musical society Concerts de la Loge Olympique in 1787, "this society, at No. 65 in the Palais Royal [where Desmoulins harangued revolutionary crowds and Bonneville cited his Cercle Social], is composed of persons whose merit commends them; their number is not limited."[19]

Particularly meaningful was the rise of the "ungendered" salons (quasi-public meeting places in private domiciles), which thrived in the capital and in which divisions of rank were, if not ignored, at least suspended. These pacific salons were instruments of a new sociability regulated not by men or by convention but by the moralizing and dignifying presence of women of rank and intelligence.

Expectedly, as the salon waxed, the hierarchic model of court life at Versailles waned. In the late seventeenth century intellectual fashions had been set by the king and his noble-born courtiers; but in the late eighteenth century fashions were invented not in Versailles but in Paris, where their purpose was to display the morality, good taste (and great wealth!) of those (women especially) who could afford them.

Art exhibits, plays, fairs, opera acquired wide audiences in theaters and cafés. (Paris alone counted 380 of the latter by 1723.) Even traditional institutions like Parisian law courts became a staging ground of discontent (one would say, in today's jargon, a discursive site), as Tocqueville observed long ago: "the law courts were largely responsible for the notion that every matter of public or private interest was subject to debate and every decision could be appealed from, as also for the opinion that such affairs should be conducted in public and certain formalities observed."[20]

Informal "institutions" contributed to societal change. Rumors and covert networks of information were well developed in France, although we do not know much about them. On September 19, 1783, for example, over a hundred thousand Parisians, forming perhaps the largest crowd that had ever been seen in France, assembled at Versailles to watch the launching of Montgolfier's new hot-air balloon.

Sociability and communication were transformed by the broader relevance of the printed page, and Kant was right to see the simple act of shared reading as a fundamental cause for the rise of enlightened public concern. Unconnected readers, simultaneously struck by the power of rational argument, would thereby, he predicted, become of their own accord a united, reformist public. The act of reading, so important to the Jacobins, was, we can surmise, more important often than what was actually being read. The life and death of a saint, after all, could be taken by non-Christians as an example of individualistic achievement or, conversely, as a sad wasted existence, as a model that no sensible and enlightened person could follow.

These various formal and informal institutions nicely extended one another. Letter writing moved from the purely private to the semipublic. Supposedly private letters, which had in fact often been written for public effect, were read in salons, where they would be discussed, copied, and recirculated. Letters to the editors of newspapers and magazines were yet another tactic, and during the Revolution, Marat in his role as a responsive journalist would carefully recycle this genre in his reply to letters that he had covertly written to himself as the wily editor of *L'Ami du peuple*.

Nationalism, Public Opinion, and Public Life

> Gentlemen who are alive and well: there is nothing as unconditional as the disdain of the dead.
>
> Machado de Assis, in *The Posthumous Memoirs of Brás Cubas*

After midcentury, French culture was transformed in ways whose significance for the politics of the Jacobins are nearly self-evident. Their clubs, their obsession with the press, their sharply different definitions of the rights of man and the responsibilities of women, and their anticlericalism all have roots in the breakdown of the Old Regime.

But without eliciting the disdain of the dead, we can go beyond such important connections, of which contemporaries were quite aware, and strive to understand more subtle cultural transformations that contemporaries— or so we can suppose—intuited rather than acknowledged. For in the second half of the eighteenth century the nation, public opinion, and public life were all redefined. And after 1789, few things had greater influence on the Jacobin worldview than prerevolutionary assumptions which held that the shapers of opinion and wielders of public authority should be judged by the same high moral standards that applied to the private lives of ordinary citizens.

The Prerevolutionary Nation

After 1750, the flow of energy from the public to the private that had prevailed in the previous century was reversed. In the absolutist state, atomized society (in theory, though not in fact, of course) had existed only through the sun king at Versailles. Sovereignty rested exclusively in the monarch. But once the king's political existence was held to depend on the beneficial effect he might have on an immanent nation and self-standing civil society that were ends in their own right, French taxpayers—in their own minds at least—a sovereign force, no longer felt obliged to pay and pay again. In the words of Rivarol—an enlightened traditionalist who despised both the Jacobins and the new money men—the king was powerless now that so many of his subjects had become the creditors of their master: "a parsimonious king is always the master of his subjects . . . a debtor king is nothing more than a slave."[21]

In the Christian and absolutist system, subjects had expected no more than fair justice. Now they wished to assert their rights as citizens,[22] and the realm of the civic domain was extended outward from domestic life to include nationwide concerns, like taxes, religion, and economics: taxes because the monarchic state was seen as a system of out-relief paid by the poor to support the rich; religion because mainstream Catholicism was now at odds with not just Gallicans and Jansenists but freethinkers as well; and economics because traditional statism, defended by economic conservatives like Jacques Necker and Ferdinando Galiani, was vigorously attacked by modernizers like Turgot, the king's first minister from 1774 to 1776.

The term "nationalism" was not coined until the Jacobinized and imperial armies of the Grande Nation rampaged through the length and breadth of Europe from Madrid in 1807 to Moscow in 1812, but the reality (if not the politicization) of French nationalism and of militarized patriotism was everywhere present in French culture long before the Revolution.[23] The French language, already Europe's international idiom,[24] gained prestige within France at the expense of Latin. A general propensity for conversation (or communication) and the universality of the French language were seen by the French (and Immanuel Kant) as proof of their enlightened and international vocation. Local languages were demoted to the rank of mere dialect. The history of the French state, of French chivalry, and of the French nation—which heretofore had not been academic subjects—attracted unprecedented interest. Many French kings—and Joan of Arc as well—were popularly perceived as quasi-religious figures. Schemes of "national education" were floated here and there, one of them, incongruously, in 1763, by the otherwise extremely reactionary and noble-born lawyer and Parlementaire Louis de Caradeuc de la Chalotais (1701–1785).[25] The Académie Française's prize for poetry, originally created to sing the praise of the sun king, was reshaped in 1759 to salute the feats of the "nation's celebrated men" (les hommes célèbres de la nation).[26]

By the time of their Revolution, the French had also developed a national musical canon, a repertoire of frequently performed works that emphasized patriotic continuity rather than aesthetic novelty. Administratively, the nation likewise became a standard unit of social measurement with the development of statistics and social analysis. In 1789 only the national, Jacobin anthem was waiting to be born, and Sieyès by then had already concluded that "the nation is strictly and without any difference as a man is in the state of nature, where he is always effortlessly himself."[27]

The ambivalent attitude of the prerevolutionary elites toward Britain reveals the new strength of French national feeling. In Paris, Britain was admired because it was victorious in war, modern, constitutional, and free. In 1777 a French art critic said of the salon of the Louvre, where rich and poor, men and women, noble and non-noble alike came to admire new paintings, that it was "the only public place in France where he could find that precious liberty visible everywhere in London."[28] Edward Gibbon, on a visit to Paris in the mid-1760s, wrote that "our opinions, our fashions, even our games, were adopted in France; a ray of national glory illuminated each individual, and every Englishman was supposed to be both a patriot and a philosopher."[29]

And yet, England was also "perfidious Albion," France's hereditary enemy and the national embodiment of selfish greediness. In the 1770s Holbach, one of the most intellectually radical of the philosophes, reminded his friends north of the Channel, "never did the love of gold make good citizens."[30] Frenchmen marveled at Britain's domestic economic gains and efficient agriculture; but from midcentury on, they also detested Britain's mortifying, worldwide military successes.[31] By 1789 nationalistic Anglophobia was as common in France as was political Anglophilia.[32] Frenchmen criticized British food, the British climate, and the moodiness of the British temperament. Suicide was known in France as the "English disease."

The War of American Independence against France's hereditary enemy, Britain, was widely supported in Paris. Forty-six thousand French soldiers and sailors took part in that North American conflict, generally with great enthusiasm.[33] "Since my Arrival here," wrote a delighted John Adams, "I never yet found one Man, nor heard of more than one who doubted

[American Independence]. If the Voice of Popularity is any Thing, I assure you that this Voice was never so unanimous in America, in Favor of our Independence as it is here."[34]

The popularity of the war had much to do with the nature of its funding, as this was the first major conflict the French Crown financed largely from loans and not from taxes (thereby, as it happens, sealing the doom of the Old Regime, now headed toward unavoidable bankruptcy). Still, in the longer view, latent nationalism was far more relevant than "nontaxation" to the zeal aroused in the late 1770s by the joint war of France and America against England's world domination.

Pétion's successful visit to London in 1791 and Robespierre's egalitarian philippic in February 1794 against the English nation, which he said he "hated," had in their background a long and growing tradition of political Anglophilia and Anglophobia, of nationalist and militarist resentment.

Public Opinion

Thanks to the idea of Nation, the public sphere, so important to the Jacobins, acquired new specificity. As Tocqueville put it, next to "society proper," resting on a framework of tradition, there now emerged "an imaginary society, in which everything was simply, harmoniously, equitable, uniform, and reasonable. The minds of the people gradually withdrew from the former to take refuge in the latter. Men became indifferent to the real by dint of dwelling on the ideal, and established a mental domicile in an imaginary city which the authors had built."[35]

Men of letters who shaped this new public opinion held themselves in high esteem. It was to general applause that the minor philosophe Antoine Thomas, when elected to the Royal Academy in 1766 (in itself a noteworthy—and scandalous—event since the man was a resolute modernizer), took as the subject of his inaugural peroration "the man of letters as citizen."[36] References to the *Respublica literaria* go back to 1417, but the philosophes managed to reconceptualize the Republic of Letters as the frame not of scholarship but of opinion.[37]

In politics, the best known apologist of this newly created public opinion in the 1780s was none other than Necker, the king's first minister. Public opinion was, in his celebrated words, "the queen of the world,"[38] an ironic twist since the man, as a private person, was conservative, quite religious, and more inclined to favor enlightened despotism than parliamentary monarchy, not to speak of republicanism. Necker, it may be added, practiced what he preached and was the first French financier to make state loans and bonds into a kind of political plebiscite.[39] His *Compte rendu,* a disingenuous account of the royal budget, which he claimed to have restored to health, was an instant best-seller.

The Moralization of Public Life

The nation existed. Public opinion existed. These were cultural innovations that would soon be critical to the Jacobin mind. Of equal if not greater consequence was the extension outward to the public realm of the moral rules that had previously been thought appropriate only to the domestic sphere.

Why and how this all-important transformation took place is a riddle for us, even if we can see its effects in many domains of public life. It is a striking fact, for example, that amoral *raison d'état,* which the king's ministers practiced with both foreigners and docile subjects, no longer seemed acceptable to French opinion in the later decades of the Old Regime. In the previous century, guided by this cynical principle, European rulers and their servants—Richelieu and Olivares, Louis XIV and the Great Elector—had behaved with little regard to established moral or Christian norms, especially in their dealings with foreigners. Under Cardinal Richelieu, a prince of the Roman Church, France did not scruple to ally itself with Protestant princes against the pope.

But the idea developed in France after the middle of the eighteenth century that international relations and war itself should, like domestic politics, be regulated by moral convention. In contrast to Grotius (1583–1645), who had upheld the absolutist states' right to act as best suited them, Vattel (1714–1767) opposed the principles of international law. Truth—rather than reason of state—should, he thought (as did the Jacobins), become the benchmark of high politics.

Jansenism was an important factor in this tectonic cultural shift. After 1770, this religious and moralizing sensibility, which had so well expressed the mood of the late-seventeenth-century French elites, was vigorously and visibly redeployed and politicized. Jansenist affinities, for example, were the cultural foundation that enabled Parisian barristers to oppose the "despotic" acts of Joseph Terray and his colleague René de Maupeou—two ministers of Louis XV—who in 1771 suspended (momentarily) the then socially sacrosanct venality of judicial office. Many barristers were Jansenists and they now drifted to what was already called "patriotism."[40]

(Eighteenth-century French justice, as has been explained, was administered not by professional judges appointed by the king but by the law courts, the Parlements, whose members bought their office and were in the main paid by the litigants and not the state. Ideologically, this "venal" system of officeholding made no sense either from a Christian or an absolutist point of view.[41] Jacobins would despise it as Richelieu also had. But it had worked well enough in the past since it had bound traditional wealth to the then new and absolutist state.)

In these same years, many publications—among them the *Journal des dames,* edited by Louis-Sébastien Mercier, a future Jacobin—diffused this new "patriotic" vocabulary in coded, Aesopian language.[42] Indeed, many of the political pamphlets that appeared in 1787–88 were reprints of Jansenist tracts that had first surfaced in the early 1770s.

Foreign influences strengthened this renewed current of Jansenist dissidence. Just as French Jansenist and Protestant texts were well known in eighteenth-century Britain and America, so were many radical English texts known in France. (A *History of Ancient Rome* by the Jansenist historian Charles Rollin [1661–1741], long the rector of the Sorbonne, captivated both the novelist Stendhal in France and Abigail Adams in America.)

But Jansenism mattered yet more to the French, and especially to the Jacobins, as an informal cultural tradition;[43] and in 1801 Grégoire rightly (and approvingly) wrote of the "political theology" of the Jansenists that their principles "can be cited as precursors of the Revolution . . . not as regard its excesses, which were the despair of every honest soul, but as regards its patriotic principles."[44]

Obviously, Jansenism (a religious doctrine) and Jacobinism (an Enlightenment worldview) hardly overlapped. The emphasis on a civic rebirth so dear to the Jacobins was, for example, completely removed from the Jansenists' Augustinian focus on original sin and irremediable corruption. Likewise, though the Jansenists had applied their principles to a limited private sphere, their Jacobin successors applied their moralizing judgments through the new mechanisms of public opinion to the reconquered public sphere.

And yet, many points of contact connected these two sensibilities. Jansenists had prided themselves on their exemplary behavior as private persons, as the Jacobins also would. Most critical—and, as events would reveal, most catastrophic—was the shared penchant for soul-searching and condemnatory statements and the common disinterest toward the circumstances of material life.

It was bad enough that the *patriotes* imagined their political opponents to be irreconcilable *aristocrates*, but it mattered perhaps more that these *aristocrates* were imagined to be mendacious and immoral.

In 1793 the Jacobins considered themselves good and their political enemies evil. "It is a calumny against nature to believe that the mass of the people could be corrupt," wrote the Jacobin terrorist Fouché to justify the executions of supposed conspirators at Lyons.[45] And how revealing the title chosen in March 1793 by the treasurer of the Paris club, Annibal Ferrières, for a newspaper he thought that local clubs affiliated to Paris should be required to buy: *Le Mensonge et la vérité* (Lies and truth).[46]

It is tempting to suppose that without this judgmental reflex, derived in part from Jansenist instincts, the application of Jacobin principles, however contradictory, would hardly have been as tyrannical as it was.

The "Great Transformation": France between Caste and Class

If the Jacobins' moralizing desire to reorient the line between the private and the public had roots in the Old Regime's decline, so did their universalizing passions. France after 1750 was not radically transformed economically, and its irreversible industrialization traditionally dates to the 1830s. Nonetheless, prerevolutionary material change, deployed as it was by cultural upheaval, had significant sociological effects, the first of which was to make many previous social arrangements seem unacceptable.

Consider demographic growth. France's population was nearly one-fourth larger in 1789 than it had been in 1700. Peasants numbered 2 million more in 1790 than three decades before, a large increase since rural productivity gains were low and efforts to increase the surface of arable land, not successful. Wages rose less than prices, which concerned not just artisans but food-purchasing and landless peasants also. Seigneurial dues were increasingly questioned. Some rural communities became quite aggressive.

After 1750, urban France changed as well. Some important cities developed rapidly, especially those situated along land or seaborne trade routes, as contemporaries increasingly noticed. In 1725 4 million people lived in towns of more than 2,000 inhabitants. By 1789 that figure had risen by a million, an increase which reminds us that Jacobinism had a largely urban base. Paris, particularly important to the Jacobins, nearly doubled its size under the last two Louis, from less than 300,000 to well over half a million.

The volume of prerevolutionary foreign trade also grew. Though still quite small in terms of overall figures (imports or exports of grain seldom rose above 2 percent of national production), trade increasingly affected urban dwellers, and colonial commerce—closely tied to the slave trade—rose ten-fold in seven decades. Much money was to be made in Atlantic and Channel seaports like Nantes, Saint-Malo, and Bordeaux, the capital of the department of the Gironde from which were elected many of the appropriately named Girondins. The fortunes of many liberal noble families were built on the colonial trade, for example, that of the Lameth brothers, among the first members of the Jacobin club in Paris and eventually critical figures in the Jacobin-Feuillant schism. (By contrast, the waning income of the counterrevolutionary anti-Jacobin theoretician Louis vicomte de Bonald [1754–1840] was largely derived from shrinking, traditional, feudal dues.)

In many large cities poverty was endemic—especially among young female migrants and old widowed women. Overall, one French person in ten was on relief in 1789. Relations between town and country soured. Incipient manufacturers, who were engaged in the putting-out system, as protoindustrial spinners and weavers on commission, made peasants dependent on the work that city entrepreneurs farmed out on terms favorable to themselves.

Cultural and material changes were necessarily entwined. Individuated cultural transformation made entrepreneurialism more acceptable; and the impact of bourgeois enterprise in turn widened the audience of the philosophes, as it did of Jacobinism later. Money—and profit—increasingly underpinned any number of social situations. The size of the national debt rose dramatically, and the income it generated for bondholders figured prominently in the portfolio of many bourgeois families, in Paris especially, a fact that serves to explain why even the most draconian Jacobins hesitated to renege on the crushing debt the Republic inherited from the monarchy.

The cash nexus influenced the countryside significantly. In Picardy, Babeuf, the first revolutionary communist, observed the gradual displacement of sharecropping by leaseholding and the consolidation of large farms. He also witnessed the proletarianization of small or landless peasants.

Although both urban and rural wages continued to be regulated by a complicated web of rules, legal decisions, and economic happenstance, the prerevolutionary period marked the beginning of regional specialization and industrialization. Prices drew closer in what would soon be a national market for commodities of all kinds.

Prerevolutionary attitudes to the nature of human labor shifted. Though workers continued to think of labor and skill as kinds of property, and of wages as a function not just of supply and demand but of needs and traditional reward, they nonetheless altered their understanding of master-worker relations. Many owners employed workers by the hundreds and dealt with them impersonally. Strikes became more common.

The concepts of national income, national investment, national savings, and economic growth were developed by French economists between 1760 and 1789. French Physiocracy stands as the first modern school of economic analysis. Because it assumed, absurdly, that city workers consumed as much wealth as they produced, this ruralist doctrine was an incomplete understanding even of its own preindustrial times; but its conceptualization of investment, wages, and profits was an important achievement, as Marx fully understood.

Many social historians, especially those who see the world through Marxist lenses, have used this kind of evidence to develop arguments of class formation. In doing so, they overinterpret their findings. Indeed, the prerevolutionary bourgeoisie was *not* a class and only became one after 1789 with the failure of its universalizing vision. Jacobinism did not—and could not—come forward as the expression of a self-conscious, economically determined social group.

But economic change was a necessary—if not sufficient—cause of Jacobinism's inception. Jacobinism was first and foremost an urban movement. And it rose at that unique juncture of world history which the sociologist Karl Polanyi appropriately described as "the great transition." The issue obviously requires some elaboration.

France before 1750, despite absolutism's corrosive institutional effects, had still been in its cultural sensibility a (constraining) corporate society of interlocking orders.[47] On the other side of the revolutionary divide, after 1800, nineteenth-century France became a constraining society of classes. Individuals were divided by class when it came to law (the rich voted, the poor did not), legal disputes (the word of employers invariably took precedence over that of their employees), and any number of informal transactions. In mid-nineteenth-century France social stratifications were reflected in everything from dress, manners of speaking, and taste, to profession, education, literacy, and definitions of gender.

Placed between these two different social poles, between the seventeenth and the nineteenth centuries, between a society of castes and a society of classes, the prerevolutionary audience of the philosophes and, after them, the Jacobins was uniquely sited.

Many instances of their "incredible lightness of (social) being" have come down to us. In the 1780s, for example, many noble army officers optimistically prepared to reconsider their ancient status as members of the Second Estate. Many nobles appreciated the necessity of their becoming either a nationally useful and mercantile group or a remilitarized fraternity of trained and skilled officers charged with defending the fatherland efficaciously and professionally.

A juxtaposition of the nobility's *cahiers de doléances* with those of the bourgeoisie shows nobles to have been politically *more* liberal than their bourgeois neighbors. Jean-Jacques Rousseau and his readers may have idealized the people, but his patrons were often rich and, above all else, titled. Nobles like Lafayette, Condorcet, Soubrany, Antonelle, and Le Peletier (not to speak of Barras, Talleyrand, and Bonaparte) were to play an important role in Jacobin and revolutionary politics.

In many ways, the various prerevolutionary elites of the French nation (nobles and non-nobles) came to share a new and ubiquitous cultural sensibility. New familial models were not "estate"-specific. The *drame bourgeois,* a down-to-earth and prosaic genre invented by Diderot in 1757, portrayed ordinary non-noble people in extraordinary situations that brought out their inner nobility. The philosophes had a broad audience, and both nobles and bourgeois enthusiastically read Rousseau. Most members of provincial learned societies were priests, or nobles, or both. Aesthetic tastes reflected geography more than social rank. Noble and non-noble elites alike intently agitated for social improvements of all kinds, from tolerance for the socially marginal, to the decriminalization of suicide and homosexuality, to the reform of the penal system, madhouses, foundling homes, and other institutions. Most of the members of the Philanthropic Society founded in 1780 were nobles, and its governing board included twenty-four of the kingdom's thirty-four dukes.

United in common cultural pursuits, France's propertied elites had a charitable attitude toward the poor. Although poverty was not particularly more visible than before, its eradication weighed heavily on all enlightened minds, whether noble or bourgeois. Many instances of propertied benevolence were notorious, like the founding of a children's hospital by Necker, or the creation of prizes for work of social value, such as the French Academy's Prix Montyon, that was intended to reward virtuous self-sacrifice. In 1788 Mercier, soon to be a Conventionnel, remarked, "never has a century seen *charity* and *good works* more active than in recent times . . . what might you not need with a people like this, if we knew how to guide it by its own virtues."[48] (These examples stand, of course, as one more antecedent of revolutionary sensibilities, given the importance of charity and compassion in the Jacobin worldview.) Based on these many bits of evidence—contrary to what Marxist historians of previous generations assumed—we might conclude that on the eve of Revolution, social tensions in France had loosened rather than tightened.

By 1789, it had become feasible to suppose that civil society, were it unencumbered by feudal institutions, would of its own accord find its immanent harmonious balance; and Jacobins after 1789 acted on that worldview. Certainly, institutional barriers to social harmony were deeply resented before the Revolution, especially when loudly proclaimed as right and proper by the self-seeking aristocratic Parlements or by many of the king's closest and most obscurantist relatives, as happened in late 1788. Yet, in contradistinction, to the Marxist historiography of the late nineteenth century, we can now once again believe—as did universalist-minded contemporaries before the Revolution—that these reactionary calls were an affront less to a feeling of self-seeking or "class" than to a growing sense of enlightened fairness, fraternity, and humanity. Class and division were much less at issue than a broad—and among the propertied elite—widely shared sense that civil society was inherently ordered and equitably balanced between town and country, between landed and landless, between rich and poor.

Anthropologists have used the idea of "liminality" to describe a condition of "betwixt and between" when the fear of ongoing, daily constraint is limited and participants in communitarian rituals feel a sudden and transforming kinship that cannot be ordinarily understood.[49] *Mutatis mutandis*, we can see this condition as applicable to the politicized French public in the 1780s when faced with the accelerating decomposition of the Old Regime. In the context of liminal transition many prerevolutionary cultural couplings become less paradoxical.

On the face of things, it is hard to see why (pre-Jacobin) universalist yearning should have coincided with a distinct acceleration of economically individuated forms (more private trade, more credit, more exchanges, more dependence on the market, and so on). Nor is it self-evident that on the eve of the Revolution, the prestige of (prebourgeois) constitutionalist, English-oriented libertarians like Montesquieu and Voltaire should have waned precisely as individuating economic transformations acquired ever more momentum. It is puzzling also that in the 1770s and 1780s, the French should have disjoined their social and political visions, and wished henceforth to connect the possession of civil rights to equalizing nature, rather than, as in the past, to the settled and unequal prerogatives of varyingly prestigious professions.[50]

In other words, Rousseau's equalizing and civic vision "ought" to have become *less* relevant as France became richer and, in its day-to-day life, more focused on individual values and private gain.

But the reverse happened instead; and we can hypothesize an explanation for this anomaly in the particular sociology of France's path to modernity between caste and class. In the 1780s individualism's ongoing destruction of tradition neither instilled in future Jacobins a fear of freedom nor heightened their sensitivity to the imminent appearance of renewed conflict. The progress of individuation and the declining prestige of a society of orders enabled them instead to dream of the coming end of the Old Regime as the dawn of a newly harmonious age.

Frenchmen in 1788 had a sense of the irrelevance of birth but little sense of class constraint. Wordsworth expressed their ensuing feelings with unrivaled grace:

> O pleasant exercise of hope and joy!
> For mighty were the auxiliars which then stood
> Upon our side, us who were strong in love!
> Bliss it was in that dawn to be alive,
> But to be young was very heaven!

Myths of Togetherness

It is reasonable to infer, of course, that France in the 1780s was *not* in its daily practice a more fraternal society than it had been half a century before. And yet, the yearning for a universalizing society where the one and the many would come together was widely rhapsodized. Tens of thousands of readers seemed fascinated by works which explained that self-becoming and self-sacrifice were overlapping values.

After 1791, David made his mark as perhaps the most political of all great modern artists, as a militant, aggressive Jacobin and as a close friend of Robespierre. This revolutionary trajectory—as we can see with hindsight—was clearly prefigured in his prerevolutionary canvases of self-sacrificing heroes, ready to die for the public good. How revealing, then, that it was the Crown and not "the rising bourgeoisie" which subsidized David's first universalizing canvases.

The need to redefine and conciliate the private and the public was felt even at Versailles, and in tens of thousands of noble and bourgeois homes as well. Enlightened thinking on gender, for example, sharply distinguished—and then redefined as *complementary*—the uneven roles of men and women, whose purposes would become wholly distinct but mutually enhancing.

True, women (and children, whom they were held by most philosophes to resemble psychologically and physiologically, in the pitch of their voices, for example) were to be removed from the enlightened public eye.[51] Diderot, in the *Encyclopédie,* considered citizenship an exclusively masculine concern: "the title of citizen is granted to women, young children, and servants only insofar as they are the members of the family of a citizen, but they are not really citizens."[52]

But women were also seen in the late French Enlightenment as the premier agents of selflessness and politicized community. "Republican motherhood" (women at home training their children to assume the responsibilities of public life) would unite in a single purpose husbands and wives, home and country, child and nation.

In the two decades before 1789, women's bodies and the joys of marital sex took on a renewed ideological relevance. So did the virginal white muslins with which women were ordinarily enrobed, both in the paintings of the counterrevolutionary painter Vigée-Lebrun, a protégée of Marie Antoinette, and in the elaborate settings of the revolutionary *fêtes* of David, whose chosen victim Marie Antoinette was to be. The perils of solipsistic masturbation were learnedly described. Pornographic writing was popular for many reasons, but one of them was that it served as a (perverse) reminder of how important ordinary and licit, marital sexuality was thought to be.

Symptomatically, the family—the ultimate Jacobin symbol of social harmony—acquired in France a prestige it had never had and no longer has today. Domestic life, marital fidelity, and loving families became the favored topoi of painting, music, letters, and bourgeois cookbooks. As a sequel to the glorification of the abstracted, ideal, and harmonious home came the invention of domestic comforts, like fireplaces and rocking chairs, as well as children's literature, birthday celebrations, and a greater interest in the education of the (suddenly individualized) young. Bedrooms were designed to be secluded, private places. (That had certainly not been so in the frigid, absolutist palaces like Versailles.) The layout and decoration of late-eighteenth-century apartments took on a gay and cozy look, which remains a model of practical elegance admired today.

Rousseau, the universally famous and solitary "Armenian" hermit of the Île Saint-Pierre, a man whose life and works were to be a model for Jacobin revolutionaries great and small, male or female, became famous by explaining how man and woman could become themselves in finding others. In this Genevan's worldview, man's nature, though not invariably communitarian and good, was nonetheless pliable. With the help of his fellow human beings, especially his fellow woman, man the citizen, now touched by social grace, could make the best of himself. He could in a happy private life find the strength to be a good citizen as well.

Of course, few Jacobins had read any of his works in any detail. Certainly they had not digested his *Social Contract,* in which he developed the idea of the general will, a kind of collective conscience whose dictates might or might not overlap with the stated but possibly corrupted will of a majority. (In 1789 this text had not been reprinted for seventeen years. It would be republished twenty times between 1790 and 1800.)

Nevertheless, Rousseau was already an immensely popular figure. At the Trianon, her private minipalace within the great complex of Versailles, Marie Antoinette dared to stage one of his operas. "It is impossible to express or imagine the enthusiasm of this nation in his favour," wrote Hume of the French on Rousseau in 1762. "I am persuaded that, were I to open a subscription with consent, I should receive 50,000 Pounds in a fortnight . . . Voltaire and everybody else are quite eclipsed by him."[53]

Jean-Jacques's novel *La Nouvelle Héloïse* attracted widespread attention. Tens of thousands of French men and women—like Mme. Roland—com

muned with Saint-Preux (its excessively individuated, suicidally prone, nar-
cissistic, self-obsessed, and sensual hero), who was saved by finding a place
in the simultaneously patriarchal and fraternal family that revolved around
his beloved Julie, herself described as an ideal mother, wife, *and* mistress.

(In 1793, it might be added, Mme. Roland imitated Julie directly in the
respect she showed to her aging husband and in the [platonic] passion she
felt for another man—in the event, the Girondin leader Buzot. But like a
true Jacobin, she stoically subordinated the private dictates of her heart to
the public need for Jacobin decorum.)

Rousseau's view of children also became popular, supplanting the theory
of Saint Vincent de Salles, a famous educator of the previous century who
had explained that the purpose of a Christian upbringing was to break the
sinful nature of the individual child. Rousseau proposed instead to nurture
the child's desire to love and to be loved by others. "The vices and misfor-
tunes of children," he warned the subjects of the patriarchal French king,
"are chiefly the effect of what is unnatural."

His readers responded to that message, in the realm of thought at least.
Prerevolutionary French men and women whose patriarchal family lives
were not very orderly (especially in the upper reaches of society, where
infidelity was widely accepted) began to dream of integrative families in
which equal individuals would find the strength to become the fully participating members of a revivified and quasi-Republican public sphere.

Institutional Decline and Institutional Precedents

In this context of moralized universalism, the monarchy's halting attempts
to improve absolutist institutions so as to meet the needs and wants of an
enlightened public seemed increasingly inconsequential.

Traditional institutions that were neither clearly public nor clearly private in the new senses of these words were now universally decried as
proof of intolerable abuse. Everyone despised the oddities of the tax system; and most unacceptable of all was the fabled "venality" of officehold-
ers, of the Parlementaires in particular. In their judicial judgments, these
officials were neither uninformed nor savage. Royal judges were ordinarily
humane and conscientious men. Prerevolutionary French justice was far
more lenient than that of Hanoverian Britain.[54] But what struck the public
were egregious cases of injustice, specifically those with a political dimen-

sion, such as the egregious condemnation of the Protestant Calas, whose family was indemnified thanks to Voltaire; or the execution of a young man, the Chevalier de la Barre, who had mocked a religious procession; or the treatment of the baron de Lally-Tollendal, a war hero unjustly accused of treason and wrongfully executed in 1766.

Public opinion was also aroused by the rivalries of institutions within the Old Regime. An ongoing quasi-religious miniwar opposed the vestigially rigorist Jansenist and antipapalist Gallican Parlementaires to the laxist Jesuits, on the one hand, and to the royal bureaucracy, on the other.[55] This set of muted conflicts Thomas Paine aptly described in his *Rights of Man* of 1791 as a "rivalship of despotism."[56]

By the 1780s if not well before—since the middle decades of the century perhaps—more and more literate Frenchmen gradually gave up on the idea of enlightened "reform from above." They abandoned the program urged on the king by many philosophes, including Voltaire, and by reforming ministers like Maupeou in the early 1770s, Turgot in the years 1774–1776, and Malesherbes on the eve of Revolution. At this juncture, what the public saw in the monarchy's desultory attempt to reform itself was not good will but an admission of defeat and a renunciation of ancient and religious mandates. Whatever reforms the monarchy did carry out—like the abolition of torture or the official granting of religious tolerance to Protestants in 1787—went almost unnoticed. (Emblematically, Malesherbes, the minister most responsible for carrying them out and one of the king's lawyers in 1793, was executed in April 1794 at the age of seventy-three, together with his daughter and granddaughter and her husband.)

Existential distaste for the practice of administrative dictate confirmed the abstract and now corrosive message of the philosophes. Political Anglophilia waxed. Memories of the Estates General, which had not met since 1614, were revived. In the 1780s the Crown's indecisive management of its debts was read as a sign of incompetence. In these same years, the royal family was widely lampooned. The queen was rumored to be a lesbian, a groundless accusation that resurfaced at her trial in October 1793 when—to Robespierre's honest dismay—she was publicly accused of having sexually corrupted her own son.

In eighteenth-century Britain nationalism crystallized around the twinned idea of empire and Protestant monarchy.[57] In America a new sense of nation coalesced around the idea of consensual self-rule. But in France the idea of Nation was gradually dissociated from the monarchy and identified instead (for many members of the possessing class, in any case) with the universalist values of the Enlightenment.

Jacobin antimonarchism after Louis XVI's flight to Varennes in June 1791, toward the Austrian army, was the end point of a long estrangement.

Proofs: The American Republic and the Ancient City-States

To bolster their hopes for reconciling private good with moralized public good prerevolutionary French men and women looked beyond their own times and borders to find cases that might prove their point. The first of these foreign models was the newest of all nations, the recently created United States. Had not the embattled farmers of the newly emancipated thirteen colonies succeeded in reaching their Republican and fraternal goal, regenerated as they were by independence and war? Americans, the French concluded—somewhat to the surprise of their Yankee friends—had managed to bring forth in their wilderness perfect modern replicas of Athens, Rome, and Sparta. (Benjamin Franklin, who had been in Philadelphia a most respectable bourgeois gentleman, became world famous by tailoring a new republicanized public persona—complete with a beaver fur hat!—to fit the French expectation of Americans as noble Republican savages.)

The French, deeply struck by the Americans' success, attributed it in part to the effect of French intellectual ministrations. On a visit to Harvard College, Brissot in 1788 wrote that "the heart of a Frenchman palpitates on finding the works of Racine, of Montesquieu, and the Encyclopaedia, where 150 years ago, arose the smoke of the savage calumet."[58] Ten years after America had achieved true greatness, its teachers were eager to replicate at home their students' successful text. In 1791 Tom Paine boldly said that "the American constitutions were to [French] liberty, what a grammar is to language: they define its parts of speech, and practically construct them into syntax."[59]

What the French did not see, of course, was the cultural and locational specificity of the American Republic. Although the principles of the American radicals were often rhetorically truculent, the American historical experience, born of geographical isolation and constant social change, was far more conducive to the acceptance of consensual rather than confrontational politics. Outside New England no one ethnic or religious community could hope to impose its views on its rivals for any length of time. In 1776 Americans were a profoundly religious people, habituated to internal self-government, with a multisecular history of compromises that brought together a sharply defined, communitarian, and biblical golden past with a recklessly individuated, day-to-day, economic, and pioneering experience.

Although the restless subjects of Louis XVI may have wished to be free and independent-minded men and women, communitarian values were much more deeply implanted in their hearts than they were in the free-wheeling, socially mobile, ethnically and religiously varied English colonies of North America.

In revolutionary America, individualist realities always had precedence over universalist ambition: there, private property could not be attacked, even as regarded its most egregious anti-Republican incarnation, slavery. In revolutionary France, however, as was to become obvious with the quasi-suspension of the rule of law in the spring of 1794, universalist argument could take precedence over the most essential right of the individual, the claim to fair and impartial justice.

But during Jacobinism's gestation, these discrepancies went unnoticed, however clearly they stand for us in hindsight, as omens of future political misfortune.[60]

The second French model was the ancient polis. In the 1750s Lafont de Saint-Yenne, "the first modern art critic," whose presence symbolized the displacement of the court by the public as the arbiter of good taste, urged French artists to imitate Roman models because in that ancient republic, with "every private person having his part in governance" of the state, "the good constitution of the state became his private and personal interest."[61] This fetish for the classical was ubiquitous by the 1780s, in the neoclassical, monumental architecture of Ledoux, in the paintings of David, in the popularity of the newly discovered Roman ruins of Pompeii, and in the vogue for Plutarch's lives.

Jacobinism was to be a politicized ideology of self-becoming and universalism. But it was prefigured in the civil society of the 1780s as an imagined way of living.

To analyze historically, we think in terms of distinct narratives, analyses, and themes. But in the end, to understand historically, we have to reassemble our findings. How then can we comprehend the Jacobins' decision—to choose but one case among so many—to execute Marie Antoinette?

A narration of ongoing revolutionary politics reminds us that the Jacobins in late October 1793 did not want to cross the sans-culotte leaders who were at that time pushing for her trial. Moreover, many Jacobins were by then resigned to thinking that terrorism was a good way out, not just as regarded the queen but for political impasses of all kinds. And no less pertinent were the unspoken legacies of prerevolutionary times. By 1789 already, Marie Antoinette had long since been branded by the public as an unsuccessful public figure, a bad mother, and a disloyal wife.

Every level of explanation has a distinctive message. When juxtaposed and interwoven, these strands reinforce one another, and then become more compelling—up to a point. To paraphrase Roland Barthes, the French Revolution was a *scriptible* ("writable") event, and therefore of the kind that we turn over ceaselessly in our mind but cannot resolve. The Terror of 1793–94 is not and never will be a *lisible* ("readable") event that we can describe briefly in order to move on. Like Sisyphus, we write and rewrite the script of revolutionary history, although we know that we can never grasp it fully.

Some frameworks do help us understand, just as others hinder us hopelessly. But as we move from ostensible events to analyses, and then turn back to covert cultural motivation, it is wise to remember that links of cause to effect slacken ceaselessly as we rehearse them better.

Why did men who truly were humane become terrorists? And why did they choose this ideological option rather than another? Why did Rousseau matter more than Montesquieu or Voltaire? Why did Marie Antoinette have to be executed? No one answer clearly emerges, and it is a most curious fact that Marx, so deeply concerned with the causal connection from "base" to "superstructure," never did spell out precisely—whether historically or psychologically—how private persons, taken one by one, sometimes internalize their public situation, and sometimes fail to do so.

The lasting message of the revolution's history is dauntingly ambiguous. Perhaps it is that dreams are costly. Or, perhaps—less nobly but more scientifically—it says that vast impersonal forces and their serendipitous opposites (bad harvests, the character of the king, military happenstance) together frame each and every action so complicatedly that we cannot readily make them out. Or, more grandly, as we would like to think and as has been argued here, it tells us that some men and women really do have free will, at least some of the time.

We cannot tell. But it is because 1789 elicits our constant puzzlement that its varied meanings will never disappoint us.

12

Looking Forward: Jacobinism in World History

> If the French Revolution were to recur eternally, French historians would be less proud of Robespierre. But because they deal with something that will not return, the bloody years of the Revolution have turned into mere words, theories, and discussions, have become lighter than feathers, frightening no one. There is an infinite difference between a Robespierre who occurs only once in history and a Robespierre who eternally returns, chopping off French heads.
>
> Milan Kundera, *The Unbearable Lightness of Being*

> Though I abhor the sanguinary ferocity of the late Jacobins in France, yet their principles . . . are the most consonant with my ideas of reason, and the nature of man, of any that I have met with.
>
> John Thelwall, *Rights of Nature*

$\mathscr{A}$s "decentered" moderns, we feel distaste for the anomie of contemporary commercialized social life and revulsion for the horrors of our own century. We also have a strong nostalgia for the sustaining sense of order and integrative social purpose that was the essence of the prerevolutionary, pre-Jacobin, premodern, and organicist Old Regime. But this preindustrial, traditional, and (supposedly) integrated and golden past is wholly lost to us. It has no relevance to our modern lives.

Instead, 1789 is our starting point. Jacobinism brings us back to a nearby, more credible, but still golden—and Republican—past, a happy summit between the trough of vanished traditions and the depths of our own dismaying century. The French Revolution (together with 1776 in America) stands as that elating moment when Western culture, still blissfully innocent, began anew its now secularized and postreligious quest for an invariably elusive blend of private happiness and universalist public good.

This modern and Sisyphean search, at once liberating and constraining, still sets the boundaries of our public life. As Marx reminded us in the first paragraphs of his *Eighteenth Brumaire*, men make their history, but they do not make it just as they desire. Persistently, then, obsessively even, we must try to understand why Jacobinism—this most universalist version of the Republican doctrines that we need to remember and applaud—succumbed to terrorist temptation.

A narrative of events reveals that *some* ideological continuities and practices linked liberalism, as the Jacobins defined it in 1789, to the authoritarianism of 1794. But these links, though troubling, were not determining. Jacobins stumbled into the Terror. They did not plan for it to happen. They were dismayed when it unfolded and relieved when it stopped.

Jacobinism's ideological dichotomies, at once universalist and individualist, were obviously unstable. But so are all of the world's great religions and man's very essence, for that matter, at once sacred and profane. It is indeed in the nature of such contradictions to be problematic; but contrary to what Hegel blithely assumed, it is not in their nature invariably to be resolved through terrorist escapism. The search for absolute freedom does not automatically lead to tyranny and bloodshed.

Moreover, as we look forward from 1799 through the nineteenth century and into the early twentieth, our sense of the avoidable particularities of Jacobinism's revolutionary terrorist decay (and with this, the question of its relevance to our own contemporary dilemmas) is bolstered once again by a consideration of Jacobinism's place in the unfolding of its two most famous avatars (or supposed avatars): the highly positive example of the Third French Republic from 1870 to 1940 and the dreadful example of Russian Bolshevism from 1917 to 1989.

In the neo-Jacobin days of the Third Republic, French men and women, however rich or poor, were probably happier than ever before—an unusual achievement in the one European country that has traditionally accepted millions of foreigners but has itself no tradition of outward migration.[1]

Nineteenth-century French history, despite its famous ups and downs (two empires, two monarchies, three republics), gives us in the Third Republic a democratic and parliamentary incarnation of Jacobin ideals that the Enlightenment's philosophes would not have disavowed and that most historians by far would judge to have been a highly positive regime.

But Russians under a Soviet rule that also claimed to be Jacobinism's heir were as miserable as they have ever been, an unusual achievement given that country's difficult history. "Has anyone ever been happy in Russia?" asked the nineteenth-century poet Nikolay Nekrasov, whose dismay is even more relevant to the Soviet Union of the twentieth century than to his own tsarist Russia.

The French and Russian Revolutions

The opponents of Russian autocracy were fascinated by French revolutionary politics. For Thomas Jefferson, every universal-minded person had two countries, his own and Republican France. But in the words of Saltykov-Schedrin, every patriotic Russian had two homelands, not-yet revolutionized Russia and revolutionary France. Herzen, the great figure of midcentury Russian liberalism and decency, wrote—somewhat exaggeratedly—that every young Russian secretly possessed portraits of both Danton and Robespierre. Russian intellectuals of the 1840s weighed the merits of Girondins (taken to be wise liberals) and Jacobin Montagnards, who (they thought) had understood the need to go beyond formal freedoms so as to secure social justice. Nikolay Chernyshevsky called for the creation of a new man modeled on the patriot of the French Revolution. In 1856 he proclaimed himself a Jacobin. In 1862 Petr Zaichnevsky, in a populist proclamation entitled "Young Russia," argued for a revolutionary seizure of power on the French model by a ruling elite of intellectuals, an idea taken up in the 1870s by Pyotr Tkachev and Pyotr Lavrov. Russian Social Democrats of the 1890s were far better informed about the sans-culottes of 1793 than they were about Pugachev's peasant revolt in the Russian countryside in the period 1773–1775. French historians like Taine were readily translated into Russian. Jaurès's *Histoire socialiste de la France* appeared in two simultaneous Russian translations in 1908, a useful complement to the twenty-six Russian books then in print on the leftist Paris Commune of 1871, only one of them, it might be added, hostile to the Communards.

The Revolution of 1917 quickened Russian interest in the French Revolution. Terms like "Constituent Assembly" and "political commissar" were probably borrowed from French precedent. Revolutionaries often played "La Marseillaise." Stalin read the historical novels of Victor Hugo. The Petrograd garrison anticipated repetitions of the Saint-Bartholomew and September massacres of 1572 and 1792, respectively.[2] In the spring and summer of 1917 Kerensky fully expected that Russian patriotism, regenerated by revolution, would be as effective against the Germans of 1917 as French patriotism had been in 1792. Aware of the fate of the Girondins, he feared that the Bolsheviks might prove to be his own Montagnards. And did there not lurk another Bonaparte in General Kornilov, whom he wrongly accused of having tried to stage a military coup?

After the Russian civil war, the Bolsheviks assessed their own prospects by comparison to the French Thermidorian politics from the fall of Robespierre in 1794 to Bonaparte's success in 1799.[3] When Lenin decreed the New Economic Policy as a pause on the way to true communism, many Bolsheviks, himself included, worried that this step marked the crest of their revolutionary adventure. It was to appease such fears that Lenin carefully distinguished between the French Thermidor, forced onto the Jacobins by "bourgeois" civil society, and the Bolsheviks' "auto-Thermidorization," which was carried out voluntarily by the Russian revolutionaries for tactical reasons of their own and which could be stopped at any time.

Likewise, at Lenin's death in 1924, the Bolsheviks were mindful of the Bonapartist sequel to the French Thermidor when they chose Joseph Stalin, the faceless bureaucrat, over the flamboyant military expert Leon Trotsky.

Jacobins and Bolsheviks

Within Russian political culture, then, the revolutionary myth of 1789 mattered deeply, and Russian theoreticians focused much attention on a central aspect of this myth, namely, the Terror's purpose and its relevance to the politics of their own revolution.

Before the Revolution of 1917, Georgy Plekhanov (1856–1918), a populist turned Marxist, had contradictorily argued both for and against the Terror. At times, he accepted a ruthless party-run dictatorship as a historical necessity. But in other moments, after 1903 especially, Plekhanov was taken aback by the growing terrorist truculence of Lenin, who rejected the

Mensheviks' plan to cooperate with "bourgeois" liberals in order to secure parliamentary rule: "Lenin," he wrote, "is baked of the same dough as Robespierre."[4]

Lenin followed an inverse trajectory. In *What Is to Be Done?* Lenin had at first defined intellectuals as those people who could present a convincing truth to a proletariat ready for conversion. But he gradually concluded that what might not be secured through consent could be extracted by brute force. Terror gradually took on the guise of political necessity: "it is a struggle to achieve the end in view, with no shying away from drastic plebeian measures, a struggle without kid gloves, without tenderness, without fear of resorting to the guillotine . . . a proper bourgeois revolution cannot be carried out without a Jacobin purge—to say nothing of a socialist revolution. It requires a dictatorship, and the dictatorship of the proletariat requires a Jacobin mentality."[5]

In Lenin's evolving thought, Jacobin authoritarianism seemed a convincing precedent, an inspiration to call "for a centralized Party structure in order that this dictatorship [of the proletariat] be brought about. Rejection of this truth leads to organizational opportunism." The enemy of the Jacobin, he concluded, was "the Girondin timidity of the bourgeois intellectual."[6] Lenin went on to praise the Terror of 1794. He compared the Girondins to the conciliatory Georgian Social Democrats of his day, whom he despised. So completely did Lenin succeed in imposing his definition of what a Jacobin was, that in 1929 one Menshevik said of another Menshevik (who was, like him, an enemy of Lenin), "Dan is a half-Jacobin, and to be one entirely he lacks only the necessary unscrupulousness and *Konsequenz*."[7]

Many French apologists of Russian terrorism reasoned in that same authoritarian way. After 1917, for example, the eminent communist historian Mathiez pointed out that Lenin and Lev Kamenev, like Hérault and Couthon, though "subjectively" members of the old ruling class, were "objectively" reliable because they were driven leftward by universalist concern. Mathiez linked the communists of 1917 to the Jacobins of 1794. Their relationship in contemporary time, he said, was like the Jacobins' to the Hébertists. Each group "perfected" the other's methods of revolutionary government.

Such statements still matter to us because recent juxtapositions of communist and Jacobin universalisms have allowed anticommunist critics of

Jacobinism's relevance to modern life to work backward from the disastrous experience of Soviet communism to present a wholesale condemnation first of Jacobin principles and, by implication (if in lesser measure), of 1789 as well.

In retrospect, however, despite Lenin, Plekhanov, Trotsky, and their academic heirs, it is becoming increasingly difficult to draw a meaningful connection between 1789 and 1917. Instinctively, we sense a key difference in the relationship of Jacobinism and Bolshevism to patriotism, class, and class-consciousness. Jacobins were confirmed nationalists. Bolsheviks were resolutely antipatriotic. Soviet communism was or wanted to be class-based. Jacobinism aimed for the reverse. The Jacobins of 1790–91 were a cross section of the entire elite of their nation, noble and non-noble. They may have numbered as many as half a million in an apolitical nation of 27 million. The Bolsheviks, by contrast, never won a free election and were a completely unrepresentative minority of 300,000 in a highly politicized nation of more than 100 million. True, both Jacobins and Bolsheviks were enthusiasts who looked forward to the creation of a unified and fraternal society; but where the Jacobins assumed this universalist unity to be latently immanent in society as it was, Bolsheviks assumed instead, in Hegelian manner, that social unity would come through ideological negation and bloody conflict, itself defined as an inevitable ruse of history that was above moral judgment.

Another key difference between Jacobin and Bolshevik concerns their varying interpretations of popular sovereignty. Given their communistic and revolutionary purpose, Marx and Lenin were certainly right to be fascinated by the conspiratorial and antiparliamentarian communism in 1795–96 of Gracchus Babeuf, who was indubitably abetted by many prominent Jacobins. But most Jacobins, far from seeing Babouvism as an extension of Jacobin principles, considered it a denial of their ideas of representative government and free elections. At his trial Babeuf, like numerous Jacobins, quoted from Rousseau at great length. Better than Robespierre, he understood the antiparliamentary uses to which Jean-Jacques's notion of a free-floating general will might be put. But Babeuf completely ignored Voltaire and Montesquieu, whose enlightened message also fed Jacobin sensibilities. Jacobins were not born conspirators. They were confirmed parliamentary democrats, however confusedly they expressed that feeling.

Historical reflections of a broader kind also throw doubt on the identity of Jacobin and Bolshevik terror. It seems highly implausible today to assert—as was commonly done in the first half of this century—that proletarian Bolshevism in 1917 was the historical extension of the Jacobin-guided French bourgeoisie of 1789, because the successive rise and fall of different social classes in one country or another are historically and inexorably connected.

French Marxist historians like Mathiez—and Russian Marxist political figures like Lenin—felt justified in describing 1789 as the preface for 1917 with little concern for differences between Jacobin and Bolshevik word and deed (as in their respective views on property, class war, and terror). Their eyes were set on the supposedly identical world-historical situations of eighteenth-century Jacobinism and twentieth-century Bolsheviks. But Lenin's teleological belief—assuming that he was sincere not just in espousing Marxist eschatalogy but also in thinking the Jacobins to have been as he described them—hardly needs to be our own. The recent collapse of Soviet communism enables us to sense the unreality of the Hegelian model of social becoming that loomed so large (or so he claimed) in Lenin's imagination.

Paradoxically, our own ahistorical presentism is a better framework for understanding the distant Jacobin past better than was the theorizing of our Marxist predecessors, who were closer to 1789 in time but not in thought or sensibility. Instinctively, today, we sense that the terrorist vagaries of Bolshevism were far more particular to the brutality of Russian culture and history than to some (nonexistent) mechanism of unfolding (West) European class structure. Bolshevism had an East European, archetypical Russian specificity. Its relationship to Jacobinism is a social-scientific fiction. Communism in Russia originated, as the exiled historian Pavel Milyukov laid out in the years 1921–1924, in the peculiarities of Russian life, which included a bloated, peasantist absolutism and a hyperradicalized, marginalized intelligentsia.

Contrary to what Lenin said, a composite Russian working class of urban proletarians and landless peasants did not exist in 1917. The goals of ordinary Russian working people were not universalist. It was preposterous for Lenin to assume that Russian peasants were ready to act in accord with politically conscious Russian workers in 1917 just as French peasants had been ready to work with the French middle class in 1789. Indeed, millions of politically unsuitable Russian and Ukrainian peasants would soon be pushed toward their death by the Bolsheviks precisely because they did not wish to ally themselves to the "proletariat."

Russian terrorism had its roots in the Russian past, just as Jacobin terrorism—if in a very different way—had its origins in French politics and religious culture. But these two pasts were not the same; and, in any instance, neither one of them is our own.

Better than ever before, as students of world history, we can appreciate that the Hegelian-Marxist teleology of class formation, universalist consciousness, and political method—though an interesting way to understand French and Continental European history in Marx and Hegel's time from the end of the eighteenth century to the middle of the nineteenth—has limited applicability in world history, as regards the history of Europe since 1900 or, for that matter, of America at any moment in its history.

And this renewed understanding of our (noncommunist) present alters our sense of its relation to the (Jacobin) past. In the words of the late-nineteenth-century German philosopher-historian Wilhelm Dilthey, "Was wir unserer Zukunft als Zweck setzen, das bedingt die Bestimmung der Bedeutung der Vergangenheit" (The purpose of our future sets the direction for the meaning that the past has for us). Works of history as written by historians may or may not be, in the words of Henry Ford, "bunk"; but in the optic of this book, History, as lived by succeeding and anguished generations, is not "junk."[8]

The Republican Idea Today

These historical matters concern us not just as historians but as citizens of the world. The ebbing of Leninist and communist assumptions enables us to realize anew the strength of the Jacobin and Republican idea, which we can again envisage not as a stepping stone to an elusive socialist nirvana but as a free-standing, real-life principle of social fairness.

Of course, the Jacobins of 1793–94 were foolish to suppose that citizens would effortlessly find in their public role the strength to transcend their social situation. They were wrong to think that regenerated men would immediately have the strength to dispense with envy if they were poor or to be generous if they were rich. They aimed too high—for universal justice rather than mere social decency, as we do today. We see the historical naïveté implicit in Jacobinism's assertion of individualism without limits and of universalism unbounded. We understand the dangers implicit in the Jacobins' excessive polarization of the private and the public. And we can conclude that Jacobinism's underestimation of the power of bureaucracies in an age of disenchanted mass politics was a grievous error, particularly in France, where modern bureaucratic forms were invented in the seventeenth century by the new (at the time) Old Regime.

But despite these many lapses, Jacobinism deserves our esteem and recognition. We are not so far along in history's trajectory as to be unmoved by its central truth. We can still learn from Jacobinism's desire to harmonize the private and the public through purposeful and libertarian civic-mindedness.

True enough, universalism seems to be a distant social goal today. In 1958 Hannah Arendt, a pessimist Hegelian, argued that a public space of shared values of community had shrunk so drastically as to become unrecoverable. Moderns were fated to be isolated individuals whose lives were devoid of any lived, authentic commonality, she believed.[9]

In 1962 Jürgen Habermas likewise disabusedly suggested that our modern public sphere had been "refeudalized." Its "equilibration of power" now involved exclusively administrators and private corporations, the broader public being "included only sporadically in this circuit of power, (and) even then . . . only to contribute its acclamation." Just as eighteenth-century capitalistic individualism generated a public sphere to suit its purpose, so had its late-twentieth-century avatars emptied it of any meaning.[10]

But why not assume that such judgments are unduly dour? Modern individuated civil society is not necessarily oblivious to the public good. Giant corporations can have a conscience. Pressure groups can have the public interest at heart. The market can inform. The widening gap between the beginning of a still active age of retirement and a functionally defined extreme old age implies that millions of retired citizens from their fifties to their nineties have today the energy (and time) to reinvolve themselves in communal life as ambitious young people cannot hope to do.

In many other respects, modern life is quite well suited to carry through the universalist values that the Enlightenment and Jacobinism both embodied. Through dramatically improved communication and from the mass movements of population also the idea of universality has gained obvious actuality. We have realized the Jacobin ideal of communicative transparence more fully than ordinary Frenchmen in the eighteenth century ever could have. Divisions of class, race, and gender—so deeply embedded in the civil society of nineteenth-century Europe and America—have lost their ideological edge for us. They remain strong in daily life, but they have lost their relevance as guiding principles of Western public life. The incompatibility of republicanism and religion, which the Jacobins (unlike their American cousins) soon took for granted, has also lapsed. Finally, for better or for worse, the modern, nuclear, and all too often disintegrated family no longer stands between the individual and the universal as did the extended quasi-tribal and clientelistic families of the Old Regime, which the Jacobins (vainly and touchingly) hoped to make the vehicles of Republican community.

In many unforeseen respects, then, our current "existential" situation is reminiscent of their own. An economically collectivist solution to the tension between individual and community did not exist for the Jacobins, and it no longer exists for us. The surprising collapse of the Bolshevist authoritarian communist project has reshuffled those cards completely.

We too, as it happens, are well situated to understand that collective freedom can come through the expansion of individualized consciousness to all rather than through authority from above. And so, our assignment today, as we stand in the ruins of nineteenth-century liberalism, as theirs was in 1789 amid the ruins of the Old Regime, is to imagine the ways in which our spontaneous and privatist creativities can be fitted into a larger and liberating global public vision.

Jacobinism fused into the temporarily uplifting cult of Nation a diverse sensibility that had found isolated expression in prerevolutionary institutions of local sociability, like Masonic lodges, reading circles, salons, and local academies. This fusion must be an example for us. The perfect opposite of Jacobinism's vision—namely, our own inactive allegiance to socially inert and pluralistic democracy—is no more than a tired and fatalistic response to the (temporary) failure of their larger and more noble worldview.

The Jansenists' hidden deity spoke thunderously, but in riddles. What man or woman, thought these Catholic Calvinists, can truly know if he or she has been touched by God's grace?

Clio's message is no doubt less profound, but it is (at times) more clear; and among her most favored words, when the muse does decide to speak, are those of the Jacobins of 1789 to 1799: *liberté, égalité, fraternité*. Jacobinism's goal of informed and fraternal liberty "sans laquelle l'homme n'est point homme" (without which man is not man)[11] has indestructible relevance for us still.

In the age of Wordsworth, Beethoven, Goya, and Foscolo (all of them close to the Jacobins' message at some point in their lives), French revolutionaries daringly (and disastrously) tried to transcend lived circumstance to politicize Western culture's age-old longing for freedom and social complementarity. We should not ignore that historical experience. Jacobinism's triumphs and disasters are our own. Our task is not just to understand their failure but also to see why the Jacobins sensibly hoped to succeed; and it is these hopes that should be most vivid to us.

"Remember me," sighs the impassioned, spurned, self-destructive, and dying queen of Carthage in Purcell's *Dido and Aeneas*, "remember me, but forget my fate."

Notes

1. A Narrative of the French Revolution from a Jacobin Perspective

1. An argument of this kind is developed at some length by François Furet in *Le Passé d'une illusion* (Paris: Laffont, 1995).

2. A study of rural Jacobins in Normandy indicates, however, that half of the members signed up but attended no meetings and that 10 percent of the *clubbistes* were genuine militants. See Danièle Pingué, "Une première forme de politisation de masse: les Sociétés Jacobines en Normandie orientale (1793–1794)," in Claude Mazauric, ed., *La Révolution française et les processus de socialisation de l'homme moderne* (Rouen: IRED and Université de Rouen, 1989), p. 139.

3. See Mercier, *Paris pendant la Révolution, 1789–1798*, 2 vols. (1862), 2:63. In a study of six towns with a membership of 2,221, Brinton found that about one third of the members sat through both 1792 and 1793–1795: "31% of the members were Jacobins throughout the Revolution." See *The Jacobins: An Essay in the New History* (New York: Macmillan, 1930), p. 58.

4. Brinton's estimate is probably too high. Gérard Maintenant and François Furet argue for 150,000. The higher estimate is endorsed by Claude Mazauric in Albert Soboul, ed., *Dictionnaire de la Révolution française* (Paris: Presses Universitaires de France, 1989), p. 590. Historians who emphasize the sectarian power of Jacobin ideology have an obvious interest in minimizing their numbers.

5. See Lefebvre, *The Great Fear*, first published in 1932.

6. *Tableau chronologique de l'Ancien Moniteur* (Paris, 1801), p. 223.

7. See Gramsci, *Quaderni del Carcere*, folio 19 (Turin: Gerraratana, Torino, 1975), p. 229.

8. See Keith Baker, "The Idea of a Declaration of Rights," in Dale van Kley, ed., *The French Idea of Freedom and the Declaration of Rights of 1789* (Stanford: Stanford University Press, 1994), pp. 154–196.

9. Among the 661 deputies of the Third Estate, nearly 200 lawyers clearly outnumbered 100 businessmen. Revealingly, legislators connected to trade and banking became fewer as the Revolution progressed.

10. Quoted by Marcel Gauchet, "La Question du jansénisme dans l'historiographie de la Révolution," in Catherine Maire, ed., *Jansénisme et Révolution* (Paris: Bibliothèque Mazarine, 1990), p. 18. Some prominent Jansenists, it should be added, were hostile to the Civil Constitution.

11. Some anti-Catholic clubs were founded—as at Tulle and at Bergerac—in the wake of that debate.

12. The figures are 52 percent for the entire nation, and as much as 80 percent around Paris. In the Var 96 percent of priests took the oath. By contrast, in the Bas-Rhin only 8 percent of them did so.

13. On February 28, 1791, a noble deputy named Foucauld de Lardimalie had proposed the suppression of the clubs, but unsuccessfully.

14. Thomas Carlyle, *The Diamond Necklace* (1833; reprint, Boston: Houghton Mifflin, 1913), p. 86.

15. W. D. Edmonds, *Jacobinism and the Revolt of Lyon, 1789–1793* (Oxford: Clarendon Press, 1990), p. 108.

16. Michael Kennedy, *The Jacobin Clubs in the French Revolution*, 2 vols. (Princeton: Princeton University Press, 1982), 1:276.

17. Another 350, though all of them militant "patriots" by the standards of 1789, joined neither of the two clubs.

18. Kennedy, *The Jacobin Clubs*, 1:231.

19. Ibid., 2:128.

20. Ibid., 2:374.

21. Ibid., 1:236. As a libertarian, Robespierre would have rejected all of these models: "Je n'aime pas plus Cromwell que Charles Ier," he stated on May 19, 1792. See Maximilien Robespierre, *Le Défenseur de la Constitution,* in Gustave Laurent, ed., *Oeuvres complètes,* vol. 4 (Paris: Société des Études Robespierristes, 1939), p. 9.

22. Edmonds, *Jacobinism and the Revolt of Lyon,* p. 136.

23. "Je me fous bien des prisonniers; qu'ils deviennent ce qu'ils pourront."

24. *Archives Parlementaires,* henceforth *AP,* 53:161. These were published in 99 volumes, vols. 1–82 (Paris: Dupont, 1879–1914); vols. 83–99 (Paris: CNRS, 1961–1995).

25. On September 28, 1793, in his "Rapport sur les Moyens de rassembler les matériaux nécessaires à former les Annales de Civisme, et sur la Forme de cet Ouvrage": see Grégoire, *Oeuvres,* 14 vols. (Paris: KTO-HDIS, 1977), 3:3.

26. Nationwide, only 15 percent of eligible voters had bothered—or dared—to appear at the polls; but for the moment, the legitimacy of the assembly was unchallenged even by the Paris Commune.

27. Kennedy, *The Jacobin Clubs,* 2:156.

28. *AP,* 53:161.

29. Cited in Kennedy, *The Jacobin Clubs*, 2:307.

30. Ibid., 2:336.

31. *La Vedette de Besançon*, June 21, 1793.

32. The phrase is Lynn Hunt's.

33. Formerly Bourg Saint-Andéol, on August 3, 1794. See *AP*, 93:92.

34. The CPS was a reduced and more efficacious version of an earlier and ineffective Committee of General Defense, created in January 1793, whose membership had included both Montagnards and Girondins.

35. Cited in Heinrich Blömeke, *Revolutionsregierung und Volksbewegung (1793–1794): Die "Terreur" im Departement Seine-et-Marne (Frankreich)* (Frankfurt: Peter Lang Verlag, 1989), p. 177.

36. In the torrential politics of 1789–1794, the meaning of even the most commonly used words gyrated dramatically. What had happened to the term "popular society" had also happened to the word *fédérés:* in 1790 these had been the partisans of the new national government, as in related and current American usage. But in 1793 the term *fédéré* was used to describe the provincial enemies of the Paris-based Jacobins. Likewise, the *enragés* of 1790 became the conservative Feuillants in 1791, who were to the right of the Gironde, in contrast to the *enragés* of late 1793, who were to the left of the Montagnards.

37. Cited by Louis de Cardenal, *La Province pendant la Révolution* (Paris: Payot, 1929), pp. 417–418.

38. The most reliable numbers are based on comparisons of adjusted population levels before and after the period 1793–1797.

39. Yann Fauchois, *Chronologie politique de la Révolution* (Alleur: Marabout, 1989), p. 242.

40. *AP*, 79:457–458.

41. Gérard Maintenant, *Les Jacobins* (Paris, 1984), p. 100.

42. Cited by George Rudé, "The French Revolution and 'Participation,'" in Eugene Kamenka, ed., *A World in Revolution?* (Canberra: Australian National University, 1970), p. 20.

43. *AP*, 78:151. Given the Jacobins' fear of these autonomously politicized women, it is ironic that after the fall of Robespierre, his friends were often to be caricatured as feminine and furious harpies whose cries and deeds undid the natural order of social life.

44. Picardy, the Île-de-France around Paris, and areas to the north and east of Lyons were more heavily involved.

45. See Richard Cobb, *Les Armées révolutionnaires: instrument de la Terreur dans les départements avril 1793–floréal an II*, 2 vols. (The Hague: Mouton, 1961–1963), 2:777.

46. See Raymonde Monnier, "La Dissolution des sociétés populaires parisiennes au printemps de l'an II," *Annales historiques de la Révolution française*, 58, no. 268 (April–June 1987), p. 186.

47. At Artonne, on 6 Thermidor, Year II, "un membre observe que la séance est très peu nombreuse." See Fernand Martin, *Les Jacobins au village Artonne* (Clermont-Ferrand: Juliot, 1902), p. 89.

48. See Léon Seilhac, *Scènes et portraits de la Révolution en bas-Limousin* (Paris, 1878), p. 711.

49. Anacreon was an ancient Greek poet who wrote in praise of creature comforts.

50. On 9 Fructidor, see L. Constans, "La société populaire de Millau (Aveyron)," *Révolution française,* 14 (January–June 1888), p. 783.

51. See Chapter 10.

52. "While avoiding Charybdis, let's not fall into Scylla," August or September 1794. See Société populaire des sans-culottes régénérés de Bessan, Archives Départementales de l'Hérault, L 5531.

53. Archives Départementales de l'Hérault, L 5531.

54. From J. B. Galley, *Saint Étienne pendant la Révolution,* 2:749–750, cited by Michael Kennedy, "The Last Stand of the Jacobin Clubs," *French Historical Studies,* 16, no. 2 (fall 1989), p. 312.

55. On February 22, 1795. See *Réimpression de l'Ancien Moniteur,* vol. 22 (Paris: Plon, 1854), p. 535.

56. On August 11, 1794. See *AP,* 94:494, 495.

57. On the Ideologues, see Sergio Moravia, *Il pensiero degli idéologues: scienza e filosofia in Francia, 1780–1815* (Florence: La Nuova Italia, 1974).

58. See Isser Woloch, *The New Regime: Transformations of the French Civic Order, 1789–1820* (New York: Columbia University Press, 1994).

59. I owe this idea to Gerard Livesey.

60. On 17 Pluviôse, Year IV (February 6, 1794), *AP,* 84:330.

61. Baudot, *Notes historiques* (Geneva: Slatkine, 1974), p. 43.

62. Cited in Pierre Rosanvallon, *Le Sacre du citoyen* (Paris: Gallimard, 1992), p. 88. See also Jean-Paul Belin, *La Logique d'une idée force, l'idée d'utilité sociale pendant la Révolution française* (Paris, 1934).

63. No less instructive, if in a darker register, is the juxtaposition of the Jacobins' indeterminate *aristocrate* to the imprecise use of the word "Jew" by the authors of the four Gospels, so eager to explain the passion of their Savior by reference to the conspiratorial malevolence of his "Jewish" enemies, meaning at various times all Jews, some Jews, or some leaders of some Jews. See Elaine Pagels, *The Origins of Satan* (New York: Random House, 1995).

64. Cited in Jean-Pierre Gross, *Fair Shares for All: Jacobin Egalitarianism in Practice* (Cambridge: Cambridge University Press, 1997), p. 24.

65. Augustin Cochin, "Les Philosophes," in *L'Esprit du Jacobinisme* (Paris: Presses Universitaires de France, 1979), p. 35.

66. Holbach, *Système social,* 1:87–88, cited by Daniel Gordon, *Citizens without Sovereignty* (Princeton: Princeton University Press, 1994), p. 84.

67. Lucien Jeaume has developed this theme at fruitful length.

68. Desmoulins, *Le Vieux Cordelier,* no. 7 (Paris: Belin, 1987), p. 123.

69. Bibliothèque Municipale de Poitiers, S 12.

70. In June 1793. See E. Leleu, *La Société populaire de Lille,* p. 74.

71. The executioner did slap Charlotte Corday's decapitated head, however.

72. Michel Foucault, *Discipline and Punish* (New York: Vintage, 1979), p. 48.

73. Benjamin Constant, *Principes de politique* (Paris: Gallimard, 1957), p. 1004. Edgar Quinet (1803–1875) also pointed out that the revolutionaries were as impatient and intolerant of dissent and disobedience as had been the absolutist monarchy they overthrew. The king had been absolutely sovereign. But for the Jacobins, the people, were a no less absolute sovereign. Marcel Gauchet and Antoine de Baecque have also written on the transposition after 1789 to the people of images of corporeal unity that had for centuries been associated with the king's sacred body. See Marcel Gauchet, *La Révolution des Droits de l'Homme* (Paris: Gallimard, 1989), pp. 23–28, and Antoine de Baecque, *Le Corps de l'histoire* (Paris: Calmann-Lévy, 1993), p. 128. See also Jeffrey Merrick, "Fathers and Kings: Patriarchalism and Absolutism in Eighteenth-Century French Politics," *Studies on Voltaire and the Eighteenth Century,* 308 (1993), pp. 281–303.

74. See, for example, Arlette Farges, *Subversive Words* (Cambridge: Polity Press, 1995), pp. 149–175.

75. Cited by Patrice Gueniffey, *Le Nombre et la raison: La Révolution française et les elections* (Paris: EHESS, 1993), p. 392.

76. Jean Favier, *Paris, deux mille ans d'histoire* (Paris: Fayard, 1997), p. 155.

77. Cited in Blömeke, *Revolutionsregierung und Volksbewegung,* p. 262. Blömeke's excellent book is one of the best guides to the interweaving of the private and the public during the Revolution.

78. Cardenal, *La Province pendant la Révolution,* p. 429.

79. See Colin Lucas, *The Anatomy of the Terror: The Example of Javogues and the Loire* (Oxford: Oxford University Press, 1973).

80. Alain Corbin, *The Village of Cannibals* (Cambridge, Mass.: Harvard University Press, 1992), p. 91.

2. The Limitless Claims of Individual Liberty

1. Robespierre, *Le Défenseur de la Constitution,* p. 358.

2. From a statement of 1791 drawn up by the Jacobin club of Rennes. See Archives Départementales de l'Ille et Vilaine, L 1557.

3. Bibliothèque Municipale de Poitiers, S 23.

4. Cited in Gross, *Fair Shares,* p. 59.

5. On 24 Nivôse, Year II. See Archives Départementales du Vaucluse, 6 L 6, Courthézon. "L'idée du bonheur est nouvelle en Europe," the most poetic of

all Jacobin injunctions, and a remark that Saint-Just added to a short speech, nearly as an afterthought. See *AP*, 86:23.

6. Albert Denis, *Le Club des Jacobins de Toul* (Paris: Berger-Levrault, 1895), p. 11.

7. In a speech to the Jacobin club of Paris, cited in F. A. Aulard, ed., *La Société des Jacobins*, 6 vols. (Paris: Joualt, 1889–1897), 2:396.

8. Cited in Blömeke, *Revolutionsregierung und Volksbewegung*, p. 268.

9. Ibid., p. 250.

10. *AP*, 95:298

11. David painted this canvas, *The Friend of the People*, in the fall of 1793. Marat was murdered on July 13, 1793.

12. From a speech to the Bédarieux club on 20 Fructidor, Year II. See Archives Départementales de l'Hérault, L 5531.

13. On December 2, 1792. See *AP*, 54:43.

14. Cited by Colin Lucas in "Denunciation in the French Revolution," *Journal of Modern History*, 68, no. 4 (December 1996), p. 782.

15. See Seilhac, *Scènes et portraits de la Révolution en bas-Limousin*, p. 711.

16. A law passed in Vendémiaire, Year II (October 5, 1794) instructed juries to consider whether a crime had been committed with or without intent to harm.

17. On November 13, 1792. See *AP*, 53:392.

18. Gamon, on December 1, 1792. See *AP*, 54:31.

19. At Nay in December 1793. See Jean Annat, *La Période révolutionnaire dans les Basses Pyrénées: les sociétés populaires* (Pau: Lescher-Montoué, 1940), p. 225.

20. On September 22. See *AP*, 52:86.

21. Jean Starobinski has of course traced this theme in the work of Jean-Jacques Rousseau as well.

22. Pol Gosset, *La Société populaire de Reims: 1790–1795* (Reims: Imprimerie Matot-Braine, 1898), p. 21.

23. See Monbrion, *Manuel du laboureur et de l'artisan* (summer 1793), cited in Kennedy, *The Jacobin Club of Marseilles* (Ithaca: Cornell University Press, 1973), p. 185.

24. See Annat, *Basses Pyrénées*, p. 93. The Bayonne motion was endorsed by the *clubbistes* of Pau on July 19, 1794. See also Brinton, *The Jacobins*, p. 161.

25. On 28 Messidor, Year II (July 16, 1794). Cited in Aulard, *La Société des Jacobins*, 6:222–223.

26. See Annat, *Basses Pyrénées*, p. 190.

27. On October 20, 1793. See Victor Forot, *Le Club Jacobin de Tulle* (Tulle, 1912), p. 304.

28. Fire insurance was introduced in 1754. After the fall of the Girondins, life insurance companies were abolished in August 1793. They were reintroduced in 1816.

29. See Michèle Ruffat et al., *L'UAP et l'histoire de l'assurance* (Paris: J. C. Lathès, 1990), p. 53.

30. Camille Richard, *Le Comité de Salut-Public et les fabrications de guerre sous la Terreur* (Paris: Rieder, 1922), p. 136.

31. Gross, *Fair Shares*, p. 147.

32. Louis Hugueney, *Les Clubs Dijonnais sous la Révolution, leur rôle politique et économique* (Dijon: Nourry, 1905), p. 183, refers to 4–6 Vendémiaire, Year III.

33. As in the title of his book, *Every Cook Can Govern: A Study of Democracy in Ancient Greece,* 1956.

34. Richard, *Le Comité de Salut-Public et les fabrications de guerre*, p. 42.

35. Cited by Gary Kates, *The Cercle Social: The Girondins and the French Revolution* (Princeton: Princeton University Press, 1985), p. 209.

36. On April 9, 1792, at Tulle. See Seilhac, *Scènes et portraits de la Révolution en bas-Limousin*, p. 299.

37. Ibid.

38. Cited in Walter, *Histoire des Jacobins*, p. 163.

39. In his *Institutions républicaines.*

40. Cited by Charles C. Gillispie, *Science and Polity in France at the End of the Old Regime* (Princeton: Princeton University Press, 1980), pp. 274–275. Drawn from the "Point central des arts et métiers . . . composé de tous artistes vrai sans-culottes," on September 26, 1793, B.N.Inv.Rz3001; also Archives Nationales, AD series VIII, 40, T.1 pièce 18.

41. Henri Labroue, *Le Club Jacobin de Toulon (1790–1796)* (Paris: Alcan, 1907), p. 40. Less stern, a Jacobin of Montellier suggested that the Poles had been betrayed by their king. Their flag should be furled "jusqu'à ce qu'un nouveau 10 aoust rende aux polonais leur liberté entière." Archives Départementales de l'Hérault, L 5500.

42. Grégoire, *Opinion . . . concernant le jugement de Louis XVI* (November 15, 1792), p. 10.

43. Quoted by Elizabeth Roudinesco, *Théroigne de Méricourt: A Melancholic Woman during the French Revolution,* trans. Martin Thom (London: Verso, 1991), pp. xi, 166. See also Nicholas Mirzoeff, *Silent Poetry, Deafness, Sign, and Visual Culture in Modern France* (Princeton: Princeton University Press, 1995), p. 53.

44. From the charter of a "Board to Help the Poor," read at the Jacobin club of Dreux. See Georges Champagne, *La Société populaire de Dreux* (Dreux: Champagne, 1908), p. 67.

45. In part 1, letter 32. In a perfect modern analogy, the duchess of Windsor is said to have opined that "a woman can never be too thin or too rich."

46. Daniel Bernard and Jacques Tournaire, *L'Indre pendant la Révolution française* (Limoges: Lucien Souny, 1989), p. 119.

47. Denis, *Toul*, p. 76.

48. Olwen Hufton, *Women and the Limits of Citizenship in the French Revolution* (Toronto: University of Toronto Press, 1992), p. 112.

49. Cardenal, *La Province pendant la Révolution,* p. 426.

50. R. Rumeau, "Le club de Grenade pendant la Révolution," in *Société de Géographie de Toulouse,* 1908; reprinted in 1908 as a pamphlet; see p. 7.

51. Dominique Dessertine, *Divorcer à Lyon sous la Révolution et l'Empire* (Lyons: Presses de l'Université de Lyon, 1981), suggests that the possibility of divorce strengthened the bargaining hand of women.

52. I am indebted to Amanda Kessler for this idea.

53. Annat, *Basses Pyrénées,* p. 260.

54. On February 26, 1794. Cited by Dominique Godineau, *Citoyennes tricoteuses* (Paris: Alinéa, 1988), p. 264.

55. Cardenal, *La Province pendant la Révolution,* p. 70.

56. Gosset, *Reims,* p. 41.

57. Cited on p. 26 of Susan Desan's insightful overview of the women's clubs, "Constitutional Amazons: Women's Clubs in the French Revolution," in Bryan T. Ragan, Jr., and Elizabeth Williams, eds., *Recreating Authority in Revolutionary France* (New Brunswick: Rutgers University Press, 1992).

58. In the *Journal de la société de 1789,* cited by Elisabeth Badinter, *Paroles d'hommes* (Paris: POL, 1989), p. 54. Other voices were raised from time to time to ask for women's right to act politically as at Besançon, where Jacobins in February 1793 gave sustained thought to petitioning the Convention to that effect. See Henriette Perrin, "Le Club des femmes de Besançon," *Annales révolutionnaires* 9–10 (1917–1918), 9:633.

59. See Gerard Livesey's forthcoming "Virtue, Commerce, and Farming," in *Past and Present, 1998.*

60. Edmond Poupé, "La Société populaire de Callas (Var)," *Révolution française* (December 1902), pp. 481–503, see specifically p. 502.

61. Badinter, *Paroles d'hommes,* p. 99.

62. Gosset, *Reims,* p. 12.

63. Edmonds, *Jacobinism and the Revolt of Lyon,* p. 95.

64. Isabelle Bourdin, *Les Sociétés populaires à Paris pendant la Révolution jusqu'à la chute de la royauté* (Paris: Sirey, 1937), p. 150.

65. Godineau, *Citoyennes tricoteuses,* p. 115.

66. These students and patriots, the society asserted, were guided by "de bons principes se sont séparés de la tourbe des méchants qui abondent dans l'endroit." Bibliothèque Municipale de Poitiers, S 19 (June 14, 1791).

67. Guy Lemarchand, *La Fin du féodalisme dans le pays de Caux, 1640–1795* (Paris: CTHS, 1989), p. 477.

68. Ernest Jovy, *Documents sur la Société populaire de Vitry-le-François pendant la Révolution* (Vitry-le-François: J. Denis, 1892), p. 39.

69. Cited in Walter, *Histoire des Jacobins,* p. 189.

70. On 12 Prairial, Year II (May 31, 1794). See *Réimpression de l'Ancien Moniteur,* vol. 20 (Paris: Plon, 1854), p. 603.

71. Elie Rossignol, *Histoire de l'arrondissement de Gaillac* (Toulouse: Chauvin, 1890), p. 309.

72. In some sense, the Convention was at this point merely ratifying a decision taken earlier in Haiti for strategic reasons on August 29 by the French representative there, Sonthonax.

73. See Anne Pérotin Dumon, "A Turbulent Time: Revolution and the Emergence of Politics," in D. Geggus and B. Gaspar, eds., *The French Revolution and the Greater Caribbean* (Bloomington: University of Indiana Press, 1997), pp. 30–31.

74. The color black was distasteful to the Jacobins, who associated their own clubs with whiteness, which, in the nineteenth century, was identified in France with royalism. The Jacobins described their opponents on the extreme left as red and those on the right as black, an echo perhaps of the black robes of priests. Vadier, a member of the Committee of General Security, even referred to his enemies as Ethiopians.

75. Cited in Jean Tarrade, "Les Assemblées révolutionnaires et le problème de l'esclavage," in Jean Tarrade, ed., *La Révolution française et les colonies* (Paris: Société Française d'Histoire d'Outre Mer, 1989).

76. The abbé Grégoire, for example, penned in the fall of 1789 a *Mémoire en faveur des gens de couleur ou sang-mêlés*. See Bernard Plongeron, *L'Abbé Grégoire, ou l'arche de la fraternité* (Paris: Letouzey et Ané, 1989), pp. 55–56.

77. Frédérick Charles Heitz, *Les Sociétés politiques de Strasbourg pendant les années 1790 à 1795*: extraits de leurs procès-verbaux (Strasbourg, 1863), p. 141.

3. *The Indisputable Claims of Civil Society*

1. On this theme, see Gordon, *Citizens without Sovereignty*.

2. Cited in Cardenal, *La Province pendant la Révolution*, p. 255.

3. Cited in Brinton, *The Jacobins*, p. 161.

4. On February 5, 1794. See *AP*, 84:332.

5. Cited in Hannah Arendt, *On Revolution* (New York: Viking, 1965), p. 273.

6. See Ferguson, *An Essay on the History of Civil Society*, repr., ed. L. Schneider (New Brunswick: Transaction Press, 1980).

7. Hippolyte Taine, *The Origins of Contemporary France*, vol. 2, trans. John Durand (New York, 1876), p. 113, cited by Kennedy, *Marseilles*, pp. 152–153.

8. Ironically, most of the Communards whom he so despised were themselves respectable shopkeepers and artisans. Moreover, the repressive Versaillais government of 1871 was far more brutal in dealing with its enemies than the leftist Communards ever were.

9. Cited in Cardenal, *La Province pendant la Révolution*, p. 506. Napoleon's younger brother Joseph Bonaparte had likewise joined the Ajaccio Jacobins in 1791.

10. Ted W. Margadant, *Urban Rivalries in the French Revolution* (Princeton: Princeton University Press, 1992), p. 37.

11. Labroue, *Toulon*, p. 27, n. 1.

12. Cardenal, *La Province pendant la Révolution*, pp. 22–27, 80.

13. Kennedy, *The Jacobin Clubs*, 1:127.

14. *AP*, 64:431.

15. Crane Brinton, for example, probably overestimated this connection. See Kennedy, *The Jacobin Clubs*, 1:5.

16. François Furet, *Interpreting the French Revolution* (Cambridge: Cambridge University Press, 1981), p. 180.

17. See Margaret Jacob, *Living the Enlightenment: Free Masonry and Politics in Eighteenth-Century Europe* (New York: Oxford University Press, 1991).

18. Masonic influences were far-reaching geographically as well. Anne Pérotin-Dumont speculates, for example, that Masons may have contributed to the founding of Jacobin clubs in the Caribbean. See her "Les Jacobins des Antilles ou l'esprit de liberté dans les iles-du-vent," *Revue d'histoire moderne et contemporaine*, 35 (April–June 1988), pp. 275–304.

19. Desmoulins, *Révolutions de France et de Brabant*, no. 41.

20. Barral-Montferrat and Savoye-Rollin were among them.

21. Archives Départementales du Tarn, L 1531. Its rules had been very strict. Any member who spoke without respect of "religion, government, or mores" was subject to immediate exclusion.

22. Hugueney, *Dijon*, p. 100.

23. Gillispie, *Science*, p. 267.

24. See Dena Goodman, *The Republic of Letters* (Ithaca: Cornell University Press, 1994), p. 267, n. 106.

25. Kennedy, *Marseilles*, p. 218.

26. There were about 6,027 clubs in 5,510 different townships. By excluding duplications due to youth clubs and women's clubs, researchers have concluded that in late 1793 and early 1794, 98 percent of communes had but a single *société populaire*. Jean Boutier, Philippe Boutry, and Serge Bonin, *Les Sociétés politiques* (Paris: EHESS, 1992), p. 15.

27. Gosset, *Reims*, p. 49.

28. In Labroue, *Toulon*, p. 15.

29. Jacques Guilhaumou, *Marseille républicaine* (Paris: Presses de la Fondation des Sciences Politiques, 1992), p. 53.

30. Kennedy, *The Jacobin Clubs*, 2:16. See also Chapter 9.

31. On October 31, 1790. See Archives Départementales de l'Hérault, L 5531, Agde.

32. Georges Lefebvre, *La Société populaire de Bourbourg* (Lille: Lefebvre-Ducrocq, 1913), p. 100.

33. Kennedy, *The Jacobin Clubs*, 2:101.

34. Ted Margadant, in the fourth chapter of his *Urban Rivalries*, provides a description of local manipulations of national politics for municipal advan-

tage. It is also striking that rates of condemnations varied widely from one area to the next despite similarities of circumstance and local culture: many more people were condemned to death in the Vaucluse than in the neighboring department of the Drôme, for instance. See Alan Forrest, "The Local Politics of Repression," in Keith Baker, ed., *The Terror* (London: Pergamon, 1994), p. 82.

35. At Pau, on May 19, 1793; see Annat, *Basses Pyrénées*, p. 197.

36. Edmund Poupé, "La Société populaire de Villecroze," *La Révolution française*, 40, no. 7 (February 14, 1901), p. 150.

37. For instance, Batbedat at Dax denounced Ramenbordes but failed to send him to Paris though instructed to do so. See Forrest, "The Local Politics of Repression," p. 93.

38. Georges Darney, *Lagny, Thorigny, Pomponne, Dampmart* (Lagny-sur-Marne: Librairie du Centre, n.d.), p. 198.

39. Cited in Blömeke, *Revolutionsregierung und Volksbewegung*, p. 263.

40. At Aix in September 1791 a member was expelled for making the society's debates known abroad; but in all likelihood that was because this club was highly politicized, and the dissident member was in fact conspiring with anti-Jacobins.

41. At Provins on 20 Ventôse, Year II. Cited in Blömeke, *Revolutionsregierung und Volksbewegung*, p. 256.

42. Kennedy, *Marseilles*, p. 58.

43. Kennedy, *The Jacobin Clubs*, 2:43.

44. On August 25, 1793. See Archives Départementales du Vaucluse, 6 L 6 (formerly 6 L 25).

45. Paul Granié, *De l'Ancien Régime à Thermidor: une commune du Quercy pendant la Révolution* (Cahors: Girma, 1905), p. 144.

46. On December 2, 1792. See *AP*, 54:43.

47. On March 13, 1793. See *AP*, 86:438.

48. On 23 Pluviôse, Year II. See Ulysse Chevalier, *Le Comité de Surveillance révolutionnaire et la société Républico-populaire de Romans, 1793–1794* (Valence: Céas, 1890), p. 37.

49. Cardenal, *La Province pendant la Révolution*, p. 256.

50. On January 11, 1791. See Archives Départementales du Lot et Garonne, L 1131.

51. Typically, Crèvecoeur's *Letters of an American Farmer* had been translated into French as *Lettres d'un cultivateur américain*.

52. On March 11, 1793, at Lioux in the Vaucluse. See Archives Départementales du Vaucluse, 6 L 17.

53. Bibliothèque Municipale de Poitiers, S 11 (1791).

54. Archives Départementales des Bouches du Rhône, L 2026.

55. Poupé, "La Société populaire de Callas," p. 500.

56. Cited by P. M. Jones, *The Peasantry in the French Revolution* (Cambridge: Cambridge University Press, 1988), pp. 214–215.

57. Darney, *Lagny,* p. 230.

58. Burke satirized the airy, abstract words of Jacobinism as the "desperate flights [of] the aeronauts of France."

59. So did the Protestant Jacobin Jeanbon Saint-André at Brest in the fall of 1793. See William S. Cormack, *Revolution and Political Conflict in the French Navy, 1789–1794* (Cambridge: Cambridge University Press, 1995), p. 255.

60. Louis Bresson, "Une Petite Ville du sud-ouest en l'an II de la République: Tonneins la Montagne," *Révolution française,* 3 (July–December 1882), pp. 173–175, 231–240, esp. p. 235.

61. See her letter to Bancal dated August 4, 1790, cited in Edmonds, *Jacobinism and the Revolt of Lyon,* p. 55. "Lyon est un cloaque de tout ce que l'ancien régime produisait de plus immonde." The idea of urban refuse likewise came to the mind of Jefferson, whose thinking closely resembled that of the Jacobins. For him, not Lyons but New York was as "a cloacina of all the depravities of human nature" (see his letter to William Short of September 8, 1823).

62. "La mère des moeurs." Saint-Just, *Esprit de la Révolution,* in Alain Lénard, ed., *Théorie politique* (Paris: Seuil, 1976), p. 115.

63. Émile Dellas, *La Société populaire d'Auch sous la Révolution* (Auch: Foix, 1898), p. 27.

64. *Sur le Gouvernement de Pologne* (Paris: Gallimard, 1964), 3:1019.

65. Lefebvre, *Bourbourg,* p. 48.

66. Hubert C. Johnson, *The Midi in Revolution* (Princeton: Princeton University Press, 1986), p. 180; for Strasbourg, see Kennedy, *The Jacobin Clubs,* 1:85.

67. Forot, *Tulle,* p. 557.

68. I have adressed this issue in "Jacobins and Girondins," *English Historical Review,* 100, no. 396 (July 1985), pp. 513–544. See also M. J. Sydenham, *The Girondins* (London: London University Press, 1960), and Alison Patrick, *The Men of the First French Republic* (Baltimore: Johns Hopkins University Press, 1972).

69. See Chapter 10.

70. Cited by Kates, *Cercle Social,* pp. 212–213.

71. Georges Lefebvre, in an uncharacteristic moment, described the Jacobins as having a simultaneously energetic and authoritarian temperament rooted in biology and typical of leaders. From a Marxist perspective (which usually informed Lefebvre's point of view), this distinction between personal strength and weakness seems largely irrelevant. But it takes on more meaning if we see that the two groups split not on strategy but on tactics. To save the Revolution, some Jacobins (the strongest ones?) were willing to shoot Niagara. The Girondins (more pusillanimous?) were more cautious, and were pushed aside. Energy was a prized quality in the spring and summer of 1793!

72. Cited in Albert Kuscinski, *Dictionnaire des Conventionnels* (Paris: Société des Études Robespierristes, 1917), p. 516. Rabaut was executed in December 1793. His wife then took her own life.

73. Starting in 1792, the property of émigrés and convicted counterrevolutionaries was included as well. About 10 percent of France's landed wealth changed hands during the Revolution.

74. On October 23, 1790. See Bibliothèque Municipale de Poitiers, S 1.

75. Martin, *Artonne*, p. 89.

76. Cited by Cardenal, *La Province pendant la Révolution*, p. 352.

77. On April 14, 1794. See Henri Labroue, *La Société populaire de Bergerac pendant la Révolution* (Paris: Société d'Histoire de la Révolution Française, 1913), p. 241.

78. See the passage of his *Phenomenology* entitled "Absolute Freedom and Terror." Although Hegel's basic message is plain enough, its insertion in his philosophical system is extremely complex. See Joachin Ritter, *Hegel and the French Revolution* (Cambridge, Mass.: MIT Press, 1982).

79. At Gaillac, on 21 Frimaire, Year II. See Archives Municipales de Gaillac, 1 D (10) 3: "Après avoir détruit le despotisme, il est temps que le peuple s'élève à la hauteur de la Révolution."

80. At this point, Hegel's odd—and Germanic—simile compares the heads Jacobins chopped off to cabbages.

81. François Furet, *Revolutionary France: 1770–1880* (Oxford: Blackwell, 1992), p. 153.

82. *AP*, 85:519.

83. "Il parait convenable de fixer le nombre de fermes qu'un seul pourrait posséder." On 29 Messidor, Year II. *AP*, 94:161. In the Convention, however, it is true, Jacobins coolly received such proposals, though many petitions were filed to that effect between August 1792 and July 1794. See J. P. Jessene, "La Terre: redéfinition de la communauté rurale" (unpublished paper, Stanford University), p. 15.

84. Described in Jean-Pierre Gross, "Progressive Taxation and Social Justice," *Past and Present*, 140 (1993).

85. Relevant legislation on inheritance for legitimate male and female children was passed in 1791 and for illegitimate children in November 1793. In January 1794 its effects were made retroactive to July 14, 1789.

86. Combes de Patris, *Procès-verbaux des séances de la société populaire de Rodez* (Rodez: Carrère, 1912), p. 53.

87. Albert Soboul, *Le Mouvement populaire* (Paris: Flammarion, 1973), p. 295.

88. In their circular of June 7, 1793, whose purpose was to justify the illegal exclusion of the Girondin deputies, the Paris club denounced the agrarian law as "an absurd lie."

89. R. Chervy and L. Chervy, "La Société de Guréret, 1791–1794," in *Mémoires de la Société des Sciences Naturelles et Archéologiques de la Creuse*, vol. 34 (Gueret: Imprimerie Lecante, 1962), p. 142.

90. Léon Lévy-Schneider, *Le Conventionnel Jeanbon Saint-André* (Paris: Alcan, 1901), p. 228, n. 5.

91. Kennedy, *The Jacobin Clubs,* 1:97.

92. As described in Jacques Revel, *Jeux d'Echelles* (Paris: Gallimard, 1996).

4. The Limitless Claims of the Public Sphere

1. Among the basic texts on this issue are Keith Michael Baker, "Public Opinion as Political Invention," in Baker, *Inventing the French Revolution* (Cambridge: Cambridge University Press, 1990); and Mona Ozouf, "L'Opinion publique," in K. M. Baker, ed., *The French Revolution and the Creation of Modern Political Culture,* vol. 1 (Oxford: Oxford University Press, 1987).

2. Albert Kuscinski, *Dictionnaire des Conventionnels* (Paris: Société des Études Robespierristes, 1917), p. 25.

3. See Bernard Lehembre, *Naissance de l'école moderne: les textes fondamentaux, 1791–1804* (Paris: Nathan, 1989), p. 89.

4. *AP,* 93:611.

5. M. Henriot, *Le Club des Jacobins de Semur* (Dijon: Rebousseau, 1933), p. 212.

6. On November 5, 1792. See *AP,* 53:159.

7. Keith Baker and François Furet have rightly emphasized the importance of this idea in revolutionary Jacobin politics. See K. M. Baker, "Politics and Public Opinion under the Old Regime: Some Reflections," in J. R. Censer and J. Popkin, eds., *Press and Politics in Pre-Revolutionary France* (Berkeley: University of California Press, 1987), and François Furet, *Penser la Révolution française* (Paris: Gallimard, 1978), p. 72.

8. On 10 Thermidor. See *AP,* 93:611.

9. *AP,* 67:140.

10. On June 11, 1793. See *La Vedette de Besançon,* no. 44, p. 349.

11. Laplanche, in a letter of October 4, 1793, to the Committee of Public Safety, cited in François Aulard's *Recueil des Actes du Comité de Salut Public,* vol. 7 (Paris, 1894), p. 219.

12. In modern jargon, public opinion from 1750 onward (after 1770 especially) was a dominant discourse, elaborated by Enlightenment writers, their defeated enemies, and their own admiring readers before 1789 and by the revolutionaries after that.

13. From the records of the Committee of Surveillance of Provins, on 6 Frimaire, Year II, cited in Blömeke, *Revolutionsregierung und Volksbewegung,* p. 308.

14. Robespierre, *Oeuvres,* vol. 9, ed. Marc Bouloiseau (Paris: Société des Études Robespierristes, 1958), p. 452.

15. Aulard, *La Société des Jacobins,* 5:492.

16. Jeremy D. Popkin, *Revolutionary News: The Press in France, 1789–1792* (Durham: Duke University Press, 1992), p. 171.

17. Bernard Lepetit et al., *Atlas de la Révolution, population* (Paris: EHESS, 1995), 8:31.

18. See Pierre Rosanvallon, *Le Sacre du citoyen* (Paris: Gallimard, 1992), pp. 152–153.

19. Cited in Guilhaumou, *Marseille républicaine*, p. 129.

20. *Réimpression de l'Ancien Moniteur*, vol. 1 (Paris: Plon, 1854), pp. 181 and 183.

21. Alessandro Galante Garrone, *Gilbert Romme: histoire d'un révolutionnaire (1750–1795)* (Paris: Flammarion, 1971), p. 173.

22. The reaction of deputies, who in the course of a parade celebrating the anniversary of the king's death had inadvertently crossed the path of a tumbril on the way to execution, was revealing: they decided to move the guillotine to a more distant site.

23. See Aulard, *Société des Jacobins*, 1:223. For Vannes, see René Kerviler, *Armorique et Bretagne*, vol. 3 (1893), p. 25. See also George Arsmtrong Kelley, "Duelling in Eighteenth-Century France: Archaeology, Rationale, Implications," *The Eighteenth Century*, 21 (1980), p. 3.

24. On November 14, 1790. See Aulard, *La Société des Jacobins*, 1:374–375.

25. Lefebvre, *Bourbourg*, p. 165.

26. *AP*, 64:430.

27. On December 12, 1789. See *AP*, 10:521.

28. On August 5, 1793. See Hugueney, *Dijon*, p. 190, n. 5.

29. Cited in Rosanvallon, *Le Sacre du citoyen*, p. 84.

30. Lefebvre, *Bourbourg*, p. 10.

31. Cited in Desan, "Constitutional Amazons," p. 28.

32. Some of them, like Sieyès, were familiar with the outline of Kant's philosophy.

33. Jean Starobinski, *1789, Les Emblèmes de la raison* (Paris: Flammarion, 1979), p. 32.

34. Cited in F. Furet and M. Ozouf, eds., *Critical Dictionary of the Revolution* (Paris: Flammarion, 1988), p. 793.

35. Cited in his "Rapport sur l'ouverture d'un concours pour les livres élémentaires de la première éducation," in *Oeuvres* (Paris: EDHIS, 1977), 2:188.

36. In his *Essai sur les moyens de faire participer l'universalité des spectateurs à tout ce qui se pratique dans les fêtes nationales* (Paris, 1798–99), p. 5.

37. Cited by Edouard Pommier in Philippe Bordes, ed., *Aux Armes et aux arts!* (Paris: Biro, 1988), p. 175.

38. A Jacobin circular of June 7, 1793, legitimated the constitutionally illegal purge of the Girondins by making reference to Plato, Cicero, and Seneca. Literally thousands of other examples could be brought to bear here, like Hérault de Séchelles's request to the National Library that a copy of the laws of the Medes and the Persians be required reading for the Convention's legislative committee!

39. Cited in Kennedy, *The Jacobin Clubs,* 2:43.

40. Cited by Kates, *Cercle Social,* p. 231.

41. In his *Memoirs* (Paris: Dupont, 1837), 1:346.

42. On November 24, 1793. See Heitz, *Strasbourg,* p. 302.

43. A first step at Montpellier had been the suggestion on July 26, 1791, that a sign be affixed to the statue of Louis XIV to remind spectators that the royal statue had been preserved only for "la beauté de l'ouvrage." Archives Départementales de l'Hérault, L 5498.

44. See Lemarchand, *La Fin du féodalisme dans le pays de Caux,* p. 478, for a discussion of Eu.

45. Bibliothèque Municipale de Poitiers, S 3.

46. Pommier, *Aux Armes et aux arts,* p. 177.

47. Populist dechristianizing celebrations often went through three phases: a parade ridiculing clerical vestments and dumb animals (especially donkeys); a moment when revolutionaries would rid themselves of older vestments and appear in revolutionary costumes: and a last paroxysm of destruction when the vestments were set on fire.

48. I must confess to having had extremely mixed feelings while reading books taken from executed collectors and placed in the Bibliothèque de l'Arsenal.

49. Archives Départementales du Vaucluse, 6 L 12 (12 Messidor, Year II [June 30, 1794]).

50. On November 20, 1793. See Lucien Guillemaut, *Petite Histoire illustrée de la Révolution dans le Louhannais, 1789–1800* (Louhans: Romand, 1906), p. 46.

51. See Chapter 10.

52. Described by Grégoire in his "Rapport et projet de décret sur les moyens d'améliorer l'agriculture en France, par l'établissement d'une maison d'économie rurale dans chaque département," in September 1793; see his *Oeuvres,* 2:7–8.

53. See Marcel David, *Fraternité et Révolution française, 1789–1799* (Paris: Aubier, 1987).

5. The Indisputable Claims of the Nation

1. Marcel Gauchet has written fruitfully on the "ontological independence of the political body" in *Le Désenchantement du monde, une histoire politique de la religion* (Paris: Gallimard, 1985).

2. "La patrie . . . la mère commune . . ." See Émile Le Gallo, "Les Jacobins de Cognac," *La Révolution française,* 43, no. 3 (September 1902), p. 240.

3. For an overview, see Anthony Smith, *National Identity* (Harmondsworth: Penguin, 1991). Linda Colley's *Britons* is a particularly useful example of this renewed literature.

4. At "Aigues Vives" in February 1791. See Archives Départementales de l'Hérault, L 5531.

5. Robespierre, *Discours sur l'inviolabilité royale*, July 14, 1791, in *Oeuvres complètes*, vol. 7 (Paris: Société des Études Robespierristes, 1950), p. 555.

6. On July 14, 1790. See Paul Nicolle, *Histoire de Vire pendant la Révolution* (Vire: Peaufils, 1923), p. 85.

7. Explained, for example, by Jean-Baptiste Leclerc, in his *Essai sur la propagation de la musique en France, sa conservation et ses rapports avec le gouvernement* (Paris: Imprimerie Nationale, 1796).

8. Instead of the traditional "petits pois à la française," or a "filet de boeuf à la française," Barras, in a *Carte Dinatoire* of Ventôse, Year IV, offered his guests a "Glace Nationale."

9. The Montellier *clubbistes* suggested on June 28, 1791, the creation of "une décoration [nationale] à la place de la croix de Saint-Louis." Archives Départementales de l'Hérault, L 5498.

10. Kennedy, *The Jacobin Clubs*, p. 265. Norman Hampson, *Saint-Just* (London: Blackwell, 1991), p. 60.

11. On the emergence of a two-France model during the *monarchie censitaire*, see Roger Chartier, "The Two Frances," in *Cultural History* (Ithaca: Cornell University Press, 1988).

12. Heitz, *Strasbourg*, pp. 42–43.

13. Dagobert Fischer, *La Société populaire de Saverne pendant les années 1791 à 1794* (Mulhouse, 1869), p. 36.

14. On Jacobinism and Judaism, see Chapter 7.

15. René Moulinas, *Les Juifs du pape en France* (Paris: Privat, 1981), p. 453.

16. On March 13, 1794. See *AP*, 86:440.

17. See Jean-Claude Halpern, "Le mouvement populaire et l'abolition de l'esclavage en l'an II," in Michel Vovelle, ed., *L'Image de la Révolution française* (Paris: Pergamon, 1990), p. 174.

18. On October 25, 1793. See Annat, *Basses Pyrénées*, p. 268.

19. On June 11, 1793. *La Vedette de Besançon*, no. 44, p. 349.

20. On November 17, 1791. See J. Mathez, "Pontarlier sous la Révolution," *Révolution française*, 10 (1885–86), p. 2036.

21. On February 1, 1793. Archives Départementales du Vaucluse, L 8143.

22. In June 1791 some clubs (in Dunkirk, for example) had convoked primary assemblies in the aftermath of the flight of the king. Lefebvre, *Bourbourg*, p. 16.

23. In July of 1791, after the king's flight to Varennes, Laclos proposed to Parisian Jacobins a kind of plebiscite on the future of the king. He recommended a petition be circulated nationally by local Jacobins, which for good measure might be signed on separate lists by women and children too. Ten million signatures, he thought, could be so secured.

24. Furet, *Penser la Révolution*, p. 86.

25. When Robespierre defended the clubs on September 29, 1791, against Barnave's majority (which wanted to cripple them), he did so with the loud support of spectators in the gallery. The historian Taine wrongly attached a great deal of importance to this tolerance of street pressure. See his *Les Origines de la France contemporaine* (Paris: Robert Laffont, 1986).

26. Kennedy, *The Jacobin Clubs*, 1:277–278.

27. In a circular dated January 18, 1793, Archives Départementales du Vaucluse, 8 L 43: "L'appel au peuple est un déchirement de notre unité et indivisibilité . . . ils veulent nous perdre en perdant le centre de notre souveraineté."

28. See Lucien Jeaume, "Garantir les droits de l'homme," *La Revue Tocqueville*, 14, no. 1 (1993), p. 54.

29. On September 6, 1791. Archives Départementales des Bouches-du-Rhône, L 2026.

30. In a message from the Loudun Society, on August 1, 1791. Bibliothèque Municipale de Poitiers, S 19.

31. Antoine-Jean Bonnemain, *Institut républicain, ou Développement analytique des facultés naturelles, civiles, et politiques de l'homme* (Paris: Imprimerie du Cercle Social, 1792), p. 13, cited in Kates, *Cercle Social*, p. 264.

32. Labroue, *Bergerac*, p. 199.

33. On March 23, 1791. Cited in Jovy, *Documents sur la Société populaire de Vitry-le-François*, p. 7.

34. *Social Contract*, bk. 2, chap. 12.

35. In January 1792. See Nicolle, *Vire*, p. 188.

36. Sieyes's inclination to constitution mongering and to representative rather than direct government is the most non-Jacobin aspect of his thinking.

37. Guilhaumou, *Marseille républicaine*, p. 185.

38. André Fribourg, "Le Club des Jacobins en 1790," *Révolution française*, 59 (1910), p. 75.

39. In his speech of 17 Pluviôse, Year II (February 4, 1794).

40. On December 12, 1789. Archives Départementales de l'Héraut, L 5531, Bédarieux.

41. In 1795 Sieyès proposed the creation of a "jury constitutionnaire" whose task it would be to conserve the laws, but the Convention refused to approve it. See Baczko, *Comment sortir de la Terreur* (Paris: Gallimard, 1989), p. 343.

42. On March 13, 1794. See *AP*, 86:438.

43. "Quand ils s'isolaient de leur propre ouvrage," in a speech of 1791 on the eligibility of incumbent deputies.

44. Robespierre, *Le Défenseur de la Constitution*, p. 328.

45. Bibliothèque Municipale de Poitiers, S 23.

46. Aulard, *La Société des Jacobins*, 5:263.

47. Bibliothèque Municipale de Poitiers, December 19, 1791.

48. On July 21, 1791, at Tulle. See Seilhac, *Scènes et portraits de la Révolution en bas-Limousin*, p. 450.

49. On 1 Brumaire, Year II. Hugueney, *Dijon,* pp. 157–158, n. 2.

50. On October 4, 1793. See Léonard Thiot, *Les Sociétés populaires de Beauvais* (Beauvais: Imprimerie du Département de l'Oise, 1910), p. 13.

51. Gérard Walter, *Histoire des Jacobins* (Paris: Aymery Somogy, 1946), p. 137.

52. On June 24, 1792. See Aulard, *La Société des Jacobins,* 4:39.

53. Jovy, *Documents sur la Société populaire de Vitry-le-François,* p. 19.

54. See, for example, Pierre Flottes, "Le Club des Jacobins de Bordeaux et la Monarchie Constitutionnelle, 1790–92," *Révolution française,* 69, nos. 25–26 (July–August 1916), pp. 337–362, esp. p. 351.

55. On August 1, 1791. Archives Départementales de l'Hérault, L 5498.

56. On 4 Frimaire, Year II. See Louis Fochier, *Souvenirs historiques sur Bourgoin* (Vienna: Savigne, 1880), p. 457.

57. Condorcet, on June 1, 1793.

58. On 24 Nivôse, Year II. Archives Départementales du Vaucluse, 6 L 6, Courthézon.

59. On June 27, 1793. Archives Départementales du Vaucluse, 8 L 43, Venasque.

60. Baczko, *Comment sortir de la Terreur,* p. 63.

6. Jacobins as the Free Citizens of a One-Party State

1. On Maréchal, see Peter Brooks, "The Revolutionary Body," in Bernadette Fort, ed., *Fictions of the French Revolution* (Evanston: Northwestern University Press, 1991), and Beatrice Didier, *Ecrire la Revolution* (Paris: Presses Universitaires de France, 1989).

2. As explained by Gueniffey in his *Le Nombre et la raison.*

3. Ibid., p. 253.

4. For the Paris club, these were initially quite high: 12 livres to join and an annual fee of 24 livres, while workers made as little as 2 livres a day.

5. At Fontainebleau, 27 Pluviôse, Year II, cited in Blömeke, *Revolutionsregierung und Volksbewegung,* p. 276.

6. Hugueney, *Dijon,* p. 55, n. 3.

7. Jovy, *Documents sur la Société populaire de Vitry-le-François,* p. 38.

8. On November 3, 1793. See Annat, *Basses Pyrénées,* p. 21.

9. At Chateau-Landon, for example. See Blömeke, *Revolutionsregierung und Volksbewegung,* p. 276.

10. On January 1, 1793. Archives Départementales du Gard, L 2133, Peyrolas.

11. On March 29, 1994. Annat, *Basses Pyrénées,* p. 269.

12. On 9 Brumaire, Year II (October 30, 1793). Ironically the decree which required this publicity was also the one that ordered the women's clubs shut down.

13. Albert Soboul, *La Civilisation et la Révolution française,* 3 vols. (Paris: Arthaud, 1970–1983), 2:338.

14. Brinton, *The Jacobins,* p. 38.

15. Jovy, *Documents sur la Société populaire de Vitry-le-François,* p. 7.

16. On October 18, 1790. See Fernand Martin, *Les Jacobins au village* (Clermont-Ferrand: P. Juliot, 1902), pp. 242–243.

17. Cited in Martin, *Artonne,* pp. 242–243.

18. Walter, *Histoire des Jacobins,* p. 35.

19. Described at the Montpellier Society, September 27, 1793. Archives Départementales de l'Hérault, L 5501.

20. At Lidon, on June 9, 1791: "Paris est le coeur de la République et les blessures faites au coeur sont toujours mortelles." See Seilhac, *Scènes et portraits de la Révolution en bas-Limousin,* p. 411.

21. See Louis de Cardenal, *La Société populaire de Monpazier* (1924), p. 65. This view is also cited and endorsed by Gueniffey, *Le Nombre et la raison,* p. 457.

22. Heitz, *Strasbourg,* p. 261.

23. Cardenal, *La Province pendant la Révolution,* p. 445.

24. Cited in Pierre Serna, *Antonelle, Aristocrate Révolutionnaire, 1747–1817* (Paris: Editions du Félin, 1997), p. 146.

25. As stated at the Mayenne Society: "l'exécrable gouvernement militaire," in A. Galland, *Les Sociétés populaires de Laval et de Mayenne, 1791–1795* (Laval: Lelièvre, 1902), p. 26.

26. On November 30, 1790. Archives Départementales du Tarn, Castres. See also H. Baumont, "La Société populaire de Lunéville," *Annales de l'Est* (1889), p. 2.

27. Maurice Cousin, *Histoire d'un club révolutionnaire à Vesoul* (Dijon, 1922), p. 110, cited in Kennedy, *The Jacobin Clubs,* 1:22.

28. Lemarchand, *La Fin du féodalisme dans le pays de Caux,* p. 475.

29. Alan Forrest, *The Soldiers of the French Revolution* (Durham: Duke University Press, 1990), p. 114.

30. At Carcassonne on 11 Pluviôse, Year II, the club "apporte le secours de la fraternité dans les hôpitaux de l'armée." See J. Mandoul, "Le Club des Jacobins de Carcassonne," *Révolution française,* 43, no. 1 (July 14, 1893), p. 239.

31. François Galabert, *Le Club Jacobin de Montauban: son rôle politique pendant la Constituante* (n.p., n.d.), p. 56. This text also appeared in somewhat different form in *Revue d'histoire moderne et contemporaine,* 1 (1899), pp. 124–168, 236–258, 457–474, and 10 (1900), pp. 5–27, 273–317.

32. Gosset, *Reims,* pp. 7, 25.

33. On 8 Floréal, Year II. See *AP,* 89:412–413.

34. On July 26, 1794, the Poitiers club proposed a subscription to build a frigate that would bear the name *La Vienne.* The Poitevins cited Chambéry and Reims as examples. (Bibliothèque Municipale, S 35.) More ambitious yet, the

clubbistes of the Hérault looked to funding a ship of the line on 20 Ventôse, Year II. Archives Départementales de l'Hérault, L 5531.

35. Historical opinions on this issue differ. Samuel Scott plays down the Jacobin role, which Jean-Paul Bertaud emphasizes. See Scott, *The Response of the Royal Army to the French Revolution: The Role and Development of the Line Army, 1787–1793* (Oxford: Oxford University Press, 1978), p. 100; and Bertaud, *The Army of the French Revolution: From Citizen-Soldiers to Instruments of Power* (Princeton: Princeton University Press, 1988), pp. 31–34. The role of the clubs in naval matters was also important. See William S. Cormack, *Revolution and Political Conflict in the French Navy* (Cambridge: Cambridge University Press, 1995), p. 121.

36. Kennedy, *The Jacobin Clubs*, 2:133.

37. René Ducret, *Les Sans-culottes de Lunéville* (Nancy: Imprimerie Bastien, 1967), p. 27.

38. For some months, in 1793, exporting essential, nonluxury goods was forbidden altogether.

39. Gérard de Puymège, *Chauvin, le soldat laboureur* (Paris: Gallimard, 1993), p. 23.

40. Kennedy, *The Jacobin Clubs*, 2:84.

41. The printing of paper money, which enabled the state to pay its bills for a while, eventually caused destructive hyperinflation.

42. Mandoul, "Le Club des Jacobins de Carcassonne," p. 241.

43. On July 4, 1793, at the *société populaire* of Rennes. Archives Départementales de l'Ille et Vilaine, L 1557.

44. Cited in Kennedy, *The Jacobin Clubs*, 2:19.

45. Ibid., 1:36.

46. Jacques Bernet, "La Sociabilité Jacobine," in Claudine Vidal and Marc Le Pape, eds., *Des Provinciaux en Révolution: le district de Vervins* (Vervins: Société d'Archéologie et d'Histoire de Vervins et de la Thiérarche, 1992), p. 32.

47. At Carcassonne the visiting Conventionnel *en mission*, Chaudron-Rousseau, simply withdrew from the *société populaire* the right to issue these certificates. See Mandoul, "Le Club des Jacobins de Carcassonne," p. 312.

48. On April 25, 1792. See Aulard, *La Société des Jacobins*, 3:527.

49. Robert Anchel, "Les Jacobins de Breteuil," *Révolution française*, 65 (1913).

50. Kennedy, *Marseilles*, p. 127.

51. *Nouvelles politiques*, May 21, 1794.

52. On 13 Thermidor, Year II. See *La Vedette de Besançon*, no. 65, p. 483. Of course this was the same point the Girondins had made before June 1793, when they had faced exclusion. In the words of some deputies, about to be driven from the Convention, all Jacobins should look to the National Assembly in the capital: "Unite yourselves from the ends of the universe, in spirit and in truth, to the National Convention of France . . . If peace and fraternity reign in the Convention, it will reign in Paris, in all the whole country and in

the armies. Then neighboring peoples will unite with you against their tyrants in order to share your happiness." (Cited by Kates, *Cercle Social*, p. 254.)

53. In September 1792 the Convention decided that deputies could not hold any other office, thus making their national function more obvious yet.

54. Cited in Blömeke, *Revolutionsregierung und Volksbewegung*, p. 204, and in Cardenal, *La Province pendant la Révolution*, p. 423.

55. Cited by Raymonde Monnier, "La Dissolution des sociétés populaires parisiennes au printemps de l'an II," *Annales historiques de la Révolution française*, 58, no. 268 (April–June 1987), p. 179.

56. Cited by Cardenal, *La Province pendant la Révolution*, p. 198.

57. François Baque et Antoine Roquette, *Un Village du Littoral au cours des siècles* (Saint-Pons: Frances, 1960), p. 223.

58. This is one of the themes of Lynn Hunt's suggestive *Family Romance of the French Revolution* (Berkeley: University of California Press, 1992).

59. In a speech to the Convention, *AP*, 53:426.

60. "Un jour de deuil," in Vendémiaire, Year III. See Lefebvre, *Bourbourg*, p. 88.

61. On 12 Floréal, Year II. See Léon Bultingaire, *Le Club des Jacobins de Metz* (Paris and Metz: Champion, 1906), p. 12.

62. Antoine de Baecque, *La Gloire et l'effroi: sept morts sous la Terreur* (Paris: Grasset, 1997), p. 167.

63. Robert Darnton, *The Literary Underground of the Old Regime* (Cambridge, Mass.: Harvard University Press, 1982), p. 40.

64. At Guignes, on 4 Pluviôse, Year II. Cited in Blömeke, *Revolutionsregierung und Volksbewegung*, p. 302.

7. Social Reconciliation

1. Guillemaut, *Petite Histoire illustrée de la Révolution dans le Louhannais*, p. 46.

2. *AP*, 72:677.

3. Hyacinthe Chobaut, *La Société populaire d'Aigues Vives* (Nîmes: Chastanier, 1924), p. 19.

4. A rare exception came in a speech by Clavière to the Paris club on September 13, 1790, in which he refuted a pamphlet by Dupont de Nemours. Clavière humorously described a patriotic lady's reaction to this economic text, murmuring as she did at every phrase, "Dupont, mon ami, qui t'a fait si..." Cited in Fribourg, *Le club des Jacobins en 1790*, p. 76.

5. Denis, *Toul*, p. 15.

6. Bibliothèque Municipales de Poitiers, S 1 (July 1790). The instinct of complementarity which incited some Jacobins to suppose—to the distress of the interested parties—that the deaf-mute and the blind might be housed in a single building would be comic if it were not so cruel.

7. Archives Départementales de l'Hérault, L 5531. By a *commissaire civil* to the citizens of Bédarieux, as reported to the club in May 1792.

8. In 1793. See Murray Forsyth, *Reason and Revolution: The Political Thought of the Abbé Sieyès* (New York: Leicester University Press, 1987), p. 122.

9. In his *Palingénésie philosophique.*

10. Cited in Antoine de Baecque, *Le Corps de l'histoire, métaphores et politique (1770–1800)* (Paris: Calmann-Lévy, 1993), pp. 118–119.

11. On November 13, 1792. See *AP,* 53:392.

12. On December 26, 1791. See Seilhac, *Scènes et portraits de la Révolution en bas-Limousin,* p. 367.

13. Francisque Mège, *Le Puy-de-Dôme et 1793 et le pro-consulat de Couthon* (Paris: Aubry, 1877), p. 257.

14. Cardenal, *La Province pendant la Révolution,* pp. 393–394.

15. On 6 Frimaire, Year II. Couthon was "jaloux de ramener la paix et la concorde partout où autrefois l'on ne voyait respirer que la haine, et de ne laisser aucune trace de ce qui pourrait rappeler des souvenirs qu'il importe d'éteindre pour établir le règne de la fraternité." *Correspondance de Georges Couthon* (Paris: Aubry, 1872), p. 306.

16. In the founding document of the club at Béziers.

17. On August 4, 1791. Archives Départementales du Vaucluse, 6 L 6, Courthézon.

18. On April 15, 1791. See *AP,* 25:115. I owe this note to Nina Kaplan.

19. Walter, *Histoire des Jacobins,* p. 165.

20. Martin, *Artonne,* p. 75.

21. In Prairial, Year II. M. Brégail, *La Société populaire d'Auch et les sociétés affiliées* (Paris: Imprimerie Nationale, 1912), p. 79.

22. On December 26, 1793 (6 Nivôse, Year II).

23. At the time the Convention debated outlawing the use of *vous* altogether. This it did not do, but *tutoiement* nonetheless became the standard form of Jacobin address in both private and public correspondence.

24. *Les Révolutions de Paris* in April 1791, cited by Christian Bosseno, "Acteurs et spectateurs," in *Fêtes de la Révolution* (Paris: Direction Arististique de la Ville de Paris, 1989), p. 112.

25. Galabert, *Le Club de Montauban,* p. 81.

26. On 10 Nivôse, Year II. Bultingaire, *Metz,* p. 66.

27. On 9 Germinal, Year II, at Bourg-en-Bresse. See *AP,* 87:561–562.

28. James Johnson, *Listening in Paris* (Berkeley: University of California Press, 1995), p. 154.

29. Charles Rosen, *The Romantic Generation* (Cambridge, Mass.: Harvard University Press, 1995), p. 602.

30. Charles Constant, *Histoire d'un club jacobin en province pendant la Révolution* (Paris: Champion, 1875).

31. *AP,* 59:588.

32. On 21 Pluviôse, Year III. See Edouard Poumeau, *La Société populaire de Périgueux pendant la Révolution* (Périgueux: Joucle, 1907), p. 8.

33. As at Carcassonne. See Mandoul, "Le Club des Jacobins de Carcassonne," p. 239.

34. A. Fray-Fournier, *Le Club des Jacobins de Limoges* (Limoges: Vauzelle, 1903), pp. 14–27, cited in Kennedy, *The Jacobin Clubs*, 1:127–128.

35. Kennedy, *The Jacobin Clubs*, 1:99.

36. On October 24, 1790. Méjanes MS. 872.

37. Bibliothèque Municipale de Poitiers, S 23.

38. At Confolens, on January 9, 1791. L. Babaud-Laribière, *Lettres charentaises: études historiques et administratives* (Marseilles: Laffilte, 1979), p. 88.

39. On June 19, 1790, in Paul Nicolle, *Histoire de Vire pendant la Révolution* (Vire: Beaufils, 1923), p. 81.

40. Labroue, *Toulon*, p. 45.

41. Kennedy, *Marseilles*, p. 66.

42. Chobaut, *Aigues Vives*, p. 18.

43. Heitz, *Strasbourg*, p. 178.

44. Félix Ponteil, "La Société populaire des antipolitiques d'Aix-en-Provence d'après des documents inédits," *Revue historique de la Révolution française et de l'Empire*, 13–15 (1918–1923), 13:30–47, 266–290, 454–474, 577–589; 14:40–45, 263–271; 15:16–26, 146–161.

45. Kennedy, *The Jacobin Clubs*, 1:287.

46. Cited in Cardenal, *La Province pendant la Révolution*, p. 176.

47. Brégail, *La Société populaire d'Auch et les sociétés affiliées*, p. 6.

48. Ducret, *Lunéville*, p. 31.

49. See Judith Schlanger, *Métaphores de l'organisme* (Paris: Vrin, 1971), pp. 42–45, cited in Baecque, *Le Corps de l'histoire*, p. 17.

50. On October 5, 1792. See Kennedy, *The Jacobin Clubs*, 2:296.

51. On 16 Pluviôse, Year II. Archives Municipales de Gaillac, 2 I 1: "Il tient à une famille qui nous a toujours donné des marques d'un patriotisme pur et éclairé."

52. Cited by Bernard Lehembre, *Naissance de l'école moderne, les textes fondamentaux, 1791–1804* (Paris: Nathan, 1989), p. 105.

53. Roger Tissot, *Société populaire de Grenoble* (Grenoble: Jules Rey, 1910), pp. 186–187.

54. In February 1791 in Aigues Vives. See Archives Départementales de l'Hérault, L 5531.

55. Archives Départementales de l'Ille et Vilaine, L 1557.

56. On May 9, 1793. See François Aulard, ed., *Recueil des actes du Comité de Salut Public*, vol. 4 (Paris: Imprimerie Nationale, 1891), p. 76.

57. Cited in Raoul Girardet, *Mythes et mythologies politiques* (Paris: Seuil, 1986), p. 147.

58. In August 1793. See Henri Labroue, "Les Évêques Torné et Pontard et la société populaire de Périgueux," *Révolution française,* 61 (September 1911), p. 231.

59. At Pau, on November 21, 1793, they named commissaries to escort a young man to his aged father's home "pour lui rappeler ses devoirs que lui impose la nature envers celui qui lui a donné le jour." Annat, *Basses Pyrénées,* p. 206.

60. Antonin Soucaille, *Historique de la société populaire de Béziers d'après les procès-verbaux de ses séances 3 juillet 1790–30 ventôse an 3 (20 mars 1795)* (Béziers: Sapte, 1892), pp. 75–76.

61. See Seilhac, *Scènes et portraits de la Révolution en bas-Limousin,* p. 512.

62. *AP,* 91:213.

63. On July 7, 1792. Bibliothèque Municipale de Poitiers, S 23.

64. On December 25, 1790. Archives Départementales de l'Hérault, L 5531.

65. On December 26, 1791. Hugueney, *Dijon,* p. 145.

66. Cited in Walter, *Histoire des Jacobins,* p. 237.

67. They did not like badinage. There are no Jacobin counterparts to the subversive jokes that were so common in modern totalitarian states.

68. On July 12, 1793. *La Vedette de Besançon,* no. 54, p. 425.

69. On March 22, 1793. See Thiot, *Beauvais,* p. 69.

70. On July 14, 1794. See *AP,* 94:154.

71. P. Butet-Hamel, "La Société populaire de Vire pendant la Révolution," *Comité des travaux historiques: bulletin historique et philologique* (1900), p. 23.

72. Cited in Desan, "Constitutional Amazons," p. 12.

73. *Correspondance de Georges Couthon,* p. 302.

74. As described in his *Cahiers, 1716–1755* (Paris: Grasset, 1941), p. 236.

75. On March 21, 1793. See *AP,* 60:411.

76. On October 6, 1793. Henriot, *Semur,* p. 286.

77. For a sensitive description of this painting, see Abigail Solomon-Godeau, *Male Trouble: A Crisis in Representation* (New York: Thames and Hudson, 1997), pp. 134–139.

78. On 26 Messidor, Year II. See *La Vedette de Besançon,* no. 56, p. 444.

79. *Mercure Universel,* June 17, 1793.

80. Denis, *Toul,* p. 57.

81. Labroue, "Périgueux," p. 233.

82. See "Sodomie," in Condorcet, *Oeuvres complètes,* ed. D. Garat and P. Cabanis, vol. 7 (Paris, 1802), p. 374, cited in Lynn Hunt, *The French Revolution and Human Rights* (Boston: St. Martin's Press, 1996), p. 31, n. 10.

83. On September 4, 1793. Archives Départementales de l'Hérault, L 5501.

84. As explained by Joan Landes in a forthcoming work.

85. On September 26, 1793. See "Point Central des arts et métiers . . . composé de tous artistes vrai sans-culottes." Archives Nationales, AD series VIII, 40, T.1 pièce 18.

86. On September 16, 1790. Henriot, *Semur,* p. 113.

87. On July 29, 1791. Forot, *Tulle,* p. 130.

88. Much is to be said for François Furet's view of Jacobinism as an "anonymous oligarchy" where interchangeable and mediocre men like Brissot, Danton, and Robespierre were less the leaders of the Jacobin movement than the (inconsequential) effects of a Jacobin turn of mind. And since Jacobin words had become a self-referential discourse, increasingly meaningless words could—and were—mouthed by nearly anyone, regardless of intrinsic talent. See his *Penser la Révolution,* p. 228.

89. In the *Manuel du laboureur et de l'artisan* (spring 1792), quoted in Guilhaumou, *Marseille républicaine,* p. 85.

90. Cited in Saint-Just, *Discours et rapports,* ed. Albert Soboul (Paris: Editions Sociales, 1957), p. 208.

91. In a speech of May 10, 1793, to the Convention, *AP,* 64:429.

92. On April 13, 1791. Annat, *Basses Pyrénées,* p. 81.

93. At Guéret the *sociétaires* wore mourning clothes at his memorial service. See Chervy and Chervy, "La Société populaire de Guéret," p. 429.

94. Pierre Flottes, "Le Club des jacobins de Bordeaux et la monarchie constitutionnelle," *Révolution française,* 69, nos. 25–26 (July–August 1916), p. 341.

95. Kennedy, *The Jacobin Clubs,* 2:304.

96. Cardenal, *La Province pendant la Révolution,* p. 96.

97. Kennedy, *The Jacobin Clubs,* 2:340.

98. Archives Départementales de l'Hérault, L 5501, September 7, 1793; and L 5501, October 11, 1793.

99. On 8 Frimaire, Year II. Archives Départementales du Vaucluse, 6 L 6, Courthézon.

100. Danièle Pingué, "L'Implantation des sociétés populaires," *Annales historiques de la Révolution française,* 58 (1986), pp. 394–421.

101. Robert Anchel, "Les Jacobins de Breteuil-sur-Hon, (Eure)," *Révolution française,* 45 (1913), p. 494.

102. On 27 Prairial, Year II, and 10 Germinal, Year II. Archives Départementales du Vaucluse, 6 L 6, Courthézon.

103. Grégoire, *Apologie de Barthélémy de Las-Casas* (1800), cited in Plongeron, *L'Abbé Grégoire,* p. 7.

104. In 1791 or 1792. See Norman Hampson, *Saint-Just* (Oxford: Basil Blackwell, 1991), pp. 33–34.

105. In September 1792 at Montpellier. Archives Départementales de l'Hérault, L 5500.

106. In October 1793. Cited by Albert Kuscisnki, *Dictionnaire des Conventionnels* (Paris: Rieder, 1917), p. 147.

107. On 8 Thermidor. Cited by Albert Ollivier, *Saint-Just et la force des choses* (Paris: Gallimard, 1954), pp. 504–505.

108. Anne-Marie Duport, "Recherches sur la Terreur a Nîmes et dans son district" (unpublished thesis, Paris 1 [Panthéon] University, 1984), p. 292.

109. Michael Kennedy, "The 'Last Stand' of the Jacobin Clubs," *French Historical Studies*, 16, no. 2 (fall 1989), p. 320.

110. Félix Clérembray, *La Terreur à Rouen* (Rouen: Lestringant, 1901), p. 424.

111. On November 24, 1793. Martin, *Artonne*, p. 87.

112. On March 27, 1791. Archives Départementales du Vaucluse, 6 L 6, Courthézon.

113. Cited in Blömeke, *Revolutionsregierung und Volksbewegung*, p. 299.

114. In October 1792 the clubs praised Benjamin Franklin for having consolidated liberty in his fatherland by creating "des écoles de civisme," namely, patriotic societies, where he laid the groundwork for "la constitution sublime des Américains."

115. The words of a clerical *clubbiste* of Beauvais in December 1791. See Kennedy, *The Jacobin Clubs*, 2:9.

116. At Gueret on May 25, 1794 (6 Prairial, Year II). See Chervy and Chervy, "La Société populaire de Guéret," p. 76.

117. Labroue, "La Mission de Lakanal dans la Dordogne en l'an II," *Révolution française*, 69 (May–June 1916), pp. 225–242.

118. Grégoire, June 17, 1794. Cited from Bernard Lehembre, *Naissance de l'école moderne, les textes fondamentaux, 1791–1804* (Paris: Nathan, 1989), p. 90.

119. Collot argued that excessive erudition was incompatible with republicanism, and Robespierre criticized Condorcet's proposals (which were designed to identify unusual talent) as "aristocratic."

120. G. Sprigath, "Sur le Vandalisme révolutionnaire," *Annales historiques de la Révolution française*, 52 (1908), pp. 522–523.

121. Cited by Lynn Hunt, *Family Romance*, p. 75.

122. On 27 Thermidor, Year II. See A. Galland, *Les Sociétés populaires de Laval et de Mayenne, 1791–1795* (Laval: Lelièvre, 1902), p. 27.

123. *La Vedette de Besançon*, nos. 62–63, pp. 489–491.

8. Spreading the Word

1. Kennedy, *The Jacobin Clubs*, 2:103.

2. Cardenal, *La Province pendant la Révolution*, p. 376.

3. Michel Vovelle, *La Révolution contre l'Église* (Brussels: Editions Complexe, 1988), p. 224, cited in Olwen Hufton, *Women and the Limits of Citizenship in the French Revolution* (Toronto: University of Toronto Press, 1992), p. 111, n. 24.

4. Jean Falconetti, "Un Aéronaute patriote en 1791," *Révolution française*, 29 (March 14, 1910), p. 271.

5. Cited by Kates, *Cercle Social*, p. 180.

6. On July 3, 1793. Annat, *Basses Pyrénées*, p. 23.

7. On February 26, 1793: "Lisez les journaux anglais!" Kuscinski, *Dictionnaire*, p. 25.

8. For an excellent survey of the field, see Jack Censer, *The French Press in the Age of the Enlightenment* (London: Routledge, 1994).

9. In May 1792. Kates, *Cercle Social*, p. 228.

10. In 1783 he was already of the mind that "the Correspondence which we are announcing . . . will form [a] center where all the ideas, the observations, the facts, the projects relative to the happiness of the individual and society will come together; from there, Enlightenment will spread and circulate throughout Europe." Cited in Goodman, *The Republic of Letters*, p. 283. Regarding newspapers versus clubs, see Kates, *Cercle Social*, p. 177 (August 2, 1791).

11. On March 23, 1791. Jovy, *Documents sur la Société populaire de Vitry-le-François*, p. 7.

12. See Hugh Gough, *The Newspaper Press in the French Revolution* (London: Routledge, 1989), p. 107.

13. See Albert Mathiez, *Annales révolutionnaires* (1918).

14. Aulard's reconstitution of the debates of the Paris Jacobin club is heavily dependent on newspaper accounts.

15. Hugh Gough, "The Provincial Jacobin Club Press during the French Revolution," *European History Quarterly*, 16 (1986), p. 51.

16. See Melvin Edelstein, *La Feuille villageoise: communication et information dans les régions rurales pendant la Révolution française* (Paris: Commission d'Histoire Économique, 1977).

17. Cited in Blömeke, *Revolutionsregierung und Volksbewegung*, p. 282.

18. Godineau, *Citoyennes tricoteuses*, p. 217.

19. It was eventually supplanted by Lequinio's *Journal des laboureurs*.

20. Blömeke, *Revolutionsregierung und Volksbewegung*, p. 279. In the department as a whole, the *Journal de la Montagne* counted 79 subscribers. See also Harvey Chisick, "Politics and Journalism in the French Revolution," *French History*, 5 (1991), p. 355.

21. Thomas Carlyle, *The French Revolution*, part 2, bk. 1, chap. 5.

22. On October 12, 1792. See L'abbé Gros, *Le Club des Jacobins de Saint-Jean-de-Maurienne* (Saint-Jean de Maurienne: Imprimerie J. Salomon, 1908), p. 7.

23. Kennedy, *Marseilles*, p. 64.

24. Cited in Kuscinski, *Dictionnaire*, p. 16.

25. Furet, *Interpreting the French Revolution*, p. 130.

26. Consider Roland's letter of July 29, 1792, to the Jacobin club of Beauvais: "Pardonnez, mes frères, ces long épanchements d'un coeur pénétré; je réponds aux expressions affectueuses que vous avez bien voulu m'adresser; c'est

vous qui m'avez ainsi autorisé à vous répéter encore une fois à tous avec l'abandon de la confiance . . . aimons nous, puisque nous sommes frères . . . soyons prêts à mourir pour être invincibles." See L. Thiot, "Roland et les Jacobins de Beauvais," *Révolution française*, 58, no. 8 (February 14, 1910), p. 165.

27. Archives Départementales du Vaucluse, 6 L 6.

28. Camille Desmoulins, *Histoire secrète*, in *Oeuvres*, vol. 1 (Paris: Charpentier, 1874), p. 349.

29. Albert Maurat-Bellange, *Une Commune de la Haute-Vienne pendant la Révolution, 1790–1795* (Limoges: Ducourtieux, 1910), p. 54.

30. On this theme, see Peter Brooks, *The Melodramatic Imagination: Balzac, Henry James, Melodrama, and the Mode of Excess* (New Haven: Yale University Press, 1976).

31. Cited in Cardenal, *La Province pendant la Révolution*, p. 151.

32. On September 26, 1791. In an address to the Paris Jacobins, cited in Grégoire, *Oeuvres*, 4:149.

33. Cited in Edmonds, *Jacobinism and the Revolt of Lyon*, p. 288.

34. Cited in Cardenal, *La Province pendant la Révolution*, p. 294.

35. "Ce que la mousse est aux végétaux, ce que la rouille est aux métaux." In Grégoire, *Oeuvres*, 4:236.

36. As described in Mirzoeff, *Silent Poetry*, p. 47. One young deaf-mute dedicated his *Almanach de la raison pour l'an II* to the embattled Jacobins because his aim was "to give to youth an ideal of the natural religion of the *honnête homme*."

37. Stephanie Caroll, "David and Theater," *Art in America* (May 1990), p. 203.

38. On February 15, 1793. See *AP*, 54:27–28.

39. In his "Rapport sur le gouvernement révolutionnaire," cited in Alain Liénard, ed., *Théorie politique* (Paris: Seuil, 1976), p. 244.

40. See Marie-Hélène Huet, "Performing Arts: Theatricality and the Terror," in James Heffernan, ed., *Representing the French Revolution, Literature, Historiography, Art* (Hanover: University Press of New England, 1992).

41. Bibliothèque Municipale de Poitiers, S 19. In August 1792: "Vous n'y trouverez point d'éloquence. Je ne m'attache qu'aux vérités capables de faire sensation et de détruire les maux et les dangers dont le fanatisme et l'ignorance nous environnent sans cesse."

42. Jovy, *Documents sur la Société populaire de Vitry-le-François*, p. 8.

43. *Annales patriotiques*, May 5–10, 1792, cited in Kennedy, *The Jacobin Clubs*, 2:251.

44. Grégoire, "Discours . . . au service célébré par les citoyens morts à Paris le 10 août," in *Oeuvres*, 4:226.

45. On 15 Ventôse. See Soboul, *Mouvement populaire*, pp. 261–262.

46. Félix Ponteil, "La Société populaire des antipolitiques d'Aix-en-Provence d'après des documents inédits," *Revue historique de la Révolution française et de l'Empire*, 10 (1916–1918), p. 278.

47. Marc-Antoine Julien, in the Paris club, on August 30, 1793.

48. Cited by Cardenal, *La Province pendant la Révolution,* p. 9.

49. Billaud-Varennes, on November 18, 1793, *AP,* 79:458.

50. Starobinski, *1789, Les Emblèmes de la raison,* p. 45.

51. Aix, Bibliothèque Méjanes MS 872, October 23, 1790, p. 265.

52. On 13 Messidor, Year II (July 1, 1794). See *AP,* 92:315.

53. Urbain Domergue, "Adresse aux Communes et aux Sociétés populaires de la République française," in Guillaume, *Procès verbaux d'instruction publique de la Convention Nationale,* vol. 3 (Paris, 1897), pp. 444–448. See also Françoise Dougnac, *François-Urbain Domergue: le grammairien patriote, 1745–1810* (Tübingen: Gunter Narr, 1992).

54. Described by Philippe Bordes in his talk at the 1996 College Art Association meeting.

55. On this issue, see Michel de Certeau, Dominique Julia, and Jacques Revel, *Une Politique de la langue: la Révolution française et les patois—l'enquête de Grégoire* (Paris: Gallimard, 1975); and Patrice Higonnet, "The Politics of Linguistic Terrorism and Grammatical Hegemony in the French Revolution," *Social History,* 5, no. 1 (1980), pp. 41–69.

56. On 18 Prairial, Year II (June 6, 1794). See *Reimpression de l'Ancien Moniteur,* 20:648.

57. Cited by Jacques Guilhaumou, "Antoine Tournon et la grammaire des sans-culottes (1794)," *LINX,* 15 (1987), pp. 46–47.

58. Explained by William Sewell in a forthcoming publication.

59. In his tract *Des effets de la Terreur.*

60. Robespierre and Saint-Just would surely have seen the merit of Derrida's definition of texts as self-enclosed and self-referential statements that are only incidentally connected to historical reality: "reading . . . cannot legitimately transgress the text towards something other than it, towards a referent (a reality that is metaphysical, historical, psychobiographical, etc.) or towards a signified outside the text whose content could take place, could have taken place, outside of language, that is to say, in the sense that we give here to the word outside of writing in general [*Il n'y a pas de hors-texte*]." Jacques Derrida, *Of Grammatology,* trans. Gaytri Spivak (Baltimore: Johns Hopkins University Press, 1976), p. 158. Derrida's message, though ordinarily absurd, unfortunately makes a lot of sense for the Jacobins' words of 1793–94.

61. Thomas Crow, *Emulation* (New Haven: Yale University Press, 1995), p. 177.

62. On March 3, 1794. See *AP,* 86:23.

63. Baecque, *Le Corps de l'histoire,* p. 223.

64. Cited in Blömeke, *Revolutionsregierung und Volksbewegung,* p. 288.

65. On March 8, 1793. See Galland, *Laval et Mayenne,* p. 11.

66. Cardenal, *La Province pendant la Révolution,* p. 384.

67. Jonna Kitchin, *Un Journal "philosophique," la décade 1794–1807* (Paris: Lettres Modernes, 1965), p. 6.

68. On 18 Thermidor, Year III. Poumeau, *Périgueux*, p. 31.

69. On 22 Pluviôse, Year II (February 12, 1794). See Eugène Le Roy, *La Société populaire de Montignac* (Bordeaux: Delagrange, 1888), p. 63.

70. Mona Ozouf, *Festivals and the French Revolution* (Cambridge, Mass.: Harvard University Press, 1988), p. 210.

71. J. B. Leclerc, *Essai sur la propagation de la musique en France, sa convention et ses rapports avec le gouvernement* (Paris, Year IV), pp. 62–63, cited in Malcolm Boyd, ed., *Music and the French Revolution* (Cambridge: Cambridge University Press, 1992), p. 218.

72. Jovy, *Documents sur la Société populaire de Vitry-le-François*, p. 16.

73. On July 13, 1791. Fochier, *Bourgoin*, p. 215.

74. On March 13, 1794. See *AP*, 86:436.

75. Cardenal, *La Province pendant la Révolution*, p. 90.

76. Wisely, the Convention eventually decided that no one should be given national honors until ten years after his death.

77. Mirabeau's was removed as well, on December 5, 1792.

78. At Orthez the society's decision was "as they wished." See Annat, *Basses Pyrénées*, p. 353.

79. On December 26, 1791, a member at Dijon had already proposed the *clubbistes* should wear it. See Hugueney, *Dijon*, p. 145.

80. L. Dorey, "La Société populaire et Républicaine de Montaigut-en-Combrailles," *Révolution française*, 59 (December 14, 1910), pp. 533–551.

81. "Soit remise dans sa plus grande rigueur." Cited in Mandoul, "Le Club des Jacobins de Carcassonne," p. 240.

82. See Ewa Lajer-Burcharth, "David's Sabine Women: Body, Gender, and Republican Culture under the Directory," *Art History*, 14 (1991), pp. 397–430.

83. Kennedy, *The Jacobin Clubs*, 1:163.

84. On 14 Brumaire, Year II. See Seilhac, *Scènes et portraits de la Révolution en bas-Limousin*, p. 426.

85. G. Mutte, *La Société populaire de Lauris (Vaucluse) 11 nov. 1790–16 nivôse an III*, D.E.S. Histoire, Université de Grenoble, Archives Départementales du Vaucluse, microfilm Mi 4, p. 29.

86. On February 3, 1793. See Fischer, *Saverne*, p. 23.

87. Cited by Johnson, *Listening in Paris*, p. 116, who identifies the line from the third act of Calderón de la Barca's *La Vida es sueno* of 1636.

88. Mandoul, "Le Club des Jacobins de Carcassonne," p. 328. The Jacobins of Dreux also asked that citizenesses be forbidden to wear crosses.

89. Archives Départementales de l'Hérault, L 5501.

90. On October 7, 1793. See Guillemaut, *Petite Histoire illustrée de la Révolution dans le Louhannais*, p. 43.

91. Mirzoeff, *Silent Poetry*, p. 55.

92. Brégail, *La Société populaire d'Auch et les sociétés affiliées*, p. 47. At Colmar the club owned a "mortuary tricolor flag." See Paul Leuillot, *Les Jacobins de Colmar* (Paris: Librairie Istra, 1923), p. 444.

93. "Il soit fixé un mode par le conseil général pour rendre aux citoyens les devoirs que l'humanité exige." A councillor would appear "à tour de role" and "remplira cette fonction importante . . . revêtu des signes de la liberté." Archives Municipales de Gaillac, I D (10) 3 (15 Frimaire, Year II).

94. Pommier, *Aux Armes et aux arts*, p. 176.

95. Kennedy, *The Jacobin Clubs*, 2:168.

96. Pommier, *Aux Armes et aux arts*, p. 226.

97. On 23 Messidor, Year II. *La Vedette de Besançon*, no. 55, p. 436.

98. On 11 Ventôse, Year III. Archives Départementales du Vaucluse, 6 L 6.

99. Henry Poulet, *L'Esprit public à Thann pendant la Révolution: la Société des amis de la Constitution* (Thann, 1919), pp. 126–127.

100. Many people assumed that the festival would mark the end of the Terror and a new political beginning.

101. *The Old Regime and the Revolution,* bk. 1, chap. 3.

102. Louis de Bonald, *Oeuvres*, vol. 2 (Paris: Migne, 1859), pp. 930–931.

103. On July 11, 1791. Archives Départementales du Tarn, L 1531.

104. In October 1790. Bibliothèque Municipale de Poitiers, S 1.

105. Kennedy, *The Jacobin Clubs*, 1:85.

106. Chervy and Chervy, "La Société populaire de Guéret," p. 432.

107. On May 2, 1791. Archives Départementales du Vaucluse, 6 L 15.

108. Desmoulins, *Oeuvres,* 1:90, cited in Kates, *Cercle Social,* p. 101.

109. Émile Le Gallo, "Les Jacobins de Cognac," *Révolution française* (September 1902), p. 238.

110. The terms "clerical" and "anticlerical" came into common French usage after 1848. Ironically, Isnard converted to a mystical brand of Roman Catholicism in his postrevolutionary days.

111. Montauban was also one of the clubs with the highest proportion of peasant and artisan members. It had a large number of rich Protestant businessmen and a women's organization. Its politics were radical and, at first, Anglophile.

112. Anne Marie Duport, *Recherches sur la terreur* (Paris: Tourzot, 1987), p. 204.

113. Denis, *Toul,* p. 41.

114. On 11 Germinal, Year II. See Hugueney, *Dijon,* p. 117.

115. On 13 Thermidor, Year II. *La Vedette de Besançon,* no. 61, p. 487.

116. Cited in Aulard, *La Société des Jacobins,* 5:479.

117. These were first described by Albert Mathiez and Crane Brinton.

118. Described by George Rudé, *The Crowd in the French Revolution* (Oxford: Oxford University Press, 1967), p. 476.

119. Eric Goodheart's dissertation at Harvard University on adoption in revolutionary thinking develops this theme in some detail.

120. I am indebted for this idea to David Bell's unpublished paper "*Lingus Populi, Lingus Dei:* Nationalism, Language, and Religion in the French Revolution," given at the American Historical Association meeting in 1995.

121. Cited in Kennedy, *The Jacobin Clubs*, 2:211.

122. Michel Vovelle, *Religion et Révolution: la déchristianisation de l'an II* (Paris: Hachette, 1976), p. 183.

123. Kennedy, *The Jacobin Clubs*, 2:14.

9. Unifying Enmities at Home and Abroad

1. Cited by Lemarchand, *La Fin du féodalisme dans le pays de Caux*, p. 477.

2. Cited by Colin Lucas, "Urban Popular Violence in 1789," in Alan Forrest and Peter Jones, eds., *Reshaping France: Town, Country, and Region during the French Revolution* (Manchester: Manchester University Press, 1991), p. 132.

3. On 11 Messidor, Year II. Eugène Le Roy, *La Société populaire de Montignac, 1791–1795* (Bordeaux, 1888), p. 179.

4. Robespierre, *Le Défenseur de la Constitution*, p. 274.

5. Aulard, *La Société des Jacobins*, 5:222.

6. On March 1, 1791. Kerviler, *Armorique et Bretagne*, p. 58.

7. On 16 Pluviôse, Year II (February 4, 1794). Henriot, *Semur*, p. 336.

8. See Jean-Claude Martin, *Révolution et Contre-Révolution en France de 1789 à 1995* (Rennes: Presses Universitaires de Rennes, 1996).

9. Archives Nationales, F 15 2584.

10. As explained in the *Chronique de Paris* of July 16, 1790, cited in "Le Chantier national," by Valerie Jouffre, in *Fêtes et Révolution* (Paris: Délégation à l'Action Artistique de la Ville de Paris, 1989), p. 52.

11. Poupé, "La Société populaire de Villecroze," pp. 136–137.

12. Mona Ozouf, "'Jacobin' fortune et infortunes d'un mot," in *L'École de la France* (Paris: Gallimard, 1984).

13. On September 18, 1792. Archives Départementales de l'Hérault, L 5500.

14. In the Year III, at Tulle. See Seilhac, *Scènes et portraits de la Révolution en bas-Limousin*, p. 704.

15. Jacques Guilhaumou, "A Discourse of Denunciation," in Keith Baker, ed., *The Terror* (London: Pergamon, 1994), p. 141.

16. See *La Chronique de Paris*, no. 75, for November 6, 1789, cited in Claude Labrosse and Pierre Rétat, *Naissance du journal révolutionnaire* (Lyons: Presses Universitaires de Lyon, 1989), p. 201.

17. Guilhaumou, "Discourse of Denunciation," p. 142.

18. On June 4, 1794. Denis, *Toul*, p. 94.

19. "I denounce Germany / Portugal and Spain / Mexico and Champagne / The Limagne and Peru / I denounce Italy / Africa and the Turks / England and Russia / Inclusive of Moscow too." Alphonse Jouet, *Les Clubs, leur histoire et leur rôle depuis 1789* (Paris: Girard, 1891), p. 36.

20. Edmonds, *Jacobinism and the Revolt of Lyon*, p. 222.

21. The club at Lescar did on January 23, 1794. See Annat, *Basses Pyrénées,* p. 309.

22. At Lausanne, in 1795, the embittered victims of the Lyonese Jacobins printed a list of their persecutors and denunciators together with their addresses.

23. *Réimpression de l'Ancien Moniteur,* 22:487.

24. The Conventionnel Auguis, quoted in Kuscinski, *Dictionnaire,* p. 14.

25. At Courthézon, on 28 Frimaire, Year II, in a letter to the Paris club: "Nous l'avons purifié de toute la crasse de l'aristocratie." Archives Départementales du Vaucluse.

26. At Nérac and Saint-Girons. See Kennedy, *The Jacobin Clubs,* 2:280.

27. Ibid., 2:305.

28. He was murderous as well. See Baecque, *Le Corps de l'histoire,* p. 348.

29. *AP,* 54:121.

30. On November 15, 1792. See *AP,* 53:427.

31. The Academician Morellet was denounced by his washerwoman for being unhappy, presumably, about the course of events. See his *Mémoires sur le dix-huitième siècle et la Révolution,* with an introduction by Pierre Guicciardi (Paris: Mercure de France, 1988), p. 384.

32. Suggestively, Freud equated decapitation and emasculation. The scientifically minded Jacobin mechanically cleanses the body politic by decapitating or emasculating the falsely virile *aristocrate.*

33. As such, Jacobin cartoons were much closer to the bitter traditions of British mockery displayed in the ferocious works of Hogarth and Gilray than to edulcorated prerevolutionary French cartoons.

34. Kennedy, *Marseilles,* p. 183.

35. See, for example, letters written to the Convention after her death by the clubs at Garlin, near Pau in the Pyrénées, and at Rozoy, in the Seine-et-Marne, close to Paris. Cited in Hector Fleischmann, *Marie-Antoinette, libertine* (Paris: Bibliothèque des Curieux, 1911), p. 76.

36. In a cartoon entitled "La Fuite du roi, ou l'égout royal," reproduced in Antoine de Baecque, *La Caricature révolutionnaire* (Paris: CNRS, 1989), p. 180.

37. Edmonds, *Jacobinism and the Revolt of Lyon,* p. 215.

38. On 12 Thermidor, Year II. See Galland, *Laval et Mayenne,* p. 26.

39. *AP,* 98:255.

40. On March 1, 1792, in a circular from the Paris club to its affiliates. Bibliothèque Municipale de Poitiers, S 23.

41. On October 13, 1790. Bibliothèque Municipale de Poitiers, S 1. On November 29, 1790, the Paris society circularized its affiliates about this issue also.

42. On November 15, 1793. See Baumont, "La Société populaire de Lunéville," p. 345.

43. Kennedy, *The Jacobin Clubs,* 2:123.

44. Cited by Guilhaumou, *Marseille républicaine,* p. 240.

45. Archives Départementales du Vaucluse, 8 L 43.

46. In Pluviôse, Year II. Louis de Cardenal, *Les Sociétés populaires de Monpazier, 1790–1795 (Dordogne)* (Lille: Marquant, 1924), pp. 31–32.

47. On April 21, 1793. See Tzetan Todorov, "France's Nationalism," *Salmagundi*, 84 (fall 1989), p. 152.

48. On May 28, 1792. Henriot, *Semur*, p. 128.

49. Michael Sonenscher, "Artisans and Sans-Culottes," in Alan Forrest and Peter Jones, eds., *Reshaping France: Town, Country, and Region during the French Revolution* (Manchester: Manchester University Press, 1991), p. 116.

50. Kennedy, *The Jacobin Clubs*, 2:153–154.

51. Robespierre, *Oeuvres complètes*, vol. 10 (Paris: Société des Études Robespierristes, 1967), p. 349.

52. On 2 Germinal, Year II. See *AP*, 87:64.

53. Labroue, *Bergerac*, p. 347.

54. Jean-Jacques Rousseau, *Écrits sur l'Abbé de Saint-Pierre, l'état de guerre*, in *Oeuvres complètes* (Paris: Gallimard, 1964), 3:614.

55. Norman Hampson, "The Idea of Nation," in Alan Forrest and Peter Jones, eds., *Reshaping France: Town, Country, and Region during the French Revolution* (Manchester: Manchester University Press, 1991), p. 22.

56. In a letter of 15 Frimaire, cited by Herriot, *Lyon n'est plus* (Paris: Hachette, 1937), 3:172, in Edmonds, *Jacobinism and the Revolt of Lyon*, p. 289.

57. Paolo Viola, "Il Banchetto di Atro," in *Il Trono vuoto* (Turin: Einaudi, 1989).

58. Walter, *Histoire des Jacobins*, p. 7, cites the comte de Puisaye's *Mémoires* of 1803, 1:283–285.

59. Maurice de Montgaillard, *Mémoires diplomatiques* (Paris: Ollendorf, 1896), 4:290.

60. Cited in Jean-Paul Bertaud, *Les Amis du roi: journaux et journalistes royalistes en France de 1789 à 1792* (Paris: Perrin, 1989), p. 72.

61. See also François Marchand, *La Jacobinade, ou le délire et l'agonie des Jacobins, poeme héroi-comique* (Paris, 1794), p. 47:

> Pendant ce tems, livrée à des remords
> Ou n'écoutant que ses derniers transports,
> De désespoir, Erynnis va se pendre
> A certain croc, ayant su se suspendre,
> Elle s'étrangle à l'aide d'un lacet.

62. Maurice Mökli-Cellier, *La Révolution française et les écrivains Suisses-Romands (1789–1815)* (Neuchatel: Attinger, 1931), p. 143.

63. Labroue, *Toulon*, p. 20.

64. Boissy d'Anglas, *La Constitution française décrétée par la Convention* (Paris, 1795), p. 5.

65. On October 16, 1794. See *AP*, 99:210.

66. Published in Paris in 1799.

67. Pierre Irénée Dupont (de Nemours), *Avant dernier chapitre de l'histoire des Jacobins* (Paris, Year IV), p. 23.

68. Serna, *Antonelle*, p. 274.

69. Cited by Augustin Cochin, *L'Esprit du Jacobinisme* (Paris: Presses Universitaires de France, 1979), p. 123.

10. Applied Jacobinism

1. See Richard Andrews, "Republican Patriotism and the French Revolution" (unpublished paper, Center for European Studies, Harvard University, December 1988).

2. This is the central insight of the work of Keith Baker.

3. For a geographical and statistical breakdown of the Terror, the basic text is still Daniel Greer, *The Incidence of the Terror during the French Revolution* (Cambridge, Mass.: Harvard University Press, 1935).

4. Cited in Walter, *Histoire des Jacobins*, p. 44.

5. Edmonds, *Jacobinism and the Revolt of Lyon*, p. 153. The following account of Jacobinism in Lyons is heavily dependent on Edmonds's work.

6. Archives Nationales, Series AB XIX, *cahier* of the Third Estate of Lyons, p. 17.

7. In 1806 Marseilles was reckoned to have just under 100,000 inhabitants and Lyons, just over that. See R. Le Mée, "Population agglomérée, population éparse au début du XIXe siècle," *Annales de démographie historique* (1971), pp. 470, 487.

8. Cited in Guilhaumou, *Marseille républicaine*, p. 180.

9. Ibid., p. 198.

10. Ibid., p. 199.

11. Margadant, *Urban Rivalries*, p. 233.

12. Claude Wanquet, "Révolution française et identité réunionnaise," in Jean Tarrade, ed., *La Révolution française et les colonies* (Paris: Société Française d'Histoire d'Outre Mer, 1989), pp. 55–56.

13. See William B. Cohen, *The French Encounter with Africans* (Bloomington: Indiana University Press, 1980), p. 115.

14. The freed men led by André Rigault were defeated in 1799 by the former black slaves led by Toussaint l'Ouverture. The island secured its independence in 1804. In the 1810s Haiti was divided in half, with a black kingdom in the north and a colored republic in the south and west.

15. Jean Boutier, Philippe Boutry, Serge Bonin, and Jacques Bernet's *Atlas de la Révolution: les sociétés populaires*, vol. 6 (Paris: EHESS, 1992), gives the best overall statistical description of Jacobin establishments and memberships.

16. The classic work on the sans-culottes is Albert Soboul's *Les Sans-culottes parisiens en l'an II: mouvement populaire et gouvernement révolution-*

naire, 2 juin 1793–9 thermidor an II (Paris: Clavreuil, 1962). The theme of the sans-culottes as a political and cultural rather than a social category is also developed in R. A. Andrews, "Social Structures, Political Elites, and Ideology in Revolutionary Paris: A Critical Evaluation of Albert Soboul's *Les sans-culottes parisiens en l'an II*," *Journal of Social History*, 19 (1985), pp. 71–112.

17. Michael Sonenscher, *Work and Wages: Natural Law, Politics, and the Eighteenth-Century French Trades* (Cambridge: Cambridge University Press, 1989), p. 73.

18. The sans-culottes' zeal was sharpened by a newly created network of twenty-odd "fraternal societies"—popular societies, clubs, and associations—including a "société fraternelle des deux sexes." The most prominent of their associations was the Cordelier club, founded in April 1790, dormant in 1791, and resurgent in 1792. In provincial France, local sans-culottes sometimes managed to find institutionalizing stability by taking over the bourgeois Jacobin clubs. At Eu, for example, thirteen of the twenty-three original founding members were pushed out by socially less-eminent newcomers. But such cases were relatively rare, and in Paris, that principle did not apply at all.

19. Bonneville and his milieu are described in Kates, *Cercle Social,* from which much of the following material is drawn.

20. Fifty of the 413 associates of Bonneville belonged to the Paris Jacobin club. See Catherine Duprat, *Le Temps des philantropes: la philantropie parisienne des Lumières à la monarchie de Juillet* (Paris: CTHS, 1993), p. 229.

21. Kates, *Cercle Social,* pp. 169–170.

11. Looking Backward

1. Diderot cited in Daniel Roche, *La France des Lumières* (Paris: Fayard, 1993), p. 554.

2. The connections between Protestantism and Jansenism were quite numerous. Symbolically if not wholly representatively, the Jansenist and Burgundian family members of the gutter novelist Restif de la Bretonne were converts from Protestantism who had reluctantly changed their ways when the toleration of Protestantism had been suspended in 1685. In a more general way, in the later decades of the century, many prominent Jansenists like the jurist Saint-Vincent worked hard to secure the toleration of Protestantism. Likewise, Desmoulins once explained that John Bull—i.e., England—in Cromwell's time had been "presbytérien et janséniste." See C. H. O'Brien, "The Jansenist Campaign for the Toleration of Protestants in Late Eighteenth Century France," *Journal of the History of Ideas* (1985), pp. 523–538.

3. The painters Philippe de Champaigne and Georges de la Tour gave pictorial form to this moralized, searching consciousness.

4. See Hélène Martin, "Langue et souveraineté en France au XVIIe siècle," *Annales: histoire, sciences sociales,* 49, no. 2 (1994).

5. *Le siècle de Louis XIV,* in Voltaire, *Oeuvres historiques* (Paris: Gallimard, 1957), p. 1247.

6. Letter D20118, May 15, 1776, to Jacques Delacroix, in Voltaire, *Correspondence,* vol. 127, ed. Theodore Besterman (Oxford: Oxford University Press, 1975).

7. See Norbert Elias, *The Civilising Process* (New York: Pantheon, 1982). This work was first published in German in 1939.

8. A. Molinier, *Inventaire sommaire de la collection Joly de Fleury* (Paris: Picard, 1881), p. ix.

9. For a suggestive discussion of the de-feudalization and "de-oralization" of an increasingly bureaucratic monarchy, see Michel Antoine, *Le Conseil du roi sous le règne de Louis XV* (Geneva: Droz, 1970).

10. The question of the monarchy's prestige and desacralization is ably outlined in Roger Chartier, *The Cultural Origins of the French Revolution* (Durham: Duke University Press, 1991), esp. pp. 128–134. Chartier's work has likewise renewed the question of print culture. Keith Baker's more abstract view of opinion, its causes and effects, is described in his collection of essays *Inventing the French Revolution.*

11. Cited in Jennifer Mori, "The British Government and the Bourbon Restoration: The Occupation of Toulon, 1793," *Historical Journal,* 40, no. 3 (September 1797), pp. 711–712.

12. The term was invented by the Physiocrats, who also coined the expression "laissez-faire." By their emphasis on rural life, Physiocrats were backward looking. By their emphasis on individual freedom—on the connections among private profit, investment, and social progress—they were the harbingers of modern capitalism. Adam Smith's initial intention was to dedicate his *Wealth of Nations* of 1776 to Dr. Quesnay (1694–1774), the king's physician and the founder of the Physiocratic "sect."

13. Jürgen Habermas, *Structural Transformation* (Cambridge, Mass.: MIT Press, 1984), p. 48. The next pages elaborate on the arguments of Habermas and Reinhard Koselleck.

14. See Jean Marie Goulemot, *Ces Livres qu'on ne lit que d'une main: lecture et lecteurs de livres pornographiques au XVIIIe siècle* (Paris: Alinéa, 1991), p. 24.

15. Johnson, *Listening in Paris,* p. 59.

16. Anne Vincent-Buffault, *Histoire des Larmes: XVIIIe–XIXe siècle,* cited in Johnson, *Listening in Paris,* p. 65.

17. See Hervé Guénot, "Musées et lycées parisiens (1780–1830)," *Dix-huitième siècle,* 18 (1985), pp. 249–267.

18. See Daniel Roche, *Le Siècle des Lumières en provinces: académies et académiciens provinciaux* (Paris: Mouton, 1978); E. François and Rolf Reichardt, "Les formes de sociabilité en France du milieu du XVIIIe siècle au milieu de XXe siècle," *Revue d'histoire moderne et contemporaine* (1985),

pp. 453–471; and Ran Halévi, *Les Loges maçonniques dans la France d'Ancien Régime: aux origines de la sociabilité démocratique* (Paris: Colin, 1984).

19. Cited in Johnson, *Listening in Paris*, p. 75.

20. Tocqueville, *The Old Regime and the Revolution*, trans. Stuart Gilbert (Garden City, N.Y.: Anchor, 1957), p. 117.

21. Cited in Jean Dutourd, *Rivarol* (Paris: Mercure de France, 1963), p. 143.

22. Brian Singer, Marcel Gauchet, Keith Baker, and Daniel Gordon have developed these important insights in great detail.

23. For an excellent overview of the subject, see David Bell, "Recent Works on Early Modern French Identity," *Journal of Modern History*, 68, no. 1 (March 1996).

24. Curiously, French language had first been taken up as an international medium by the Dutch, who despaired of finding any foreigner who might understand their own peculiar tongue!

25. In his *Essai sur l'éducation nationale, ou plan d'études pour la jeunesse.*

26. Marc Fumaroli, *Trois institutions littéraires* (Paris: Gallimard, 1994), p. 69.

27. In his *Délibérations à prendre*, cited by G. Benrekassa, "Sieyès: crise de l'Ancien Régime, crise des idéologies," in *Annales, E.S.C.*, 44, no. 1 (January 1989), p. 41.

28. Pidansat de Mairobert, cited in Thomas Crow, *Painters and Public Life in Eighteenth-Century Paris* (New Haven: Yale University Press, 1985), p. 4.

29. Cited in Roy Porter, "The Enlightenment in England," in Roy Porter and Mikulas Teich, eds., *The Enlightenment in National Context* (Cambridge: Cambridge University Press, 1981), p. 1.

30. Holbach, *Système social ou principes naturels de la morale et de la politique,* 3 vols. (London, 1773), 2:74, cited in Sarah Maza, "Sensibility and Social Change: Why There Was No Middle-Class Consciousness in Pre-revolutionary France," unpublished paper given at the New York Association of French Historians.

31. Émile Léonard, *L'Armée et ses problèmes* (Paris: Plon, 1958), pp. 157–160.

32. Described by Josephine Grieder, *Anglomania in France, 1740–1789* (Geneva: Droz, 1985).

33. Count Fersen, who orchestrated the king's flight to Varennes in 1791, was shocked by the Americans' practice of democratic sociability.

34. In a letter to Samuel Adams of February 14, 1779. Gregg Lint et al., eds., *Papers of John Adams*, vol. 7 (Cambridge, Mass.: Harvard University Press, 1989), pp. 412–413.

35. Tocqueville, *The Old Regime*, pp. 145–146.

36. See Goodman, *The Republic of Letters*, p. 46. With the election in 1771 of d'Alembert as its perpetual secretary, the French Academy—an offi-

cially sanctioned institution—itself came close to being a subversive *société de pensée.* See Fumaroli, *Trois institutions littéraires,* p. 73.

37. Cited by Goodman, *The Republic of Letters,* p. 15. The discussion of salons and sociability in these pages owes much to her work.

38. This expression was often picked up, even in the backcountry of central rural France. See Martin, *Artonne,* p. 20. Definitions did change with time: Napoleon, for example, also grew concerned about public opinion, which, however, he interpreted differently: "There must not be any opposition. What is a government? Nothing, if it does not have public opinion on its side. How can it hope to counterbalance the influence of a tribune if it is always open to attack." Cited by Warren Roberts, *Jacques-Louis David* (Chapel Hill: University of North Carolina Press, 1989), p. 151.

39. See Thomas E. Kaiser, "Money, Despotism, and Public Opinion in Early Eighteenth-Century France: John Law and the Debate on Royal Credit," *Journal of Modern History,* 63 (1991). The first general work on French finances was Véron de Forbonnais (1722–1800). *Recherches et considérations sur les finances de France depuis l'année 1595 jusqu'à l'année 1721* was published at Basel in 1758. Interest in this issue was strong and led also to the posthumous publication in 1789 of the *Comptes rendus de l'administration des finances du royaume de France* by Jean-Roland Malet (who had died in 1736). See Margaret Bonney and Richard Bonney, *J. R. Malet, premier historien des finances de la monarchie française* (Paris: Comité pour l'Histoire Économique, 1993).

40. See Dale Van Kley, "Du Parti janséniste au parti patriote: l'ultime sécularisation d'une tradition religieuse à l'époque du chancellier Maupeou 1770–1775," in Catherine Maire, ed., *Jansénisme et Révolution* (Paris: Bibliothèque Mazarine, 1990), pp. 115–130.

41. Most French nobles came from families that had been ennobled since 1600. Nobility was ordinarily inherited, but it could be purchased outright; the ennobling title of "secretaires du roi," for example, could be had for a fee of about 80,000 gold francs (1.5 million of our dollars) in 1788. In the last fifteen years of the Old Regime about fifty such purchases occurred each year.

42. See Nina Rattner Gelbart, *Feminine and Opposition Journalism in Old Regime France: Le Journal des Dames* (Berkeley: University of California Press, 1987).

43. See Suzanne Desan, *Reclaiming the Sacred: Lay Religion and Popular Politics in Revolutionary France* (Ithaca: Cornell University Press, 1990).

44. Cited by Catherine Maire in her introduction to *Jansénisme et Révolution* (Paris: Bibliothèque Mazarine, 1990), p. 10.

45. Fouché, letter to the Convention, 21 Ventôse, Year II, in François Aulard, ed., *Recueil des actes du Comité de Salut Public,* vol. 10 (Paris: Imprimerie Nationale, 1897), p. 653.

46. Kennedy, *The Jacobin Clubs,* 2:290.

47. Best described in Roland Mousnier, *Les Hiérarchies sociales* (Paris: Presses Universitaires de France, 1969).

48. Cited by Catherine Duprat, *Le Temps des philantropes: la philantropie parisienne des Lumières à la monarchie de Juillet* (Paris: CTHS, 1993), pp. xviii, xix, 73.

49. Described by Victor Turner, "Betwixt and Between: The Liminal Period in *Rites de Passage*," reprinted from *The Proceedings of the American Ethnological Society* (Saint Louis: Washington University Press, 1964). See also Turner, *The Ritual Process, Structure, and Anti-Structure* (Ithaca: Cornell University Press, 1969), p. 95, as well as "Passages, Margins, and Poverty: Religious Symbols of Communitas," in his *Dramas, Fields, and Metaphors: Symbolic Action in Human Society* (Ithaca: Cornell University Press, 1987). These pages owe much to my conversations with Jeremy Kleiner.

50. This shift is described by Pierre Rosanvallon in his excellent *Le Sacre du citoyen*, p. 68.

51. Traditional definitions of femininity had been ambiguous: women had had few rights in the traditionally defined private sphere (they were ordinarily disinherited). But they could accede (more or less) to the public sphere as reigning queens, royal mistresses, or, more humbly, owners of fiefs. Thus, a handful of women were allowed to act vicariously as voters in elections to the Second (noble) Estate in 1788–89; so were widows of men who had been "masters" of a professional corporation in the elections of the Third Estate.

52. Cited by Godineau, *Citoyennes tricoteuses*, p. 15.

53. Cited by Benedetta Cravieri, *Madame du Deffand and Her World* (Boston: David Godine, 1994), p. 260.

54. Surrey, with 80,000 inhabitants, saw as many condemnations as did the entire province of the Languedoc. Britain counted twice as many capital crimes as did France. See Roche, *La France des Lumières*, p. 281.

55. These conflicts are discussed in Durand Echeverria, *The Maupeou Revolution: A Study of Libertarianism in France, 1770–1774* (Baton Rouge: Louisiana State University Press, 1985).

56. Paine, *Collected Writings*, ed. Eric Foner (New York: Library of America, 1995), p. 445.

57. Described in Linda Colley, *Britons, Forging the Nation* (New Haven: Yale University Press, 1992).

58. Brissot de Warville, *New Travels in the United States of America, Performed in 1788* (Dublin: W. Corbet, 1792), p. 107, cited in Paul Merrill Spurlin, *The French Enlightenment in America: Essays on the Times of the Founding Fathers* (Athens: University of Georgia Press, 1984), p. 116.

59. Paine, *Rights of Man*, in *Collected Writings*, p. 492.

60. I have developed this comparatist theme at some length in my *Sister Republics: The Origins of French and American Republicanism* (Cambridge, Mass.: Harvard University Press, 1988).

61. Lafont de Saint-Yenne, *Sentiments sur quelques ouvrages de peinture, sculpture et gravure, écrits à un particulier en province* (Paris, 1754), pp. 91–92.

12. *Looking Forward*

1. Norway, with a population one-tenth that of France, has sent more immigrants to America than the Grande Nation.

2. As explained in Pitirim Sorokin, *Leaves from a Russian Diary* (Boston: Beacon Press, 1950), p. 123.

3. The importance of Thermidor as a frame of reference for communist politics is ably described in Tamara Kondraiteva, *Bolsheviks et Jacobins* (Paris: Payot, 1989). See also D. Shlapentoch, "The French Revolution in Lenin's Mind: The Case of the False Consciousness," *World Futures,* 44 (1995), pp. 247–262.

4. Cited in Dmitry Shlapentokh, *The French Revolution in Russian Intellectual Life, 1865–1905* (Westport, Conn.: Prager, 1996).

5. Cited by Nikolay Valentinov, *Encounters with Lenin* (New York: Oxford University Press, 1968), p. 128.

6. Ibid., p. 139.

7. Cited by André Liebich, *From the Other Shore: Russian Social Democracy after 1921* (Cambridge, Mass.: Harvard University Press, 1997), p. 22.

8. In the terms of Terry Eagleton's opposition.

9. Hannah Arendt, *The Human Condition* (Chicago: University of Chicago Press, 1958), pp. 50–59.

10. Habermas, *Structural Transformation,* p. 176.

11. In a speech at the Castres Society on July 3, 1792. Archives Départementales du Tarn, L 1531.

Index

Robespierre, Maximilien *(continued)*
  charity, 190; and citizenship, 134; and civic involvement, 133; and civil society, 102; and Clootz, 151; and clothing, 227; and clubs, 31, 71; and Committee of Public Safety, 48, 59, 282; and Condorcet, 363n119; on conspiracy, 130; conspiracy against, 59; conspiracy of, 179; and continuance of Revolution, 39; and contradiction, 216; and Convention, 60; and Cromwell, 137; and currency, 176; and Danton, 37, 198–199; death of, 60; on democracy, 156; denunciation of, 60–61, 159; on deputies, 158; and Desmoulins, 58; and Encyclopedists, 226; on enemy prisoners, 255; and exclusion of aristocracy, 246; and executions, 131, 163; fall of, 60–61, 159, 249–250; on familial guilt, 88; and *fêtes,* 189; on food prices, 79; and food riots, 55; and freedom of press, 128; and free speech, 77; on Girondins *vs.* Montagnards, 40; on government, 105; on guiding principles, 69–70; and Hébert, 56; and Helvetius, 226; and High Jacobinism, 16; and ideology, 288; image of, 243; and income redistribution, 122; influence of, 33; on insurance, 84; and international relations, 252; on Jacobins' name, 255; and journalism, 129; on Lafayette, 240–241; and language, 221; and Lenin, 329; and Louis XVI, 28, 34, 146; and Louvet, 38, 40; and Marat, 45–46; name of, 138; and National Convention, 131; and Paris club, 282; and Paris Commune, 57, 60; on passion, 79; and peasantry, 23; and plebiscite, 41; as plotter, 243; and poetry, 110; and poor, 112, 124; and power, 166; and price controls, 53; and public good, 208; and public opinion, 126; and purge of bureaucracy, 180; and réacteurs, 62; and religion, 72–73; and representation, 150; reputation, 203, 243; and Revolution, 76; and sacrifice, 187; and Sade, 188; and sans-culottes, 39, 277; on science, 141–142; on selflessness, 203; and September massacres, 37–38, 40; and sex, 194–195; and Sieyès, 67–68; as speaker, 218; and statism, 282; and suicide, 131, 206; and suspension of law, 52; and symbolism, 232; and Terror, 80, 121; and terrorism, 58, 59; on virile will, 89; and war, 32; on women, 92; on youth, 97
Roederer, Pierre-Louis, 257
Roland, Jean Marie, 36, 138, 364n26; and Bureau d'Esprit Public, 211; and civil society, 142; and elections, 167; on enlightenment of clubs, 242; and Jacobin ministry, 33, 34, 35; and work, 112
Roland, Manon Jeanne, 33, 85, 92, 115, 133, 319, 320
Rollin, Charles, 311
Roman mass, 238. *See also* Catholic Church
Rome, 138, 212, 322, 323. *See also* Classicism
Romme, Gilbert, 63, 106, 130, 141, 208
Rouen, 51
Rousseau, Jean Jacques, 1, 115, 126, 128, 210; and aristocracy, 315; and art, 224; and Babeuf, 330;

and bicameralism, 156; and Bonneville, 286; on Britain, 252; and children, 320; and civil society, 102; and compassion, 190; and conscience, 80, 82; on conspiracy, 242; and constitution, 154; and contract, 154–155; and empathy, 1; and family, 319, 320; and *fêtes,* 188; on gender roles, 94; and Hume, 319; knowledge of, 71–72; and Marie Antoinette, 319; and morality, 135; *La Nouvelle Héloïse,* 304, 319–320; and opinion, 154; relevance of, 317; and Sieyès, 156; *Social Contract,* 319; and society, 121; and terrorism, 2
Roux, Jacques, 55
Rovère, Joseph, 62
Royal Academy, 299
Royal army, 174
Royalist: and civil war, 69; and loss of rights, 88; and military, 173; and peasantry, 221; and Sieyès, 61, 63, 67
Rural population: and clubs, 104; as context, 263; and Old Regime, 295–297, 297–298; unrest among, 36, 312; and urban population, 115, 313. *See also* Provinces, provincials
Russia, 42, 210, 261
Russian Revolution, 328–332

Sacrifice, 187, 191, 205–206, 316, 318
Sade, marquis de, 155, 188, 200
Saint-André, Jeanbon, 124, 138, 235
Saint-Denis, 140
Saint-Domingue. *See* Haiti
Saint-Étienne, Rabaut, 21, 195, 269–270, 271
Saint-Just, Louis de, 58, 77; and agrarian communism, 69; and agriculture, 115; on aristocracy, 245; on Britain, 254; on Brutus, 205; and civil society, 102, 122; and decrees of Ventôse, 122; and economy, 84; execution of, 59, 60; and Hébertists, 157; on incest, 199; and inflation, 175; *Institutions républicaines,* 187; and language, 221; on Louis XVI, 159; and monarchy, 70–71; on nature, 185; on parties, 148; on passion, 89; and poor, 112; and property redistribution, 122; and rhetoric, 218; on self, 80; on self-control, 89; on selflessness, 203; and signs, 225–226; and society, 147; and statism, 157; on Terror, 181, 254; and violence, 229
Saint-Yenne, Lafont de, 323
Salles, Saint Vincent de, 320
Salon, 275, 305, 306, 308
Sans-culottes, 15, 373n18; accusations of, 118; and anticlericalism, 285; and aristocracy, 285; and artisans, 284; and *assemblées sectionnaires,* 50; character of, 283; and clothing, 226; and clubs, 56; and Committee of Public Safety, 56; control of, 56; and Convention, 55; and dechristianization, 56; demands of, 283–284; and Directory, 65; on economy, 284; and food, 283; and food riots, 53; and Girondins, 36, 44, 117; and guillotine, 283; insurrection of, 63; and intent, 81; and Jesus, 234; and justice, 284; and language, 285; and Maréchal, 165; and Marie